Culture, Migration, and Health Communication in a Global Context

This is a major volume concerning the influence that culture has on how individuals perceive, receive, and provide health care. Understanding the cultural context in which one communicates about heath is a growing concern for practitioners, researchers, and patients alike. This collection of theoretically diverse applied research in health communication provides important insights into the ways in which socio-cultural constructs influence health care.

—*Annette Madlock Gatison, Southern Connecticut State University*

Both international and internal migration brings new challenges to public health systems. This book aims to critically review theoretical frameworks and literature, as well as discuss new practices and lessons related to culture, migration, and health communication in different countries. It features research and applied projects conducted by scholars from various disciplines including media and communication, public health, medicine, and nursing.

Yuping Mao is Assistant Professor in communication studies at California State University, Long Beach, USA.

Rukhsana Ahmed is Associate Professor at the Department of Communication, University of Ottawa, Canada.

Routledge Research in Health Communication

1 **Communicating Women's Health**
Social and Cultural Norms that Influence Health Decisions
Edited by Annette Madlock Gatison

2 **Culture, Migration, and Health Communication in a Global Context**
Edited by Yuping Mao and Rukhsana Ahmed

Culture, Migration, and Health Communication in a Global Context

Edited by Yuping Mao and Rukhsana Ahmed

Routledge
Taylor & Francis Group
LONDON AND NEW YORK

First published 2018 by Routledge

2 Park Square, Milton Park, Abingdon, Oxfordshire OX14 4RN
52 Vanderbilt Avenue, New York, NY 10017

Routledge is an imprint of the Taylor & Francis Group, an informa business

First issued in paperback 2019

Library of Congress Cataloging-in-Publication Data
CIP data has been applied for.

ISBN: 978-1-138-22489-6 (hbk)
ISBN: 978-0-367-88518-2 (pbk)

Typeset in Sabon
by codeMantra

Contents

Acknowledgements

We begin by profusely thanking the authors for their fine contributions and patience to make *Culture, Migration, and Health Communication in a Global Context* possible. It has been a privilege to work with a group of enthusiastic and committed scholars whose unique voices and visions make us even more aware of the importance and meaning of this project. We also remember with heavy heart the untimely loss of one of our contributors and colleagues, Dr. Mahmoud Eid.

Our sincere thanks go to the Routledge team, especially Felisa Salvago-Keyes and Christina Kowalski, for their enthusiasm, guidance, and patience from inception to completion of this project. We gratefully acknowledge reviewers of the book proposal and chapters for their informative and insightful comments and suggestions that have helped improve the final product. We also recognize the intellectual curiosity of our students and colleagues in the classroom and at conferences for providing the impetus to work on this project.

Lastly, we dedicate this book to our families and all the migrants' families. We could not have started this book without the inspiration and shared experiences of migrants all over the world, and we could not have completed this book without the support, sacrifice, and encouragement of our family members. Yuping truly appreciates her husband Anming Wu's unconditional support in accompanying her along her journey from Europe to the United States in the process of working on this book project. Yuping also gives special thanks to her son Alistair Wu for being very adaptable in his linguistic and cultural transition across different countries at a young age. Alistair has been a great inspiration and motivation for her to complete this book project. She also wants to say "Xie Xie" ("thank you" in Chinese) to her father Wanliu Mao and mother Yuanshou Huang, for supporting her to pursue her dream and live the life she desires far away from them. Rukhsana is most grateful to her husband Dr. Zahirul Hasan Khan, her daughter Zerin Mahzabin Khan, and her cat Pancakes for their continued love, patience, and inspiration. She would also like to thank her mother Momena Ahmed and her father Dr. Momtaz Uddin Ahmed for their unconditional love and support.

Introduction

Health Communication at the Crossroads of Culture and Migration

Rukhsana Ahmed and Yuping Mao

In her opening remarks at a technical briefing on migration and health during the 69th World Health Assembly in May 2016, WHO Director-General Dr. Margaret Chan called migration "a fact of life" (WHO, 2016). This observation poignantly underscores population movement in a changing and globalized world. With the rapid increase in the size of the world's population, people are moving in larger numbers than ever before to new cities or countries to work, travel, study, reunite with family members, find better economic and social opportunities, or to escape natural disaster, persecution, violence, conflict, and war (Knobler, Mahmoud, Lemon, & Pray, 2006; WHO, 2007). Migration, as a cultural phenomenon, shapes migrants' social and cultural lives in many different ways. The upsurge in migration at different scales also "poses challenges to the organization and delivery of effective and culturally sensitive social services" (WHO, 2007), including health care. Culture related communication issues and migrants' health-related communication become part of the public discourse that requires more research attention. It is in this context that this edited book integrates theoretical discussion, as well as applied research, on culture and migrants' health in order to contribute to the health communication literature.

The Changing Landscape of Migration and Health

According to WHO estimates (WHO, 2017), there are 1 billion migrants in the world today, including 250 million international migrants—people living outside their country of birth—and 763 million internal migrants—people moving from one location to another within a particular country (UN, 2015, 2016; UNFPA, n.d.). The extraordinary movement of people present enormous and growing challenges to addressing the health needs of migrants. Concerted international efforts have been underway, calling to action on comprehensively addressing and prioritizing protection of migrants' health (WHO, 2017).

Important to note is the complex nature of migrants' health needs compounded by their status as either international travelers, migrant workers, refugees and uprooted people, student, undocumented or irregular migrants, and victims of human trafficking (Knobler *et al.*, 2006; Schenker, Castaneda, & Rodriguez-Lainz, 2014; WHO, 2007). For example, migrants are more exposed to stress "arising from displacement, insertion into new environments and reinsertion into former environments" (WHO, 2007, p. 2). Migrants, especially new arrivals, often live in poverty, are marginalized, and have limited access to basic social services, including health care (Pérez-Escamilla, Garcia, & Song, 2010). Low-skilled and temporary migrant workers are more concentrated in jobs that pose a variety of occupational safety and health risks (Preibisch & Hennebry, 2011). Women and children migrants who are victims of human trafficking are especially susceptible to communicable and noncommunicable diseases, including mental health disorders (Ciment & Radzilowski, 2015; McMichael & Healy, 2017). Disaster, conflict, and disease-induced migration, "is closely linked both to the destruction of livelihoods and, often, to disruptions to the health system" (Thomas, 2016).

During the technical briefing on migration and health in May 2016, Dr. Margaret Chan outlined four priorities related to managing migration and health:

1. The necessity for better data on the health needs of migrants;
2. The need for inclusive health policies and legal frameworks in recipient countries to ensure rightful access to quality health services, notwithstanding migrant legal status;
3. The need for migrant-sensitive health services and practices that are culturally competent and linguistically appropriate; and
4. The necessity for multi-sectoral collaboration and international partnership to manage the health needs of migrants (WHO, 2016).

Improving the health and wellbeing of migrants can result in reduction of long-term health and social costs, as well as enhancement of health security, thus contributing to social and economic development. Recognizing the need for international collaboration, in February 2017, health leaders from around the world adopted the Colombo Statement at the second Global Consultation on Migrant Health (UN News Centre, n.d.). Jointly organized by the Government of Sri Lanka, International Organization for Migration (IOM), and WHO, "the Global Consultation provides an important platform for countries to share lessons learned, research and best practices on how to address the complex health needs of migrants at local, national and international level" (WHO, Sri Lanka, 2017). We situate this edited book along "a shared [global] research agenda" with the goal to inform the "development of global frameworks to ensure migrant health is protected" (UN News Centre, 2017). Collectively, the chapters in this book respond to at least three priorities related to managing migration and health by contributing to discussion on the health needs of migrants; the necessity for migrant-sensitive health services and practices that are culturally competent and linguistically appropriate; and the need for international partnership and multi-sectoral collaboration for managing migrants' health needs.

Health Communication and Culture

In the face of large movements of migrants with different economic, political, social, and environmental health determinants and needs (WHO, 2017), among other coordinated efforts, it is essential to explore the role of communication processes for health promotion among migrants. As Obregon and Waisbord (2012) postulated, "Few dispute the centrality of communication in global public health and development efforts, given the extensive research and applications in local and international aid programs" (p. 3). However, when migrant health issues are concerned, the complex interactions between communication and culture cannot be bypassed.

Hall (1959) posited that cultural frameworks help to interpret communication. Extending this notion, Gudykunst and Lee (2002) underscored that while "communication is unique within each culture, ..., there are systematic similarities and differences across cultures" (p. 26). For example, Perkins, Geppert, Gonzales, Cortez, and Hazuda (2002) found cross-cultural similarities and differences among Mexican-American, Euro-American, and African-American inpatients with regard to their decisions about performing advance care planning. Therefore, it is not only group differences, but also individual differences that influence health communication. And, understanding these complex interactions between communication and culture is important to better understand how health is communicated across different cultural contexts.

Culture has been identified as an important variable, influencing how people experience, perceive, construct, and understand health. For example, Lupton (1994) argued that a shared interpretation of the medical encounter by persons of different cultures is confounded by disagreement, debate, power struggles, and emotional conflict among different cultural groups. In a similar vein, Helman (2007) explained that different cultural, social, and ethnic groups may differently understand the causes of illness, the kinds of treatment they believe in, and to whom they would go if they are ill. Helman further argued that a better understanding of culture's roles in health beliefs will allow providers to adapt to patients' cultural needs. Other studies also demonstrate that language is a cultural difference that matters in effective health care (Meddings & Haith-Cooper, 2008). For example, minority ethnic older people in Great Britain suffer from bad health because of language and communication barriers (Mold, 2006). Also, language and communication difficulties, among other factors, act as barriers encountered by international nurses as they adjust to foreign health-care environments (Kawi & Xu, 2009). Accordingly, research has underscored the need for nurses in Great Britain to be aware of the communication patterns they use in their interactions with patients (Castledine, 2008). It is also important for nurses to use professional interpreter services to overcome language barriers when communicating with patients and provide them with culturally-sensitive palliative care (Mancuso, 2009). Cioffi (2003) found that many nurses attempted to manage communication with culturally and linguistically diverse patients with the help of interpreters, bilingual health workers, and other strategies.

Case studies of cultural difficulty in health communication demonstrate that cultural difference includes factors beyond speaking different languages. Using HIV/AIDS narrative as a case study, Geist-Martin, Ray, and Sharf (2003) described five layers of meanings in provider-patient communication: ideological, sociopolitical, institutional/professional, ethnocultural/familial, and interpersonal layers of meaning and argued accounting for semantic meaning is not enough. Likewise, Galanti's (1991) case studies outline many levels of cultural differences that can cause conflicts and misunderstandings between health care providers and patients. These case studies underscore the importance of understanding and adapting to one's individual and cultural differences to avoid conflict and misunderstanding. This can be achieved by gaining knowledge of the individual's cultural values, family structure, health care beliefs and practices, religious beliefs, diet, language and communication processes, and psychosocial interactions that may differ between and among cultures.

Therefore, providing culturally receptive health care to diverse patient populations is essential, which, in turn, necessitates a comprehensive understanding of how health communication is negotiated in relation to context, experience, and culture. Studies in health communication help us to explore "the role of communication in promoting health, establishing health care relationships, and other important health-related processes and practices" (Kreps, 2015, p. 1). Against this backdrop, this edited book takes the task to bring together an integrated set of theoretical and applied research on culture, migration, and health communication from unique local and global perspectives.

Why Focus on Culture, Migration, and Health Communication in a Global Context?

As we have discussed above, there is increasing migration happening across geographic regions within a country or across different countries. The migrant populations keep some of their original cultures with them that influence their communication about health. Meanwhile, migrant populations are constantly exposed to and adapting to cultural values and practices in their host countries or regions, which gradually alter their health related communication and behaviors. On the one hand, migrants' health communication and behaviors have become an important social topic in many countries, especially in North America (Gushulak, Pottie, Roberts, Torres, & DesMeules, 2011; Singh, Rodriguez-Lainz, & Kogan, 2013) and some European countries (WHO Regional Office for Europe, n.d.) with a relatively long history of immigration from other countries. On the other hand, in countries like China, urbanization accelerates migration within the country, primarily with economically and socially disadvantaged population migrating from rural to urban areas (Wildau, 2015). The ongoing migration flows across different countries or regions increase the complexity of the economic, political, ethnic, racial, and cultural milieu of the destination country or region. Both international and internal migrations and their changing patterns in the current global context bring new challenges to public health systems and new questions to explore the role of health communication in local, regional, national, and a larger global context.

Health communication is one of the fastest growing fields of study. Migration studies are increasing, and many scholars in health communication are seeking more diverse examinations of the health communication context. In the backdrop of the growth, scope, complexity, and impact of migration, culture-related communication issues and migrants' health communication require more research attention.

Culture is one of the most complex yet rich concepts to study. Culture can be understood as a comprehensive and integrated pattern of various socio-cultural variables such as religion, ethnicity, race, country of origin, and politics. The production of cultural knowledge involves accumulating individual experiences rooted in history. Thus, culture is "a community of meaning and shared body of local knowledge rather than a region or a nation" (González & Chen, 2016, p. 5). The understanding of culture cannot be separated from power struggles, group negotiations, social structures, and dominant ideologies. As researchers, while we attempt to understand shared cultural experiences, we also appreciate individual voices. We also embrace the dialectic approach of understanding culture and communication (Martin & Nakayama, 2013). The cultural-individual, personal-contextual, differences-similarities, static-dynamic, history/past-present/future, and privilege-disadvantage dialectics well capture the complex and paradoxical relationships between different aspects and levels of intercultural communication. Communication constructs culture, and culture shapes the way people communicate. There are numerous ways of defining cultural groups. Taking a communication perspective, this book examines how differences among different cultural communities relate to health communication at interpersonal, group, and societal levels. Health communication is always situated in certain social, political, economic, historical, and cultural contexts. This book addresses a few important contextual factors that practitioners and researchers need to be aware of in research, practice, and policy-making.

Although there is a growing scholarly interest in issues of migration and health communication, what is missing is integrated scholarly efforts at the intersection of culture, migration, and health communication. Existing literature has covered issues of health, medicine, and culture with a focus on health communication (Dutta, 2008; Kar, Alcalay, & Alex, 2001), from a public health perspective (Edberg, 2013) and adopting a medical anthropology approach (Helman, 2007; Winkelman, 2008). Although scant, scholars have also attended to the examination of globalization and health (Lee, 2003), as well as migration and health (Gushulak & MacPherson, 2006).

Over the past two decades, migration has changed the world dramatically, and there is a strong need for a more updated literature on culture and health communication. In response, this book features contributions by scholars from different disciplines in a wide geographic scope, integrating discussions on culture, migration, and health communication in a broad and inclusive manner. Specifically, it provides a wide coverage of research and applications of interdisciplinary scholarly work in communication, media, public health, and nursing, with various methodological and theoretical approaches.

This edited volume makes three key contributions: (1) it features theoretical discussion as well as applied research on culture and migrants' health. Specifically, this book provides an understanding of widely applied theoretical frameworks, embedded in public health and health communication contexts, to immigrant health research and practice. (2) This book adopts an interdisciplinary approach to discuss new practices and lessons related to culture, migration, and health communication. As a result, readers will be able to appreciate the theoretical discussion as well as applied research on culture and migrants' health from multiple perspectives. (3) This book covers international research, stimulating health communication cases on immigrants' health in different countries with in-depth analysis of their unique contexts. Particularly, it offers readers the opportunity to engage with scholarly work that adopts various methodological and theoretical approaches to study health communication issues spanning across geographic regions: North and South America, Europe, Australasia, and Asia.

Studying Culture, Migration, and Health Communication: Multiple Perspectives, Approaches, and Contexts

The collection of chapters in this edited book is divided into five parts representing the multiple perspectives, approaches, and contexts from and within which issues of culture, migration,[1] and health communication have been examined. Below, we provide a synopsis of the individual chapters under each part.

Part I, "Theoretical Discussion and Application," includes three chapters providing in-depth and critical review of some theories that have been widely used in health communication research. In Chapter 1, Mao and Ahmed review acculturation and identity management theories and the theoretical concept of cultural competence, as well as reflect on how they can inform and advance understanding of culture related health communication. These theories and concept have been frequently cited and discussed in research addressing cultural issues in communication. Each of these theories and concept provides a unique angle to understand migrants' experience in the health context. With global and local cultures being constantly changed by migration, new challenges and issues arise in health communication across different cultural groups. Within this social background, there is a need for refining and further developing the existing theories and potentially develop new theories to unpack the complicated interplay among migration, culture, and health communication.

Dearing and Cox, in Chapter 2, discuss diffusion of innovations theory, which has been widely applied to understand how innovations flow among different populations and are adopted by individuals and groups. They focus on applications of the diffusion paradigm in interdisciplinary, international, and intercultural research, as well as community health projects. In particular, this chapter provides insights on how the diffusion of innovations theory can be applied to advance our understanding of migration, cultural assimilation, migrant health, and international health communication.

Closing this Part, in Chapter 3, Dutta demonstrates how the application of the theoretical framework of the culture-centered approach creates spaces for Bangladeshi construction workers in Singapore to articulate their experiences, meanings, and negotiations of health and wellbeing. The culture-centered approach understands culture as dynamic and constituted in local contexts. Through culture-centered ethnographic interviews, Dutta weaves migrant narratives of health risks that are constituted at the intersections of migration and work. Championing a culture-centered approach to theorize immigrant health, Dutta calls for privileging subaltern voices to critically interrogate and enrich the dominant approaches to health communication.

Part II, "Cultural Differences and Disparities in Immigrants' Health Care Practices," contains four chapters devoted to discussions on immigrants' experiences of health and health care disparities related to cultural differences in various social contexts. Cultural minorities, including immigrants, encounter various barriers to effective access to health care services. Some of these barriers include limited language ability, lack of communication skills, lack of social support networks, and differences in cultural norms and health beliefs. In some situations, migrants could be constrained by their relatively disadvantaged socio-economic status and limited coverage of health insurance. In Chapter 4, Mantwill and Schulz compare the Albanian- and Serbian-speaking immigrants' culture-specific health communication and decision-making behavior during medical consultation for back pain with those of non-immigrants' in Switzerland. They also examine associations between cultural differences and back pain related outcomes among these groups. The survey findings reveal cultural differences in communication processes and decision-related behavior between immigrant and non-immigrant population during medical consultation and their possible impacts on back pain related outcomes. Mantwill and Schulz conclude by emphasizing the need to advance cultural competence training in medical education.

This recognition of the importance of cultural competence training for health professionals is also evident in Chapter 5 by Team, Manderson, and Markovic. The authors bring to light how poor health literacy, cultural differences in health care systems, health beliefs, and poor patient-professional communication can contribute to chronic illness among immigrants. Based on findings from in-depth interviews with Ukrainian Australians aged 50 years and over, Team, Manderson, and Markovic urge for integrating immigrants' culture and age-specific health beliefs and practices into clinical care.

Gong, in Chapter 6, explores Chinese migrant mothers' perceptions and experiences of health risks during pregnancy, childbirth, and early years of mothering in the UK. Based on in-depth interview findings, Gong argues that Chinese mothers' risk perceptions are rooted in Chinese values, beliefs, and the concept of health, as well as shaped by their maternity health care experiences in the UK, including lack of family and social support as well as barriers to accessing key health information and resources.

Concluding this Part, Jun, in Chapter 7, discusses the rise of medical tourism service use among immigrants as a response to health disparities they experience. Presenting the case of Korean-Americans in the US, Jun documents the health disparities that racial/ethnic minority and new immigrant groups experience in multiple contexts and the difficulties they face in navigating the health care system in the United States. Jun underscores the complexities surrounding medical tourism, including health risks, and identifies the need for accessible and culturally sensitive health information sources and services for racial/ethnic minorities and immigrants.

Digital media and information communication technologies are important channels for health education and communication, and they also become sites for health information sharing and social construction of health narratives. Part III, "ICTs and Migrants' Health

Communication," features two chapters that focus on how content and format of digital media and technology in combination with other social factors, such as social capital and social networks, shape immigrant health and influence immigrants' health beliefs and behaviors. In Chapter 8, Guntarik, Berry, and Arnoldi analyze the use of the Internet and social media by new migrants in Australia to seek health information across geographic, social, and cultural boundaries. Guntarik and colleagues show that during migration and resettlement, migrants use digital social networks as health-information seeking tools to negotiate and transform individual, family, and community health in addition to navigating the local health care system. They urge for further investigation into migrants' health information seeking activities across local and transnational digital networks.

Ending this Part, Chapter 9 by Olaniran offers a comprehensive discussion on the unique social and health challenges that migrant women workers face resulting from violence against them. Olaniran focuses on different forms of violence against migrant women workers that are exacerbated by their disadvantageous social status. He also explores the potential uses and limits of information communication technologies to help ease the plight of migrant women workers and address violence against them.

The growing literature on migrant health has often oversimplified the importance of culture as a framework for understanding migrants' health communication processes. This oversimplification of the importance of cultural frameworks tends to ignore the dynamic and complex interactions between cultural diversity, cross-cultural communication challenges, diverse health beliefs and practices, socio-political contexts, socioeconomic status, and geopolitical realities in the provision of health care, limiting the development of a comprehensive approach to meeting migrants' health needs. The three chapters in Part IV, "Culturally Grounded and Community-Based Health Intervention for Migrants," consider culturally informed health interventions for promoting migrant health and well-being. In Chapter 10, Olufowote and Aranda advocate the PEN-3 cultural model to explore how socio-cultural factors influence community health practices. Specifically, they critically review the PEN-3 cultural model in the context of health epidemics affecting African communities. In so doing, Olufowote and Aranda argue for developing culturally-unique models of health and advance the PEN-3 cultural model as a framework to examine health issues of African immigrant communities.

Nahon-Serfaty and Eid, in Chapter 11, discuss how they developed and implemented a participatory action research project involving multiple stakeholder groups for breast cancer awareness and education in Venezuela. Guided by the principles of ecological perspectives and citizenship mobilization and community action, the project aimed at empowering marginal voices of patients and social activists in their fight against breast cancer and to bring about social change. Nahon-Serfaty and Eid describe the results of a series of research activities over the five years of the project amidst high political and social polarization and changes in the Venezuelan public health care system. For success in health activism, Nahon-Serfaty and Eid underscore the importance of being cognizant of unique cultural contexts, sociocultural realities of different patients, and familial and cultural influences on health behavior.

In Chapter 12, An discusses how the significance of sociocultural factors is de-emphasized in current scholarship on dietary acculturation. An examines the influence of social support and social control, two important functions of social relationships, on dietary behavior among Asian immigrants living in the United States. In view of disparities in overweight and obesity prevalence among Asian immigrants and the importance of sociocultural factors as determinants of health behavioral change, An argues for designing interventions that are informed by an understanding of how social relationships impact health in order to promote healthy nutrition among Asian immigrants.

The final two chapters in Part V, "Methodological Reflections," offer insights into the research process and methodological considerations when examining issues of culture and migrant health in a global context. Although research on migration and health communication is on the rise, reflections on how our movement as global health researchers inform and influence our research practices remain less in focus. In Chapter 13, Bates takes us through his journey as a researcher in migratory spaces to demonstrate how the researchers' own movements shape their research and practice. Using mobile methodologies, Bates draws on four field experiences in Bangkok, Singapore, Bahrain, and Tanzania to introspectively unpack health communication research as a global practice. In so doing, Bates calls attention to the researcher as a site of analysis and reflection when researching issues of migration and health.

Finally, Chapter 14 is concerned with the importance of interdisciplinary approach to and international collaboration on migration and global health research. In this chapter, Richter and Jarvis discuss the details of developing research partnerships to research design and knowledge dissemination. Richter and Jarvis identify key methodological insights and challenges that may arise and suggest strategies and tools that may be utilized to aid in the process of conducting research in immigrant health with interdisciplinary and international research teams.

This edited book features a broad range of research contributed by scholars across different continents. It has been an exciting and educational process for us to work with contributors who not only have knowledge of disciplinary topics, but also knowledge of various cultures that they combined to explore migration and health issues in different social settings. The accumulated "local" knowledge of health communication makes this book "international" and "global." We hope this book becomes one of the starting points for researchers and practitioners to reflect and dialogue on the existing, evolving, and emerging health communication issues in local and global contexts. We look forward to future dialogues that are more inclusive of all kinds of cultural differences and more empowering for marginalized and silenced groups.

We hope students, researchers, scholars, and practitioners alike from a variety of fields will find the cross-disciplinary nature and treatment of these issues of importance and interest. In addition to an academic audience, we also hope administrators and policy makers working in the health sector will find the book valuable and resourceful. Finally, we hope this book will spur critical debate and advance further exploration of issues of culture, migration, and health communication.

Note

1 We duly acknowledge the interchangeable use of the terms *migrant* and *immigrant*, as well as *migration and immigration* in many chapters throughout the book.

References

Castledine, G. (2008). The use of language in nursing care. *British Journal of Nursing*, *17*(9), 608. doi:10.12968/bjon.2008.17.9.29250.

Ciment, J., & Radzilowski, J. (Eds.). (2015). *American immigration: An encyclopedia of political, social, and cultural change* (2nd ed.). London: Routledge.

Cioffi, J. (2003). Communicating with culturally and linguistically diverse patients in an acute care setting: Nurses' experiences. *International Journal of Nursing Studies*, *40*, 299–306. doi:10.1016/S0020-7489(02)00089-5.

Dutta, M. J. (2008). *Communicating health: A culture-centered approach*. London: Polity Press.

Edberg, M. (2013). *Essentials of health, culture, and diversity: Understanding people, reducing disparities*. Burlington, MA: Jones & Bartlett Learning.

Galanti, G. N. (1991). *Caring for patients from different cultures: Case studies from American hospitals*. Philadelphia: University of Pennsylvania Press.

Geist-Martin, P., Ray, E. B., & Sharf, B. F. (2003). *Communicating health: Personal, cultural, and political complexities*. Belmont, CA: Wadsworth/Thomson Learning.

González, A. & Chen, Y.-W. (2016). Introduction. In A. González & Y.-W. Chen (Eds.). *Our voices: Essays in culture, ethnicity, and communication* (6th ed.) (pp. 1–15). New York: Oxford.

Gudykunst, W., & Lee, C. M. (2002). Cross-cultural communication theories. In W. B. Gudykunst and B. Mody (Eds.), *Handbook of international and intercultural communication* (2nd ed.) (25–50). Thousand Oaks, CA: Sage Publications.

Gushulak, B. D., & MacPherson, D. W. (2006). *Migration medicine and health: Principles and practice*. Hamilton, ON: BC Decker.
Gushulak, B. D., Pottie, K., Roberts, J. H., Torres, S., DesMeules, M. (2011). Migration and health in Canada: Health in the global village. *Canadian Medical Association Journal, 183*(12), E952–E958. Retrieved from http://olip-plio.ca/wp-content/uploads/2013/06/Gushulak-et-al-Migration-and-health-in-Canada.pdf.
Hall, E. T. (1959). *The silent language*. New York: Fawcett.
Helman, C. G. (2007). *Culture, health, and illness* (5th ed.). Oxford: Oxford University Press.
Kar, S. B., Alcalay, R., & Alex, S. (Eds.). (2001). *Health communication: A multicultural perspective*. Thousand Oaks, CA: Sage Publications.
Kawi, J., & Xu, Y. (2009). Facilitators and barriers to adjustment of international nurses: an integrative review. *International Nursing Review, 56*(2), 174–183. doi:10.1111/j.1466-7657.2008.00705.x.
Knobler, S., Mahmoud, A., Lemon, L., & Pray, L. (Eds.). (2006). The impact of globalization on infectious disease emergence and control: Exploring the consequences and opportunities: Workshop summary. Institute of Medicine Forum on Microbial Threats. Washington (DC): National Academies Press. Retrieved from www.ncbi.nlm.nih.gov/books/NBK56593/.
Kreps, G. (2015). Health communication inquiry and health promotion: A state of the art review. *Journal of Nature and Science, 1*(2), e35. Retrieved from www.jnsci.org/index.php?journal=nsci&page=article&op=view&path%5B%5D=35.
Lee, K. (2003). *Health impacts of globalization: Towards global governance*. London: Palgrave Macmillan.
Lupton, D. (1994). Medicine as culture: Illness, disease and the body in western societies. London: Sage Publications.
Mancuso, L. (2009). Providing culturally sensitive palliative care. *Nursing, 39*(5), 50–53. doi:10.1097/01.NURSE.0000350758.93924.51.
Martin, J. N., & Nakayama, T. K. (2013). *Intercultural communication in contexts* (6th ed.). New York: McGraw-Hill.
McMichael, C., & Healy, J. (2017). Health equity and migrants in the Greater Mekong Subregion. *Global Health Action, 10*(1) (Article ID 1271594). doi:10.1080/16549716.2017.1271594.
Meddings, F., & Haith-Cooper, M. (2008). Culture and communication in ethically appropriate care. *Nursing Ethics, 15*(1), 52–61. doi:10.1177/0969733007083934.
Mold, F. (2006). Culturally competent care. *Nursing Older People, 18*(8), 3.
Obregon, R., & Waisbord, S. (Eds.). (2012). *Handbook of global health communication, development and social change*. Chichester: Wiley-Blackwell.
Pérez-Escamilla, R., Garcia, J., & Song, D. (2010). Health care access among Hispanic immigrants: ¿alguien esta` escuchando? [Is anybody listening?]. *NAPA Bulletin, 34*(1), 47–67. doi:10.1111/j.1556-4797.2010.01051.x.
Perkins, H. S., Geppert, C. M. A., Gonzales, A., Cortez, J. D., & Hazuda, H. P. (2002). Cross-cultural similarities and differences in attitudes about advance care planning. *Journal of General Internal Medicine, 17*(1), 48–57. doi:10.1046/j.1525-1497.2002.01032.x.
Preibisch, K., & Hennebry, J. (2011). Temporary migration, chronic effects: The health of international migrant workers in Canada. *CMAJ : Canadian Medical Association Journal, 183*(9), 1033–1038. doi:10.1503/cmaj.090736.

Schenker, M., Castañeda, X., & Rodriguez-Lainz, A. (Eds.). (2014). *Migration and health: A research methods handbook*. Oakland: University of California Press.

Singh, G. K., Rodriguez-Lainz, A., & Kogan, M. D. (2013). Immigrant health inequalities in the United States: Use of eight major national data systems. *The Scientific World Journal, 2013*, 1–21. doi:10.1155/2013/512313.

Thomas, F. (2016). *Handbook of migration and health*. Cheltenham: Edward Elgar Publishing.

United Nations. Department of Economic and Social Affairs, Population Division. (2015). *Population facts: Trends in international migration, 2015* (No. 2015/4). Retrieved from www.un.org/en/development/desa/population/migration/publications/populationfacts/docs/MigrationPopFacts20154.pdf.

United Nations. Department of Economic and Social Affairs, Population Division. (2016). *International migration report 2015: Highlights* (ST/ESA/SER.A/375). Retrieved from www.un.org/en/development/desa/population/migration/publications/migrationreport/docs/MigrationReport2015_Highlights.pdf.

United Nations Population Fund. (n.d.). *Migration*. Retrieved from www.unfpa.org/migration.

UN News Center. (n.d.). At global UN consultation, health leaders underline need for actieoropeanon on migrant health. Retrieved from www.un.org/apps/news/story.asp?NewsID=56237#.WNmOes91qAK.

Wildau, G. (2015). China migration: At the turning point. *Financial Times*. Retrieved from www.ft.com/content/767495a0-e99b-11e4-b863-00144feab7de.

Winkelman, M. (2008). *Culture and health: Applying medical anthropology*. San Francisco, CA: Jossey-Bass.

World Health Organization. (2016). *Technical briefing on migration and health*. Report. 69th World Health Assembly. Retrieved from www.who.int/migrants/publications/WHA69_mh-technical-breefing.pdf?ua=1.

World Health Organization. (2017). *Refugee and migrant health*. Retrieved from www.who.int/migrants/en/.

World Health Organization. Country Office for Sri Lanka. (2017). *Sri Lanka gears up to host Global Consultation on Migrant Health*. Retrieved from www.searo.who.int/srilanka/areas/global-consultation-migrant-health/en/.

World Health Organization. Executive Board. (2007). *Health of immigrants: Report by the Secretary* (EB122/11). Retrieved from www.who.int/hac/techguidance/health_of_migrants/B122_11-en.pdf.

World Health Organization. Regional Office for Europe (n.d.). *Migrant health in the European region*. Retrieved from www.euro.who.int/en/health-topics/health-determinants/migration-and-health/migrant-health-in-the-european-region.

Part I

Theoretical Discussion and Application

1 Acculturation, Identity Management, and Cultural Competence

Understanding Culture and Health Communication from Dynamic and Dyadic Approaches

Yuping Mao and Rukhsana Ahmed

Immigration has brought various social, economic, and cultural changes to Western societies in the past two decades. Some of the changes are embraced by members of host societies, while some have triggered different levels of resistance. In recent years, there have been heated social and political debates between a pro-immigration social ideology and a more conservative and restraining view toward immigration. Immigrants' roles and contributions to the changing societies are scrutinized from different perspectives and analyzed based on costs and benefits, which lead to policy changes on immigration and international relationships in many countries. Among all the discussions and debates, immigrants' health and their usage of public health resources have been brought up in various contexts. With the increasing social significance of understanding migration, culture, and health, research in this area continuously receives academic attention.

In health communication research, various theories have been advanced and applied to understand different aspects of health communication research and practice. The rising number of immigrants around the world has significantly increased the chance of communication across different cultures in the health context. Addressing migrant's health needs in a global context requires we understand the intricate web of social, cultural, psychological, and relational factors that influence their health-related communication and behavior. In the following, we discuss, make connections among, and compare two widely applied intercultural communication theories: acculturation and identity management, as well as the theoretical concept of cultural competence. These theories and concepts are essential to unpack the complexities and nuances surrounding migrant health issues.

Acculturation: Immigrants' Adaptation

Acculturation theory has been widely applied to understand minorities' and immigrants' psychological adaptation in cross-cultural contexts and can also be useful to understand their health issues and behaviors. Literature shows that immigrants tend to change their health behavior in their acculturation process (Arcia, Skinner, Bailey, & Correa, 2001). Berry's (1980, 1997) acculturation framework has two dimensions. The cultural maintenance dimension refers to immigrants' preference to maintain their own cultural heritage, while the intercultural contact and participation dimension indicates the degree to which immigrants wish to have contact with and be involved in the host society. Within those two dimensions, immigrants primarily take four acculturation strategies: assimilation, separation, integration, and marginalization. Immigrants who take an assimilation approach would give up maintaining their own cultural identities but try to adopt all the cultural norms and practices of the dominant cultural group in the host country. In contrast, immigrants may choose to fully conserve their cultural heritage and not to be in contact with members of the host country, which is defined as separation strategy. In recent years, integration has been a preferred strategy and a more 'popular' cultural ideology in many developed countries. Immigrants taking an integration approach are expected to maintain some of their cultural heritage but at the same time actively take part as a contributing member of the host country by embracing its core cultural norms and practices. Immigrants could suffer marginalization when they abandon or are unable to preserve their cultural heritage and, at the same time, when they are excluded from or discriminated by the dominant cultural group in their host country.

On the one hand, acculturation can bring significant health benefits to immigrants, for instance, higher health literacy (van Servellen, Brown, Lombardi, & Herrera, 2003) and easier communication with health care providers (Fernandez *et al.*, 2004). On the other hand, extensive literature has shown that acculturation is associated with various undesirable health behaviors. Most immigrants go through a long and challenging process to find and implement their own acculturation strategy. The stress and anxiety, along with the acculturation process, can have some negative impacts on immigrating population, for instance, poorer health behaviors and health outcomes (Finch & Vega, 2003). Newly arriving immigrants in developed nations are generally healthier than native-born populations, a phenomenon referred to as the healthy immigrant effect, although immigrants' health tends to deteriorate with more years spent in the host country (Corlin, Woodin, Thanikachalam, Lowe, & Brugge, 2014; Vang, Sigouin, Flenon, Astrid, & Gagnon, 2017). For example, studies (McDonald & Kennedy, 2005) show immigrants tend to lose their health advantages after living in the United States for a long period of time, as evidenced by increased overweight and obesity rates as well as some other health outcomes. In particular, Latino Americans with higher levels of acculturation are found to have higher rates of poor physical and mental health such as cancer and infant mortality (Clark & Hofsess, 1998; Vega & Amaro, 1994). Immigrants' use of media has been associated with their acculturation. For example, Latino adolescents' use of media is found to be a predictor of their acculturated risky health behaviors that result in getting sunburn and drinking carbonated beverages (Mao & Shi, 2015).

Food consumption is one of the most important acculturation processes that every migrant needs to navigate. How and to what extent migrants adopt the new dietary culture in the host country and abandon their home country's dietary tradition are not only about what they like to eat, but it is also a significant socializing process that involves constant negotiation of migrants' cultural identity in relation to the culture of their host countries. Lévi-Strauss (1978) argued that cooking, a human activity, is as universal as the use of language, yet the importance of cooking in social life is not sufficiently emphasized. The collective experience of identification and reproduction of dietary culture and practice plays an important role in forming and maintaining immigrant cultural communities (Parasecoli, 2014), and thusly can be seen as an important aspect of their group acculturation. As acculturation theory predicts, acculturation tends to induce more changes in the acculturating group (Berry, 1990). Research shows immigrants' assimilation into the U.S. culture is associated with selecting foods that are considered more American (Guendelman, Cheryan, & Monin, 2011). Guendelman and colleagues found that Asian-Americans were likely to order and eat dishes that are "more prototypically American" (p. 962) and contain more calories and fat when their American identity was directly challenged than not. Other research (Batis, Hernandez-Barrera, Barquera, Rivera, & Popkin, 2011) found that Mexican-Americans tend to lose the influence of the Mexican diet within one generation of moving to the United States.

The acculturation process seems to have some negative impact on immigrants' dietary habits. Research found some immigrants tend to abandon their beneficial traditional health behaviors such as fiber-rich diet and adopt negative behaviors including consuming high-calorie processed foods during their acculturation process in the United States (Lara, Gamboa, Kahramanian, Morales, & Bautista, 2005; Zambrana & Carter-Pokras, 2010). Soda consumption, smoking, and drinking alcohol are major acculturation-related health behaviors among the Latino population in the United States (Lara *et al.*, 2005). Creighton, Goldman, Pebley, and Chung (2012) found that social and linguistic acculturation level accounts for lower consumptions of fruits for second- and third-generation Mexicans in the United States.

In this edited book, Team, Manderson, and Markovic took an ethnographic approach to understand the eating habits of Ukrainian

Australians, aged 50 years and over, with respect to the way healthy eating is communicated in Australia. Their findings reveal most participants have little knowledge on the links between lifestyle factors and chronic illness, and this is partly due to their perceptions of Australian physicians' failure to discuss diet- and eating-related issues with patients. This research not only contributes to our understanding of immigrants' food acculturation process, but it also stresses the importance for the health care system to better promote and communicate healthy dietary habits that can lead to positive health outcomes. To expand the current research that focuses on environmental and individual determinants of dietary acculturation, another chapter in this book, written by An, discusses the impact of sociocultural factors, specifically social support and social control, on dietary behaviors among Asian immigrants. The findings and arguments in these two chapters underscore the importance of situating immigrants' dietary acculturation behaviors in the social, cultural, and relational contexts where the mutual exchange of information and culture between immigrants and members of host country occurs. In this way, immigrants not only adapt to the host country's culture, but also become part of the renewing culture of the host countries. Communication is a two-way process, thusly both immigrants and members of host country go through cultural adaptation simultaneously.

Acculturation theory is helpful for unpacking the different ways immigrants negotiate their relationship with their host society, but the theory does not fully capture the dynamic interaction between migrants and the members of host country and how that could influence their relationship. In addition, host country members' perceptions and preferences of migrants' acculturation strategies could also shape migrants' choices of acculturation strategies. It is evident that immigrants' acculturation strategies influence their relationship with dominant groups in the host society. Research finds that dominant group members in the host society tend to have more positive attitude toward immigrants who seem to accept the normative standards and common values of the host society, because those more assimilated immigrants are perceived as less threatening to host members' traditional way of life (Matera, Stefanile, & Brown, 2012). However, immigrants not only adopt mainstream cultural norms, but also bring in new cultural aspects to their host country. In this light, identity management theory can provide a more dyadic approach to understand how immigrants and members of the host country both adapt their communication strategies in renewing their relationships.

Identity Management: Negotiation between Two Parties

If we see that acculturation theory well captures immigrants' tendencies of adopting new culture or retaining their own cultural heritage, the identity management theory (Imahori & Cupach, 2005) focuses on the different stages that immigrants go through in acknowledging cultural differences and reforming their cultural identities. On immigrants' side, the acculturation process can be seen as a long-term identity management process. In comparison with acculturation theory, identity management theory can be more useful to understand intercultural relationships at a micro level, especially with the recognition that the "dominant" cultural rules are subject to change, or in situations where it's uncertain whether the host country's culture should be acculturated into. Identity management theory focuses on understanding intercultural communication in relational contexts and better captures the negotiation of identities between both parties in the relationship and interaction. According to identity management theory, in managing intercultural relationships, there are three stages that interactants need to go through: trial, enmeshment, and negotiation. Individuals start to acknowledge cultural differences and develop their desired cultural identity at the trial stage. Moving from differences, individuals start to find common ground in understanding one another and the intercultural relationship at the enmeshment stage. Finally, at the negotiation stage, individuals build on their understanding of cultural differences and shared common rules to elevate the intercultural relationship to a higher level, at which point they are capable of dealing with some challenging intercultural communication issues in a constructive and sometimes innovative way.

In an intercultural health communication context, it is crucial to understand individuals', especially immigrants', identity management processes. It is evident that individuals' social identity is linked to a variety of health-related behaviors (Haslam, S. A., Jetten, Postmes, & Haslam, C., 2009), and health promotion strategies can be more effective when they are linked to targeted audience's social identity (Moran & Sussman, 2014). Research has found that "individual and collective identity management strategies are related to both personal and social facets of well-being" (Bobowik, Basabe, & Páez, 2014, p. 119). Immigrants' identity transition and management is a dynamic process with constant negotiation between the culture of their home country and their host society, as Hall (1996) aptly states,

> Identities are about questions of using the resources of history, language, and culture in the process of becoming rather than being: not "who we are" or "where we came from," so much as what we become, how we have been represented and how that bears on how we represent ourselves.
>
> (p. 4)

Immigrants continuously reproduce and reform their cultural identities by practicing their homeland culture in memory and their perceived host country culture. The ways they enact and renew their identities shape their health beliefs and practices.

In understanding intercultural communication between patients and health care providers, an in-depth understanding of how each party forms their identity could help to reduce communication uncertainty and set reasonable expectations in the medical encounter and patient-provider relationships. In this book, Gong's chapter investigates Chinese migrant mothers' understandings of risks (perceived, real, and ambiguous) during pregnancy in the United Kingdom. The ways these Chinese mothers process health information during pregnancy and evaluate "risk" demonstrate a balance between their sociocultural knowledge and expectations of the health care systems and health care providers in both China and the United Kingdom. In this sense, managing and coping with "risk" is part of their identity management in a specific health care context. Gong's research, along with some other literature (e.g. Mao & Shi, 2015) focusing on immigrants' health communication experience, pointed to the lack of understanding of and emphasis on the accommodation strategies that the health care system and health care providers in the host country adopt during interaction with immigrants. The dominant expectation that immigrants should adapt their identity to fit in the current health care system is a reflection of ethnocentrism and could lead to immigrants' frustration with their host country's health care system. Therefore, we call for more research that focuses on the dyadic communication and identity management of the immigrants and members in their host countries.

The immigrant population in developed countries is very diverse in cultural backgrounds, socio-economic status, legal status, and some other parameters. It is very important for the host society to understand immigrants' identity in plural ways, as well as to recognize the uniqueness of individual and subgroup experiences. Some subgroups in the immigrant population are more vulnerable and subject to various social stigma, discrimination, and injustices. Migrant women workers face gender-specific challenges in addition to other barriers, and their relationships with other immigrant groups and dominant members of the host country are unique. In this book, Olaniran's chapter stresses the issue of violence against migrant women workers and provides suggestions on how information and communication technologies may help alleviate some of the challenges.

With the development of new technology, the Internet has broken the geographic boundaries in information sharing, social support, and interpersonal networking. Immigrants use social networking sites to manage their multicultural and multifaceted identities (Mao & Qian, 2015). One's health belief is deeply rooted in his/her cultural identity. It is not uncommon among immigrants to promote various ideologies of health and share health-related information on their social networking sites, in salient or subtle manners. Social networks have been found to be important information sources for vulnerable populations

(Liu, 1995; Metoyer-Duran, 1993), and exert significant influence on individuals' health behavior (Christakis & Fowler, 2008). Informal social networks are especially helpful for immigrants experiencing language and cultural barriers (Hernandez-Plaza, Pozo & Alonso-Morillejo, 2004). When immigrants encounter health issues, it is reasonable to assume many of them will seek relevant information from online resources in their host country, as well as in their home country. For immigrants, their complicated and fluid cultural identities can not only lead them to various health resources found in their multicultural social networks, but also shape their perceptions and evaluations of various health information they acquire. Exploring immigrants' online health information and social-support–seeking behaviors in the context of their identity management could provide meaningful insights into how the changes of cultural identity influence immigrants' health communication. In this book, Guntarik, Berry, and Arnoldi analyzed ten websites of health care providers targeting women's health in Dandenong, Australia, and found those websites were designed to present generic information to the wider English-speaking populace without addressing culture-specific needs or an understanding of health and healing from the perspective of diverse immigrant groups. Similar phenomena are likely to be found in some other developed countries. Without a comprehensive and in-depth understanding of immigrants' health identities and how they use the Internet as part of their identity management process and information exchange practices, the health system in the host country fails to adjust its core identity in building a relationship with immigrant populations. This kind of static health system is not one to accommodate the diverse health beliefs and needs of immigrants from different cultures.

When immigrants encounter barriers to accessing health care, they may find their own ways to satisfy their health needs, where one of those means is to go back to their home country for health care services. Medical tourism is becoming increasingly popular among some immigrants in the United States, Canada, Australia, and New Zealand (Lunt, Smith, Exworthy, Green, Horsfall, & Mannion, 2011). Aside from the complicated sociocultural aspects of medical tourism and health risks and challenges for medical tourists, immigrants' use of cross-border health care services also indicates the health disparity in the host country. For instance, when immigrants are underserved or do not have adequate knowledge of and access to the host country's health care system and services, they become marginalized and pushed back by the host country to seek homeland medical services (Connell, 2013; Lee, Kearns, & Friesen, 2010). This experience can reshape immigrants' understanding of their identity. Clearly, identity management is not only about immigrants' motivation for, efforts to, or actions of refusing or accepting the host country's cultural norms and traditions, but it is also a matter of mutual acceptance and an adaptation process shared by the immigrants and the dominant groups of the host country. Much scholarly research has focused on immigrants' adaptation behavior, yet future research should take a more dyadic approach to examine both the host country's health care system, and immigrants' perceptions of and experiences within the health care system. In this line of research, identity management theory could shed light on a variety of factors and contextual influences on both immigrants and host country members' identity management processes. These factors include, but are not limited to, group characteristics and individual traits, relational context, power struggle, social hierarchy, perceived differences and similarities, and interactions between different social networks.

Cultural Competence: Counting on Health Care Providers

In the literature on health care providers' efforts to serve a diverse population, cultural competence as a theoretical concept, and sometimes as a theoretical model, has been regularly emphasized. Health care providers' cultural competence can bring a wide range of benefits to patients and reduce health disparities. Providers' cultural competence can lead to the following patient outcomes: increased number of patients seeking health care; lower rates of morbidity and mortality; better adherence to treatment; improved health status; and higher levels of trust, self-esteem, and satisfaction with the service (Alizadeh & Chavan, 2016).

Cultural competence has been conceptualized in different ways. Researchers (Cross, Bazron, Dennis, & Isaacs, 1989) developed the six-stage cultural competence continuum for health care professionals: cultural destructiveness, incapacity, blindness, pre-competence, competence, and proficiency. Health care professionals advance their cultural competence through this continuum until they reach the cultural competence stage, at which point they recognize and value cultural differences. The highest stage in this continuum is cultural proficiency. At this stage, health care professionals and organizations embrace cultural diversity and are able to conduct research to develop culturally competent practices and disseminate the knowledge and practices. Taking a different approach, Campinha-Bacote (1999) described five key components of cultural competence: cultural awareness, cultural knowledge, cultural skill, cultural encounters, and cultural desire. In cultural competence training for health care professionals, the LEARN model developed by Carballeria (1997) is widely applied. This model suggests health care providers to listen, evaluate, acknowledge, recommend, and negotiate in their interactions with patients. This model "respects client centrality, avoids stereotyping, and leads to the adoption of mutually acceptable objectives-and measures-for behavior change" (Carballeria, 1997, p. 12). Based on a systematic review of literature on cultural competence, Alizadeh and Chavan (2016) summarized that although cultural competence has various definitions, most researchers emphasized that enhancing cultural competence is an ongoing process, and cultural awareness, cultural knowledge, and cultural skills/behavior are important elements of cultural competence. Hence, the features of cultural competence in health care can be broadly applicable across individual and organizational levels to bridge communication barriers and provide culturally appropriate health care (Ahmed, Bates, & Romina, 2016).

Needless to say, cultural competence entails responsiveness, knowledge, capacity, and skills for health care professionals to meet the unique needs of patients from diverse cultures. The theoretical concept and related models of cultural competence can be applicable worldwide. However, in existing literature on cultural competence in health care, there appears to be a narrow focus on health care providers' communication in different cultural settings in the United States, primarily with Caucasian-Americans, African-Americans, non-white Hispanics, and Asian-Americans (Alizadeh & Chavan, 2016). The development and application of a cultural competence framework or model have not been fully recognized or explored in multicultural health settings within a wider global context. Furthermore, many of the proposed cultural competence models have not been sufficiently validated by empirical research (Alizadeh & Chavan, 2016). The generalizability and applicability of these cultural competence models thus need to be further established. In this book, Mantwill and Schulz's chapter discovered group differences among Serbian-speaking immigrants, Albanian-speaking immigrants, and Swiss participants in their communications with health care providers on back pain in Switzerland. The group differences among the three cultural groups underline the importance for cultural competence training for health care providers in Switzerland. This chapter extends the cultural competence research to European context and supports the necessity of cultural competence training through empirical evidence.

Cultural competence has been regarded as a desired skill set for health care providers, but it is only one of many factors that influence effective provider-patient communication. Not only does patients' communicative participation matter in the health care provider-patient communication dyad, but effective medical communication is also shaped by the larger contexts in which it occurs and the conditions surrounding it—perceptions of the relationship and the other party, sociocultural factors, family communication patterns, informal networks, and health care policies, among others (Bates & Ahmed, 2012; Cegala, Street, & Clinch, 2007; McLeroy, Bibeau, Steckler, & Glanz, 1988; Street, 2003). As such, cultural competence skills building might be useful and important for patients, as well. Future research should, therefore, focus on building a more integrative cultural competence model.

Given the changing world demographics, cultural competence in health care is more timely and pivotal. In the discussion on cultural competence of health care providers, foreign-trained doctors are a unique group. Many foreign-trained doctors have a dual identity as immigrant and health care provider. They need to acculturate themselves into the new social and professional culture in the host country and work with patients of the host country who may perceive foreign-trained doctors differently (Chen *et al.*, 2011). Tsugawa, Jena, Orav, and Kjha (2017) reported that about one quarter of the physicians in the United States, United Kingdom, Canada, and Australia graduated from medical programs in other countries such as India, Philippines, and Pakistan. Those foreign-trained doctors not only bring into the Western medical system their unique cultural perspectives, but also face similar cultural and social challenges and discriminations that other migrants face. Understanding the cultural competence process of these doctors is an important new area to explore in specific relational contexts. For example, while foreign trained doctors could be perceived as cultural brokers and medical experts for patients with whom they share similar cultural backgrounds, these doctors might be considered less qualified or culturally incompetent by patients from a different culture. The cultural competence framework developed primarily in the North American context might not be sufficient to examine the medical communication processes and outcomes between foreign-trained doctors and their patients.

It is important to note that most empirical studies examining the impact of health care providers' cultural competence on patient outcomes tend to consider only patient satisfaction, and very few have focused on patient trust and health status (Alizadeh & Chavan, 2016). Not only is there a need to develop specific measures of cultural competence, but also the assessment of the impact of cultural competence on health outcomes needs to be more multidimensional and capture different aspects of the medical communication, e.g., patients' fear of physicians and perceptions of physicians' cultural competence (Ahmed & Bates, 2017). Future research should also consider interaction effect of cultural competence with other factors such as the organizational culture of health care institutions, the existing cultural differences between patients and doctors, as well as among patients, and the cultural stereotypes of patients and health care providers.

Final Reflections

The preceding discussion of commonly used theories and theoretical concepts in intercultural communication in the context of immigrant health clearly shows the relevance of cultural frameworks in understanding the dynamic, multidimensional, and complex nature of migrant health issues. Each of these theories and concepts has its own focus, along with its strengths and limitations. Acculturation theory primarily focuses on immigrants' cultural negotiation and provides insights into the "dynamic process of adaptation involving culture learning and maintenance influenced by individual, group, and environmental factors" (Cook, Brown, Loder, & Wissow, 2014, p. 1094). Migrants' adaptation process may shape their health-related communication and behavior. Identity management provides a dyadic approach that involves both migrants and the members of the host countries in understanding how they develop cultural relationships. Through the lens of identity management theory, individual traits, as well as multilevels of relational and contextual factors, are considered in the dynamic interactions between two parties. Identity management theory advances understanding of "the multidimensional character of identity management strategies" (Bobowik, Basabe, & Páez, 2013, p. 230) and how the use of these strategies may shape experiences of immigrants seeking health care. Bridging acculturation and identity management, cultural competence as an essential set of skills can help to realize a

> health care system...as one that acknowledges and incorporates—at all levels—the importance of culture, assessment of cross-cultural relations, vigilance toward the dynamics that result from cultural differences, expansion of cultural knowledge, and adaptation of services to meet culturally unique needs.
>
> (Betancourt, Green, Carrillo, & Ananeh-Firempong, 2003, p. 294)

Although patients and sometimes their important social networks are the important parties in health communication, scholarly discussions and professional training on cultural competence have put more emphasis on the health care providers' side. Put together, these theories and theoretical concepts help us understand how culture influences immigrant health; how immigrant health issues are culturally negotiated across values, beliefs, traditions, and customs, along with social, economic, and political realities; and how these issues and realities may best be harnessed to reach immigrant groups in the most meaningful manner possible.

Incorporating cultural frameworks into studying health communication aspects of immigrant health have theoretical, practice, and policy implications. Although scholarly efforts have been made to apply these theories and theoretical concepts to study issues related to immigrant's health, there is limited systematic effort in health communication literature to study immigrant health-related communication and behavior. According to Babrow and Mattson (2003), "health communication scholarship is first and foremost about concrete practices in the world" (p. 37). Theories become concrete and make more sense when they are understood in applied contexts. Efforts are essential to develop theoretically informed interventions and health promotion programs to address health challenges for immigrants. In this chapter, through our discussion on the above theories and concept, we acknowledge the need for applying multiple perspectives and approaches to ground understandings of immigrants' health communication issues.

Furthermore, health care practitioners can greatly benefit from scholarly efforts in developing new theories and refining existing theories in order to better unpack the complex interplays among migration, culture, and health communication. At the technical briefing on migration and health in May 2016, the following request, among others, was made to the World Health Organization: "To develop technical guidelines and tools and conduct research and help build the evidence base to inform migrant health policy formulation and changes" (WHO, 2016). We underscore the importance of sound theory building as the cornerstone of evidence-informed policy formulation to meet the health needs of migrants.

The purpose of this chapter has been to initiate an interdisciplinary dialogue on culture-related theories that can provide important insights into health communication research and practice. We hope our survey and discussion of acculturation, identity management, and cultural competence have demonstrated how they can be uniquely situated, as well as complementary, so as to inform examinations of the various social, cultural, and relational contexts that influence immigrant's health communication. We conclude by calling for further investigations into issues of culture, immigration, and health communication in order to help inform future directions of theoretical developments in culture and health in a global context.

References

Ahmed, R., & Bates, B. R. (2017). Patients' fear of physicians and perceptions of physicians' cultural competence in healthcare. *Journal of Communication in Healthcare: Strategies, Media and Engagement in Global Health*. doi:10.1080/17538068.2017.1287389.

Ahmed, R., Bates, B. R., & Romina, S. M. (2016). Assessing the influence of patients' perceptions of physicians' cultural competence on patient satisfaction in an Appalachian Ohio context. *Howard Journal of Communications*, 27(4), 403–421. doi:10.1080/10646175.2016.1211569.

Alizadeh, S., & Chavan, M. (2016). Cultural competence dimensions and outcomes: A systematic review of the literature. *Health and Social Care in the Community*, *24*(6), e117–e130. doi:10.1111/hsc.12293.

Arcia, E., Skinner, M., Bailey, D., & Correa, V. (2001). Models of acculturation and health behaviors among Latino immigrants to the U.S. *Social Science & Medicine*, *53*, 41–53. doi:10.1016/s0277-9536(00)00310-5.

Babrow, A. S., & Mattson, M. (2003). Theorizing about health communication. In T. L. Thompson, A. M. Dorsey, K. I. Miller, and R. Parrott (Eds.),

Handbook of health communication (pp. 35–61). Mahwah, NJ: Lawrence Erlbaum Associates.

Bates, B. R., & Ahmed, R. (2012). Introduction to medical communication in clinical contexts. In B. R. Bates & R. Ahmed (Eds.), *Medical communication in clinical contexts* (pp. 1–16). Dubuque, IA: Kendall Hunt.

Batis, C., Hernandez-Barrera, L., Barquera, S., Rivera, J. A., & Popkin, B. M. (2011). Food acculturation drives dietary differences among Mexicans, Mexican Americans, and Non-Hispanic whites. *The Journal of Nutrition, 141*, 1898–1906. doi:10.3945/jn.111.141473.

Berry, J. W. (1980). Acculturation as varieties of adaptation. In A. M. Padilla (Ed.), *Acculturation: Theory, models and some new findings* (pp. 9–25). Boulder, CO: Westview.

Berry, J. W. (1990). Psychology of acculturation. In J. Berman (Ed.), *Cross-cultural perspectives: Nebraska symposium on motivation* (pp. 201–234). Lincoln, NE: University of Nebraska Press.

Berry, J. W. (1997). Immigration, acculturation and adaptation. *Applied Psychology: An International Review, 46*, 5–68. doi:10.1111/j.1464-0597.1997.tb01087.x.

Betancourt, J. R., Green, A. R., Carrillo, J. E., & Ananeh-Firempong, O. II (2003). Defining cultural competence: A practical framework for addressing racial/ethnic disparities in health and health care. *Public Health Reports, 118*(4), 293–302.

Bobowik, M., Basabe, N., & Páez, D. (2013). Identity management strategies, perceived discrimination, and well-being among young immigrants in Spain. In R. Dimitrova, M. Bender, & F. van de Vijver (Eds.), *Global perspectives on well-being in immigrant families* (pp. 213–234). New York: Springer.

Bobowik, M., Basabe, N., & Páez, D. (2014). "Heros of adjustment": Immigrant's stigma and identity management. *International Journal of Intercultural Relationships, 41*, 112–124. doi:10.1016/j.ijintrel.2014.04.002.

Campinha-Bacote, J. (1999). A model and instrument for addressing cultural competence in health care. *Journal of Nursing Education, 38*(5), 203–207.

Carballeria, N. (1997). The LIVE and LEARN model for cultural competent family services. *Continuum, 17*, 7–12.

Cegala, D. J., Street, R. L., Jr., & Clinch, C. R. (2007). The impact of patient participation on physicians' information provision during a primary care medical interview. *Health Communication, 21*(2), 177–185. doi:10.1080/10410230701307824.

Chen, P. G.-C., Curry, L. A., Bernheim, S. M., Berg, D., Gozu, A., & Nunez-Smith, M. (2011). Professional challenges of non-U.S.-born international medical graduates and recommendations for support during residency training. *Academic Medicine, 86*(11), 1383–1388. doi:10.1097/ACM.0b013e31823035e1.

Christakis, N. A., & Fowler, J. H. (2008). The collective dynamics of smoking in a large social network. *New England Journal of Medicine, 358*, 2249–2258. doi:10.1056/NEJMsa0706154.

Clark, L., & Hofsess, L. (1998). Acculturation. In S. Loue (Ed.), *Handbook of immigrant health* (pp. 37–59). New York: Plenum Press.

Cook, B. L., Brown, J. D., Loder, S., & Wissow, L. (2014) Acculturation differences in communicating information about child mental health between

Latino parents and primary care providers. *Journal of Immigrant and Minority Health, 16*(6), 1093–1102. doi:10.1007/s10903-014-0010-2.
Connell, J. (2013). Contemporary medical tourism: Conceptualisation, culture and commodification. *Tourism Management, 34*, 1–13. doi:10.1016/j.tourman.2012.05.009.
Cook, B. L., Brown, J. D., Loder, S., & Wissow, L. (2014). Acculturation differences in communicating information about child mental health between Latino parents and primary care providers. *Journal of Immigrant Minority Health, 16*, 1093–1102. doi:10.1007/s10903-014-0010-2.
Corlin, L., Woodin, M., Thanikachalam, M., Lowe, L., & Brugge, D. (2014). Evidence for the healthy immigrant effect in older Chinese immigrants: a cross-sectional study. *BMC Public Health, 14*, 603. doi:10.1186/1471-2458-14-603.
Creighton, M., Goldman, N., Pebley, A., & Chung, C. (2012). Durational and generational differences in Mexican immigrant obesity: Is acculturation the explanation? *Social Science & Medicine, 75*(2), 300–310. doi:10.1016/j.socscimed.2012.03.013.
Cross, T., Bazron, B., Dennis, K., & Isaacs, M. (1989). *Towards a culturally competent system of care, Volume 1*. Washington, DC: CASSP Technical Assistance Center, Center for Child Health and Mental Health Policy, Georgetown University Child Development Center.
Fernandez, A., Schillinger, D., Grumbach, K., Rosenthal, A., Stewart, A. L., Wang, F., & Pérez-Stable, E. J. (2004). Physician language ability and cultural competence. *Journal of General Internal Medicine, 19*(2), 167–174. doi:10.1111/j.1525-1497.2004.30266.x.
Finch, B. K., & Vega, W. A. (2003). Acculturation stress, social support, and self-rated health among Latinos in California. *Journal of Immigrant Health, 5*, 109–117. doi:10.1023/A:1023987717921.
Guendelman, M. D., Cheryan, S., & Monin, B. (2011). Fitting in but getting fat: Identity threat and dietary choices among U.S. immigrant groups. *Psychological Science, 22*(7), 959–967. doi:10.1177/0956797611411585.
Hall, S. (1996). Introduction: Who needs identity? In S. Hall & P. du Gay (Eds.), *Questions of cultural identity* (pp. 1–17). London: SAGE Publications.
Haslam, S. A., Jetten, J., Postmes, T., & Haslam, C. (2009). Social identity, health and well-being: An emerging agenda for applied psychology. *Applied Psychology, 58*, 1–23. doi:10.1111/j.1464-0597.2008.00379.x.
Hernandez-Plaza, S., Pozo, C., & Alonso-Morillejo, E. (2004). The role of informal social support in needs assessment: Proposal and application of a model to assess immigrants' needs in the South of Spain. *Journal of Community & Applied Social Psychology, 14*, 284–298. doi:10.1002/casp.782.
Imahori, T. T., & Cupach, W. R. (2005). Identity management theory. In W. B. Gudykunst (Ed.), *Theorizing about intercultural communication* (pp. 195–210). Thousand Oaks, CA: SAGE Publications.
Lara, M., Gamboa, C., Kahramanian, M. I., Morales, L. S., & Bautista, D. E. H. (2005). Acculturation and Latino health in the United States: A review of the literature and its sociopolitical context. *Annual Review of Public Health, 26*, 367–397. doi:10.1046/10.1146/annurev.publhealth.26.021304.144615.
Lee, J. Y., Kearns, R. A., & Friesen, W. (2010). Seeking affective health care: Korean immigrants' use of homeland medical services. *Health & Place, 16*(1), 108–115. doi:10.1016/j.healthplace.2009.09.003.

Lévi-Strauss, C. (1978). *The origin of table manners*. New York: HarperCollins Publishers.

Liu, M. (1995). Ethnicity and information seeking. *Reference Library*, *49*(50), 123–134. doi:10.1300/J120v23n49_09.

Lunt, N., Smith, R., Exworthy, M., Green, S. T., Horsfall, D., & Mannion, R. (2011). Medical tourism: treatments, markets and health system implications: A scoping review. *Directorate for Employment, Labour and Social Affairs, OECD*. Retrieved from www.oecd.org/els/health-systems/48723982.pdf.

Mao, Y., & Qian, Y. (2015). Facebook use and acculturation: The case of overseas Chinese professionals in Western countries. *International Journal of Communication*, *9*, 2467–2486. Retrieved from: http://ijoc.org/index.php/ijoc/article/view/2380/1434.

Mao, Y., & Shi, L. (December, 2015). Comparing Chinese immigrant women with Caucasian women on maternal health communication with healthcare providers: Findings from the Los Angeles Mommy and Baby (LAMB) survey. In A. M. Gatison (Ed.), *Communicating women's health: Social and cultural norms that influence health decisions* (pp. 91–103). New York: Routledge.

Matera, C., Stefanile, C., & Brown R. (2012). Host culture adoption or intercultural contact? Comparing different acculturation conceptualizations and their effects on host members' attitudes towards immigrants. *International Journal of Intercultural Relations*, *36*, 459–471. doi:10.1016/j.ijintrel.2012.03.002.

McDonald, J. T., & Kennedy, S. (2005). Is migration to Canada associated with unhealthy weight gain? Overweight and obesity among Canada's immigrants. *Social Science & Medicine*, *61*, 2469–2481. doi:10.1016/j.socscimed.2005.05.004.

McLeroy, K. R., Bibeau, D., Steckler, A., & Glanz, K. (1988). An ecological perspective on health promotion programs. *Health Education Behavior*, *15*(4), 4351–4377. doi:10.1177/109019818801500401.

Metoyer-Duran, C. (1993). The information and referral process in culturally diverse communities, *Reference Quarter*, *32*(3), 359–371. Retrieved from: www.jstor.org/stable/25829307.

Moran, M., & Sussman, S. (2014). Translating the link between social identity and health behavior into effective health communication strategies: An experimental application using antismoking advertisements. *Health Communication*, *29*, 1057–1066. doi:10.1080/10410236.2013.832830.

Parasecoli, F. (2014). Food, identity, and cultural reproduction in immigrant communities. *Social Research*, *81*(2), 415–439. Retrieved from: https://muse.jhu.edu/article/549124/pdf.

Street, R. L., Jr. (2003). Communicating in medical encounters: An ecological perspective. In T. L. Thompson, A. M. Dorsely, K. I. Miller, & R. Parrott, (Eds.), *Handbook of health communication* (pp. 63–89). London: Lawrence Erlbaum Associates.

Tsugawa, Y., Jena, A. B., Orav, E. J., & Kjha, A. (2017). Quality of care delivered by general internists in US hospitals who graduated from foreign versus US medical schools: Observational study. *BMJ*, *356*, j273. doi:10.1136/bmj.j273.

van Servellen, G., Brown, J. S., Lombardi, E., & Herrera, G. (2003). Health literacy in low income Latino men and women receiving antiretroviral therapy in community-based treatment centers. *AIDS Patient Care and STDs*, *17*(6), 283–298. doi:10.1089/108729103322108166.

Vang, Z. M., Sigouin, J., Flenon, Astrid, F., & Gagnon, A. (2017). Are immigrants healthier than native-born Canadians? A systematic review of the healthy immigrant effect in Canada. *Ethnicity & Health*, 22(3), 209–241. doi:10.1080/13557858.2016.1246518.

Vega, W. A., & Amaro, H. (1994). Latino outlook: Good health, uncertain prognosis. *Annual Review of Public Health*, *15*, 39–67. doi:10.1146/annurev.pu.15.050194.000351.

World Health Organization (WHO). (2016). *Technical briefing on migration and health*. Report. 69th World Health Assembly. Retrieved from www.who.int/migrants/publications/WHA69_mh-technical-breefing.pdf?ua=1.

Zambrana, R. E., & Carter-Pokras, O. (2010). The role of acculturation research in advancing science in reducing health care disparities among Latinos. *American Journal of Public Health*, *100*, 18–23. doi:10.2105/AJPH.2008.138826.

2 On the Diffusion of People and Practices

Prospects for Health Communication Research

James W. Dearing and Jeffrey G. Cox

> Regardless of how the globalization debate is resolved, it is clear that as broad global forces transform the world in which the next generation will live and work, the choices that today's young people make or others make on their behalf will facilitate or constrain their success as adults. Traditional expectations regarding future employment prospects and life experiences are no longer valid.
>
> —National Research Council and Institute of Medicine (2005)

> Refugees from poor and war-torn places are crossing land and sea in record numbers to get to the better lives shown to them by modern communications.
>
> —Yardley, Smale, Perlez, and Hubbard (2016)

Migrant health, and the role of scholars in investigating and helping to improve migrant health, are vitally important right now. The political and policy implications of the immigration issue are far-reaching and have elicited strong populist and nativist sentiments against migrants who are swelling the ranks of immigrants in those countries where migrants arrive. Especially driven by political instability and war in the Middle East, increased emigration directly affects communities and cities in more-industrially developed countries while impacting the prospects for recovery and rebuilding in less-industrially developed countries. Local and national cultures are fused, split, and fused again as beliefs, practices, and norms move with migrants.

The movement of people has always been a very effective means of cultural transmission as anthropologists have long observed in their accounting of the spread of language, customs, and artifacts over time and across the world (Steward, 1962). Population scientists, too, have studied trends in population partly as a function of the movement of people (National Research Council, 2001). Now, the spread of information technology into the hands of ordinary people everywhere (Cortada, 2012) has accelerated decisions to emigrate, partly because early-leaving emigrants tend to post positive images of new places to their family and friends who have yet to leave, thus making later emigrants perceive less risk and lowering the emotional and relational barriers to deciding to migrate. Cellular telephones have enabled more and better communication among far-flung family members and perhaps reduced the prospect of isolation and loneliness that leaving can produce.

It is reasonable to expect that increased movement of migrants will mean increased cultural disruption where they will newly live. Assimilation, acculturation, cultural adaptation, and cultural competency are going to be controversies for years to come. Even in communities and cities that welcome immigrants with open arms, there is much work to do (Bennhold, Erlanger, & Smale, 2015). An objective such as cultural competency can take many years to master for the family that is suddenly raising sons and daughters in a new country. The need and opportunities for the expertise that health communication scholars and practitioners can provide to migrants and those who support them will be great.

Health Communication and the Migrant Experience

One of the fascinating and fundamental aspects of studying migration and immigrants is movement. Physical relocation is filled with hope and dreams for a better life, fear and terrific uncertainty about what lies ahead, and strong motivation to improve life conditions. Migrants, especially those who need the most help, may be poor with low literacy and both chronic and acute health problems. They may be politically and religiously persecuted and socially stigmatized, and physically and sexually abused. They may have experienced traumatic events and devastating personal loss. For many, migration means a break from the social support of families and friends. So immigrants can need the full array of social services including housing, language schooling, and job retraining and counseling. Elevated stress and uncertainty along with persistent financial insecurity can be expected to lead to the adoption of unhealthy habits.

Obviously, we are not painting a picture of limited opportunities for health communication scholars to add value to our understanding of this enlarged global issue and ways to possibly improve conditions. Consider, if you will, a few possibilities here of what may lie ahead for health communication scholars who are attending to the conjoint topics of culture and migration:

- The mobility that is manifest in migration is not just physical relocation. Mobility may be social. Does the immigrant benefit from social mobility as a result of migration? Does she attain higher social status? Can she eventually attain jobs and positions of authority that are out of her reach in her home country? Similarly, the migrant may experience psychic mobility by using her phone. She may see new people, places, and things, as well as the people, places, and things she left behind. This is a different mobility calculus than originally calculated by the development sociologist Daniel Lerner (1976), who theorized a linear progression for migrants from physical mobility (rural to urban) leading to social mobility (low caste to middle caste) leading to psychic mobility (education to enlightenment). Migration in 2018 is all about psychic mobility via platforms like Facebook leading to physical relocation. If Lerner and his international development colleagues in the 1950s, 1960s, and 1970s identified a pathway of rising expectations producing rising frustrations—which they famously did—then the new calculus of mobility may lead to even more frustration for migrants as rosy prospects in the pictures on phones evaporate into the harsh reality of a new country, and where the very idea of social mobility may be far, far away. What types of messages and support are most needed to offset the deleterious effects of dislocation and grueling travel? Do expectations need to be tempered with messages that counter or contextualize actual living and employment conditions? What sorts of cultural competency training can be sent to migrants so that they make fewer mistakes when they arrive? The health communication scholar could have much to study about these types of mobility and the migrant experience.

- There are better times and worse times to encourage people to change. The act of migration is transformative for many migrants, a major life event. Transformative experiences can unfreeze resistance to change, making positive cognitive, attitudinal, and behavioral responses to health communication efforts more likely. People who use tobacco products may be more willing to try quitting in a new culture. People not accustomed to discussing sex with their partner may be more accepting of such conversations in a new culture. The husband who drinks and gambles away his weekly income with his friends may, when he is removed from that social group, be newly willing to change. Health communication scholars who work on developing, testing, improving, and scaling up health promotion programs may find migrants an attentive audience if initial communication successfully occurs and if pro-social norms in the new country are perceived by immigrants.
- Information about health reaches immigrants through different channels. As migrants, they bring their own beliefs and normative practices about health with them. The hiring of external change agents in the new country and related identification of immigrants who are willing to work as para-professional aides from the inside of a neighborhood or community is another way that information about health can reach immigrant populations. Specialty and mass media and social media represent a third type of channel. As with most health communication campaigns, we can expect

that the same or consonant messages communicated through different channels and repeatedly can have a reinforcing effect on immigrants' knowledge, attitudes, and behaviors about one or a set of related health practices. However, health communication efforts are usually strapped for resources. Which type of channel can deliver health messages at both low-cost and with reasonable effectiveness?

- Producing new healthy behaviors by immigrants depends most directly on immigrants themselves. The transition to a new mode of behavior requires enabling factors or preconditions of readiness, willingness, and ability (Lesthaeghe & Vanderhoeft, 2001). Readiness means that the new behavior must be perceived as advantageous to the individual, an informal form of cost/benefit analysis. Willingness means that the new behavior must be perceived as culturally acceptable even while representing a break with past behavior. Ability means that the individual must both have access to resources they need to enact the new behavior and be skilled enough to engage in the behavior. Can international health communication scholars structure campaigns and community health outreach efforts around the attainment of preconditions such as these?
- Social support is often essential for individuals to try a new behavior. People are far from being atomized individuals. Social support can be expected to be an especially large contributor to successful health communication programs for immigrants who, in breaking with their past, are already at-risk of not being embedded in strong support systems. Working class people rely heavily on direct personal relations to find jobs. More so than for the middle class, direct ties in ethnic and kin networks are a basis for how working class people survive, learn of opportunities, and live once they are in a new city (Salaff, Fong, & Wong, 1999). Immigrant neighborhoods thrive because of small tight circles of relations (Espinoza, 1999). Are there ways for health communication scholars to learn about and collaborate with local neighborhoods and thus build outward on a basis of participation and relational strength? Which community residents are especially influential? In partnering with a community, can health communication scholars take such an approach that results in social mobilization for better health (Haider, 2005)?

The social change paradigm known as the diffusion of innovations has been used to study the spread of people and practices. We turn to it now to suggest ways in which diffusion concepts may help international health communication scholars to conceptualize and conduct studies or design health promotion programs that aim to learn about and improve the migrant experience.

The Diffusion Paradigm

The research and practice paradigm of the diffusion of innovations seeks to explain how and why certain new ideas, products, or practices are adopted by individuals within a population (Rogers, 2003). Diffusion focuses on the individual- and group-level processes of adoption and how those relate to system-level social structure. Diffusion research has its roots in sociology in the theorizing of Georg Simmel in Germany and Gabriel Tarde in France, with the key subsequent empirical studies being conducted by rural sociologists who examined the pattern of diffusion of hybrid corn seed among Iowa farmers. Since then, the diffusion framework has proven to be robust and versatile, with important applications in fields as diverse as international development, psychology, communication, marketing, management, agriculture, medicine, and epidemiology. Researchers from these fields often collaborate in the university and in the field. From an intervention standpoint, diffusion work is inherently interdisciplinary, requiring researchers and communication practitioners (often with different specialties and from different countries) to work together with influential individuals and organizations that are seen as highly credible in communities of need. The wide interest in and adaptability of diffusion research across diverse populations means that it often has an international component.

Innovations that diffuse to many individuals or organizations have key attributes that enhance their adoptability: *Observability* (how visible the innovation's outcomes are to others), *trialability* (one's ability to test the innovation before full-scale adoption), *complexity* (how simple the innovation is to understand and use), *compatibility* (how the innovation fits with established routines and norms) and *relative advantage* (how effective and efficient the innovation is when compared with alternative methods of achieving the same ends). These attributes are considered by potential adopters of an innovation as one important set of factors in the *individual adoption-process* consisting of more or less time-ordered stages.

At the *awareness/knowledge* stage, an individual is introduced to initial descriptive information about the innovation, followed by the *persuasion* stage, during which time the individual considers attribute-focused evaluative information about the innovation. At the *decision* and *implementation* stages, the individual decides whether the innovation is worth trying, and then, if the decision is made to try the innovation, a trial-and-error period of learning to use the innovation. Finally, *confirmation* is important since many adopters come to doubt their earlier decision to adopt. The success of a diffusion intervention is often dependent on hired change agents who recruit local para-professional aides with detailed knowledge of a community, the degree to which change agents are able to identify who in the community is informally influential according to others, and concentrating change agent attention on those influential community residents.

Diffusion concepts have been used many times internationally to design, launch, and then measure the effects of public health and other types of programs. Often, this type of work means that new health practices (innovations) are designed to be compatible with existing resources, have advantages relative to existing practices and training programs, be easy to understand and use, and be low cost, as well as effective. Then, the workshops, trainings, or community health outreach scripts are written to reflect positive attributes. Change agents are taught to "read" the influence structure of a community and then intervene with the right people (Dearing, 2009). Personal interaction, repeated visits, and concern for others before beginning to talk about an innovation are all important qualities of a successful change agent, in addition to the change agent's technical knowledge (Havelock & Havelock, 1973). For immigrants, it is reasonable to expect that the recruitment and training of para-professional aides (Rogers, 2003) who would probably also be recent immigrants, would be especially important so that they would be trusted by other immigrants.

The design of community interventions based on diffusion theory is necessarily interdisciplinary, as it relies on the merging of outside technical/medical expertise with insiders' knowledge of a social system such as a community, a neighborhood, or a network of immigrants. Influential opinion leaders, if they agree to help with a diffusion effort, are able to model and demonstrate the use of an innovation within their communities, allowing other individuals in their communities to observe the innovation's effects and consequences before they try it for themselves. Asking for the help of opinion leaders offers significant advantages when used in concert with mass or specialty media, because informal leaders have more influence on community members' beliefs and behaviors than do impersonal messages, especially if the topic is perceived by potential adopters to be consequential for how they live or work.

A good example of the role of opinion leaders was Coleman, Katz, and Menzel's (1966) seminal diffusion study examining the diffusion of a drug's prescription among a community of physicians in New England. Although initially started as an investigation into the effects of drug advertising on its adoption by physicians, it quickly turned into an analysis of social relations and influence among members of the population. Perhaps the most important aspect of the study was its identification of the characteristics of the most influential physicians (opinion leaders), within their own medical community. Importantly, opinion leader influence extended beyond their specialized networks of other physicians and bridged more generally into the communities in which they lived.

Kelly *et al.* (1991, 1992) conducted a series of very successful studies that applied diffusion principles to increase adoption of HIV prevention practices. Initially conducted in U.S. cities, this program of research and application expanded to more than fifty countries. Researchers from diverse backgrounds began by asking bartenders at popular bars to identify individuals whom they considered opinion leaders in the gay community, based on their influence and social ties. These men were then recruited and trained in both safe sex practices and how to lead group discussions and training sessions. Through workshops with friends and social connections, these individuals could inform members of their community about how to stay safe, as well as identifying others who could also lead such discussions. This study provides a compelling example of how a diffusion-based intervention relies on interdisciplinary collaboration, as well as how the theory can be used to engage with members of the community.

Diffusion Concepts and Immigrant Communities

The diffusion concepts of opinion leadership and innovation attributes are two obvious ways that this international literature can aid in the study of migration and, especially, attempts to improve conditions for immigrants. A number of social marketing, dissemination, entertainment-education, community-based outreach, and health communication campaigns have done so (Singhal & Dearing, 2006). In international diffusion-inspired efforts, interventions are most often combinations or bundles of components, each of which acts to reinforce or complement campaign objectives (Althabe *et al.*, 2008). Especially for insular and "hidden" populations, interpersonal discussions and demonstrations led by change agents and para-professional aides where population members live or work is exceedingly important for gradually establishing the trust required for population members to then try an innovation and see its relevance to them and their loved ones (Dearing *et al.*, 1996). These interventions have more formal components such as leaflets and brochures, social media apps, and materials such as condoms, oral rehydration kits, and anti-malaria bed nets, but it is the repeated interpersonal "touch" that leads individuals to try the innovation and take the message to heart (Gawande, 2013). The success of a change agent or their aide who is recruited from the community in question to help in spreading the word about an innovation and demonstrating its use for those they call on is directly related to the change agent's ability to correctly identify and then concentrate their time in the field on informally influential members of the community (Kim & Dearing, 2016; Kim *et al.*, 2015).

What does the change agent say to the community member who is an opinion leader for others? Specialty media, small media, and reminders of many types have important roles to play in behavior change and maintenance, but the extant influence of opinion leaders with their near-peer followers means that the opinion leader does not need instruction in how to persuade or get others to listen. They may need information about the innovation in question including descriptive knowledge (what is it? What does it do?) and evaluative information (its pros and cons, framed in terms of innovation attributes of cost, effectiveness, simplicity, compatibility, trialability, and observability) in accessible formats so that they can tell others where to find out more about the innovation. In general, however, since community members value opinion leaders for their judgment, the "ask" of opinion leaders should be for them to learn about the innovation and decide for themselves, and communicate that opinion with others. Asking them to advocate is usually a mistake unless they are comfortable doing so and it is a role they normally play.

Since community-based opinion leaders wield significant sway over specific populations to which an innovation is targeted, they can be especially important in immigrant communities where there may be considerable distrust of governmental authorities and others in formal positions of authority (Kim, Chikombero, & Modie-Moroka, 2013). Immigrants may also distrust the mass media. These preferences for information from known, informal members inside a population or community networks are at least in part culturally determined since consonance of language, customs, and beliefs will carry over from immigrants' country of origin.

Part of the reason that community opinion leaders can be influential is because they can affect different stages of the diffusion process that are difficult for formal information channels to reach. In a study aimed at increasing mammography screening among Samoan immigrants in Los Angeles, Levy-Storms and Wallace (2003) found that successful diffusion occurred only with the confluence of both professional and interpersonal influences, with different sources driving different stages of the diffusion cycle. While Samoan migrants' primary care physicians were successful in moving the women into the behavioral *implementation* and *confirmation* stages, informal social networks were found to be much more effective at influencing Samoan women's intention to use mammography screening in the future.

The impacts of innovation characteristics (e.g. observability, compatibility, relative advantage, trialability, and complexity) on diffusion are also likely to play out differently in an immigrant community than a native one. For immigrants who may be experiencing an overwhelming number of new concepts to which they must adapt, the *complexity* of an innovation may be an especially important consideration. Additionally, *compatibility,* or how well the innovation fits with existing beliefs or practices, takes on an added importance in communities where cultural and health beliefs may be quite different from established public health recommendations. In Anne Fadiman's (2012) classic case study *The Spirit Catches You and You Fall Down,* the American medical system's approaches to treating a young Hmong child's epilepsy are in stark opposition with her parents' desires for more traditional healing. A lack of compatible understanding on both sides leads to a disaster in the young child's health, as well as growing distrust of modern medicine among members of this immigrant community. Similarly, folk beliefs in ineffective, and sometimes dangerous, methods for treating HIV/AIDS in some countries in Africa (e.g. only sick-looking people are infected; having sex with a virgin girl can rid one of the disease) (*Leclerc-Madlala, 2002*) can also lead to counterproductive, and oftentimes dangerous outcomes. This is again where the coordination of formal (science-based medical sources) and informal (influential individuals in the community) communication sources can be complementary for establishing correct health knowledge and then disseminating it.

Interdisciplinary Health Research

An interdisciplinary approach to learning about and intervening in immigrant populations is almost always a good idea since the skill set and degree of knowledge required of a project team can be many times greater than what is typically required in a domestic project. In recent years, national health funding institutes in the United States, Canada, and the United Kingdom have increasingly encouraged, and sometimes required, the collaboration of individuals from diverse educational and experiential backgrounds on research projects (Clarke *et al.*, 2012). In the US, the National Institutes of Health (NIH) has pushed diverse health research collaboration with their Interdisciplinary Research Program, funding successful research consortia to take on problems such as cancer, stress, and obesity (NIH, 2016). The US Environmental Protection Agency's (EPA) Superfund Research Program brings together researchers such as biologists, toxicologists, and social scientists to study environmental contamination and its effects on human health (EPA, 2014). Such collaborations allow researchers to expand their knowledge and impact by bringing a diverse set of perspectives and competencies to approaching health issues (Gebbie *et al.*, 2008). Certainly, in our own research we have repeatedly found this to be the case.

The advantages of interdisciplinary health research include the ability to address multifaceted health problems by providing complementary perspectives and methodological approaches, and the prospect of creating and developing a comprehensive theoretical lens for these problems (Choi & Pak, 2006). For example, fighting the spread of an infectious disease requires not only medical professionals who understand the pathology of the virus, but also epidemiologists who can model its spread through populations, social scientists who have an understanding of human health behavior, and communication experts who can disseminate health and risk information and study response, and often community outreach workers to reach residents and community organizers to stage events. As diseases and health problems now frequently span international borders, experts with knowledge of specific populations, cultures, and regions are increasingly key to global approaches to health.

The input of researchers with different backgrounds and expertise is also important for the development of theoretical approaches to understanding health issues. The collaboration of health and social scientists in theory development can lead to more holistic ways of addressing complex health problems (Rosenfield, 1992). Researchers with different experiences and knowledge sets can help effectively assess, monitor, and evaluate different stages of theoretical development and translation into practice (Logan & Graham, 1998). Partly because of its broad orientation to social change, the diffusion paradigm has been used many times to organize such interdisciplinary efforts (Dearing, Smith, Larson, & Estabrooks, 2013). By focusing on the establishment of evidence-based and useful health information, mass media channels, and community engagement, a diffusionist approach requires the coming together of professionals from diverse backgrounds to address a common problem. All of these factors must be understood at the time of designing for diffusion (the planning stage) in order to maximize the effective dissemination of effective health practices. If researchers and health practitioners do not address unique social and cultural aspects of an immigrant population, any information, no matter how established or effective, will likely be ignored by the population in question.

References

Althabe, F., Buekens, P., Bergel, E., Belizan, J. M., Campbell, M. K., Moss, N., ... Wright, L. L. (2008). A behavioral intervention to improve obstetrical care. *New England Journal of Medicine*, *358*, 1929–1940. doi:10.1056/nehmsa071456.

Bennhold, K., Erlanger, S., & Smale, A. (2015, September 6). Germany welcomes thousands of weary migrants. *The New York Times*.

Choi, B. C., Pak, A. W. (2006). Multidisciplinarity, interdisciplinarity and transdisciplinarity in health research, services, education and policy: 1. Definitions, objectives, and evidence of effectiveness. *Clinical and Investigative Medicine*, *29*, 351–364.

Clarke, D., Hawkins, R., Sadler, E., Harding, G., Forster, A., McKevitt, C., ... Farrin, A. (2012). Interdisciplinary health research: Perspectives from a process evaluation research team. *Quality in Primary Care*, *20*, 179–189.

Coleman, J. S., Katz, E., & Menzel, H. (1966) *Medical innovation: A diffusion study*. Indianapolis, IN: Bobbs-Merrill. doi:10.2307/2091036.

Cortada, J. W. (2012). *The digital flood: The diffusion of information technology across the U.S., Europe, and Asia*. New York: Oxford University Press. doi:10.19093/acprof:oso/9780199921553.001.0001.

Dearing, J. W. (2009). Applying diffusion of innovation theory to intervention development. *Research on Social Work Practice*, *19*(5), 503–518. doi:10.1177/1049731509335569.

Dearing, J. W., Rogers, E. M., Meyer, G., Casey, M. K., Rao, N., Campo, S., & Henderson, G. M. (1996). Social marketing and diffusion-based strategies for communicating health with unique populations: HIV prevention in San Francisco. *Journal of Health Communication*, *1*, 343–363. doi:10.1080/108107396127997.

Dearing, J. W., Smith, D. K., Larson, R.S., & Estabrooks, C. A. (2013). Designing for diffusion of a biomedical intervention. *American Journal of Preventive Medicine, 44(1S2), 70–76. doi:10.1016/j.amepre.2012.09.038.*

Environmental Protection Agency (2014). Superfund research program: Fact sheet. www.niehs.nih.gov/research/supported/assets/docs/r_s/srp_fact_sheet_508.pdf.

Espinoza, V. (1999). Social networks among the urban poor: Inequality and integration in a Latin American city. In B. Wellman (Ed.), *Networks in the global village* (pp. 147–184). Boulder, CO: Westview Press.

Fadiman, A. (2012). *The spirit catches you and you fall down*. New York: Farrar, Straus, and Giroux. doi:10.1006/ebeh.2000.0037.

Gawande, A. (2013, July 29). Slow ideas. *The New Yorker*, pp. 36–45.

Gebbie, K. M., Meier, B. M., Bakken, S., Carrasquillo, O., Formicola, A., Aboelela, S. W., ... Larson, E. (2008). Training for interdisciplinary health research. *Journal for Allied Health, 37*, 65–70.

Haider, M. (2005). *Global public health communication*. Sudbury, MA: Jones and Bartlett.

Havelock, R. G., & Havelock, M. C. (1973). *Training for change agents*. Ann Arbor, MI: Institute for Social Research, University of Michigan.

Kelly, J. A., St Lawrence, J. S., Diaz, Y. E., Stevenson, L. Y., Hauth, A. C., Brasfield, T.L., ... Andrew, M. E. (1991). HIV risk behavior reduction following intervention with key opinion leaders of population: An experimental analysis. *American Journal of Public Health, 81*, 168–171. doi:10.2105/ajph.81.2.168.

Kelly, J. A., St Lawrence, J. S., Stevenson, L. Y., Hauth, A. C., Kalichman, S. C., Diaz. Y. E., ... Morgan, M. G. (1992). Community AIDS/HIV risk reduction: The effects of endorsements by popular people in three cities. *American Journal of Public Health, 82*, 1483–1489. doi:10.2105/ajph.82.11.1483.

Kim, D. K., Chikombero, M., & Modie-Moroka, T. (2013). Innate health threat among a visibly hidden immigrant group: A formative field data analysis for HIV/AIDS prevention among Zimbabwean workers in Botswana. *Journal of Health Communication, 18*, 146–159. doi:10.1080/10810730.2012.688252.

Kim, D. K., & Dearing, J. W. (2016). Opinion leader identification. In D. K. Kim & J. W. Dearing (Eds.), *Health communication research measures* (pp. 77–86). New York: Peter Lang. doi:10.3726/978-1-4539-1682-7.

Kim, D. A., Hwong, A. R., Stafford, D., Hughes, D. A., O'Malley, A. J., Fowler, J. H., & Christakis, N. A. (2015). Social network targeting to maximize population behavior change: A cluster randomized controlled trial. *The Lancet, 386*, 145–153. doi:10.1016/s0140-67.36(15)60095-2.

Leclerc-Madlala, S. (2002). On the virgin cleansing myth: Gendered bodies, AIDS and ethnomedicine. *African Journal of AIDS Research, 1*, 87–95. doi:10.2989/16085906.2002.9626548.

Lerner, D. (1976). Technology, communication, and change. In W. Schramm & D. Lerner (Eds.), *Communication and change: The last ten years—and the next* (pp. 287–301). Honolulu, HI: University Press of Hawaii. doi:10.2307/2577438.

Lesthaeghe, R., & Vanderhoeft, C. (2001). Ready, willing, and able: A conceptualization of transitions to new behavioral forms. In National Research Council (Ed.), *Diffusion processes and fertility transition: Selected perspectives* (pp. 240–264). Washington, DC: National Academies Press.

Levy-Storms, L., & Wallace, S. P. (2003). Use of mammography screening among older Samoan women in Los Angeles County: A diffusion network approach. *Social Science and Medicine*, *57*, 987–1000. doi:10.1016/s0277-9536(02)00474-4.

Logan, J., & Graham, I. D. (1998). Toward a comprehensive interdisciplinary model of health care research use. *Science Communication*, 20, 227–246. doi:10.1177/1075547098020002004.

National Institutes of Health (NIH). (2016). Interdisciplinary research. https://commonfund.nih.gov/interdisciplinary.

National Research Council. (2001). *Diffusion processes and fertility transition: Selected perspectives.* Washington, DC: National Academies Press.

National Research Council and Institute of Medicine. (2005). *Growing up global: The changing transitions to adulthood in developing countries.* Washington, DC: The National Academies Press, p. 1.

Rogers, E. M. (2003). *Diffusion of innovations.* (5th ed.). New York: Free Press.

Rosenfield, P. L. (1992). The potential of transdisciplinary research for sustaining and extending linkages between the health and social sciences. *Social Science and Medicine*, *35*, 1343–1357. doi:10.1016/0277-9536(92)90038-r.

Salaff, J. W., Fong, E., Wong, S. L. (1999). Using social networks to exit Hong Kong. In B. Wellman (Ed.), *Networks in the global village* (pp. 299–329). Boulder, CO: Westview Press.

Singhal, A., & Dearing, J. W. (Eds.) (2006). *Communication of innovations.* Thousand Oaks, CA: Sage. doi:10.4135/9788132113775.

Steward, J. H. (1962). *Alfred Kroeber 1876–1960. A biographical memoir.* Washington, DC: National Academy of Sciences.

Yardley, J., Smale, A., Perlez, J., & Hubbard, B. (2016, June 26). A test of Western alliances and institutions. *The New York Times*, p. 1.

3 Negotiating Health on Dirty Jobs

Culture-Centered Constructions of Health among Migrant Construction Workers in Singapore

Mohan J. Dutta

The neoliberal organizing of global health has shaped the structural determinants of health, weakening labor unions, flexibilizing the global movement of labor, and creating conditions of disenfranchisement through structural adjustment programs in the global South that have catalyzed the global movement of labor (Dutta, 2015a, b, 2016a). Essential to contemporary global patterns of migration are the exploitative conditions of labor facilitated by globalization processes, leveraging flexible labor-related policies to enable the exploitation of migrant workers to generate maximum profits for transnational capital in the most cost-effective ways. Weak global labor policies enable the exploitation of migrant workers, particularly in the lowest rungs of capitalist production processes, with little to no protection offered to them. The simultaneous minimization of opportunities for migrant workers to participate in organizing processes enable the extractive processes of profiteering, reproducing the conditions of precarity under which migrant workers toil (Dutta, 2016a).

In the dominant health communication literature on immigration, the normative idea of immigration accounts for acculturation or cultural adaptation, suggesting pathways for enabling the immigrant communities to adapt to the host culture (Dutta & Jamil, 2013; Gao, Dutta, & Okoror, 2015). The immigrant culture is constructed as a deficit in opposition to the normative health behaviors that are universally prescribed (Dutta & Jamil, 2013). A culturally colonizing model of communicating health to immigrants articulates culture as the barrier to health that needs to be overcome through tailored messaging strategies. In this framework, culture is conceptualized as a static collection of beliefs and values, mapping immigrant culture in relation to the host culture, and developing recipes for cultural transformation through communication as persuasion. Communication, connected to culture, is tailored to adapt to the characteristics of the immigrant community, with the goal of generating culturally sensitive messages that are persuasively effective with the targeted immigrant community (Dutta, 2016a). Culturally sensitive messages are based on identifying characteristics of the culture that can be spoken to in order to generate affiliation and persuasive message processing.

Another thread of health communication scholarship focuses on developing culturally adaptive communication strategies for health care practitioners and professionals, suggesting mechanisms for practitioners to understand and effectively communicate with immigrant cultures (Dutta, 2007, 2008). In this framework, the emphasis is placed on developing cultural competence among health service providers so they can appropriately communicate with immigrant communities. The emphasis is often placed on language, translation, development of cultural respect, etc. In both of these threads, the culture of the immigrant community emerges as a key construct in the development of communication characteristics. However, missing from this dominant thread of health communication are the local cultural contexts of immigrant communities (Dutta & Jamil, 2013). In configuring immigrants as passive recipients of health messaging, the agentic capacities of immigrants are erased. Also absent from dominant health communication theorizing are the voices of local communities of immigrants, their lived experiences, and their negotiations of health. Moreover, the individualistic health communication frameworks often fail take into account the broader political economy of immigrant life.

Migrant workers from Bangladesh working in the construction industry in Singapore form a part of this global flow of labor, negotiating their health amid global structures of flows of capital and labor (Baey & Yeoh, 2015; Bal, 2015). In this chapter, I apply the theoretical framework of the culture-centered approach (CCA) to listen to the voices of migrant construction workers in Singapore (Dutta, 2004a,b, 2008; Dutta & Jamil, 2013). The concepts of culture, structure, and agency are offered as conceptual anchors for foregrounding local meanings of health constituted at the intersections of migration and work (Dutta & Jamil, 2013; Gao *et al.*, 2015). Building on a growing line of existing research that connects health to the precarity of work in global processes of labor flow, this chapter elucidates the structural contexts of immigrant health, depicting the construction of meanings amid these structures, and suggesting strategies for health communication that responds to these overarching structures of health and migration. The narratives of migrant construction workers foreground the meaning of work as an organizing feature of global health communication, depicting the ways in which the conditions of/at work shape the constructions of health. Rather than suggesting the calibrated modifications in behavior that are typically recommended in emerging health communication interventions that position themselves as being structurally adaptive (Blankenship, Friedman, Dworkin, & Mantell, 2006), the voices of the participants suggest entry points for structural transformations that fundamentally invert the ways in which workplace relationships and risks of health are constituted.

Immigrant Health and Communication

The dominant approach to immigrant health in the health communication literature conceptualizes immigrant health in the context of acculturation, the movement of health of immigrants along a continuum from the point of entry to incorporation into the host culture (Dutta, 2007). Mapping the struggles faced by immigrant communities in acculturating to the host culture, the literature suggests strategies for addressing the cultural barriers that are depicted as being experienced in immigrant communities. Culture as a concept is theorized as a static characteristic of immigrant communities, and the role of health communication in immigrant contexts is to respond effectively to cultural characteristics. In contrast to this dominant framework of health communication, a culture-centered approach to communicating health takes as its entry point a framework of culture as dynamic and constituted in context through the active participation of community members in the life of the culture.

Cultural Sensitivity Approach

The cultural sensitivity approach is based on the premise that relevant cultural characteristics can be identified and selected to guide the development of persuasive health communication interventions targeting immigrant communities (Dutta, 2007). The premise of the approach is on the identification of the appropriate cultural characteristics, which can then guide the development of the messaging strategy for the health communication intervention. Existing scholarship suggests a wide array of cultural characteristics ranging from deep characteristics such as cultural values to superficial characteristics such as modification of the language or use of cultural insiders in the imagery of the message. The cultural sensitivity approach emphasizes educating the immigrant communities, taking an overarching individualistic framework to behavior change.

Culture-Centered Approach

Noting the top-down nature of health communication and health promotion approaches that fail to take the contextually situated local culture into account, Airhihenbuwa (1995) criticizes the existing trends in studying health communication and argues that health communication should be guided by culture. The conceptualization of culture offered by Airhihenbuwa is dynamic, fragmented, and ever-transforming. Building on the work of Airhihenbuwa, the culture-centered approach (CCA) to health communication views culture as constantly metamorphosing, constitutive, and transformative in the domain of health meanings, foregrounding meanings as entry points for the constructions of health and well-being (Dutta, 2004a, b, 2008, 2015a). The CCA proposes that cultural contexts are entry points to theoretical insights into the ways health decisions and meanings are negotiated in cultural communities (Dutta, 2008). It is only through engagement in dialogue with the cultural insider that the local meanings of health can be articulated and understood. Focusing on the voices from the margins, constructing epistemologies from the periphery, and by focusing on the "conceptualization of health, the culture-centered approach reverses the traditional one-way flow of communication from the core to the periphery" (Dutta, 2004a, p. 1108). Theorizing health at sites of erasure, the CCA seeks to co-construct spaces of listening to subaltern[1] voices that render impure the conceptual categories of the dominant mainstream (Guha, 1988). The presence of subaltern voices in the discursive spaces inverts the dominant articulations. For the culture-centered scholar, rather than serving as an interlocutor that represents subaltern articulations, the driving question is one of co-creating infrastructures of legitimacy that recognize the capacity of subaltern communities to represent themselves (Haig-Brown, 2003).

The CCA does not box health in terms of universals as the biomedical model prescribes, but constructs health in terms of the cultural logics of the local, attending to the cultural rationalities that emerge from communities at the margins. It co-constructs ways of understanding and articulating health from the perspectives of the cultural insider, suggesting that an entry point for addressing health and well-being of those at the margins is the creation of infrastructures of listening (Dutta, 2014). It suggests that to understand what really matters to subaltern communities at the margins, one needs to "begin by creating spaces for those voices [that has been] systematically silenced through our [the dominants] expertise and eliticism" (Dutta, 2008, p. 45). It is by creating spaces and listening to the voices from the margins that CCA tries to introduce theoretical guidelines in understanding the culture-structure-agency interactions (Dutta, 2008). Culture here is defined as a complex web of meanings (Geertz, 1973) and shared practices, beliefs, and values. So culture is fluid and dynamic, and draws from the past, present, and is modifiable in the future. Structure reflects the material realities that constrain and enable human action, and it is within these constraints that cultural insiders must enact their agency (Dutta, 2008). So in this aspect, "structures define the realm of possibilities in the context of health ... [and] through the enactment of agency in relationship with structure that individuals, communities and societies come to experience health" (p. 56).

The culture-centered approach attempts to deconstruct the taken-for-granted attitudes and assumptions of the dominant knowledge base, and tries to co-construct meanings and discursive spaces from the perspectives of cultural insiders. Such spaces in turn help in dialogic engagement with the marginalized, thus creating a bottom-up structure for articulating experiences and meanings. Positioning culture as the center of theorizing, the CCA has some key characteristics that draw attention to locally articulated meanings of health. They include voice and dialogue, structure, context, space, values, and criticism (Dutta, 2008). Voice and dialogue are central to CCA and seek to create spaces for the local communities' voices in ways that articulate their health needs, working on the basis of these articulations to build infrastructures of health. Rather than assuming the role of passive recipients of top-down solutions, communities at the margins work through the structures as active participants. According to Dutta (2008), structure refers to "those organizations, processes and systems in society which determine how that society is organized, how it functions, and how individual members within it behave with respect to each other, to social organizations, and so on" (p. 62). In the realm of migration, structures range all the way from policies defining the rules of movement, to conditions at places of work, to the organizing of resources of health. Context in CCA refers to the immediate surroundings of the cultural members in which they express their agency, and space refers to the spatial arrangement (center-periphery) of the dominant and marginalized groups. Space is closely intertwined with overarching structures, and is rendered meaningful in the local context. In the CCA, the emphasis placed on fostering spaces of legitimacy for subaltern voices to be heard means that the work of health communication is shifted from one of developing persuasive solutions prescribing individual behaviors to building methods of listening that would make space for subaltern voices in the dominant structures that produce knowledge. Finally, criticism plays a key role in the CCA as it takes a critical look at the dominant approaches to health communication by "suggesting the need to articulate the values that have driven the dominant paradigm, and by locating these values in the realm of the dominant ideology" (Dutta, 2008, p. 65). Interrogating the dominant ideologies of health serves as the backdrop for methods of listening through co-creation. This article draws from the CA and co-constructs meanings of health with Bangladeshi migrants' narratives that originate from their own discursive spaces. The narratives that appear in this article are stories shared with me by Bangladeshi migrants who work in Singapore as construction workers, about their conceptions of health that encompass their everyday lives.

Method

The chapter draws on thirty-five ethnographic in-depth interviews conducted with Bangladeshi construction workers in Singapore, part of a broader ongoing culture-centered ethnographic project initiated in 2008. The goals of the broader project are to foster infrastructures for listening to the voices of migrant construction workers in Singapore (Dutta, 2014). The in-depth interviews ranged from sixty minutes to two hours in length, with an average interview being forty-two minutes in length. The interviews were conducted in Bengali and then translated into English. The in-depth interviews resulted in three hundred twenty-five pages of single-spaced transcripts. In addition to the in-depth interviews, I conducted participant observations at public spaces where Bangladeshi construction workers hang out, spending time in Little India (space where migrant workers gather, especially on their day off on Sundays), attending performances put together by migrant workers, accompanying migrant workers during their visits to run errands, accompanying migrant workers during visits to doctors, and coordinating broader discussions with migrant workers as part of the larger culture-centered project driven toward identifying problems and developing solutions. The narratives shared by the participants in the project point toward a variety of contexts where their health is threatened and share strategies through which they secure access to health. In this chapter, we will share snippets from these conversations to elucidate the interplays of structure and agency in articulations of migrant worker health.

Agentic Expressions of Health amid Structures

The narratives shared by the participants point toward their everyday struggles for negotiating health amid the structures of migrant construction work. The everyday meanings of health are situated amid the local understandings of food, cultural approaches to health, and the structures that shape the distribution of resources. In sharing their experiences with structures, participants point toward the profit-driven framework of the structures that often directly threaten human health and well-being. Moreover, participants share their strategies of everyday health seeking amid these structural limitations.

Health as Absence

In the narratives of the participants, health is marked as an absence, primarily voiced in the realms of the absence of food from the everyday lives of the Bangladeshi construction workers in Singapore. When asked about how he comes to understand health, Rajeeb discussed that health to him is about having enough food so he could go about with the hard work on his job. He shared how construction work is heavy work, and is demanding on the body. To do such work as he did at the construction sites, often lifting heavy weight and carrying the weight for distances, called for him to have enough physical strength, which in turn, he derived from eating food. Yet he noted,

> Food is something that is often absent from the lives of Bangladeshi workers. I work long hours, and by the time I get back, the food that is catered is already stale. There are many nights when I don't get to eat anything.

The participants discussed the heavy work at construction sites, juxtaposed in the backdrop of the absence of sufficient food from their everyday lives. For Atif, "Food is the source of life, especially for a Bengali. We Bengalis work to eat, even this is what all the elders say and one has learned from childhood." On a similar note, Kareem shares,

> The hard work in the construction site goes from 7 in the morning until 8 or 9 in the evening. This is hard work. How can I do the work when I don't have enough food in my body and feel lethargic? I feel very tired and then worry that I am going to fall or have an accident. My stomach is empty.

The hard work at construction sites is juxtaposed in the backdrop of the absence of food.

Bangladeshi construction workers in Singapore often live in dormitories. While there are a wide range of dormitories in Singapore, in most of these dormitories, there are no cooking facilities. As a result, most of the workers receive food from catering agencies. Rezan shares his dependence on the catering companies,

> We can't cook our own food in the dormitory. There is no facility to cook own food. So I will have to depend on the catering company. Even though the quality of the food delivered by the catering company is of poor quality, I have no other choice.

Many Bangladeshi construction workers share similar problems with the quality of the food delivered by the catering company. This is what Zoeb shares,

> The problem is with the workers having to get the food from a catering company, and the catering company does not really care about the quality of the food we get. It just gets something to the workers. For most days, I can't just eat the food because it has gone stale.

Participants share,

> The food is so unhealthy that it can get you sick. There are many times I have had to take a medical certificate (MC) for a leave because I have gotten sick from eating the food. One time, it was stale. I knew it when I ate it. But I was so hungry that I ate it. Later it made me sick.

In the narrative shared by Mustaq, we hear the experience of unhealthy food that made him sick. Along similar lines, Saleem shares,

> The food has often gone stale by the time I eat it. It is delivered in the dorm at 5 a.m. in the morning and is cooked the previous night.

> I eat it only at noon during lunch time and that's when it has already become stale. So many times I just skipped the meal because the food had gone bad.

The story of food that has gone bad is shared by a number of participants. The poor quality of food emerges as a consistent theme in participant narratives of health, situating food within their cultural contexts and depicting the structures of the dormitories and catering companies that limit their access to healthy food.

Health as Indecent Work

In the lives of the participants, the absence of health is marked by the stressors experienced at worksites, often tied to the experiences of indecency, reflected in uncivil communication directed at the workers. Participants often share stories of being mistreated at work by the supervisor and this threatens their health by creating stressors that they feel in their body, and by making them vulnerable to accidents at construction sites. Koreem shares, "The boss is always shouting. Shouting and calling names. I get nervous, trying to hurry, and that's when I make mistakes on the job." On a similar note, Sajal shares, "I try very hard to follow what the boss says, but sometimes I can't understand and the boss gets angry." In these narratives, participants share the ways in which being mistreated at work makes them vulnerable to making errors, which in turn, threatened their health. Salient across the participant narratives is the interplay of being mistreated and the risks of workplace injuries. Rajib,

> I have injured my hand at work because the boss was shouting at me and asking me to hurry, voices this. I could not understand what the boss was saying and so was trying to carry the crates even faster, and twisted my wrist.

Not understanding the supervisor is a theme that emerges across the in-depth interviews, with participants noting the pressures on the work that are related to not understanding the supervisor.

Reyaz shares,

> The work is very hard, and I try to work hard so the boss will not abuse me. One time, I fell down while trying to hurry. The boss did not even let me rest properly, and I went on with the work.

This notion of "trying to hurry" is voiced throughout the interviews, with participants noting that their work is constituted amid demands of workplace efficiency and productivity. This is articulated by Shobuj,

> The foreman needs to meet his quota for the day. So he is going to push, push, push. The quota cannot be met it is so high. So he is going to keep pushing. And what that means is that I am going to face the stress of moving fast, fast, fast.

Similarly, articulates Abdul, "I am very tired with the work. Push my body really hard and the boss is still not happy. The boss will yell, and call us lazy. And I work hard so the boss will not call me lazy."

Moreover, Jalal recounts the verbal abuse hurled at workers by the supervisor, "The boss is always angry and always calling names. I am not used to this, as I have always had my decency back in Bangladesh. I lose my decency working here, being called names, and being made to feel low." This experience of being called names affects Jalal's health, being internalized in his bodily experiences. Similarly, Paresh recounts the experience of being verbally abused:

> The boss will call names, and say things about Bangladeshis. That makes me upset. Makes me very sad. I do not know what to do. Just be quiet and try keeping to work. Only work and no respect. This makes me sad, and makes me stay up at night. Some nights, I cry. Why did I come here? What brought me here to this life?

The sense of losing one's dignity in the workplace broadly translates into an overarching sense of living a life that is not worthy. The participants share how their low sense of self-worth translates into their overarching experiences of health and well-being.

Health and Uncertainty

Participants note the uncertainty of everyday life that takes its toll on their health and sense of well-being. Particularly salient in the narratives is the articulation of struggles to make a living, the economic hardships, and the anxieties around high debts which are often taken to make the trip to Singapore. Jamil shares, "I took all this debt when I came here. My father put the land on mortgage. So I have to keep working, no matter what. Just keep working so I can pay back the debt." Similarly, for Mohsin, "The agent fees in Bangladesh so high that I will work for two years to return it." In this backdrop of the high agent fees, participants often share stories of putting their wife's jewellery with the money lender or mortgaging one's land in order to deposit the money. This translates into being under constant mental pressure to return the money, articulated by the participants as the uncertainties of everyday life of migrant construction work.

Hamid shares, "I don't know what will happen. If the boss says, don't want, send you back, then have to go back. This is the reality of my life."

The uncertainties of the job translate into power in the hands of employers, with workers often experiencing this power as a direct threat to their everyday health. Moynul shares, "I am always stressed and worried about the money. Always thinking about how I am going to pay the money back." The sense of worry that Moynul experiences is often voiced by participants, sharing the challenges to health that are routinized in this everyday worrying about the debts that many of the Bangladeshi migrant workers in construction industries in Singapore are under.

Health and Workplace Injuries

For many workers, workplace injuries constitute a life event that can transform their lives and push them into immobility. Shares Sejal, "It all can change just in a few seconds. That you don't think about, but when someone falls down or is hurt badly, you see that, that could be you. You always have that knowledge." Participants share stories of workplace deaths (although Singapore has worked to develop strong policy frameworks and workplace solutions for minimizing these deaths) and workplace injury-related disabilities. They note how injuries at work are significant threats to their health, livelihoods, and economic immobilities of their families. Shares Ahmed, "I broke my toe one day while carrying a load and fell down. I had to be in rest, and could not go to work. Did not get my salary for those days." Ahmed's experience of workplace injuries is intertwined with experiences of economic vulnerabilities at work shared in the previous section. Having a workplace injury meant the inability to earn money, which translated into a weakened ability to send money back home to family. He went on to note, "This month, I will have very little to send home. So no matter what, I just let it get better a little and went back (to work)." Even though Ahmed was still experiencing the pain, he noted that being absent from work any longer would mean his family in Bangladesh wouldn't have the resources needed for the coming month. The physical threats to health posed by workplace injuries translate into worries about what would happen to their economic condition and to their ability to return the debt or take care of their families. This means that in spite of their injuries, workers often go back to work just to earn the money needed to support their families.

Although existing policy frameworks dictate that workers qualify for medical leaves when injured, a number of participants discussed the ways in which the doctors the company arranged them to see were reluctant to issue medical certificate as that would mean less money for the company. A number of participants felt that company-assigned doctors often worked in collusion with the company. When asked why they didn't seek other options, they often noted that they were constrained by their company with respect to which doctor they could see. Also, not being aware of the health care infrastructure in Singapore, they often did not know where to go to or how to navigate the structure. This point is shared by Najmool,

> I cut my finger, and went to the company doctor because that's where the boss sent me. The doctor was no good, just gave me a bandage and no MC (referring to medical certificate). I did not know anyone else. I went back to work the next day, and my finger was still hurting.

Amid these structural limitations to seeking health care amid risks experienced in workplaces, participants shared that they often relied on their social networks to secure access to health. Noted Zayed, "I will talk to my friends from my village who are here in Singapore. They will know where to go to, and tell me what to do." Social networks that share and draw upon kinship ties in Bangladesh serve as key resources of health. This point was also articulated by Bashir,

> I have my uncle here. He has been here a long time. When the company doctor did not give the MC, my uncle told me about this place I can go to where I can get a free check-up. I went to the doctor there and the doctor gave the MC. I brought the MC back to company.

In this narrative, resources in interpersonal networks offer sources of support for seeking out and securing access to health care, amid the structural inaccessibility to care constituted by the limitations experienced at workplaces.

Discussion

In the narratives of the participants, we hear stories of migrant health as constituted in the realm of structure. Structures of health are expressed in experiences of poverty and marginalization that flow from the lives of the participants in Bangladesh to their lives in Singapore, depicting the interconnected threads of health risks that flow across global boundaries. Risks to health flow through global chains of movement of labor. Although the nature of structurally constituted health risks changes in the trajectories of global flow, taking on different features within specific local-national contexts, what remains salient is the narrative of economic deprivation that is experienced across the various layers of movement, and the health risks that are intertwined with these economic vulnerabilities. The mobility of contractual labor in global networks, uprooted from sources of livelihood in the realm of the local, is marked by the immobility of labor. Approaching immigrant health communication as structurally constituted attends to the constraining features of work amid globalization that produce vulnerabilities of health. Moreover, challenging the dominant theorizing of structurally-based health interventions (Blankenship *et al.*, 2006; Cohen, Scribner, & Farley, 2000), rather than featuring the challenges of health as built around the diffusion and consumption of a product (such as condoms or micronutrient foods), the localized articulations of structures attend to the materiality of access to resources, relationships, and dynamics of power that constitute these relationships. The voices of the participants point toward articulation and implementation of policy features that would offer the necessary social protections to contractual laborers in global migration networks. The experiences of the migrant construction workers shared in this chapter point toward the much-needed work of health communication as health advocacy that seeks to develop global infrastructures for securing health at work. Frameworks of collaboration that emerge from these journeys of listening open up discursive spaces for building infrastructures of health and well-being that are locally grounded and voiced in relationship to structures of global health.

In other words, the definition of structures is rearticulated (Dutta, 2016a, b; Dutta & Basu, 2007), from the availability of products and commodities promoting behavior change (Blankenship *et al.*, 2006) to relationships, patterns, and networks. The shift in focus from products to networks and modes of local-global organizing attends to the constructions of health amid the differentials in distribution of power in society. Rather than placing the onus on group norms or generating solutions within product-driven consumerist frameworks of health, the articulation of structures attends to the overarching contexts of organizing and the differentials in power in relationships. The voices of the participants attend to the importance of conceptualizing and addressing the broader structures of local, national, and global organizing that constitute work, health, and vulnerabilities of health. The interplays between the national and global structures attends to the neoliberal organizing of structures globally that constitute health vulnerabilities and place bodies of contractual migrant laborers at health risk. The participants in our culture-centered project contextualize the vulnerabilities of health that flow from Bangladesh to Singapore, and are situated amid neoliberal global policies that produce precarious conditions that threaten human health and well-being.

Contributing to a growing body of literature on immigration and health communication (see Dutta & Jamil, 2013; Gao *et al.*, 2015; Sargent & Larchanché, 2011), this chapter highlights the role of work as a defining feature of migrant health amid neoliberal flows of labor. Health is constituted in the vulnerabilities of/at work. The precarious nature of construction work with limited to no security renders workers vulnerable. The health of migrant construction workers is threatened by unprotected working conditions. Particularly salient in this context is the development and implementation of adequate policy frameworks that offer the needed protections to migrant construction workers in global flows. Creating infrastructures of listening to the voices of migrant construction workers in urban spaces of neoliberal cities disrupts the erasure that is built into the everyday logics of global organizing of labor. The urban subaltern in the neoliberal city, voices pathways of representation and recognition by challenging structures that constrain subaltern agency. Future scholarship on immigrant health ought to examine the challenges of communication work that seeks to interrogate the structures and make entry points for listening to subaltern voices.

The CCA co-creates entry points for inverting the marginalization experienced by contractual migrant workers, and it does so by disrupting the dominant discourses of migrant work. For instance, dominant articulations of migrant labor to be strategically managed through efficiency (Kaur, Tan, & Dutta, 2016) is shifted into the hands of migrant workers, who point toward the necessity for creating the very infrastructures of listening that offer contractual migrant workers modes of access to addressing the health threats they experience, and opportunities for meaningfully participating in platforms that enable their articulations to be heard in ways that matter. The narratives sharing the role of health service providers who work in collusion with employers to deny medical leave or treatment to workers points toward the need for the development of measures that hold health service providers and employers accountable in addressing the health needs of construction workers. Similarly, the experiences of being mistreated by employers and the effects of such mistreatment on health point toward the importance of addressing the stigmatization of work and the cultural codes of inequality that are built into workplace management. The articulations of health as dignity point toward the need for developing health communication that is directed at addressing the overarching inequalities in the distribution of power and the ways in which these inequalities play out in relationships.

Note

1 Subalternity refers to the condition of being erased (Guha, 1988).

References

Airhihenbuwa, C. (1995). *Health and culture: Beyond the Western paradigm.* Thousand Oaks, CA: Sage.

Baey, G., & Yeoh, B. (2015). Migration and precarious work: Negotiating debt, employment, and livelihood strategies amongst Bangladeshi migrant men working in Singapore's construction industry. *Migrating Out of Poverty Working Paper No. 15.*

Bal, C. S. (2015). Production politics and migrant labor advocacy in Singapore. *Journal of Contemporary Asia, 45*(2), 219–242. doi: 10.1080/00472336.2014.960880

Blankenship, K. M., Friedman, S. R., Dworkin, S., & Mantell, J. E. (2006). Structural interventions: concepts, challenges and opportunities for research. *Journal of Urban Health, 83*(1), 59–72. doi: 10.1007/s11524-005-9007-4

Cohen, D. A., Scribner, R. A., & Farley, T. A. (2000). A structural model of health behavior: A pragmatic approach to explain and influence health behaviors at the population level. *Preventive medicine, 30*(2), 146–154. doi: 10.1006/pmed.1999.0609

Dutta, M. (2004a). Poverty, structural barriers and health: A Santali narrative of health communication. *Qualitative Health Research, 14*, 1–16. doi: 10.1177/1049732304267763

Dutta, M. (2004b). The unheard voices of Santalis: Communicating about health from the margins of India. *Communication Theory, 14*, 237–263. doi: 10.1093/ct/14.3.237

Dutta, M. J. (2007). Communicating about culture and health: Theorizing culture-centered and cultural sensitivity approaches. *Communication Theory, 17*(3), 304–328. doi:10.1111/j.1468-2885.2007.00297.x

Dutta, M. J. (2008). *Communicating health: A culture-centered approach.* London: Polity Press.

Dutta, M. J. (2014). A culture-centered approach to listening: Voices of social change. *International Journal of Listening, 28*(2), 67–81. doi: 10.1080/10904018.2014.876266

Dutta, M. J. (2015a). Decolonizing communication for social change: A culture-centered approach. *Communication Theory, 25*(2), 123–143. doi: 10.1111/comt.12067

Dutta, M. J. (2015b). *Neoliberal health organizing: Communication, meaning, politics.* New York: Routledge. doi:10.4324/9781315423531

Dutta, M. J. (2016a). Cultural context, structural determinants, and global health inequities: The role of communication. *Frontiers in Communication, 1*, 5. doi:10.3389/fcomm.2016.00005

Dutta, M. J. (2016b). Violence in Gaza: an academic-activist agenda for health communication. *Health communication*, 1–3. doi: 10.1080/10410236.2015.1089455

Dutta, M. J., & Basu, A. (2007). Health among men in rural Bengal: Exploring meanings through a culture-centered approach. *Qualitative Health Research, 17*, 38–48. doi:10.1177/1049732306296374

Dutta, M. J., & Jamil, R. (2013). Health at the margins of migration: Culture-centered co-constructions among Bangladeshi immigrants. *Health communication, 28*(2), 170–182. doi:10.1080/10410236.2012.666956

Gao, H., Dutta, M., & Okoror, T. (2015). Listening to Chinese immigrant restaurant workers in the Midwest: Application of the culture-centered approach (CCA) to explore perceptions of health and health care. *Health communication, 31*(6), 727–737. doi:10.1080/10410236.2014.989383

Geertz, C. (1973). *The interpretation of cultures: selected essays.* New York: Basic Books.

Guha, R. (1988). *Selected subaltern studies.* New York: Oxford University Press.

Haig-Brown, C. (2003). Creating spaces: Testimonio, impossible knowledge, and academe. *International Journal of Qualitative Studies in Education*, *16*(3), 415–433. doi:10.1080/0951839032000086763

Kaur, S., Tan, N., & Dutta, M. J. (2016). Media, migration and politics: The coverage of the Little India Riot in The Straits Times in Singapore. *Journal of Creative Communications*, *11*(1), 27–43. doi:10.1177/0973258616630214

Sargent, C., & Larchanché, S. (2011). Transnational migration and global health: The production and management of risk, illness, and access to care. *Annual Review of Anthropology*, *40*, 345–361. doi:10.1146/annurev-anthro-081309-145811

Part II

Cultural Differences and Disparities in Immigrants' Health Care Practices

4 Patient Involvement

Exploring Differences in Doctor–Patient Interaction among Immigrants and Non-immigrants with Back Pain in Switzerland

Sarah Mantwill & Peter J. Schulz

Introduction

Inclusive health care that allows patients to be autonomous decision-makers with regard to their own health has become an essential part of many countries' health care policies (Thompson, 2007). International and supranational organizations have issued directives that strongly favor active patient participation (Thompson, 2007; Williamson, 2014; World Health Organization (WHO), 1978, 2006). Particularly in primary care, patient involvement has come to be an important quality standard (Entwistle & Watt, 2006). Patient involvement, as well as autonomous decision-making, implies familiarity with the health care system, including having the knowledge and skills to successfully navigate the medical encounter (Paasche-Orlow & Wolf, 2007).

Minority and immigrant populations are more likely to experience less patient involvement, especially during medical encounters. One study from the US found, for example, that immigrants rated perceived quality of health care lower than the native population, which in turn was related to less perceived patient-centered communication (Orom, 2016). Other studies from the US have found similar results, showing that minorities are less likely to experience, and to be satisfied with, patient-centered communication (Schouten & Meeuwesen, 2006). Explanations for these findings are manifold. Some of the key factors that influence intercultural doctor-patient communication are, for instance: (1) differences in understanding what the doctor-patient relationship entails and one`s individual role in this relationship, (2) differences with regard to explanatory models of illness and disease, as well as (3) language-related barriers (Paternotte, van Dulmen, van der Lee, Scherpbier, & Scheele, 2015; Schouten & Meeuwesen 2006; Suurmond & Seeleman, 2006). The latter is probably the most evident factor. Besides compromising the overall satisfaction with the medical encounter (Carrasquillo, Orav, Brennan, & Burstin, 1999; Nápoles-Springer, Santoyo, Houston,

Pérez-Stable, & Stewart, 2005), language barriers are likely to reduce information provision (Ferguson & Candib, 2002; González, Vega, & Tarraf, 2010). Further, language barriers impede the establishment of affective relationships with health care providers (De Maesschalck, Deveugele, & Willems, 2011; Ferguson & Candib, 2002), the patient's active participation during the medical encounter (August, Nguyen, Ngo-Metzger, & Sorkin, 2011) and, subsequently, shared decision-making processes (Ferguson & Candib, 2002; Mead *et al.*, 2013; Suurmond & Seeleman, 2006).

Even though in many parts of the world shared decision-making and related communication processes have been commonly accepted and advocated in clinical practice (Flynn, Smith, & Vanness, 2006), they might still not be universally accepted and experienced by different cultures (Charles, Gafni, Whelan, & O'Brien, 2006; Schouten & Meeuwesen, 2006). Shared decision-making involves the participation of two or more parties, meaning that not only health care providers need to be invested in the deliberation and eventual treatment decision but also the patients (Charles, Gafni, & Whelan, 1997, 1999). Cultural background is one of the factors that might influence in how far patients want to actively participate in the decision-making process and thus in the overall medical encounter (Schouten & Meeuwesen, 2006). The ethical emphasis on patient autonomy has been mainly brought forward in the western parts of the world, and it has been argued that it is not easily transferable to other cultural contexts (Charles *et al.*, 2006; Obeidat, Homish, & Lally, 2013). Studies from Europe, for example, have shown variations in preferences for treatment decision-making and participation. Results partially show that in particular citizens from southern and eastern parts of Europe are less likely to prefer active participation in decision-making or the medical encounter as compared to their counterparts from northern and central European countries (Bär Deucher *et al.*, 2016; Coulter & Jenkinson, 2005; O'Donnell, Monz, & Hunskaar, 2007). Accordingly, also in the context of immigrant and ethnic minority health, different cultural norms are likely to influence the role that patients assign to themselves and their health care providers (Charles *et al.*, 2006; Meeuwesen, van den Brink-Muinen, & Hofstede, 2009). Studies from different countries have shown that minority and immigrant groups, including groups from non-western cultures and former socialist countries, are less likely to show participatory behavior during the medical encounter and are more likely to accept a paternalistic approach to treatment (Kokanovic & Manderson, 2007; Paternotte *et al.*, 2015; Pavlish, Noor, & Brandt, 2010; Remennick & Ottenstein-Eisen, 1998; Schouten, Meeuwesen, Tromp, & Harmsen, 2007; Searight & Gafford, 2005; Suurmond & Seeleman, 2006; Young & Klingle, 1996). In addition, adding another layer to the complexity of the medical encounter, in some cultures medical decisions are more likely to be made in concordance with patients' family members than by the individual alone (Charles *et al.*, 2006; Mead *et al.*, 2013; Nápoles-Springer *et al.*, 2005; Searight & Gafford, 2005).

Switzerland

In 2012, it was found that about forty percent of the population in Switzerland suffered from back pain (including low back pain) (Swiss Federal Statistical Office (FSO), 2014a). Particularly among immigrants and asylum-seekers in Switzerland, back pain is one of the most frequently cited health complaints (Bischoff, Schneider, Denhaerynck, & Battegay, 2009; Swiss Federal Office of Public Health (FOPH), 2007). Further, one intervention study from Switzerland found that chronic pain patients with an immigration background were more likely to suffer from higher pain severity, as well as worse psychological functioning. Additionally, they were also more likely to engage in passive coping behaviors, such as catastrophizing (Kellner, Halder, Litschi, & Sprott, 2013).

In Switzerland about thirty-five percent of the population has an immigration background (including first and second generation immigrants) (FSO, 2014b), thus constituting an important group that deserves further in-depth exploration with regard to back pain related factors. Among the largest immigrant groups in Switzerland who do not speak one of the official Swiss languages as their native language are Albanian- and Serbian-speakers (FSO, 2014b). The majority of Albanian-speakers comes from Kosovo (*ca.* 100,000), and most Serbian-speakers come either from Serbia (*ca.* 78,000) or Bosnia and Herzegovina (*ca.* 100,000) (FSO, 2014b). Particular Kosovars and Serbians are in relatively good physical and psychological health when they first move to Switzerland. Yet, data from Switzerland also shows that with increasing age, immigrants become less healthy than non-immigrants (Guggisberg *et al.*, 2011). Part of the explanation might lie within the health care encounter but very little is known about it in the Swiss context so far (see, for example, Swiss Federal Office for Migration (FOM), 2014). What is known is that in general people from former Yugoslavia are less likely to need language-related assistance as compared to the majority of other immigrants with a background in a language other than one of the Swiss languages (Weilandt, Rommel, Eckert, & Azmat, 2006). Further, women and men from Kosovo are in general less likely than native Swiss to consult a physician (Guggisberg *et al.*, 2011), which is also partly reflected in differences for uptake of preventive health care behaviors, such as cancer screening (Bischoff, Fontana, Wanner, & Greuter, 2009; Fontana & Bischoff, 2008; Guggisberg *et al.*, 2011). Yet, women from Kosovo and Serbia, as well as men from Serbia, have been found to consult more frequently their general practitioner (Guggisberg *et al.*, 2011).

Objective

The chapter at hand aims at examining cultural differences in communication and decision-related behaviors that are likely to occur during medical consultations among Albanian- and Serbian-speaking immigrants in Switzerland who are suffering from back pain. In particular it aims at identifying differences between immigrants and non-immigrants.

Furthermore it aims at investigating in how far cultural differences are associated with back pain related outcomes. Even though the evidence shows that ineffective communication between health care providers and patients influences health(-related) outcomes (Kaplan, Greenfield, & Ware, 1989; Stewart, 1995; Stewart *et al.*, 1999; Street, Makoul, Arora, & Epstein, 2009), there is still a lack of research on the influence of cross-cultural variations in the medical encounter on actual outcomes (Schouten & Meeuwesen, 2006).

Methods

Data for this study came from a cross-sectional survey among people suffering from back pain in Switzerland, which was conducted in summer/fall 2013. Included in the study were Swiss natives from the German- and Italian-speaking part of Switzerland, as well as first- (born outside of Switzerland) and second-generation Albanian- and Serbian-speaking immigrants living in the respective parts.

Data was collected via self-administered paper and pencil, as well as online questionnaires. Participants were recruited using snowball sampling. Trained recruiters who were native speakers of the respective languages recruited participants through their social networks. In addition, participants were also recruited via cultural organizations and community outreach. Local community members were identified who were able to promote the study (Swanson & Ward, 1995; Yancey, Ortega, & Kumanyika, 2006). Questionnaires were available in different languages, and participants could choose the language of their choice, namely German, Italian, Albanian or Serbian. Participants were eligible if they had suffered from back pain (including lumbago and cervical pain) during the 12 months prior to participation in the study (*"In the last 12 months, have you suffered from back pain (including lumbago and cervical pain)?"*). Further, due to the sponsor of the study (Swiss National Accident Insurance Fund - SUVA), participants had to be gainfully employed. As a thank you, participants had the possibility to take part in a prize draw.

Measures

The complete questionnaire included a number of different measures, including scales on coping behaviors and causal attribution of back pain. The study at hand focuses only on items that were related to the (1) medical encounter and (2) back pain related outcomes, such as severity of back pain, receipt of diagnosis and medication use. The German and Italian versions of the questionnaire were taken from a prior study (for details see Schulz, Hartung, & Riva, 2013). The Albanian and Serbian versions were translated from English using forward- and back-translations. Discrepancies between translations were resolved by consensus finding among the translators and project coordinators. The scales were pretested and, if necessary, adaptations were made.

Predictor Variables

The survey included a variety of items inquiring about what participants normally do before or during a doctor's visit. Further, how they would characterize themselves during the medical consultation. *((1) "What do you usually do before and during your doctor's visit?", (2) "How would you characterize yourself during the medical consultation?").* Participants were asked to rate items on a scale from 0 (not at all/never) to 6 (completely/always) in how far the situations described would apply to them. Items included *"I discuss the different therapies with my physician."* or *"I ask questions when I do not understand the content of the conversation (e.g. when I do not know the meaning of a word or when instructions are not clear)."* (For a complete list of items, please see Table 4.3.) The aim was to include a relatively broad range of possible situations, including those that were related to communication processes, as well as decision-making behavior during the medical encounter.

The questionnaire also included questions that specifically asked about potential language barriers among immigrant participants and included items such as: *"I do not speak my doctor's language well enough to understand everything he/she is saying."* or *"I bring someone to my appointment to translate for me (e.g. a family member or professional translator)."*

Outcome Variables

Severity of back pain was one of the outcomes that was analyzed for this study. Participants were asked to indicate the intensity of their back pain on a scale from 0 (not at all strong) to 6 (extremely strong) at the moment they were responding to the questionnaire. Further, participants were asked whether they had already received a diagnosis for their back pain, assessed as a dichotomous variable (yes/no). The questionnaire also inquired about medication use and asked respondents whether they had taken any medication because of their back pain or any related condition (e.g. insomnia or depression) in the last seven days prior to the study (yes/no). In addition, among those who indicated to have taken medication, the questionnaire asked about the frequency.

Initially measured on a continuous scale, the variable was transformed into a dichotomous variable (*"less or equal to once a day"* vs. *"equal or more than twice a day"*).

Data Analysis

Descriptive statistics for the participants' characteristics were calculated. Mann-Whitney U Tests and Kruskal-Wallis H Tests were run to investigate group differences for the predictor variables. For the Kruskal-Wallis H Test a Bonferroni correction for multiple comparisons was applied with statistical significance accepted at the $p < 0.016$ level. In a second step a principal component analysis was conducted to investigate the underlying component structure.

Pain severity was assessed using linear regression, while all other outcomes were assessed using logistic regression calculating odds ratios. Unadjusted, as well as adjusted associations were investigated. Adjusted models were controlled for gender, age, education, region of residence, and immigration status (Albanian- and Serbian-speaking participants vs. Swiss participants).

Results

Demographics

Data was analyzed for overall 495 participants, of which 27.9% ($n = 138$) had an Albanian-speaking and 39.6% ($n = 196$) a Serbian-speaking background (hereafter referred to as Albanian-speaking and Serbian-speaking). Most participants indicated to have either a high school diploma or to have finished vocational training (Table 4.1).

Outcome Variables

The overall mean value for back pain was 2.86 (SD = 1.733). Participants with an immigration background were significantly more likely to have stronger back pain than Swiss participants, $F(2, 491) = 14.688$, $p < 0.001$. The majority of participants indicated that they had not yet received a diagnosis regarding their back pain ($N = 287$, 58.0%). Yet, Swiss participants were significantly more likely to have received a diagnosis, $x^2(2) = 14.994$, $p = 0.001$.

34.6% ($n = 168$) indicated to have taken medication for their back pain and any related condition within the last seven days. Serbian-speaking participants were significantly more likely to have taken medication as compared to the two other groups, $x^2(2) = 11.672$, $p = 0.003$. Among those that had indicated to have taken medication no significant differences were found with regard to frequency of medication use (Table 4.2).

Table 4.1 Participants` Characteristics

Demographics	*Language Groups*			
	Albanian-speaking (%)	*Serbian-speaking (%)*	*Swiss German- and Italian-speaking (%)*	*p*
Age				
16–20	3 (2.2)	14 (7.1)	6 (3.7)	
21–40	79 (57.2)	119 (60.7)	58 (36.0)	
41–60	51 (37.0)	52 (26.5)	87 (54.0)	
61 and above	1 (0.7)	7 (3.6)	4 (2.5)	<.*001*
Missing	4 (2.9)	4 (2.0)	6 (3.7)	
Gender				
Female	39 (28.3)	97 (49.5)	87 (54.0)	
Male	93 (67.4%)	94 (48.0)	67 (41.6)	<.*001*
Missing	6 (4.3)	5 (2.6)	7 (4.3)	
Education				
No degree/ elementary school	32 (23.2)	8 (4.1)	3 (1.9)	
Secondary school	41 (29.7)	53 (27.0)	10 (6.2)	
High school/ vocational training	40 (29.0)	51 (26.0)	85 (52.8)	
Higher educational degree	18 (13.0)	79 (40.3)	55 (34.2)	<.*001*
Missing	7 (5.1)	5 (2.6)	8 (5.0)	
Region of Residence				
German-speaking part	82 (59.4)	96 (49.0)	69 (42.9)	
Italian-speaking part	56 (40.6)	100 (51.0)	92 (57.1)	<.*05*
Generation				
First generation	120 (87.0)	140 (71.4)		
Second generation	13 (9.4)	51 (26.0)		<.*01*
Missing	5 (3.6)	5 (2.6)		

Predictor Variables

The most striking differences were found between Swiss and immigrant participants with regard to responsiveness to information. Participants with an immigration background were significantly more likely to state that too much information would make them insecure and that they rather preferred not to know everything, $x^2(2) = 13.870$, $p = 0.001$. Also did they indicate significantly more often that they preferred *not* to receive a diagnosis, since otherwise they would feel ill, $x^2(2) = 18.782$,

Table 4.2 Differences in Outcome Variables

Outcome	*Language Groups*			
	Albanian-speaking (%)	*Serbian-speaking (%)*	*Swiss German- and Italian-speaking (%)*	*p*
Receipt of diagnosis				
Yes	38 (27.5)	72 (36.7)	79 (49.1)	
No	92 (66.7)	120 (61.2)	75 (46.6)	<.*001*
Missing	8 (5.8)	4 (2.0)	7 (4.3)	
Medication last seven days				
Yes	49 (35.5)	81 (41.3)	38 (23.6)	
No	88 (63.8)	112 (57.1)	117 (72.7)	<.*01*
Missing	1 (0.7)	3 (1.5)	6 (3.7)	
Frequency of medication use				
≤once a day	29 (59.2)	46 (56.8)	28 (73.7)	
≥twice a day	20 (40.8)	35 (43.3)	8 (21.2)	>.*05*
Missing	0 (0.0)	0 (0.0)	2 (5.3)	

$p = 0.000$. In addition, Serbian-speakers were significantly less likely than Swiss participants to want to know everything concerning their back pain, $x^2(2) = 6.432$, $p = 0.040$.

With regard to decision-making behavior, no significant differences were identified, except for Albanian-speaking participants who preferred their physician to decide on the appropriate therapy for their back pain, $x^2(2) = 51.318$, $p = 0.000$.

With regard to possible language barriers, it was found that Albanian-speakers were more likely to ask their doctor questions during a medical visit because of language barriers, $U = 6353.500$, $z = -1.980$, $p = 0.048$. Further, they were more likely to not speak their doctor's language well enough to understand everything she/he was saying, $U = 6121.000$, $z = -2.082$, $p = 0.037$.

Unadjusted Regression Analysis

Pain Severity

In unadjusted regression analysis only three out of nine items were significantly associated with severity of back pain in the overall sample (Table 4.3). When split into the different language groups, results were slightly different. Notably in Albanian- and Serbian-speaking participants being insecure because of too much information was in both cases significantly associated with increased severity of back pain. In Albanian-speaking participants only, preference for not receiving a diagnosis was associated with less back pain. Yet, a preference for letting the physician decide about the appropriate therapy was associated with increased back pain, which was also found in the Swiss sample. In addition, in the Swiss sample discussing personal issues with the physician was associated with increased severity of pain (Table 4.3). When language-related items were included, the overall models were not significant anymore. Yet, none of the language-related variables was significantly associated with pain severity (not shown in the table).

Diagnosis and Medication Use

With regard to diagnosis and medication outcomes, no clear patterns emerged across the different groups. In the overall sample, the only item that was significantly associated with all outcomes was "*I am happy to let my physician decide about the appropriate therapy*". When language-related items were included, unadjusted analysis showed that among Serbian-speakers those who indicated that they did not speak their doctor's language well enough were twice as likely to take medication (OR: 2.038, CI: 1.103–3.766, $p = 0.023$) and to have received a diagnosis (OR: 1.856, CI: 1.015–3.394, $p = 0.045$).

Prinicipal Component Analysis

A principal component analysis (PCA) with Varimax orthogonal rotation was run on the predictor variables (except for the language-related variables). Suitability of PCA was assessed by checking the correlation matrix. Further, the overall Kaiser-Meyer-Olkin (KMO) measure was 0.707 with individual KMO measures all >0.05. Bartlett's test of sphericity was statistically significant ($p = 0.000$). Three components were identified that had eigenvalues greater than one, explaining in total a variance of 61.725. A three-component solution met the interpretability criterion. The three components were named: (1) "Engagement", (2) "Information Responsiveness", (3) "Decision-Making" (Table 4.4).

Swiss participants scored significantly higher on "Information Responsiveness" than the other two groups, $x^2(2) = 16.846$, $p = 0.000$. Albanian-speaking participants scored significantly lower than Serbian-speaking and Swiss participants on "Decision-Making", $x^2(2) = 16.123$, $p = 0.000$, and scores for "Engagement" were significantly lower for Serbian-speakers, as compared to Swiss participants, $x^2(2) = 10.664$, $p = 0.005$.

Table 4.3 Unadjusted Regression Analyses. Back Pain Severity (Only Significant Coefficients Shown)

Predictor Variables	*Language Groups*											
	Overall sample			*Albanian-speaking participants*			*Serbian-speaking participants*			*Swiss participants Italian- and German-speaking*		
	B	*SE*	*β*	*B*	*SE*	*β*	*B*	*SE*	*β*	*B*	*SE*	*β*
Prior to the visit, I prepare a list of things that I want to discuss with my physician.[a]												
I ask questions when I don't understand the content of the conversation (e.g. when I don't know the meaning of a word or when instructions are not clear).[a]												
I want to know everything concerning my back pain.[b]												

I discuss the different therapies with my physician.[b]												
I would like to decide myself which therapy to undergo.[b]												
I am happy to let my physician decide about the appropriate therapy.[b]	.131	.044	.150**	.253	.101	.262*				.235	.080	.260**
I also discuss personal issues with my physician that might be related to my back pain.[a]	.146	.044	.179**							.186	.072	.229*
Too much information makes me insecure; I'd rather not know everything.[b]	.176	.051	.187**	.272	.104	.285*	.154	.076	.184*			
I prefer to not get a diagnosis, otherwise I would feel ill.[b]				−.284	.109	−.292*						
Adj. R^2	.087				.107			.074			.105	

***$p < .001$; **$p < .01$; *$p < .05$.

Note: Question format: [a]What do you usually do before and during your doctor's visit? (0 = Never – 6 = Always); [b]How would you characterize yourself during the medical consultation? (0 = Not at all – 6 = Completely).

Table 4.4 Principal Component Analysis

Items	*Engagement*	*Information Responsiveness*	*Decision-Making*
I discuss the different therapies with my physician.	**.804**	.078	–.058
I want to know everything concerning my back pain.	**.699**	.216	.138
I also discuss personal issues with my physician that might be related to my back pain.	**.696**	–.102	.107
I ask questions when I don't understand the content of the conversation (e.g. when I don't know the meaning of a word or when instructions are not clear).	**.683**	.187	–.139
Prior to the visit, I prepare a list of things that I want to discuss with my physician.	**.591**	–.235	–.050
I prefer to not get a diagnosis, otherwise I would feel ill.¶	.087	**.857**	–.100
Too much information makes me insecure; I'd rather not know everything.¶	.003	**.843**	.109
I would like to decide myself which therapy to undergo.	.311	–.160	**.786**
I am happy to let my physician decide about the appropriate therapy.¶	–.347	.200	**.732**

Note: ¶Reverse coding was applied.

Adjusted Regression Analysis

Pain Severity

Controlling for gender, age, education, region of residence and immigrant status (reference group Swiss participants), a stepwise multiple regression analysis for the complete sample was run. The overall model was significant, adj. $R^2 = 0.123$, $F(9, 432) = 7.895$, $p = 0.000$. "Engagement" and "Information Responsiveness" were significantly associated with pain severity, $p < 0.01$ (Table 4.5). The same pattern was also observed when analyses were run for Swiss and Serbian-speaking participants respectively. Whereas "Engagement" was positively associated with pain, meaning that more engagement was linked to increased pain severity, "Information Responsiveness" was negatively associated with severity of back pain, meaning the more people were willing to receive information on their back pain the less severe their back pain was. For Albanian-speaking participants the overall model was not significant and only "Decision-Making" was significantly negatively associated with pain severity (Table 4.6).

Table 4.5 Regression Analyses – Overall Sample: Receipt of Diagnosis, Medication Last Seven Days, Frequency of Medication, Pain Severity

	Outcome Variables							
	Receipt of diagnosis		*Medication last seven days*		*Frequency of medication*		*Pain severity*	
	Unadj. OR (CI)	*Adj. OR (CI)*	*Unadj. OR (CI)*	*Adj. OR (CI)*	*Unadj. OR (CI)*	*Adj. OR (CI)*	*Unadj. β (CI)*	*Adj. β (CI)*
Albanian-speaking¶	.33 (24, .64)***	.49 (.27, .89)*	1.71 (1.03, 2.84)*	1.22 (.63, 2.34)	2.41 (.91, 6.37)	1.07 (.28, 4.03)	.23 (.52, 1.29)***	.15 (.11, 1.01)*
Serbian-speaking¶	.57 (.37, .88)*	.72 (.44, 1.17)	2.23 (1.40, 3.54)**	2.88 (1.67, 4.96)***	2.66 (1.08, 6.55)*	5.25 (1.55, 17.71)**	.24 (.51, 1.21)***	.27 (.58, 1.33)***
Engagement	1.44 (1.18, 1.76)***	1.31 (1.06, 1.64)*	1.58 (1.28, 1.95)***	1.68 (1.32, 2.12)***	.56 (.75, 1.48)	1.55 (.97, 2.46)	.14 (.09, .40)**	.16 (.12, .44)**
Information Responsiveness	1.21 (1.04, 1.54)*	1.20 (.97, 1.49)	.76 (.62, .92)**	.79 (.63, .98)*	.65 (.46, .91)*	.59 (.39, .89)*	−.19 (−.48, −.17)***	−.14 (−.40, −.08)**
Decision-Making	1.00 (.83, 1.21)	1.00 (.82, 1.23)	.74 (.61, .91)**	.68 (.54, .85)**	.87 (.60, 1.25)	.73 (.46, 1.15)	−.11 (−.35, −.03)*	−.09 (−3.05, .01)

*<.05; **<.01; ***<.001.

Note: Complete Sample, adjusted for gender, age, education, region of residence.
¶Reference Group: Swiss participants.

Table 4.6 Regression Analyses – Subgroups: Pain Severity

	Albanian-speaking participants		*Serbian-speaking participants*		*Swiss participants (German- and Italian-speaking)*	
	Pain severity[§]		*Pain severity*		*Pain severity*	
	Unadj. β (CI)	*Adj. β (CI)*	*Unadj. β (CI)*	*Adj. β (CI)*	*Unadj. β (CI)*	*Adj. β (CI)*
Engagement	.12 (–.09, .50)	.07 (–.20, .44)	.21 (.09, .55)**	.20 (.09, .54)**	.22 (.11, .70)**	.22 (.10, .73)*
Information Responsiveness	–.08 (–.44, .17)	–.08 (–.45, .16)	–.25 (–.59, –.16)**	–.18 (–.49, –.05)*	–.10 (–.53, .12)	–.17 (–.68, –.02)*
Decision-Making	–.26 (–.74, –.15)**	–.27 (–.77, –.15)**	.05 (–.17, .35)	.04 (–.18, .30)	–.11 (–.45, .09)	–.12 (–.49, .80)

*<.05; **<.01; ***<.001.

Note: Subgroups, adjusted for gender, education, age, region of residence. Medication frequency no included since cell sizes were too small.
§Adjusted model not significant.

Table 4.7 Regression Analyses – Subgroups: Receipt of Diagnosis, Medication Last Seven Days

	Albanian-speaking participants				*Serbian-speaking participants*				*Swiss participants (German- and Italian-speaking)*			
	Receipt of diagnosis§		*Medication last seven days*§		*Receipt of diagnosis*§		*Medication last seven days*		*Receipt of diagnosis*		*Medication last seven days*	
	Unadj. OR (CI)	*Adj. OR (CI)*	*Unadj. OR (CI)*	*Adj. OR (CI)*	*Unadj. OR (CI)*	*Adj. OR (CI)*	*Unadj. OR (CI)*	*Adj. OR (CI)*	*Unadj. OR (CI)*	*Adj. OR (CI)*	*Unadj. OR (CI)*	*Adj. OR (CI)*
Engagement	1.36 (.92, 2.00)	1.25 (.82, 1.93)	1.53 (1.05, 2.23)*	1.35 (.89, 2.05)	1.24 (.91, 1.69)	1.24 (.89, 1.73)	1.54 (1.12, 2.12)**	1.71 (1.18, 2.48)**	1.74 (1.18, 2.56)**	1.53 (.99, 2.36)	2.52 (1.52, 4.19)***	2.22 (1.31, 3.75)**
Information Responsiveness	1.17 (.79, 1.73)	1.16 (.77, 1.75)	.70 (.49, 1.01)	.72 (.49, 1.06)	1.05 (.78, 1.41)	1.12 (.81, 1.54)	.75 (.56, 1.00)	.79 (.56, 1.10)	1.45 (.97, 2.18)	1.38 (.88, 2.19)	1.07 (.68, .1.70)	.89 (.51, 1.53)
Decision-Making	.80 (.55, 1.18)	.84 (.55, 1.28)	.87 (.61, 1.25)	.84 (.56, 1.28)	1.02 (.73, 1.44)	1.03 (.72, 1.47)	.62 (.44, .89)*	.58 (.39, .86)**	.98 (.72, 1.34)	1.33 (.89, 1.97)	.68 (.46, .99)*	.72 (.46, 1.14)

*<.05; **<.01; ***<.001.

Note: Subgroups, adjusted for gender, education, age, region of residence. Medication frequency not included since cell sizes were too small.
§Adjusted model not significant.

Diagnosis and Medication Use

In the overall sample, "Engagement" was significantly associated with the receipt of diagnosis (Table 4.5), yet among the separate language groups none of the variables under investigation was significantly associated with receipt of diagnosis (Table 4.7). With regard to medication use, analysis of the complete sample showed that all components were significantly associated with it. Analyses of the subgroups showed that in the Serbian-speaking, as well as in the Swiss group, "Engagement" was associated with increased likelihood of medication use. Yet, at the same time it was found that in the Serbian-speaking group those who wanted to be more involved in the "Decision-Making" process were less likely to take medication. No such a relationship emerged for the Albanian-speaking or Swiss participants (Table 4.7).

Cell sizes for frequency of medication intake were too small for subgroup analyses but the analysis of the overall sample showed that those who scored higher on "Information Responsiveness" were less likely to take medication more than once a day.

Discussion

Results of this study show that cultural differences in medical encounters are likely to occur when comparing immigrants to non-immigrants in Switzerland. The study highlights a potential preference for paternalistic decision styles, as well as more passive participation during the medical encounter for Albanian- and Serbian-speaking immigrants in Switzerland. Yet, responses of Albanian- and Serbian-speaking participants did not necessarily show the same patterns. Albanian-speakers were less likely to prefer active participation in decision-making with regard to therapies concerning their condition, which also showed to be related to the severity of their back pain (even though the overall model was not significant). On the other hand, Serbian-speakers were less likely to actively engage in medical encounters; however active participation was in their case associated with increased severity of back pain and increased likelihood for medication use, a pattern that also held true for Swiss participants. Part of the explanation might lie in the fact that increased back pain might be associated with increased communication to influence and convince the health care provider of the urgency of the pain (Craig, 2009).

As outlined in the introduction the idea of shared-decision making and related patient autonomy has been mainly brought forward in the western parts of the world (Charles *et al.*, 2006; Obeidat *et al.*, 2013). The socialist past of the countries that immigrant participants in this study came from might still shape their approach to health care, including a tendency for less perceived patient autonomy and increased expectations of paternalism (Prodanov, 2001; Rechel, Kennedy, McKee, & Rechel, 2011). This might be further amplified by lower social status and related perceptions of power inequalities (Schouten & Meeuwesen, 2006).

Detailed analyses showed that immigrants were more likely to avoid information that would make them feel insecure or sick. Yet, only among Serbian-speaking participants it was significantly related to one of the outcomes in adjusted analysis. It showed that those who were more likely to adjust to unwanted information and diagnosis were suffering from less severe back pain, and vice versa. So-called "information avoidance" has been observed throughout a variety of health conditions (Howell & Shepperd, 2013). Engaging in information avoidance is likely to occur when people believe it to produce unwanted or undesired behaviors or negative emotional responses (Howell & Shepperd, 2013; Sweeny, Melnyk, Miller, & Shepperd, 2010). A study with immigrants in the US partly confirms our results. It showed that Bosnian immigrants preferred not to be directly informed about a serious illness and a preference for physician-centered decision-making (Searight & Gafford, 2005). Further, it has been found that Eastern-European immigrants in the US are less likely to prefer direct disclosure of bad news as compared to Americans (Larkin & Searight, 2014). In our case, the purposeful avoidance of relevant information might lead to increased back pain due to under-diagnosis and under-treatment. Besides the attempt to forego potential unpleasant emotions (Sweeny *et al.*, 2010), it might also reflect the participants' living and working situations. Immigrants tend to work in less secure jobs with often short-term contracts, extra hours or changing shifts (Ronda Pérez *et al.*, 2012). The receipt of an official diagnosis, as well as possible treatment recommendations that might include behavioral changes (Sweeny *et al.*, 2010) potentially influences work presence and performance. A situation many immigrants might want to forego due to their lack of job security and to prevent any socioeconomic disadvantages (Galon *et al.*, 2014; Soler-González *et al.*, 2008). So-called "sickness presenteeism", meaning presenting to work while being sick, has been in particular observed in populations that e.g. work regularly overtime or shifts, as well as in sectors that have seen recent cutbacks (Aronsson, Gustafsson, & Dallner, 2000; Böckerman & Laukkanen 2010). This is potentially aggravated by immigration background (Agudelo-Suárez *et al.*, 2010).

The study predominantly focused on differences between immigrants and the native population. However, for the immigrant groups specifically it was observed that language issues seemed to play only a minor role with regard to back pain outcomes. Detailed analyses showed that language-related variables were not associated with pain severity. Only one language-related variable was significantly associated with receipt of diagnosis and medication use among Serbian-speaking participants. Yet, the directionality was unexpected. Those who indicated to have difficulties in understanding their doctor were more likely to have received a diagnosis and to use medication. Whereas the latter might be potentially explained by patterns of self-medication, due to foregoing medical visits because of language issues (Derose & Baker, 2000), explanations for the receipt of diagnosis are less obvious. One potential reason might be related to patients' understanding of what exactly a diagnosis entails and the different meanings that are attached to it (Baumann, 2003; Karasz, Dempsey, & Fallek, 2007), possibly explained in this case by language and translation issues.

Limitations

There are a number of limitations to this study. First of all, participants were recruited via snowball sampling, meaning participants were recruited via their social networks or local organizations. This might have led to the inclusion of participants from socially cohesive groups with similar backgrounds, thus making the results not representative at large. Further, the questionnaire was self-reported which might have let to the exclusion of participants with low literacy skills. Yet, this was partly accounted for by giving participants the option to fill out the questionnaire in the language of their choice. Another limitation is related to the fact that only participants who were gainfully employed were eligible to participate in the study. This is particularly important as unemployment rates are twice as high for foreigners in Switzerland than for Swiss citizens; including additional regional differences between the different language regions (FSO, 2016). Moreover, the study did not look into micro-cultural differences related to the region of residence. In adjusted analyses it was found that relatively often region of residence was associated with one of the outcomes (not shown in results section). A couple of studies have studied micro-cultural differences in health behaviors in Switzerland and have found that some differences do indeed occur (Camerini & Schulz, 2016; Filippini, Masiero, & Moschetti, 2006; Schulz *et al.*, 2013; Schulz, Nakamoto, Brinberg, & Haes, 2006). Further, the study did not include an actual measure of language proficiency, which could have explained some of the differences found.

Future Research and Implications

This study was a first step to explore quantitatively cultural differences in communication processes and decision-related behavior during the medical encounter among immigrants, and to compare them to the non-immigrant population in Switzerland. Besides its methodological limitations, the study was able to show that cultural differences during the medical encounter are likely to occur. However, the results also showed that findings cannot easily be generalized for different immigrant groups, as different patterns for the two immigrant groups appeared. Especially immigrants from former Yugoslavia are often grouped into one large cluster, with little attention to differences among subgroups; a pattern that has also been observed for Latino or Asian populations in the US and which deserves further examination (see e.g. Kagawa-Singer & Kassim-Lakha, 2003). An additional cultural layer in this study was its setting in a multilingual country. Future research might want to explore in how far countries' multilingualism and related cultures might produce different health behaviors and related communication processes not only in the native population but also in immigrants.

The study also investigated in how far cultural differences in communication processes and decision-related behavior were associated with health(-related) outcomes, a relationship that has been largely neglected until now (Schouten & Meeuwesen, 2006). By providing proof on its possible impact on health outcomes, this study adds to the scientific evidence for promoting training in cultural competence in medical education (Kripalani, Bussey-Jones, Katz, & Genao, 2006). In Switzerland training in intercultural competence and communication among medical students has been a relatively recent addition to the medical curriculum (Hudelson, Perron, & Perneger, 2011). Showing, for example, that patients' expectations for authoritarian health care delivery are not meant as a means to pressure health care providers for additional examinations (Hudelson, 2006) but are rather an expression of learned experience and culture, will help to sensitize health care providers to the influence of culture on medical communication and care. Similar effects might be observed by showing that different preferences for information provision are not necessarily related to the inability to understand information (Hudelson, 2006) but rather to the patients' background and culture.

References

Agudelo-Suárez, A. A., Benavides, F. G., Felt, E., Ronda-Pérez, E., Vives-Cases, C., & García, A. M. (2010). Sickness presenteeism in Spanish-born and immigrant workers in Spain. *BMC Public Health, 10*(1), 791. doi:10.1186/1471-2458-10-791.

Aronsson, G., Gustafsson, K., & Dallner, M. (2000). Sick but yet at work. An empirical study of sickness presenteeism. *Journal of Epidemiology and Community Health, 54*(7), 502–509. doi:10.1136/jech.54.7.502.

August, K. J., Nguyen, H., Ngo-Metzger, Q., & Sorkin, D. H. (2011). Language concordance and patient–physician communication regarding mental health needs. *Journal of the American Geriatrics Society, 59*(12), 2356–2362. doi:10.1111/j.1532-5415.2011.03717.x.

Bär Deucher, A. B., Hengartner, M. P., Kawohl, W., Konrad, J., Puschner, B., Clarke, E., ... & Süveges, Á. (2016). Participation in medical decision-making across Europe: An international longitudinal multicenter study. *European Psychiatry, 35*, 39–46. doi:10.1016/j.eurpsy.2016.02.001.

Baumann, L. C. (2003). Culture and illness representation. In L. D. Cameron & H. Leventhal (Eds.), *The self-regulation of health and illness behaviour* (pp. 242–254). New York: Routledge.

Bischoff, A., Schneider, M., Denhaerynck, K., & Battegay, E. (2009). Health and ill health of asylum seekers in Switzerland: an epidemiological study. *The European Journal of Public Health, 19*(1), 59–64. doi:10.1093/eurpub/ckn113.

Bischoff, A., Fontana, M., Wanner, P., & Greuter, U. (2009). Cervical cancer screening among immigrants in Switzerland. *Diversity & Equality in Health and Care, 6*, 159–169.

Böckerman, P., & Laukkanen, E. (2010). What makes you work while you are sick? Evidence from a survey of workers. *The European Journal of Public Health, 20*(1), 43–46. doi:10.1093/eurpub/ckp076.

Carrasquillo, O., Orav, E. J., Brennan, T. A., & Burstin, H. R. (1999). Impact of language barriers on patient satisfaction in an emergency department. *Journal of General Internal Medicine, 14*(2), 82–87. doi:10.1046/j.1525-1497.1999.00293.x.

Camerini, A. L., & Schulz, P. J. (2016). Patients' need for information provision and perceived participation in decision making in doctor-patient consultation: Micro-cultural differences between French-and Italian-speaking Switzerland. *Patient Education and Counseling, 99*(3), 462–469. doi:10.1016/j.pec.2015.10.018.

Charles, C., Gafni, A., & Whelan, T. (1997). Shared decision-making in the medical encounter: what does it mean? (or it takes at least two to tango). *Social Science & Medicine, 44*(5), 681–692. doi:10.1016/S0277-9536(96)00221-3.

Charles, C., Gafni, A., & Whelan, T. (1999). Decision-making in the physician–patient encounter: revisiting the shared treatment decision-making model. *Social Science & Medicine, 49*(5), 651–661. doi:10.1016/S0277-9536(99)00145-8.

Charles, C., Gafni, A., Whelan, T., & O'Brien, M. A. (2006). Cultural influences on the physician–patient encounter: The case of shared treatment decision-making. *Patient Education and Counseling, 63*(3), 262–267. doi:10.1016/j.pec.2006.06.018.

Coulter, A., & Jenkinson, C. (2005). European patients' views on the responsiveness of health systems and healthcare providers. *The European Journal of Public Health, 15*(4), 355–360. doi:10.1093/eurpub/cki004.

Craig, K. D. (2009). The social communication model of pain. *Canadian Psychology/Psychologie Canadienne, 50*(1), 22–32.

De Maesschalck, S., Deveugele, M., & Willems, S. (2011). Language, culture and emotions: Exploring ethnic minority patients' emotional expressions in primary healthcare consultations. *Patient Education and Counseling, 84*(3), 406–412. doi:10.1016/j.pec.2011.04.021.

Derose, K. P., & Baker, D. W. (2000). Limited English proficiency and Latinos' use of physician services. *Medical Care Research and Review, 57*(1), 76–91.

Entwistle, V. A., & Watt, I. S. (2006). Patient involvement in treatment decision-making: the case for a broader conceptual framework. *Patient Education and Counseling, 63*(3), 268–278. doi:10.1016/j.pec.2006.05.002.

Ferguson, W. J., & Candib, L. M. (2002). Culture, language, and the doctor-patient relationship. *Family Medicine, 34*(5), 353–361.

Filippini, M., Masiero, G., & Moschetti, K. (2006). Socioeconomic determinants of regional differences in outpatient antibiotic consumption: evidence from Switzerland. *Health Policy*, *78*(1), 77–92. doi:10.1016/j.healthpol.2005.09.009.

Flynn, K. E., Smith, M. A., & Vanness, D. (2006). A typology of preferences for participation in healthcare decision making. *Social Science & Medicine*, *63*(5), 1158–1169. doi:10.1016/j.socscimed.2006.03.030.

Fontana, M., & Bischoff, A. (2008). Uptake of breast cancer screening measures among immigrant and Swiss women in Switzerland. *Swiss Medical Weekly*, *138*(49–50), 752–758.

Galon, T., Briones-Vozmediano, E., Agudelo-Suárez, A. A., Felt, E. B., Benavides, F. G., & Ronda, E. (2014). Understanding sickness presenteeism through the experience of immigrant workers in a context of economic crisis. *American Journal of Industrial Medicine*, *57*(8), 950–959. doi:10.1002/ajim.22346.

González, H. M., Vega, W. A., & Tarraf, W. (2010). Health care quality perceptions among foreign-born Latinos and the importance of speaking the same language. *The Journal of the American Board of Family Medicine*, *23*(6), 745–752. doi:10.3122/jabfm.2010.06.090264.

Guggisberg, J., Gardiol, L., Graf, I., Oesch, T., Künzi, K., Volken, T., … Müller, C. (2011). *Zweites Gesundheitsmonitoring der Migrationsbevölkerung (GMM) in der Schweiz – Schlussbericht* [Health monitoring of the migrant population in Switzerland – Final Report]. Bern: Swiss Federal Office of Public Health, Swiss Federal Office for Migration.

Howell, J. L., & Shepperd, J. A. (2013). Reducing health-information avoidance through contemplation. *Psychological Science*, *24*(9), 1696–1703. doi:10.1177/0956797613478616.

Hudelson, P. (2006). Contextualizing cultural competence training of residents: Results of a formative research study in Geneva, Switzerland. *Medical Teacher*, *28*(5), 465–471. doi:10.1080/01421590600607567.

Hudelson, P., Perron, N. J., & Perneger, T. (2011). Self-assessment of intercultural communication skills: A survey of physicians and medical students in Geneva, Switzerland. *BMC Medical Education*, *11*(1), 63–63. doi:10.1186/1472-6920-11-63.

Kagawa-Singer, M., & Kassim-Lakha, S. (2003). A strategy to reduce cross-cultural miscommunication and increase the likelihood of improving health outcomes. *Academic Medicine*, *78*(6), 577–587.

Kaplan, S. H., Greenfield, S., & Ware, J. E. Jr, (1989). Assessing the effects of physician-patient interactions on the outcomes of chronic disease. *Medical Care*, *27*(3), 110–127.

Karasz, A., Dempsey, K., & Fallek, R. (2007). Cultural differences in the experience of everyday symptoms: a comparative study of South Asian and European American women. *Culture, Medicine and Psychiatry*, *31*(4), 473–497. doi:10.1007/s11013-007-9066-y.

Kellner, U., Halder, C., Litschi, M., & Sprott, H. (2013). Pain and psychological health status in chronic pain patients with migration background—the Zurich study. *Clinical Rheumatology*, *32*(2), 189–197. doi:10.1007/s10067-012-2099-9.

Kokanovic, R., & Manderson, L. (2007). Exploring doctor–patient communication in immigrant Australians with type 2 diabetes: a qualitative study. *Journal of General Internal Medicine, 22*(4), 459–463. doi:10.1007/s11606-007-0143-2.

Kripalani, S., Bussey-Jones, J., Katz, M. G., & Genao, I. (2006). A prescription for cultural competence in medical education. *Journal of General Internal Medicine, 21*(10), 1116–1120. doi:10.1111/j.1525-1497.2006.00557.x.

Larkin, C., & Searight, H. R. (2014). A systematic review of cultural preferences for receiving medical "bad news" in the United States. *Health, 6*(16), 2162–2173. doi:10.4236/health.2014.616251.

Mead, E. L., Doorenbos, A. Z., Javid, S. H., Haozous, E. A., Alvord, L. A., Flum, D. R., & Morris, A. M. (2013). Shared decision-making for cancer care among racial and ethnic minorities: a systematic review. *American Journal of Public Health, 103*(12), 15–29. doi:10.2105/AJPH.2013.301631.

Meeuwesen, L., van den Brink-Muinen, A., & Hofstede, G. (2009). Can dimensions of national culture predict cross-national differences in medical communication? *Patient Education and Counseling, 75*(1), 58–66. doi:10.1016/j.pec.2008.09.015.

Nápoles-Springer, A. M., Santoyo, J., Houston, K., Pérez-Stable, E. J., & Stewart, A. L. (2005). Patients' perceptions of cultural factors affecting the quality of their medical encounters. *Health Expectations, 8*(1), 4–17. doi:10.1111/j.1369-7625.2004.00298.x.

Obeidat, R. F., Homish, G. G., & Lally, R. M. (2013). Shared decision making among individuals with cancer in non-Western cultures: a literature review. *Oncology Nursing Forum, 40*(5), 454–463. doi:10.1188/13.ONF.454-463.

O'Donnell, M., Monz, B., & Hunskaar, S. (2007). General preferences for involvement in treatment decision making among European women with urinary incontinence. *Social Science & Medicine, 64*(9), 1914–1924. doi:10.1016/j.socscimed.2007.01.017.

Orom, H. (2016). Nativity and Perceived Healthcare Quality. *Journal of Immigrant and Minority Health, 18*(3), 636–643. doi:10.1007/s10903-015-0218-9.

Paasche-Orlow, M. K., & Wolf, M. S. (2007). The causal pathways linking health literacy to health outcomes. *American Journal of Health Behavior, 31*(Supplement 1), 19–26.

Paternotte, E., van Dulmen, S., van der Lee, N., Scherpbier, A. J., & Scheele, F. (2015). Factors influencing intercultural doctor–patient communication: A realist review. *Patient Education and Counseling, 98*(4), 420–445. doi:10.1016/j.pec.2014.11.018.

Pavlish, C. L., Noor, S., & Brandt, J. (2010). Somali immigrant women and the American health care system: Discordant beliefs, divergent expectations, and silent worries. *Social Science & Medicine, 71*(2), 353–361. doi:10.1016/j.socscimed.2010.04.010.

Prodanov, V. (2001). Bioethics in Eastern Europe: a difficult birth. *Cambridge Quarterly of Healthcare Ethics, 10*(1), 53–61.

Rechel, B., Kennedy, C., McKee, M., & Rechel, B. (2011). The Soviet legacy in diagnosis and treatment: Implications for population health. *Journal of Public Health Policy, 32*(3), 293–304. doi:10.1057/jphp.2011.18.

Remennick, L. I., & Ottenstein-Eisen, N. (1998). Reaction of new Soviet immigrants to primary health care services in Israel. *International Journal of Health Services, 28*(3), 555–574.

Ronda Pérez, E., Benavides, F. G., Levecque, K., Love, J. G., Felt, E., & Van Rossem, R. (2012). Differences in working conditions and employment arrangements among migrant and non-migrant workers in Europe. *Ethnicity & Health, 17*(6), 563–577. doi:10.1080/13557858.2012.730606.

Schouten, B. C., & Meeuwesen, L. (2006). Cultural differences in medical communication: A review of the literature. *Patient Education and Counseling, 64*(1), 21–34. doi:10.1016/j.pec.2005.11.014.

Schouten, B. C., Meeuwesen, L., Tromp, F., & Harmsen, H. A. (2007). Cultural diversity in patient participation: The influence of patients' characteristics and doctors' communicative behaviour. *Patient Education and Counseling, 67*(1), 214–223. doi:10.1016/j.pec.2007.03.018.

Schulz, P. J., Hartung, U., & Riva, S. (2013). Causes, coping, and culture: A comparative survey study on representation of back pain in three Swiss language regions. *PLoS One, 8*(11), e78029. doi:10.1371/journal.pone.0078029.

Schulz, P. J., Nakamoto, K., Brinberg, D., & Haes, J. (2006). More than nation and knowledge: Cultural micro-diversity and organ donation in Switzerland. *Patient Education and Counseling, 64*(1), 294–302. doi:10.1016/j.pec.2006.03.009.

Soler-González, J., Serna, M. C., Bosch, A., Ruiz, M. C., Huertas, E., & Rué, M. (2008). Sick leave among native and immigrant workers in Spain—a 6-month follow-up study. *Scandinavian Journal of Work, Environment & Health, 34*(6), 438–443.

Searight, H. R., & Gafford, J. (2005). "It's like playing with your destiny": Bosnian immigrants' views of advance directives and end-of-life decision-making. *Journal of Immigrant Health, 7*(3), 195–203. doi:10.1007/s10903-005-3676-7.

Stewart, M. A. (1995). Effective physician-patient communication and health outcomes: A review. *Canadian Medical Association Journal, 152*(9), 1423–1433.

Stewart, M., Brown, J. B., Boon, H., Galajda, J., Meredith, L., & Sangster, M. (1999). Evidence on patient-doctor communication. *Cancer Prevention & Control, 3*(1), 25–30.

Street, R. L., Makoul, G., Arora, N. K., & Epstein, R. M. (2009). How does communication heal? Pathways linking clinician–patient communication to health outcomes. *Patient Education and Counseling, 74*(3), 295–301. doi:10.1016/j.pec.2008.11.015.

Suurmond, J., & Seeleman, C. (2006). Shared decision-making in an intercultural context: Barriers in the interaction between physicians and immigrant patients. *Patient Education and Counseling, 60*(2), 253–259. doi:10.1016/j.pec.2005.01.012.

Swanson, G. M., & Ward, A. J. (1995). Recruiting minorities into clinical trials toward a participant-friendly system. *Journal of the National Cancer Institute, 87*(23), 1747–1759. doi:10.1093/jnci/87.23.1747.

Sweeny, K., Melnyk, D., Miller, W., & Shepperd, J. A. (2010). Information avoidance: Who, what, when, and why. *Review of General Psychology, 14*(4), 340–353. doi:10.1037/a0021288.

Swiss Federal Office for Migration (FOM). (2014). The population of Bosnia and Herzegovina in Switzerland. Retrieved from www.bundespublikationen.admin.ch/cshop_mimes_bbl/2C/2C59E545D7371EE495A4A6B21623F42A.pdf.

Swiss Federal Office of Public Health (FOPH) (2007). *Wie gesund sind Migrantinnen und Migranten?* [How healthy are female and male migrants?]. Bern: Swiss Federal Office for Public Health.

Swiss Federal Statistical Office (FSO). (2014a) *Gesundheitsstatistik 2014* [Health Statistics 2014]. Neuchâtel: Swiss Federal Statistical Office.

Swiss Federal Statistical Office (FSO). (2014b). *Migration und Integration – Indikatoren: Ausländische Bevölkerung: Staatsangehörigkeit* [Migration and Integration – Data, Indicators: Nationality]. Retrieved from: www.bfs.admin.ch/bfs/portal/de/index/themen/01/07/blank/key/01/01.html.

Swiss Federal Statistical Office (FSO). (2016) *Arbeitslosigkeit, offene Stellen – Detaillierte Daten – Detaillierte Ergebnisse der SAKE* (Unemployment, Open Positions – Detailed Data – Detailed Results from SAKE). *Erwerbslosenquote gemäss ILO nach Geschlecht, Nationalität und anderen Merkmalen* [Unemployment rate by ILO standard according to gender, nationality and other characteristics]. [Data file]. Retrieved from www.bfs.admin.ch/bfs/portal/de/index/themen/03/03/blank/data/02.html.

Thompson, A. G. (2007). The meaning of patient involvement and participation in health care consultations: A taxonomy. *Social Science & Medicine, 64*(6), 1297–1310. doi:10.1016/j.socscimed.2006.11.002.

Weilandt, C., Rommel, A., Eckert, J., & Azmat, R. G. (2006). Gesundheitsmonitoring der Migrationsbevölkerung in der Schweiz. [Health Monitring of the Migrant Population in Switzerland]. *Bundesgesundheitsblatt-Gesundheitsforschung-Gesundheitsschutz, 49*(9), 866–872. doi:10.1007/s00103-006-0020-x.

Williamson, L. (2014). Patient and citizen participation in health: The need for improved ethical support. *The American Journal of Bioethics, 14*(6), 4–16. doi:10.1080/15265161.2014.900139.

World Health Organization (WHO). (1978). *Declaration of Alma-Ata*, International Conference on Primary Health Care, Alma-Ata, USSR, 6–12, September 1978. Retrieved from www.who.int/publications/almaata_declaration_en.pdf.

World Health Organization (WHO) World Alliance for Patient Safety. (2006). *Global Patient Safety Challenge 2005–2006: Clean Care is Safer Care.* Retrieved from www.who.int/patientsafety/events/05/GPSC_Launch_ENGLISH_FINAL.pdf.

Yancey, A. K., Ortega, A. N., & Kumanyika, S. K. (2006). Effective recruitment and retention of minority research participants. *Annual Review of Public Health, 27*, 1–28. doi:10.1146/annurev.publhealth.27.021405.102113.

Young, M., & Klingle, R. S. (1996). Silent partners in medical care: a cross-cultural study of patient participation. *Health Communication, 8*(1), 29–53. doi:10.1207/s15327027hc0801_2.

5 Cultural Competence in Health

Understanding the Food Choices of Older Ukrainian Australians

Victoria Team, Lenore Manderson, & Milica Markovic

Introduction

Increased life expectancy in Australia and other developed countries highlights the need for health promotion focused on chronic disease prevention and improvements in quality of life (Nay, Garratt, & Fetherstonhaugh, 2014). Although there are many factors that may predispose to chronic diseases, including genetic, social, environmental, and financial factors, preventive advice has frequently focused on modifying personal lifestyle (Willcox, 2014), on the grounds that this approach is both effective and cost-effective (Ananthapavan, Sacks, Moodie, & Carter, 2014; Carter *et al.*, 2009). Despite recent advances in health promotion and disease prevention in Australia, some disadvantaged groups, including immigrant populations, still experience a higher than average burden of chronic disease, disability and premature mortality (AIHW, 2014). Furthermore, a recently published finding from the analysis of the longitudinal Household, Income, and Labour Dynamics in Australia (HILDA) survey data indicated that after twenty years of residing in Australia, immigrants who were of good health upon arrival reported as many chronic diseases as the Australia-born population (Jatrana, Pasupuleti, & Richardson, 2014).

The links between overweight and obesity and a range of chronic illnesses are well established. In Australia, the proportion of people who are overweight and obese is increasing, and 28 percent of the population is reported to be obese (ABS, 2013). Some population groups, including older Australians and people from different cultural backgrounds, experience higher rates of obesity and these rates are projected to increase (Hauck, Hollingsworth, & Morgan, 2011; Nepal & Brown, 2013; Renzaho, Bilal, & Marks, 2014; Shahwan-Akl, 2010). At the same time, perceptions of normal variation of body weight may differ across community groups. For example, in some Aboriginal communities, people may underestimate their body weight and would be less interested in weight management strategies (Cunningham, O'Dea, Dunbar, & Maple-Brown, 2008). Socio-economic circumstances, too, shape people's health behaviors. People from low socio-economic backgrounds have fewer opportunities to engage in healthy eating behaviors (Crawford *et al.*, 2014; Warin, Turner, Moore, & Davies, 2008), and the greater availability of cheap fast food restaurants in low socio-economic suburbs may also influence food choice (Thornton, Lamb, & Ball, 2016). Problems related to purchasing and carrying groceries, and limited access to transport, appear also to affect the ability of some elderly people to purchase a variety of food products (Burns, Bentley, Thornton, & Kavanagh, 2011).

The current Australian Healthy Eating Guidelines, including for older people, were developed by the National Medical Research Council (NHMRC, 2013) and are available online for download; print versions can be ordered. However, older people may not have IT skills nor own a computer, and so would be unable to access this information and place an order. Translated versions of these guidelines are available in eleven community languages (although not in Russian and Ukrainian) through the Multicultural Health Communication (www.mhcs.health.nsw.gov.au/publicationsandresources/pdf/publication-pdfs/oth-9450).

Immigrants are less likely than other people to be involved in preventive activities due to insufficient knowledge, language issues, lack of priority at the time of resettlement, limited access to health care, and differences in health care policies and health systems in Australia and countries of their origin (Lee, Sulaiman-Hill, & Thompson, 2013; Team, Manderson, & Markovic, 2013; Vasey & Manderson, 2012). Research in Australia and elsewhere illustrates a range of attitudes that negatively influence peoples' engagement in healthy practices: the cultural perceptions of health as an absence of illness and/or a belief that a health condition in an individual is determined by God, independently of his or her behavior, for instance, as found in a study with people from United Arab Emirates (Baglar, 2013); or fatalistic beliefs regarding their lack of control, as documented in a study with Chinese and Korean Americans (Heiniger, Sherman, Shaw, & Costa, 2015). Other factors, such as social isolation and limited social relationships, adjustment-related increased levels of stress, other family members' food preferences, the absence of traditional foods and the availability of cheap animal products and fast food products, may all result in adopting unhealthy diets, as illustrated in research with Australian Iranians (Delavari, Farrelly, Renzaho, Mellor, & Swinburn, 2012), first generation Greek Australians (Kouris-Blazos, 2002) and Filipino Australians (Maneze, DiGiacomo, Salamonson, Descallar, & Davidson, 2015). Post-traumatic stress disorder among Cambodian refugees in Australia has been associated with emotional eating (Wagner *et al.*, 2015). Food-related behaviors and practices may be passed through generations, and dietary acculturation, including the adoption of 'healthier' behaviors (as defined by health professionals), can be a long-term process, as found in a study with Chinese and Italian Australians (Rhodes *et al.*, 2016) and Australian refugees from the Horn of Africa (Wilson & Renzaho, 2015). Acculturation too may have advantages and disadvantages in relation to lifestyle behaviors. For example, with an increased level of acculturation, Vietnamese Australians were involved in higher levels of physical activity, but also increased levels of meat consumption (Tran, Jorm, Johnson, Bambrick, & Lujic, 2013).

Background

According to the latest available data from the 2011 Census, approximately 14,000 Ukrainian people reside in Australia (Commonwealth of Australia, 2014). People in the age groups 45–64 years (~23%) and 65 years and over (~40%) comprised the greatest proportion of the population. Significant numbers of Ukraine-born people are of Russian (24%) and Jewish (~15%) ancestries. The main languages spoken at home are Russian (~58%) and Ukrainian (~24%) (Commonwealth of Australia, 2014). The majority of older Ukrainians arrived in Australia from displaced persons camps after the World War II. Additional numbers of Ukraine-born people emigrated as skilled and family migrants after the collapse of the USSR in 1991 (Commonwealth of Australia, 2014).

Although Ukrainian people are described as being 'well known' for their extensive culinary preparations (LeBlanc, 1999), traditionally, their diet has been characterized as high in fat and rich in animal food products (Biloukha & Utermohlen, 2001; Kollegaeva, 2012). The eating behavior of Ukrainians was influenced by former USSR policies recommending greater intake of daily protein, which was also associated with greater fat intake (Biloukha & Utermohlen, 2000), and by the relative availability and affordability of different food items (Phillips, 2002). Environmental factors also influenced eating habits. For example, seasonality, including the absence of fresh green vegetables and some fruits during winter, contributed to diets high in protein and animal fat (Biloukha & Utermohlen, 2001; Shanahan, Carlsson-Kanyama, Offei-Ansah, Ekström, & Potapova, 2003). In addition, after the Chernobyl disaster (1986), Ukrainians were less likely to consume local fresh fruits, vegetables, milk and meat due to increased amounts of radioactive substances in these products. If they could afford to do so, they purchased processed milk, and canned fruits, vegetables and meat imported from other countries (Phillips, 2002). Furthermore, although they were exposed to health promotion messages on healthy eating, people necessarily consumed food products that were available and affordable rather than 'healthy' (Cockerham, 2005; Honkanen & Frewer, 2009).

A number of researchers have emphasized that Ukrainians do not trust media messages, including those related to healthy eating, because during the USSR era, the media served the government (Benisovich & King, 2003; Biloukha & Utermohlen, 2000). Ukrainian people appear to regard health practitioners' advice on healthy eating as most accurate and trustworthy (Biloukha & Utermohlen, 2001), and generally believe that good health depends largely on the quality of health care rather than on individual health promoting behaviors (Abbott, Turmov, & Wallace, 2006a; Cockerham, Hinote, Cockerham, & Abbott, 2006). Factors contributing to ill health, such as genetic factors, environmental pollution, infectious agents and heavy workloads, are all seen to be beyond individual control (Abbott *et al.*, 2006a).

Below, we explore the relationship between the communication of healthy eating in Australia and the eating behaviors of Ukrainian Australians aged 50 years and over. This age group was selected as particularly disadvantaged because many have insufficient English language skills and lack information technology skills. The aim of the research project on which we draw here was to investigate the factors which influence lifestyle, exploring the personal experiences of Ukrainian immigrants. Convenience sampling was applied as a sampling strategy, with participants recruited through ethnic community and religious organizations in Melbourne. Face-to-face in-depth interviews were selected as a method of data collection. Data collection and data analysis were conducted concurrently. In total, thirteen Ukrainian immigrants, including six men and seven women, were interviewed, including an informal community leader. In this work, we used pseudonyms.

We draw on ideas of the 'four-dimensional cultural competence in health' model developed by the National Health and Medical Research Council (NHMRC, 2006, p. 45), in accordance with which health professionals as a group and as individual practitioners should ensure that 'the different needs of different groups within the community are recognized.' According to this guideline, health professionals should 'contact community health services and multicultural resource centers for respected community workers/peer educators who have knowledge and expertise in the values and norms of their respective communities in relation to dietary habits, norms, practices' (NHMRC, 2006, p. 38). An example of cultural competence in relation to healthy eating on an individual level could be health professionals' tailored messages on 'appropriate foods and food preparation techniques both from the culture of origin and the host country' (NHMRC, 2006, p. 39).

Results

Study Participants

We interviewed six men and seven women. The mean age of participants was 69 years (range 51–87). Five participants had completed undergraduate university courses in the former Soviet Union, seven had completed post-secondary technical or vocational courses, and one had completed primary education. At the time of interview, two participants were in full-time employment and 11 participants received the old age pension; of those receiving a pension, five were involved in voluntary work in local community and religious organizations. All participants resided in Melbourne; four of them owned their own homes and nine lived in the Housing Commission (public housing) apartments. Most participants had some basic spoken English language skills, but none were able to read or write English. Nine participants spoke Russian at home and four spoke Ukrainian.

"A Stockpile in the Body": Pre- and Post-immigration Experiences

Most participants explained that food insecurity in Ukraine contributed to unhealthy eating habits. The seasonality of some fruits and vegetables and lack of imported fresh products resulted in people eating a lot of fruits when they were available. For example, Vasily explained:

> When cherries and strawberries were in season, we ate as much as we could fit in [our bodies]. We were making a stockpile of these foods in our bodies, so that there would be enough for the whole year [until the next season].

Other participants too mentioned this. These beliefs and practices contributed to overeating some foods during the early re-settlement period, as Galya explained:

> I came to Australia hungry. I bought a six-hundred-millilitres packet of sour cream, tasted it, and the cream was sweet and rich. I ate it all at once with a bread roll. My husband saw this and said: You will feel bad after eating this. I laughed and told him: You will feel bad without sour cream; with sour cream, you will never feel bad. At first, I was eating bread with butter. My body had this need, but after one or two years, I was satiated. Now I do not take butter and fats; my body does not require these calories.

Other participants, who in Ukraine had experienced food shortages due to financial problems, food shortages or post-Chernobyl restrictions on certain types of food, also pointed out their tendency to overeat during their early years in Australia. They ate a lot because many products were available and affordable, and some products they wanted to try because they did not know about them in Ukraine. They believed that they had had insufficient calories and vital nutrients, which could be restored. Romero-Gwynn *et al.* (1997), exploring eating habits of immigrants from the former Soviet Union, also noticed an increased consumption of familiar products that were available and affordable in the United States.

All participants continued to eat pork lard, except for one participant who observed kosher law and consumed only kosher products. All tried to substitute lard with similar products that were available in Australia, but felt that they did not necessarily feel full after eating these. Participants spoke of their desire to eat traditional foods, as Marusya explained:

> In Ukraine, I can say, there were not many food varieties, but you'd eat a piece of bread and a piece of lard, and you would no longer be hungry. Here – you have this and that, and you don't know what to eat, and you always think of bread and lard.

Most participants purchased home-made lard, or made their own, as Mycola explained:

> Once we were hunting wild boars with my friends. There are millions of them in Australia. We killed one, and it was a female, who had piglets. I took two of them home and gave them to Liusya [his wife]. Well, how do you think a wild boar differs from a domestic pig? Meat and lard from the wild boar are harder. Why? Because they eat grass... Liusya fed the piglets with bread, vegetables, and various leftovers. Believe me or not, their lard was better than that of domestic pigs.

In Australia, some participants, especially from lower socio-economic backgrounds and those with large families, experienced financial difficulties, and took discarded products from the recycling bins of bakeries, local butcher shops, vegetable shops in local markets, and food stores. They also purchased and utilized discounted products when the use-by date was close to expiring. Feeling full at the time was more important than eating healthy food. For example, Galya said that she purchased 25 packages of buckwheat for 20 cents each from the local NQR ('Not Quite Right') shop. The date indicated on the package was close to the expiry date at the time of purchase, but Galya explained, grains can be stored forever. She also used to pick out chicken bones from the rubbish bin of the butcher's shop at the local market in order to make broth. She continued to do this until the market expanded and the rubbish bins were placed in a secure area to which she had no access. Marusya too said: "I live economically. I buy what other people would say is rubbish." They did not discard food leftovers, as Roza said:

> Yosef [her husband] never eats leftovers and does not allow me to finish them. However, as soon as he goes to the main room... from time to time, I throw some food in my mouth rather than in the rubbish bin.

Personal experiences of food availability also affected food choice and quantity. Two relatively wealthy participants said that all types of food available in Australia had been available for them in Ukraine, and their eating patterns upon immigration had not changed. By contrast, in Ukraine, Ivan had lived close to the Chernobyl zone, and his wife died of leukaemia soon after the blast. He then married an Australian woman of Russian background, and immigrated to Australia with his three children. They did, he explained, have some unhealthy food practices, such as serving cakes frequently as desired by his children. However, they consumed many fruits and vegetables, which they were not allowed to eat in Ukraine. Ivan became concerned about the potential health risks of eating fresh products in Australia too, because of the use of chemicals in growing and storing the food, as he shared:

> There were a lot of precautions about not eating anything from the radioactive zone... People did not buy vegetables and fruits either; they were afraid to buy them. People stopped to eat fruits and vegetables. Immediately, after the blast, no one sold them and no one purchased them. For about two or three years we were told not to buy fruits and vegetables. When we came here, the children wanted to try everything, but they ate mostly fruits and vegetables, which was bad because all fruits here are sprayed with chemicals.

Other researchers, who conducted studies in Ukraine soon after the Chernobyl disaster and decades later, have reported that people ate what was available, even when knowing the risks associated with the consumption of some products with high content of radionuclides (Abbott, Wallace, & Beck, 2006b; Phillips, 2002). Upon immigration to Australia, people's fear of contamination was translated into a fear of toxins in food due to the use of chemical fertilizers, pesticides, preservatives, and hormones.

In Australia, although the focus is on healthy eating, participants noted the contradictory attitude in relation to some practices, such as community barbecue events. Yasha, an informal Russian and Ukrainian Jewish community leader in the Housing Commission apartments, said that in terms of healthy eating, the local council organized 'inappropriate' activities, including free barbecue events and the distribution of unsold bread instead of promoting healthy cooking skills.

> They make free barbecues for us. Well, this is good for people in terms of communication, but our oldies won't benefit from eating these sausages. You see them eating sausages there and putting a couple of sausages in their bags to take home. And they don't need these sausages, but they take them because they are free... I was talking to the council committee about planning some other activities, but they said that they plan these activities themselves (Yasha).

Health Literacy and Understanding the Concept of 'Healthy Eating'

Most participants had poor health literacy and did not have access to educational material on healthy eating, except for two women who had been given printed language-specific educational material as part of diabetes education, and one man who used an old health advice book written in Polish. Some participants were anxious about eating particular foods, after seeing food labels with listed additives, which they did not understood. Lacking reading and IT skills, some participants relied on their adult children to get information on eating, the nutrient values of foods, and other issues.

> You look at the label, and you see all these numbers, and you never know if this ingredient is good or bad for your health. For example, you read that additive 456 was included in this product. What does it mean to you? How would you interpret this number? I understand nothing from the information they provide [on the label]. Why don't they teach us how to interpret these numbers (Lena)?
>
> When you read the ingredients [on the label] ...oh, there are carbonates and gluconates, and preservative number this and preservative number that. Here, if you die, you will never know what preservative number has caused your death. If you read the composition [label], it is horrible, you will be scared to eat. Our products were unlabelled because they were organic. Here, products won't expire until the year 2030... I purchase products that have fewer ingredients on the label (Galya).

Similar to our findings, former Soviet Union immigrants in Israel (Gesser-Edelsburg, Endevelt, Zemach, & Tirosh-Kamienchick, 2015) and the United States (Lubman, Doak, & Jasti, 2012) have also been reported to have poor label use and interpretation skills. But in addition, the current Australian food labelling system is complicated. Although many Australians claim that they use the information on the labels, the actual use and understanding of label information appears to be limited (Mhurchu & Gorton, 2007). On a positive note, the Australian Government (Commonwealth Department of Health, 2014) has developed the Food Star Rating system for labelling packaged products, which is easier to understand; the system is currently voluntary.

People may have various interpretations of the concept of 'healthy eating,' as Bisogni, Jastran, Seligson, and Thompson (2012) conclude from their review study. Our participants generally linked eating and health, for example, the consumption of radioactively contaminated food with leukaemia and other cancers, and the consumption of food with additives with allergies and unknown impacts on health. However, most participants did not link unhealthy eating behaviors with risks for or the development of chronic diseases, excepting for some participants who linked overeating to obesity. Most participants were unable to list any chronic diseases related to unhealthy lifestyle behaviors, and did not link 'unhealthy' eating behaviors and chronic diseases. They did not understand the concept of 'healthy eating,' and rather, believed that for a healthy person any type of food is healthy. Moreover, they perceived the concept of 'healthy eating' to refer to maintaining a diet as part of a disease management plan or dieting for the purpose of weight loss.

RESEARCHER: Can you list some healthy foods?

IVAN: I don't know these [health] recommendations. In my understanding, if you have a need and if you have a chance to buy the product, you need to eat everything without limiting yourself. For a healthy person any type of food is healthy.

RESEARCHER: How do you understand healthy lifestyle?

IVAN: When you can eat whatever you want without any problem and feel well with this. But if you ate something, this harms you and that harms you, this means that it is not a healthy lifestyle…

RESEARCHER: Do you know any diseases related to unhealthy eating?

IVAN: No

RESEARCHER: Diabetes?

IVAN: Diabetes... I heard that this is a hereditary disease, or maybe they eat a lot of sugary foods. They cannot maintain a healthy lifestyle despite wanting to. For them a diet is suitable; it is necessary for them, otherwise they cannot maintain a healthy lifestyle...

A lack of understanding the links between individual lifestyle and chronic illness has also been reported by studies conducted in Ukraine and other countries of the Former Soviet Union (Abbott *et al.*, 2006a; Cockerham *et al.*, 2006). Insufficient understanding of this link, in addition to inappropriate economic policies in relation to food products and the marketing and sale of unhealthy products, can contribute to increases in chronic illness.

On the other hand, participants associated malnutrition during childhood with all health problems in older age, and two participants linked chronic health problems with adult hunger and starvation. A question regarding their choice of eating either white or wholemeal bread brought back their memories of starvation during the post-war period:

> All my life I was starving. All my life I was chasing a piece of bread. At times, I was dreaming of white bread. My husband died during the war. I was raising my only son alone, saving the last piece of bread for him. You can never imagine these long queues and us standing in the freezing cold from early morning to get your ration.

> You bring it home, and it does not even look as bread. I don't want to deprive myself of a piece of white bread, especially now at the end of my life (Tanya).
>
> Enough, I ate enough dark bread in the '40s. After the war we had no white bread, only dark and soggy (bread). We lived such a difficult life, expecting that things would become better with time. Socialism… we were on the horizon of communism, as they said. Thank God that he helped me to move from their horizon to Australia where I can eat as much as I want before I die (Galya).

Varieties of dark bread as well as portion control were therefore unpleasant reminders of war, poverty and the struggle to survive. Similar findings were reported by Teshuva (2010), who investigated ageing and aged care among genocide survivors, including older Holocaust survivors in Jewish Care in Melbourne. Aged care staff looking after Holocaust survivors reported that elderly people were hoarding food and did not want to discard it even it was clearly spoiled. Bezo and Maggi (2015), conducting a study involving Ukrainian Canadians, also found that memories of hunger and starvation tend to pass from one generation to the next in the form of personal and collective memories. Some practices, such as purchasing more products than required, stockpiling food at home because of uncertainty, never discarding leftovers, and treating food with a special reverence, were observed even in second and third generations of hunger survivors. Memories of hunger have also influenced the eating behaviors of the first generation of Greek Australians (Kouris-Blazos, 2002) and arguably would influence the eating practices among other groups for whom the abundance and variety of foods are highly valued.

"Doctor, What Am I Allowed Eat?" Health Communication and Information Provision

In Ukraine, health professionals, and particularly medical doctors, provided patients with health information on healthy eating and dieting for weight and disease management purposes (Biloukha & Utermohlen, 2001), and people externalized their health locus of control to the health care system (Cockerham *et al.*, 2006; Team *et al.*, 2013). Upon immigration, most Ukrainian Australians who participated in this project relied on their GPs (general practitioners) and were critical that their GPs did not provide eating-related advice and rarely discussed lifestyle issues. Immigrants suspected that their GPs lacked time, but also that they viewed eating and dieting as contributing little to a disease management compared to medication. As a result, participants said that their GPs provided simplistic advice, such as 'eat less' and 'start exercising,' and undermined patients' diet-related concerns and cultural beliefs. For example, Sonya believed that her physician simply lacked time: "He always runs. I asked him: 'Doctor, what am I allowed eat?' He said: 'You know this better than me.'" Rita believed that her physician did not discuss with her lifestyle behaviors because of her insufficient English language skills:

> Even if I will go to the doctor to seek his advice, how will he talk to me if I cannot speak English properly? I cannot connect even a few words together. If you know English well, then the doctor definitely would advise you on what to eat and how to exercise.

Vasily said that the doctor had found his question funny: "I asked my doctor if chili sauce is good for your heart because if I take a spoon or two I feel better; I can breathe easier. He just laughed..."

Petya thought that doctors were not concerned about older people's health:

> No, the doctors talk nothing about food; only once they told me to eat less meat. I'll tell you openly, when you are becoming older, they don't care... One doctor even told me: 'You should learn how to help yourself.' But how can I help myself if I don't know how. I just trust in God...

Petya did not understand the concept of self-care; he perceived it as neglect and associated it with age-related discrimination of older people by health professionals. Other studies with immigrants from the former USSR have also revealed insufficient understanding of self-care (Team *et al.*, 2013).

Marusya believed that Australian doctors were insufficiently trained to provide eating-related advice, and that they considered diet to contribute less to disease management than medications. Diagnosed with hypertension, Marusya decided to ask her doctors about a specific diet for her health condition:

> Don't you remember when you were sick (in Ukraine), the doctor first of all would suggest to you to follow a diet? Something you should include in your diet and something you should abstain from. Then he would suggest you take some herbs and vitamins and, if these do not help, then medications would be prescribed. Here, it is opposite... They told me: 'Take your medications regularly and decrease salt.' Australian doctors know nothing about diets.

Bella, too, was willing to follow the doctor's advice related to weight loss. Aiming to clarify this advice, she asked her overseas-trained Russian-speaking doctor about further steps: "I said: 'I know that I need to lose my weight, just tell me how.' She [the doctor] said: 'Stop stuffing your guts.'" Bella was also involved in the informal care of her husband, who had an advanced form of schizophrenia, and she had asked his doctor for suggestions about diet:

> I asked his doctor if I could cook any special food for my husband. He said: 'I don't know any special food that might help people with schizophrenia.' He said something else... The interpreter translated this as meaning, 'stop making waves in a glass of water.'

While most participants depended on their GPs for all health matters, they were concerned with their failure to discuss diet and eating-related issues.

Lifestyle focused interventions, including suggestions on healthy eating and reducing energy intake, are considered primary steps in management of overweight and obesity, which are in turn linked to chronic illnesses (Grima & Dixon, 2013). Lifestyle modification advice provided by GPs has been shown to be effective because of its potential to influence patients' attempts to modify their lifestyle-related behaviors (Dorsey & Songer, 2011; Egede, 2003). However, despite increasing evidence of its value, some health professionals may see healthy lifestyle advice as of little clinical relevance and potentially not beneficial for patients (Jacka & Berk, 2012). Other studies, too, highlight that lack of time in a busy practice was a common reason for this. For example, in a survey of overweight and obese patients in New South Wales, most participants believed that they would benefit from a physician's advice on healthy eating; however, almost half of them thought that their physician lacked the available time to provide quality advice (Tan, Zwar, Dennis, & Vagholkar, 2006).

Concluding Remarks

Ukrainian immigrants aged 50 years and over had low levels of health literacy upon immigration and followed unhealthy eating diets. Lack of educational materials on healthy eating in Russian and Ukrainian languages, as well as lack of advice from general practitioners, contributed to this. Participants did not seek information on healthy eating, believing that for a healthy person any type of food was healthy, but also, with poor English language and IT skills, they were unable to find this information from other sources. Furthermore, mass media campaigns on healthy eating can be easily misunderstood, particularly by older immigrants, who may have different understandings of the concept of 'healthy eating' and see no links between eating behaviors and chronic illness. Although younger and middle-aged Ukrainian immigrants have better English language and IT skills, and so may be able to find nutrition guidelines online, older people may benefit from face-to-face verbal communication with their GPs with the help of Ukrainian or Russian interpreters.

GPs are well-positioned to provide information on lifestyle behaviors to older people since they are the most frequent users of their services (Brownie, Muggleston, & Oliver, 2015). If GPs have developed a chronic illness management plan, they can refer patients to a dietitian/nutritionist who could provide counselling to patients, which is covered by Medicare. Yet, health professionals would need to explain this clearly to patients. Patients, however, may perceive dietary advice from a health professional other than a GP as inferior. The provision of printed information on healthy eating in the language of their preference would be beneficial, particularly if this information was provided by a physician. As stated in the Australian Medical Association's (AMA, 2010) position statement on preventative care, information provision, health education, improving health literacy, and building patient's capacity to manage their own health are the key roles of medical doctors and core elements of preventative care, which should be better integrated into general practice. Moodie and associates (2013) have argued that most of the determinants of obesity in Australia are outside of the health sector. They suggested that both better health promotion and creating supporting environments are required to address these determinants. Our own research suggests, however, that in some communities or age groups within these communities, health-sector–based, physician-led health promotion activities remain important on an individual level.

There are benefits to increasing the cultural awareness of physicians practicing in a multicultural country and developing their cultural competence. However, physicians may not be aware of all culture-specific issues related to various health conditions and different aspects of patients' life, including healthy eating. To date, we have limited evidence of the effectiveness of training physicians on 'cultural practices' and difference (Lie, Lee-Rey, Gomez, Bereknyei, & Braddock, 2011), particularly in relation to the prevention and management of chronic illnesses (Henderson, Kendall, & See, 2011). Cultural competence training may improve health professionals' knowledge of some cultural issues, but not all health professionals apply their knowledge and skills into practice (see, for example, Chevannes, 2002). The results of a recent study in Australia indicated that even senior staff members, such as clinical supervisors, lacked cultural competence and were unable to communicate cultural competence messages to their junior colleagues (Berger, Conroy, Peerson, & Brazil, 2014). Developing cultural competence would require continuity and "the goal of integrating culture into clinical care is [to] remain elusive" (Berger & Peerson, 2015, p. 515). To improve patient-professional communication, we suggest a cultural communication approach, whereby a physician asks patients about their culture-specific beliefs and practices related to their health condition, and then together they select the optimal preventive or management approach. Asking a patient is the first step of the '5As framework'

(Dosh *et al.*, 2005)—Ask, Assess, Advise, Assist, Arrange—adopted by the Royal Australian College of General Practitioners (RACGP, 2012) for preventive activities in general practice.

The significance of our study is that it further contributes to the existing knowledge base in the field of health promotion and health communication, focusing on cultural and age specific issues of immigrant communities. As we have discussed, people from different backgrounds may have different understandings of the health promotion concepts and practices, including 'healthy eating,' 'healthy lifestyle,' and 'self-care.' Their understanding of these concepts is informed by their past experience with health policies and practices in their countries of origin. Differences in health care systems and people's individual understanding of health behaviors, and the links between these and the development of chronic illness, should be acknowledged and reflected in health communication and health promotion. We anticipate that this is relevant for immigrants, particularly for older people who lack health literacy, and whose demographic and historical circumstances render them vulnerable to chronic disease.

Acknowledgments and Funding

The content of this chapter draws on the doctoral thesis of the first author. She was supported by the University of Melbourne Fay Marles Scholarship; Population Health Investing in Research Students' Training Funding Scheme; and an Australian Federation of University Women (AFUW-Vic) Scholarship. Sections of this chapter were presented at the Sociopolitics of Food Workshop, Monash University, May 28, 2012, and at the Conference of the Mykola Zerov Centre for Ukrainian Studies, Monash University, February 15–16, 2013.

References

Abbott, P., Turmov, S., & Wallace, C. (2006a). Health world views of post-Soviet citizens. *Social Science & Medicine*, *62*(1), 228–238. doi:10.1016/j.socscimed.2005.05.019.

Abbott, P., Wallace, C., & Beck, M. (2006b). Chernobyl: Living with risk and uncertainty. *Health, Risk & Society*, *8*(2), 105–121. doi:10.1080/13698570600677167.

ABS. (2013). *Australian Health Survey: Updated results, 2011–2012. ABS cat. no. 4364.0.55.003*. Canberra: Australian Bureau of Statistics.

AIHW. (2014). *Australia's health 2014. Australia's health series no. 14. Cat. no. AUS 178*. Canberra: Australian Institute of Health and Welfare.

AMA. (2010). *Doctors and Preventative Care – 2010*. Barton: Australian Medical Association.

Ananthapavan, J., Sacks, G., Moodie, M., & Carter, R. (2014). Economics of obesity—Learning from the past to contribute to a better future.

International Journal of Environmental Research and Public Health, *11*(4), 4007–4025. doi:10.3390/ijerph110404007.

Baglar, R. (2013). "Oh God, save us from sugar": An ethnographic exploration of diabetes mellitus in the United Arab Emirates. *Medical Anthropology*, *32*(2), 109–125. doi:10.1080/01459740.2012.671399.

Benisovich, S. V., & King, A. C. (2003). Meaning and knowledge of health among older adult immigrants from Russia: A phenomenological study. *Health Education Research*, *18*(2), 135–144.

Berger, G., Conroy, S., Peerson, A., & Brazil, V. (2014). Clinical supervisors and cultural competence. *The Clinical Teacher*, *11*, 370–374. doi:10.1111/tct.12170.

Berger, G., & Peerson, A. (2015). Cultural competence lessons learned: The continuum model. *Medical Education*, *49*(5), 515–516. doi:10.1111/medu.12685.

Bezo, B., & Maggi, S. (2015). Living in "survival mode:" Intergenerational transmission of trauma from the Holodomor genocide of 1932–1933 in Ukraine. *Social Science & Medicine*, *134*, 87–94. doi:10.1016/j.socscimed.2015.04.009.

Biloukha, O. O., & Utermohlen, V. (2000). Correlates of food consumption and perceptions of foods in an educated urban population in Ukraine. *Food Quality and Preference*, *11*(6), 475–485. doi:10.1016/S0950-3293(00)00020-3.

Biloukha, O. O., & Utermohlen, V. (2001). Healthy eating in Ukraine: Attitudes, barriers and information sources. *Public Health Nutrition*, *4*(2), 207–215. doi:10.1079/PHN2001213.

Bisogni, C. A., Jastran, M., Seligson, M., & Thompson, A. (2012). How people interpret healthy eating: Contributions of qualitative research. *Journal of Nutrition Education and Behavior*, *44*(4), 282–301. doi:10.1016/j.jneb.2011.11.009.

Brownie, S., Muggleston, H., & Oliver, C. (2015). The 2013 Australian dietary guidelines and recommendations for older Australians. *Australian Family Physician*, *44*(5), 311–315.

Burns, C., Bentley, R., Thornton, L., & Kavanagh, A. (2011). Reduced food access due to a lack of money, inability to lift and lack of access to a car for food shopping: A multilevel study in Melbourne, Victoria. *Public Health Nutrition*, *14*(6), 1017–1023. doi:10.1017/S136898001000385X.

Carter, R., Moodie, M., Markwick, A., Magnus, A., Vos, T., Swinburn, B., & Haby, M. (2009). Assessing cost-effectiveness in obesity (ACE-Obesity): An overview of the ACE approach, economic methods and cost results. *BMC Public Health*, *9*(1), 419. doi:10.1186/1471-2458-9-419.

Chevannes, M. (2002). Issues in educating health professionals to meet the diverse needs of patients and other service users from ethnic minority groups. *Journal of Advanced Nursing*, *39*(3), 290–298. doi:10.1046/j.1365-2648.2002.02276.x.

Cockerham, W. C. (2005). Health lifestyle theory and the convergence of agency and structure. *Journal of Health and Social Behavior*, *46*(1), 51–67. doi:10.1177/002214650504600105.

Cockerham, W. C., Hinote, B. P., Cockerham, G. B., & Abbott, P. (2006). Health lifestyles and political ideology in Belarus, Russia, and Ukraine. *Social Science & Medicine*, *62*(7), 1799–1809. doi:10.1016/j.socscimed.2005.08.024.

Commonwealth Department of Health. (2014). *Health star rating system: cost benefit analysis. 16 May 2014*. Southbank, Australia: PricewaterhouseCoopers.

Commonwealth of Australia. (2014). *Community information summary: Ukraine-born*. Canberra: Australian Government, Department of Immigration and Citizenship. Retrieved from www.dss.gov.au/sites/default/files/documents/02_2014/ukraine.pdf.

Crawford, B., Yamazaki, R., Franke, E., Amanatidis, S., Ravulo, J., Steinbeck, K., … Torvaldsen, S. (2014). Sustaining dignity? Food insecurity in homeless young people in urban Australia. *Health Promotion Journal of Australia*, *25*(2), 71–78. doi:10.1071/HE13090.

Cunningham, J., O'Dea, K., Dunbar, T., & Maple-Brown, L. (2008). Perceived weight versus Body Mass Index among urban Aboriginal Australians: Do perceptions and measurements match? *Australian and New Zealand Journal of Public Health*, *32*(2), 135–138. doi:10.1111/j.1753-6405.2008.00189.x.

Delavari, M., Farrelly, A., Renzaho, A., Mellor, D., & Swinburn, B. (2012). Experiences of migration and the determinants of obesity among recent Iranian immigrants in Victoria, Australia. *Ethnicity & Health*, *18*(1), 66–82. doi:10.1080/13557858.2012.698255.

Dorsey, R., & Songer, T. (2011). Lifestyle behaviors and physician advice for change among overweight and obese adults with prediabetes and diabetes in the United States, 2006. *Preventing Chronic Disease*, *8*(6), A132.

Dosh, S. A., Holtrop, J. S., Torres, T., Arnold, A. K., Baumann, J., & White, L. L. (2005). Changing organizational constructs into functional tools: An assessment of the 5 A's in primary care practices. *The Annals of Family Medicine*, *3*(suppl 2), S50–S52. doi:10.1370/afm.357.

Egede, L. E. (2003). Lifestyle modification to improve blood pressure control in individuals with diabetes: Is physician advice effective? *Diabetes Care*, *26*(3), 602–607. doi:10.2337/diacare.26.3.602.

Gesser-Edelsburg, A., Endevelt, R., Zemach, M., & Tirosh-Kamienchick, Y. (2015). Food consumption and nutritional labeling among immigrants to Israel from the Former Soviet Union. *Journal of Immigrant and Minority Health*, *17*(2), 459–466. doi:10.1007/s10903-013-9885-6.

Grima, M., & Dixon, J. B. (2013). Obesity: Recommendations for management in general practice and beyond. *Australian Family Physician*, *42*(8), 532–541.

Hauck, K., Hollingsworth, B., & Morgan, L. (2011). BMI differences in 1st and 2nd generation immigrants of Asian and European origin to Australia. *Health & Place*, *17*(1), 78–85. doi:10.1016/j.healthplace.2010.08.016.

Heiniger, L. E., Sherman, K. A., Shaw, L. E., & Costa, D. (2015). Fatalism and health promoting behaviors in Chinese and Korean immigrants and Caucasians. *Journal of Immigrant and Minority Health*, *17*(1), 165–171. doi:10.1007/s10903-013-9922-5.

Henderson, S., Kendall, E., & See, L. (2011). The effectiveness of culturally appropriate interventions to manage or prevent chronic disease in culturally and linguistically diverse communities: A systematic literature review. *Health & Social Care in the Community*, *19*(3), 225–249. doi:10.1111/j.1365-2524.2010.00972.x.

Honkanen, P., & Frewer, L. (2009). Russian consumers' motives for food choice. *Appetite*, *52*(2), 363–371. doi:10.1016/j.appet.2008.11.009.

Jacka, F. N., & Berk, M. (2012). Depression, diet and exercise. *Medical Journal of Australia*, *1*(Suppl 4), 21–23. doi:10.5694/mjao12.10508.

Jatrana, S., Pasupuleti, S. S. R., & Richardson, K. (2014). Nativity, duration of residence and chronic health conditions in Australia: Do trends converge towards the native-born population? *Social Science & Medicine*, *119*, 53–63. doi:10.1016/j.socscimed.2014.08.008.

Kollegaeva, K. (2012). Eating Ukraine and its lard(er). *Gastronomica*, *12*(3), 52–58. doi:10.1525/GFC.2012.12.3.52.

Kouris-Blazos, A. (2002). Morbidity mortality paradox of 1st generation Greek Australians. *Asia Pacific Journal of Clinical Nutrition*, *11*, S569–S575. doi:10.1046/j.1440-6047.11.supp3.2.x.

LeBlanc, R. D. (1999). Food, orality, and nostalgia for childhood: Gastronomic Slavophilism in mid-nineteenth-century Russian fiction. *The Russian Review*, *58*(2), 244–267. doi:10.1111/0036-0341.701999070.

Lee, S. K., Sulaiman-Hill, C. M. R., & Thompson, S. C. (2013). Providing health information for culturally and linguistically diverse women: Priorities and preferences of new migrants and refugees. *Health Promotion Journal of Australia*, *24*(2), 98–103. doi:10.1071/HE12919.

Lie, D. A., Lee-Rey, E., Gomez, A., Bereknyei, S., & Braddock, C. H. (2011). Does cultural competency training of health professionals improve patient outcomes? A systematic review and proposed algorithm for future research. *Journal of General Internal Medicine*, *26*(3), 317–325. doi:10.1007/s11606-010-1529-0.

Lubman, N., Doak, C., & Jasti, S. (2012). Food label use and food label skills among immigrants from the Former Soviet Union. *Journal of Nutrition Education and Behavior*, *44*(5), 398–406. doi:10.1016/j.jneb.2011.08.009.

Maneze, D., DiGiacomo, M., Salamonson, Y., Descallar, J., & Davidson, P. M. (2015). Facilitators and barriers to health-seeking behaviours among Filipino migrants: Inductive analysis to inform health promotion. *BioMed Research International*, *2015*(Article ID 506269), online. doi:10.1155/2015/506269.

Mhurchu, C. N., & Gorton, D. (2007). Nutrition labels and claims in New Zealand and Australia: A review of use and understanding. *Australian and New Zealand Journal of Public Health*, *31*(2), 105–112. doi:10.1111/j.1753-6405.2007.00026.x.

Moodie, M., Carter, R., Swinburn, B., Allender, S., Osborne, R., & Lawrence, M. (2013). Moving obesity prevention to the non-health sector. *Obesity Research & Clinical Practice*, 7(Supp 2), e120–e121. doi:10.1016/j.orcp.2013.12.715.

Nay, R., Garratt, S., & Fetherstonhaugh, D. (Eds.). (2014). *Older people: Issues and innovations in care* (4th ed.). Chatswood, Australia: Elsevier Health Sciences.

Nepal, B., & Brown, L. (2013). Projection of older Australians with a history of midlife obesity and overweight 2010–2050. *Obesity Research & Clinical Practice*, *21*(12), 2579–2581. doi:10.1002/oby.20187.

NHMRC. (2006). *Cultural competency in health: A guide for policy, partnerships and participation. 9 December 2005*. Canberra, Australia: National Health and Medical Research Council.

NHMRC. (2013). *Australian dietary guidelines*. Canberra, Australia: National Health and Medical Research Council.

Phillips, S. D. (2002). Half-lives and healthy bodies: Discourses on contaminated food and healing in postChernobyl Ukraine. *Food and Foodways*, *10*(1), 27–53. doi:10.1080/07409710212483.

RACGP. (2012). *Guidelines for preventive activities in general practice* (8th ed.). East Melbourne: Royal Australian College of General Practitioners.

Renzaho, A. M. N., Bilal, P., & Marks, G. C. (2014). Obesity, type 2 diabetes and high blood pressure amongst recently arrived Sudanese refugees in Queensland, Australia. *Journal of Immigrant and Minority Health*, *16*(1), 86–94. doi:10.1007/s10903-013-9791-y.

Rhodes, K., Chan, F., Prichard, I., Coveney, J., Ward, P., & Wilson, C. (2016). Intergenerational transmission of dietary behaviours: A qualitative study of Anglo-Australian, Chinese-Australian and Italian-Australian three-generation families. *Appetite*, *103*, 309–317. doi:10.1016/j.appet.2016.04.036.

Romero-Gwynn, E., Nicholson, Y., Gwynn, D., Kors, N., Agron, P., Fleming, J., ... Screenivasan, L. (1997). Dietary practices of Refugees from the former Soviet union. *Nutrition Today*, *32*(4), 153–156.

Shahwan-Akl, L. (2010). Cardiovascular disease risk factors among adult Australian-Lebanese in Melbourne. *International Journal of Research in Nursing*, *1*(1), 1–7. doi:10.3844/ijrnsp.2010.1.7.

Shanahan, H., Carlsson-Kanyama, A., Offei-Ansah, C., Ekström, M. P., & Potapova, M. (2003). Family meals and disparities in global ecosystem dependency. Three examples: Ghana, Russia and Sweden. *International Journal of Consumer Studies*, *27*(5), 420–422. doi:10.1046/j.1470-6431.2003.00321.x.

Tan, D., Zwar, N., Dennis, S. M., & Vagholkar, S. (2006). Weight management in general practice: What do patients want? *Medical Journal of Australia*, *185*(2), 73–76.

Team, V., Manderson, L., & Markovic, M. (2013). From state care to self-care: Cancer screening behaviours among Russian-speaking Australian women. *Australian Journal of Primary Health*, *19*(2), 130–137. doi:10.1071/PY11158.

Teshuva, K. (2010). *Caring for older survivors of genocide and mass trauma*. Melbourne: Australian Institute for Primary Care & Ageing, La Trobe University.

Thornton, L. E., Lamb, K. E., & Ball, K. (2016). Fast food restaurant locations according to socioeconomic disadvantage, urban–regional locality, and schools within Victoria, Australia. *SSM – Population Health*, *2*, 1–9. doi:10.1016/j.ssmph.2015.12.001.

Tran, D. T., Jorm, L. R., Johnson, M., Bambrick, H., & Lujic, S. (2013). Effects of acculturation on lifestyle and health status among older Vietnam-born Australians. *Asia-Pacific Journal of Public Health*, *27*(2), NP2259–NP2274. doi:10.1177/1010539513491419.

Vasey, K., & Manderson, L. (2012). Regionalizing immigration, health and inequality: Iraqi refugees in Australia. *Administrative Sciences*, *2*, 47–62. doi:10.3390/admsci2010047.

Wagner, J., Berthold, S. M., Buckley, T., Kong, S., Kuoch, T., & Scully, M. (2015). Diabetes among refugee populations: What newly arriving refugees can learn from resettled Cambodians. *Current Diabetes Reports*, *15*(8), 1–14.

Warin, M., Turner, K., Moore, V., & Davies, M. (2008). Bodies, mothers and identities: rethinking obesity and the BMI. *Sociology of Health & Illness*, *30*(1), 97–111. doi:10.1111/j.1467-9566.2007.01029.x.

Willcox, S. (2014). *Chronic diseases in Australia: The case for changing course. Background and policy paper No. 02/2014*. Melbourne, Australia: Mitchell Institute for Health and Education Policy.

Wilson, A., & Renzaho, A. (2015). Intergenerational differences in acculturation experiences, food beliefs and perceived health risks among refugees from the Horn of Africa in Melbourne, Australia. *Public Health Nutrition*, *18*(1), 176–188. doi:10.1017/S1368980013003467.

6 Chinese Migrant Mothers' Perceptions and Experiences of Health Risks in the UK

Qian (Sarah) Gong

Background

With globalization and the transnational labor movement reaching another peak, health issues of migrants have drawn increasing attention among health communication scholars (Dutta & Jamil, 2013; Johnson *et al.*, 2004). Many argue that the voices of migrants are invisible from the mainstream health policy and that the migrants constitute the most underserved communities for health care within our society (Dutta & Jamil, 2013; Katbamna, 2000, p. 7). Studies within this body of work have taken an 'interpretive, critical, and cultural framework' and challenged the post-positivistic approach that used to dominate health communication research (Dutta & Zoller, 2008). Despite this welcoming progress represented by quite a few recent studies taking up the 'culture-centered approach' (Dutta, 2007), there are still limitations in the scope of sampling as well as in the engagement with wider sociological perspectives.

Previous studies of health communication of migrant mothers have largely focused on lower socioeconomic groups (Dutta & Jamil, 2013; Hogg, de Kok, Netto, Hanley, & Haycock-Stuart, 2015). While it is imperative to make visible the health care experiences of these groups and to improve health service for them, the experiences of other migrant mothers are less problematized and attract little scholarly attention. The study of health issues of other migrant groups is important in the light of a new model of social classes conceptualized by Savage *et al.* (2013). This new model reflects how 'cultural and social boundaries might suggest new lines of class division' in the current British society (2013, p. 243). In this model, Savage and colleagues have identified a new 'technical middle class' which has high economic capital (£37,428 household income), moderate cultural capital but few social contacts (2013, p. 230). Many migrants working in scientific and technical-oriented jobs, including most of the participants of the current study, belong to this class division.[1] As the link between social and cultural capitals and health has been increasingly emphasized for the general population (Carlson & Chamberlain, 2003; Colton, Janzen, & Laverty, 2015; Dubbin, Chang, & Shim, 2013), it is reasonable to speculate that the (lack of) social and cultural capitals of migrant mothers may directly link to their health experiences and outcomes. Additionally, research on Chinese migrant mothers remains largely scarce in academic literature, especially in the British context—only a few studies are in existence, two of which were conducted more than fifteen years ago (Chan, 2000; Cheung, 1997; Hogg *et al.*, 2015).

Theoretical Perspectives

Research on maternal health issues of migrant women is often conducted in health sciences scholarship with a primary focus of improving health care service, but this has limited engagement with wider sociological theories (Dowswell, Renfrew, Gregson, & Hewison, 2001; Johnson *et al.*, 2004). Existing research often draws on theoretical perspectives such as acculturation, racialization, and othering, and problematizing issues including language, access, religion, tradition, and cultural differences and their implications for accessing good quality health care service (Arora, Liu, Chan, & Schwarz, 2012; Johnson *et al.*, 2004; Katbamna, 2000; Tahseen & Cheah, 2012). Few studies have analyzed women's sociocultural and material realities that shape their health care experiences (DeSouza, 2005; Guo, Munshi, Cockburn-Wootten, & Simpson, 2014). The analysis of these sociocultural conditions in the women's home country and host country is crucial in understanding how they shape women's perceptions of 'becoming a mother,' especially for those who have migrated recently and acutely face what Liamputtong (2007, p. 16) termed 'double-transition'—'becoming mothers and bringing their children up in a new country.' Some women may well face a third 'transition' in their new host country in which the health care system takes a different approach to managing childbirth from that in their home country (see discussion of South Asian women's experiences in the UK in Katbamna, 2000, p. 1).

In the subject of mothering, motherhood, and infant health, a rich body of literature has engaged with the concept of risk. Much of the literature has been informed by risk writers including Beck (1992), Giddens (1991), and Furedi (2008) who argue that modern societies have become increasingly risk-centered. In a risk society with a prevailing neoliberal ideology, the public are highly risk-aware and risk-averse. As many health-related risks (e.g. radiation, pollution) are being identified and health itself is being defined as an individual responsibility (Beck-Gernsheim, 2000, p. 124), the solution to many health risks is based on self-management. As modern risks are complex, the public rely on scientific understanding and expert knowledge to make sense and manage these risks. In the meantime, the public are also aware of the contradictions and uncertainties within science that have rendered the role of science in risk definition and management ambiguous (Beck, 1992; D. Lupton, 1999a; Zinn, 2008). Critically engaging with these perspectives, studies have taken issue with neoliberal management of health risks, individual responsibilities and surveillance, and intensive motherhood ideology. These studies have provided rich accounts of women's situated risk experiences grounded in their everyday life, documenting tensions, contradictions, and ambivalence in individual experiences caught between the expert-guided neoliberal discourse of a self-responsible citizen and the moralized discourse of a good mother (Coxon, Sandall, & Fulop, 2014; Holland, McCallum, & Walton, 2016; Knaak, 2010; Lee, 2008; Lee, Sutton, & Hartley, 2016; Lupton, 1999; Murphy, 2000). Yet most of these studies taking a sociocultural approach to risk are conducted in advanced industrial societies, focusing primarily on the mainstream: white, middle class women. Little research has been extended to migrant mothers who also live in these societies and face pervasive 'risks' but whose experience of those 'risks' may be significantly shaped by beliefs and values carried with them from their home country. It is against this backdrop that this chapter seeks to make a modest contribution to health communication literature by focusing on Chinese migrant mothers and their perceptions of health information and experiences of health care in the UK. Their perceptions and experiences are analysed through their dealings with various health 'risks' during their pregnancy, childbirth, and early years of mothering.

Methodology

This research is part of a larger study investigating Chinese parental experiences of health care for their children. This research uses in-depth interviews to explore sociocultural underpinnings of Chinese migrant mothers' perceptions and experiences of health risks in the UK. These mothers were asked about their general mothering and baby care experiences, as well as more specific questions about their perceptions and experiences of health risks and about their engagement with health messages such as exercise, eating, and antenatal scans during pregnancy, exclusive breastfeeding, and postnatal infant nutrition. This research interviewed ten migrant mothers of Chinese origin. Except for one mother, all these women have had one child within the last three years. All of these mothers migrated to the UK within the last fifteen years and maintained strong ties with family and friends in their country of origin. All of these women are married and heterosexual and have middle-class and upper–middle-class socioeconomic backgrounds. They have varied educational levels, employment statuses, and family compositions (e.g. UK- or elsewhere-born husband). The sample is small but the in-depth interviews have generated a rich set of data. The focus on mothers of middle class and above backgrounds addresses the changing demographics in the current British society. In the remainder of the chapter, I will provide further background information of maternity care for Chinese migrant mothers in the UK, before I turn to the core analysis of the chapter.

Maternal Health Issues in the UK and China

Becoming a mother for many women is perhaps the most significant life event irrespective of their class, ethnicity, and sexual orientation. However, according to a systematic review, much of the literature on motherhood is based on samples of mainstream, white, and middle-class mothers (Brunton, Wiggins, & Oakley, 2011). Limited academic work is available on ethnocultural groups (Bhopal, 1998; Katbamna, 2000; Liamputtong, 2007). The dearth of literature becomes problematic with an increasing diverse population in the UK, resulting from waves of modern immigration since the 1940s. In 2014, 13 percent of UK's population (8.3 million) was born abroad (BBC, 2015). Latest official figures indicate that in 2013 over a quarter of births (26.5 percent) in England and Wales were to mothers born outside the UK (ONS, 2014a). Chinese mothers had 3,611 births, accounting for 0.5 percent of all births in England and Wales in 2011 (ONS, 2014b). The number of Chinese mothers is small, but statistics indicate that the Chinese is one of the fastest growing non-EU immigrant groups in the UK (ONS, 2016). Therefore, it is important for the maternity service of the National Health Service (NHS) to recognize its increasing number of users of ethnocultural backgrounds, including Chinese mothers and their needs, in order to improve the women-centered objective outlined in the recent service review (Cumberlege, 2016).

Since the last century, the discourse of science has featured strongly in childcare practices and parenting advice particularly in the West (Apple, 1987; Grant, 1998). Pregnancy and childbirth have been treated as health problems that require medical surveillance and interference from health professionals. The increasing scienticization and medicalization of the pregnancy and childbirth in the UK since the Second World War has been documented by a great volume of literature, including classic works by Kitzinger, Oakley, and Davis (Davis, 2012; Kitzinger, 1962; Kitzinger & Davis, 1978; Oakley, 1980, 1984). This body of work making visible (mostly) white women's experience together with lobbying efforts of charity groups such as the National Childbirth Trust (NCT) has significantly contributed to recent trends of maternity care in the in the UK in which a less medicalized and interventionist approach towards birth and childrearing has started to emerge (Department of Health, 2007; Katbamna, 2000, pp. 12–13; National Childbirth Trust (NCT), 2009). A key development highlighted in recent government health policies is its aim to offer a range of informed 'choices' to women regarding how to access maternity care, types of antenatal care, place of birth and place of postnatal care (Cumberlege, 2016), and to 'improve the quality of service, safety, outcomes, and satisfaction for all women' (Department of Health, 2007, p. 5). These wider choices available to women do not necessarily indicate lessened medical surveillance, because another emphasis of the same policy is firmly located around 'safety,' and the NCT has identified potential tensions between prioritizing choice and ensuring safety in clinical practices (National Childbirth Trust (NCT), 2009, p. 3). Empirical research found that the social constructions of birth risk as a normality and medical intervention as 'an essential "rescue" from the hazards or uncertainties of birth limit women's choice of their childbirth places' (Coxon *et al.*, 2014, p. 63). Nonetheless, widened choices available to women regarding their birth plans signified an important paradigm shift away from a highly restrictive set of practices of regulating and controlling women's body, epitomized by the medical practices in the 1970s discussed in Oakley's (1980) work *Women Confined.*

To the contrary, maternity care in China has been marked by increasing medicalization and intervention by health care professionals over the past three decades (Gong & Jackson, 2013; Guo *et al.*, 2014). Despite the fact that maternity health care has improved significantly over the past decade, new parents and grandparents demonstrate a high level of awareness of and anxiety about health risks for which medical science is often recommended as the remedy (Gong, 2016). Parental anxieties about risks need to be understood within the context of expanding neoliberalism in the health sector in China. Insufficient government regulation, coupled with a plethora of information from commercial sources, common practices of over-treatment and scaremongering by doctors, and increasing cost of medical treatment in the neo-liberal medical system, has created 'perfect' breeding ground for fears and anxieties for new parents in China (Gong, 2016). As increasingly medicalized and risk-centered management of pregnancy, childbirth, and childcare has become a prominent discourse, parents rely heavily on medical surveillance such as frequent antenatal scans, Caesarean section and blood tests in postnatal check-ups to monitor the health of the foetus, expectant mother and infant (Gong, 2016; Gong & Jackson, 2013).

The contrast between the medical systems and their approaches to pregnancy and birth in the UK and China does not mean that these two systems share no similarities. Both systems operate on the same basis of biomedical model in which medical surveillance is central. In the UK, the surveillance is shared between the medical institution and expectant mothers who have been educated to manage various health risks via a set of self-surveillance practices such as alcohol and cigarette avoidance, regular exercise, and avoidance of certain food items (e.g. soft cheese, soft-boiled eggs, and tuna). Whilst in China, the surveillance (mostly paid for by patients) is predominantly performed by medical professionals aided by modern technologies. Having introduced more background of maternity health care in the UK and China, I now turn to the main analysis of this chapter. I organize my discussions with three types of risks—'perceived risks,' 'real risks,' and 'ambiguous risks,' using examples of mothers' experiences from their pregnancy, childbirth, and health care provision for their young children. The 'perceived risks' section discusses how mothers conceptualize and manage risks based on their own lay knowledge and experience; the 'real risks' section discusses women's experiences of risks identified by authoritative medical knowledge; the 'ambiguous risks' section discusses women's experiences of health risks that are uncertain or have been ambiguously advised by medical knowledge (general practitioner and paediatrician) and informed by their lay knowledge.[2]

'Perceived Risks'

Influenced by their knowledge of medicalized practices in managing pregnancy, birth, and postnatal care in China, most women that I interviewed believed that they received insufficient care in the UK. The most often used example to demonstrate this is the number of ultrasound scans that they received during their pregnancy. According to the guideline of maternity service of the NHS, most women with low-risk and uncomplicated pregnancy are offered two scans—a dating scan at the fourteenth week and an anomaly scan at the twentieth week (Department of Health, 2009, p. 48). In urban China, expectant mothers usually have an ultrasound scan every two to three months, and towards the end of their pregnancy, scans are more frequently used to monitor the growth of the foetus, sometimes once a month. Most of the mothers interviewed said that there was a long gap between the second scan and delivery, and they often suspected health risks for their baby during this period. They also doubted the accuracy of health monitors because it was only based on midwife's tape measures and palpation, and mothers' urine and blood pressure tests.[3] Two of these mothers purchased a third scan in their third trimester privately to ensure everything was fine. Another mother had a third scan at the NHS hospital when her midwife suspected that her baby had slow-growth. The midwife was not very sure about referring her to another scan because she was slender and her bump was 'compact.' The midwife thought the baby was probably fine, but she 'pushed' for the scan:

> I didn't want anything to go wrong... My midwife was very experienced but the way they measure baby growth (referring to the midwife using a tape to measure the size of the bump and then anticipate the weight of the foetus according to a chart) isn't very scientific. I'd rather see my baby and measure her size on the screen, like they did in the first scan. So I really pushed for it and my midwife agreed. It turned out the growth was fine and everything else was fine. I was really glad to have an extra scan; it was a bonus because the NHS only does two scans. But I have to say my midwife was very good. The weight of my baby (from the scan result) was exactly the same as her estimate. She was spot on. (Mother A of middle-class background)

The quote above revealed this mother's anxiety about the process and outcome of her pregnancy, despite the fact that she was healthy, had been categorized as 'low-risk,' and had no problem with her pregnancy whatsoever until that point. She admitted that her decision to insist on the third scan was probably influenced by her family in China who often asked her if she had had another scan to check on the baby. For her, medical surveillance based on midwife's touching and measuring was insufficient, and surveillance aided by ultrasound technologies was thought to be accurate and 'scientific.' The use of sonogram alleviates mothers anxieties about the 'pathologized notions of pregnancy,' as also found in Theodorou and Spyros's (2013, p. 93) study of Greek Cypriot mothers' consumption of ultrasound examinations. While this mother's perception of health advice was clearly influenced by her knowledge of medical practices in China, she also demonstrated some ambiguities about her midwife's approach which was less 'instrumental' but also accurate. When asked if she would accept the midwife's assessment next time in a similar situation, she said she probably would.

Another area where 'risks' were often discussed was the health advice about staying active during pregnancy. The NHS (2009, p. 34) and its key publication for maternity care—the *Pregnancy Book*—recommend regular and light exercise (e.g. walking, dancing, or swimming) for pregnant women, but exercise in the first trimester is usually thought to be risky in China. Swimming and contact with water, which is thought to be a cold property, are even considered dangerous (for causing miscarriage). When facing such 'contradictory' health information, most mothers interviewed adhered to the Chinese assumption and not many had exercise during their pregnancy. Some of them talked about exercising with their expectant-mother friends in the UK, but only to seek assurance and affirmation from their friends who also avoided exercising, especially swimming. In fact, the *Pregnancy Book* provided to all first-time mothers in their first midwife appointment in the UK was not read by most of the Chinese mothers interviewed. The *Pregnancy Book* provided by the Department of Health is intended to be used as a 'complete guide to: a healthy pregnancy, labor, and childbirth and the first weeks with your new baby' (Department of Health, 2009, cover). It is written in plain language and has included key health information during pregnancy, birth, and early days of mothering. When asked why they did not refer to this key guidebook for information, mothers said they did not find some information relevant or useful, such as the information about swimming and balanced diet (regarding calcium intake by consuming dairy products). They commented that Chinese cuisine was not keen on dairy products, especially the ones recommended in the guidebook such as cheese and yoghurt but the book did not recommend alternatives. Modifying diet (e.g. balancing cold/hot property foods) for expectant and new mothers commonly practiced in an Asian context

(Katbamna, 2000, p. 15) was not reflected in the guidebook. Mothers also commented that the book was given to them in the first midwife appointment between eight and twelve weeks of their pregnancy but they had started searching for health information regarding pregnancy somewhere else (usually online information in Chinese) long before that.

The above discussions show that Chinese mothers made conscious choices about avoiding exercise, in particular swimming, in the first trimester. Their choice may have been mostly risk-averse and based on their awareness of common assumptions in China, but the lack of other effective and relevant English health information may have also played a part in these women's use of Chinese sources, which may further reinforce their risk perceptions. What these mothers mentioned about the late arrival of the guidebook has, indeed, indicated that these women who were probably most keen to read about pregnancy related information when they first found out about their pregnancy in weeks five to eight missed the 'window of information.' Before the arrival of the *Pregnancy Book* at their first midwife appointment, these mothers had fewer chances to receive childcare manuals and pregnancy information that were in circulation in the mainstream society from British friends due to the lack of social contacts. As online information was readily available and easily accessible, these mothers who all have good educational background and are internet-savvy, naturally resorted to such a source of information. Only two mothers read the *Pregnancy Book* from cover to cover, and others only selectively read chapters or passages. While no one mentioned that language was particularly a problem and reason for them not to use the *Pregnancy Book,* some of them did say that Chinese online information sources were easier to find, were well-directed, and more useful for specific health problems. Thus, the easier use of native language, together with other factors such as the timing of the delivery of key health information by the NHS and the lack of social network, have all contributed to women's enhanced perceptions of health risks.

'Real Risks'

While the ways in which these mothers experienced the 'perceived risks' mostly reflect their sense of anxiety, rooted in their knowledge of risk-centered management of pregnancy and childbirth in China, the ways in which some of them deal with risks defined by medical knowledge, are fraught with tension and with the 'intensive motherhood' ideology that represents a different configuration of neoliberal management of health (Hays, 1996). One mother developed a rare medical condition called obstetric cholestasis in the thirty-sixth week of her pregnancy.[4] She read information regarding this condition mostly in English as she was educated as a nutritionist and was familiar with general health literature and medical terminologies. Understanding the risk this condition carried, she discussed with her consultant and arranged for a scheduled induction in the thirty-seventh week, which is a common practice for managing this condition. She was admitted to the hospital for induced delivery in the thirty-seventh week, but none of the induction drugs, hormonal drips, or water-breaking techniques performed in week thirty-eight and thirty-nine resulted in delivery. She was in intermittent painful labor for almost three weeks, after which both she and her baby developed infections because her water had been broken for too long. Eventually, an emergent Caesarean section had to be performed to ensure both her and her baby's safety. This birthing experience, as this mother later reflected, was 'traumatic':

> I never thought it would have been so traumatic. I felt that I was going to die when they tried so many things and they didn't work… The pain was so horrendous. I didn't feel a thing when the anaesthetist poked the needle six times into my back for the epidural. I just wanted it to be over. Now I think about the whole thing, I didn't have to go through all that pain, because they could have intervened sooner. When the hormonal drips didn't work, they should have just performed a C-section to get my baby out… The NHS website clearly says there is increased risk of stillbirth with my condition and after eight months' pregnant who could afford taking that risk? In Asia, a C-section would have been performed a lot sooner. But they (the NHS) just had to stick to their procedures or protocols—if hormone drips doesn't work, try breaking waters that and C-section is only the last resort. I tried to ask for a C-section but they said no and I had no energy to argue with them. I know the NHS likes the idea of having natural birth, but is it worthwhile to take the risk on the life of my baby and give me that much pain?

This lengthy quote shows a painful experience of this mother not only in coping with extraordinary labor and delivery pain but also in managing a real life-threatening risk for her unborn son. For her, there is inconsistency between the health information about her condition published on the NHS website and the actual practices of the medical professionals in managing her condition. She also challenged the hegemonic non-intervention approach of the NHS based on her own experience, which was nothing but 'traumatic.' After the baby was born via Caesarean section, she was left alone in the hospital ward with her son for another three days. During this period of time, she was encouraged to breastfeed, but her milk had not come in. She said for two days her son suckled so hard but there was no milk. Her son was constantly crying and she wanted to give her son infant formula but was told that newborn babies had a stomach size as big as marbles and they would be fine without feeding for a few days. She was extremely worried. On day three, her son was crying particularly hard and she said she had to get the attention from the midwife and expressed her worries again. The midwife became wary and did the heel-pick test which showed the baby's glucose level was dangerously low. A consultant immediately prescribed 50 ml infant formula and her son finished it within a few minutes and stopped crying.

> I've read so much about breastfeeding, and how that is natural and good, and how that reduces the risks of having long-term health problems. I can tell you that is nonsense. My milk hadn't come in until I was out of the hospital and my son could have been starved to death. They were so sure about it (her baby would be OK with little milk for a few days) and it turned out his blood sugar was dangerously low. All these things you read about and you were told about, you can't trust them. You have to go with your gut feelings. (Mother B of middle-class background)

Mother B's experiences show on the one hand, her intention to use more medical intervention was linked to her knowledge of medical practices in China, as she clearly used that as a reference point in her discussion of her birth story. It is probably also linked to the fact that the clinical outcome (failed induction and her son was born full term) was different from the NHS's treatment recommendation, i.e. scheduled induction at the thirty-seventh week to reduce the risk of stillbirth. For her, the NHS was 'fixated' on non-instrumental delivery regardless of how much pain women had to endure. She was able to challenge some clinical practices based on her knowledge of her condition obtained from the NHS website. But, her vulnerable position (pain, disorientation, long-time hospitalization) limited her ability to make a stronger request for a Caesarean section. Her birth story shows how the hegemonic discourse of natural birth and breastfeeding is deeply inscribed in the NHS practices. An example of criticism that has long been made is that such discourse universalizes women's birth and feeding experiences and disempowers women (Almond, 2010; Striley & Field-Springer, 2014). This mother was able to make critical judgements and to challenge the monolithic discourse of 'natural' breastfeeding, but only after she returned home from the hospital.

In my sample, except for another mother who did not have milk and used infant formula exclusively, other mothers interviewed had no major problem with breastfeeding. All these mothers were clearly aware of the benefits of breastfeeding and supported the idea of feed-on-demand, which constitutes part of the intensive motherhood ideology. This shows that most Chinese migrant mothers are acceptant of certain practices of the intensive motherhood ideology, unless personal experiences are significantly (e.g. mother B) deviant from the mainstream practices.

'Ambiguous Risks'

The uncertain nature of risks which denotes the probability of something happening is an important factor that shape women's perceptions and experiences. One baby had an incident of choking on a small piece of banana, his mother was worried about incidents like this happening again and decided to take preventative measures against all (first aid) emergencies. She enrolled into a paediatrics first aid course taught by a local ambulance service to learn how to respond to or treat baby choking, burning, frozen bits, and foreign bodies in nose and ears and how to perform a cardiopulmonary resuscitation (CPR). When asked why she took such a course she said:

> I need to know how to deal with it, like the choking and other problems. The midwife said 'pat on the back' if your baby is choking but how much strength do I use? You wouldn't know for [how] long to run cold water on a burnt spot, would you? This course is very useful and I'd recommend it… We're on our own, and I feel more in control when I know all these things. (mother C from upper-middle-class background)

This mother's comment about 'we're on our own' is worth noting. She lives in a secluded large luxury house and rarely interacts with her neighbors. She and her husband have no family in the UK and their close friends live at least a three-hour drive away. This lack of family support and social connection as safety nets perhaps has contributed to her need to seek for additional health and safety information. The risks of choking and burning are possible risks but the chances of choking, burning, frostbite, and cardiac arrest all happening to her son are small. Every mother faces the uncertainty of the occurrence of the risks, but the lack of presence of family and friends made this mother felt acutely insecure and therefore she needed to be in control of all health risks and emergencies. Although previous literature on migrant parents has identified negative effects of lacking social support (Layton, 2007), evidence from my research shows that this mother mitigated some of the effects by proactively taking advantage of her information searching skills (ambulance service found online) and economic resources (the course costs £260) to manage the health risks to her son.

Another baby had several viral infections since she started nursery at the age of six months. Her mother took her to the general practitioner (GP), but each time was sent home and was told that the baby needed only rest. For her, the advice from the medical professionals was sufficient and useful, but she became uncertain about them after another viral infection for the baby:

> My daughter had a fever and coughs again so I took her to the GP for a check-up just to be sure. I thought it was just one of the infections that she got from the nursery. The GP listened to her chest and measured something with a clip attached to her finger, then he took out an emergency kit with oxygen mask. He said my daughter's oxygen level was low, and he needed to give her medication in steam to open up her airway. Then he rang the hospital which then sent out an ambulance. I had my car just outside, but the GP said the hospital insisted that we went in with an ambulance. It's my first time riding on an ambulance, holding my baby and I became very nervous... we arrived at the hospital A&E and a nurse measured her oxygen level again and attached a monitor to her toe. We waited for about two hours for a paediatrician. She came [and] asked a bunch of questions and examined my daughter again and said it was bronchiolitis and no big deal. Then she sent us home and told me only to give her Calpol (paracetamol) and water if the temperature went up again. I don't know how to interpret this. They told you viral infections were normal, and then the GP was very cautious as if it's something serious. The ambulance also made me nervous, but then the paediatrician told me it wasn't a big deal. Next time when this happens, I'll probably just take her to the A & E straightaway. The airway and oxygen stuff sounded serious. (Mother D middle class)

This mother was previously content with general medical advice given to her by medical professionals, but her last comment shows that she became more risk-averse with regard to her daughters viral infections. The practices of the medical professionals (GP, hospital ambulance department, and paediatrician at A & E) may have enhanced her risk perception, because these practices for her were inconsistent and contradictory. And one of the key features of modern risks argued by Beck (1992) is that they are undetectable without expert assistance, yet the assistance became increasing ambiguous as expert opinions and advice can be contradictory. As the practices of medical professional sent out mixed messages ('serious' or 'no big deal'), this mother lost trust in the experts and decided to use her own judgement (take her daughter to the A & E) to manage the risk of developing serious airway problems.

Conclusion

This research has attempted to make a modest contribution to fill the gap in the literature by investigating Chinese migrant mothers and their health perceptions and experiences in the UK. It studies the health experience of this minority group by discussing how they conceptualize and manage various risks in their pregnancy, childbirth and childcare as well as how they engage with health information, messages, and practices in their everyday mothering experiences. This chapter argues that the understanding of risks (perceived, real, and ambiguous) by Chinese migrant mothers have shaped the way they perceive how useful health messages are, or even how good health service is, in the UK. To a great extent, mothers' risk perceptions are influenced by their knowledge of pregnancy, childbirth and childcare practices in China which are marked by a high degree of medicalization and risk-aversion. However, their perceptions are also shaped by other sociocultural and material factors such as the lack of family and social support, late arrival of key health information (The *Pregnancy Book*), and contradictory medical practices resulting in the loss of trust in experts. The sources of risk knowledge (expert or lay) do not solely determine women's perceptions of and responses to various risks. Rather, their existing knowledge (medical/nutritional science), corporeal experience (pain) and other socio-cultural factors (social contacts with Chinese mothers and a shared belief of pregnancy risk) shape how risks are experienced and managed. It is clear from the discussions that these women are reflexive and active, using their subject positions (e.g. knowing very clearly that they are migrants with little family support), medical knowledge, technical proficiency, and financial resources to negotiate with dominant medical messages and practices (natural birth and breastfeeding) and to learn about techniques to manage health emergencies. The ways in which they engage with the dominant discourse of natural birth and breastfeeding, which can be viewed as part of the wider 'acculturation process,' is not universal. Within this small sample of middle-class and upper middle-class women, there are variations based on individual experiences.

The sociological perspective—risk—embedded in this research challenges an essentialist version of culture that differentiates these women's health communication experiences from those of the mainstream white mothers on the basis of a simplified racial description. It also challenges the essentialist view that often homogenizes ethnocultural groups and 'ignore(s) individual individuality and diversity contexts' (Anderson & Reimer Kirkham quoted in Johnson *et al.* 2004, p. 255). The Chinese migrant mothers' risk perceptions and understandings grounded in their everyday experiences share many similarities with those of white middle-class mothers (see Lupton, 1999), suggesting that socio-economic position is perhaps a more significant dimension than racial and cultural difference, in which women's maternity health care experiences (especially in risk management) converge. This is a preliminary finding based on a small-scale pilot study of middle class Chinese migrant mothers. Further research comparing health communication across class is needed to shed more insight into this finding.

Notes

1 The Chinese migrants constitute one of the UK's smallest minorities with a population under 400,000 (ONS, 2016), but they are highly dispersed geographically and socio-economically. Two recent studies conducted in London boroughs depict very different lives of the Chinese migrants situating on a broad socio-economic spectrum, ranging from millionaire investors to undocumented migrants. In the middle, a large number of Chinese migrants are business proprietors, professionals and semi-skilled workers, many of whom work in catering and restaurant trades (Knowles, 2015; Pharoah, 2009). The definition of class has always been a subject of academic debates. For consistency, here I use Savage and colleagues' (2013, p. 230) definition to indicate what 'middle class' is as understood in the British context. The 'traditional middle class' have 'very high economic capital (£47,184 household income), high social capital (social contact number 17), and very high highbrow cultural capital.

2 The sources of risk knowledge are used to separate 'real risks' (defined by authoritative medical knowledge) from 'perceived risks' (defined by lay knowledge) to organize my analysis. Quotation marks are used here to indicate that these risks defined by expert/lay knowledge cannot be accepted as unproblematic. Rather, the definition and management of these risks are linked to a 'social and cultural lens' through which we view and understand' risks (cf. Douglas & Wildavsky, 1982; Lupton, 2006, p. 15). The lens will be analysed in the following section to highlight the ambiguities and contradictories in women's risk experiences informed by both expert and lay conceptualization of risks.

3 Midwives are health professionals who are specially trained to care for mothers and babies throughout normal pregnancy, labor, and after the birth. They provide care for most women at home or in hospital' (NHS, 2016). The NHS clinical guideline suggests that 'midwife- and General practitioner (GP)-led models of care should be offered to women with an uncomplicated pregnancy' (National Institute for Health and Care Excellence (NICE), 2008, p. 13). Consultants are senior specialist doctors (e.g. obstetrician and paediatrician) based in hospitals. GPs and midwives can refer women to see a consultant or a member of the consultant-led team in hospital.

4 This is a rare liver disorder that causes bile salt to build up in the body and severe itchiness. Women with this condition have increased risks of premature birth or stillbirth (NHS, 2014).

References

Almond, B. (2010). *The monster within: The hidden side of motherhood.* Berkeley, CA: University of California Press.

Apple, R. (1987). *Mothers and medicine: A social history of infant feeding 1890–1950* Madison WI: University of Wisconsin Press.

Arora, A., Liu, M. N. M., Chan, R., & Schwarz, E. (2012). English leaflets are not meant for me: A qualitative approach to explore oral health literacy in Chinese mothers in Southwestern Sydney, Australia. *Community Dentistry and Oral Epidemiology, 40*(6), 532–541. doi:10.1111/j.1600-0528.2012.00699.x.

BBC. (2015). UK net migration hits record high. Retrieved 27 August 2015, 2015, from www.bbc.co.uk/news/uk-34071492.

Beck, U. (1992). *Risk society: Towards a new modernity.* London: Sage Publications.

Beck-Gernsheim, E. (2000). Health and responsibility: From social change to technological change and vice versa. In B. Adam, U. Beck, & J. Van Loon (Eds.), *The risk society and beyond: Critical issues for social theory* (pp. 122–135).

Bhopal, K. (1998). South Asian women in East London: Motherhood and social support. *Womens Studies International Forum*, *21*(5), 485–492. doi:10.1016/s0277-5395(98)00067-3.

Brunton, G., Wiggins, M., & Oakley, A. (2011). *Becoming a mother: A research synthesis of women's views on the experience of first-time motherhood.* London: EPPI Centre, Social Science Research Unit, Institute of Education, University of London.

Carlson, E. D., & Chamberlain, R. M. (2003). Social capital, health, and health disparities. *Journal of Nursing Scholarship*, *35*(4), 325–331. doi:10.1111/j.1547-5069.2003.00325.x.

Chan, C. (2000). The quality of life of women of Chinese origin. *Health & Social Care in the Community*, *8*(3), 212–222. doi:10.1046/j.1365-2524.2000.00243.x.

Cheung, N. F. (1997). Chinese zuo yuezi (sitting in for the first month of the Postnatal period) in Scotland. *Midwifery*, *13*(2), 55–65. doi: 10.1016/S0266-6138(97)90057-7.

Colton, T., Janzen, B., & Laverty, W. (2015). Family structure, social capital, and mental health disparities among Canadian mothers. *Public Health*, *129*(6), 639–647. doi:10.1016/j.puhe.2015.03.023.

Coxon, K., Sandall, J., & Fulop, N. J. (2014). To what extent are women free to choose where to give birth? How discourses of risk, blame and responsibility influence birth place decisions. *Health, Risk & Society*, *16*(1), 51–67. doi:10.1080/13698575.2013.859231.

Cumberlege, J. (2016). Better births: Improving outcomes of maternity services in England. Retrieved 10 March 2015, from www.england.nhs.uk/wp-content/uploads/2016/02/national-maternity-review-report.pdf.

Davis, A. (2012). *Modern motherhood: Women and family in England, 1945–2000.* Manchester: Manchester University Press.

Department of Health. (2007). *Maternity matters: Choice, access and continuity of care in a safe service.* London: DH Publications.

Department of Health. (2009). *The pregnancy book*. London: DH Publications.

DeSouza, R. (2005). Transforming possibilities of care: Goan migrant motherhood in New Zealand. *Contemporary nurse*, *20*(1), 87–101.

Dowswell, T., Renfrew, M. J., Gregson, B., & Hewison, J. (2001). A review of the literature on women's views on their maternity care in the community in the UK. *Midwifery*, *17*(3), 194–202. doi:10.1054/midw.2001.0260.

Dubbin, L. A., Chang, J. S., & Shim, J. K. (2013). Cultural health capital and the interactional dynamics of patient-centered care. *Social Science & Medicine*, *93*, 113–120. doi:10.1016/j.socscimed.2013.06.014.

Dutta, M. J. (2007). *Communicating health: A culture-centred approach.* Cambridge and Malden: Polity Press.

Dutta, M. J., & Jamil, R. (2013). Health at the margins of migration: Culture-centered co-constructions among Bangladeshi immigrants. *Health Communication*, *28*(2), 170–182. doi:10.1080/10410236.2012.666956.

Dutta, M. J., & Zoller, H. (2008). Introduction. In M. J. Dutta & H. Zoller (Eds.), *Emerging perspectives in health communication: Meaning, culture and power* (pp. 1–28). London and New York: Routledge.

Furedi, F. (2008). *Paranoid parenting: Why ignoring the experts may be best for your children*. London and New York: Continuum.

Giddens, A. (1991). *Modernity and self-identity*. Cambridge: Polity Press.

Gong, Q. (2016). *Children's healthcare and parental media engagement in urban China: A 'Culture of anxiety?*. Baskingstoke: Palgrave.

Gong, Q., & Jackson, P. (2013). Mediating science and nature: Representing and consuming infant formula advertising in China. *European Journal of Cultural Studies*, *16*(3), 285–309. doi:10.1177/1367549413476013.

Grant, J. (1998). *Raising baby by the book: The education of American mothers*. New Haven, CT: Yale University Press.

Guo, S., Munshi, D., Cockburn-Wootten, C., & Simpson, M. (2014). Cultural dilemmas of choice: Deconstructing consumer choice in health communication between maternity-care providers and ethnic Chinese mothers in New Zealand. *Health Communication*, *29*(10), 1020–1028. doi:10.1080/10410236.2013.831515.

Hays, S. (1996). *The cultural contradictions of motherhood*. New Haven, CT: Yale University Press.

Hogg, R., de Kok, B., Netto, G., Hanley, J., & Haycock-Stuart, E. (2015). Supporting Pakistani and Chinese families with young children: Perspectives of mothers and health visitors. *Child Care Health and Development*, *41*(3), 416–423. doi:10.1111/cch.12154.

Holland, K., McCallum, K., & Walton, A. (2016). 'I'm not clear on what the risk is': Women's reflexive negotiations of uncertainty about alcohol during pregnancy. *Health, Risk & Society*, *18*(1–2), 38–58. doi:10.1080/13698575.2016.1166186.

Johnson, J. L., Bottorff, J. L., Browne, A. J., Grewal, S., Hilton, B. A., & Clarke, H. (2004). Othering and being othered in the context of health care services. *Health Communication*, *16*(2), 253–271.

Katbamna, S. (2000). *'Race' and childbirth*. Buckingham, PA: Open University Press.

Kitzinger, S. (1962). *The experience of childbirth*. London: Gollancz.

Kitzinger, S., & Davis, J. (1978). *The place of birth*. Oxford: Oxford University Press.

Knaak, S. J. (2010). Contextualising risk, constructing choice: Breastfeeding and good mothering in risk society. *Health Risk & Society*, *12*(4), 345–355. doi:10.1080/13698571003789666.

Knowles, C. (2015). *Young Chinese migrants in London*. London: Runnymede Trust.

Layton, S. (2007). Left alone to hold the baby. *Infant Observation*, *10*(3), 253–265. doi:10.1080/13698030701694371.

Lee, E. (2008). Living with risk in the era of 'intensive motherhood': Maternal identity and infant feeding. *Health, Risk and Society*, *10*(5), 467–477.

Lee, E., Sutton, R. M., & Hartley, B. L. (2016). From scientific article to press release to media coverage: Advocating alcohol abstinence and democratising risk in a story about alcohol and pregnancy. *Health, Risk & Society*, 1–23. doi:10.1080/13698575.2016.1229758.

Liamputtong, P. (2007). Situating reproduction, procreation and motherhood within a cross-cultural context: An introduction. In P. Liamputtong (Ed.),

Reproduction, childbirth and motherhood: A cross-cultural perspective (pp. 3–34). New York: Nova Science Publishers, Inc.
Lupton, D. (1999a). *Risk*. London and New York: Routledge.
Lupton, D. (1999b). Risk and the ontology of pregnant embodiment. In D. Lupton (Ed.), *Risk and sociocultural theory: New directions and perspectives* (pp. 59–85). Cambridge: Cambridge University Press.
Lupton, D. (2006). Sociology and risk. In G. Mythen & S. Walklate (Eds.), *Beyond the risk society: Critical reflections on risk and human security* (pp. 11–24). Maidenhead: Open University Press.
Murphy, E. (2000). Riks, responsibility and rhetoric in infant feeding. *Journal of Contemporary Ethnography*, *29*(3), 291–325.
National Childbirth Trust (NCT). (2009). *NCT document summary: Maternity matters: Choice, access and continuity of care in a safe service*. Retrieved 10 January, 2015, from www.nct.org.uk/sites/default/files/related_documents/DS12%20Maternity%20Matters%20%5BEngland%5D.pdf.
National Health Service (NHS). (2009). *The pregnancy book: Your complete guide to a healthy pregnancy, labour and childbirth, the first weeks with your new baby*. Retrieved 20 May 2017, from https://www.stgeorges.nhs.uk/wp-content/uploads/2013/11/Pregnancy_Book_comp.pdf.
National Institute for Health and Care Excellence (NICE). (2008). Antenatal care for uncomplicated pregnancies: Clinical guideline. Retrieved 10 November 2015, from www.nice.org.uk/guidance/cg62.
NHS.(2014).Itchingandobstetriccholestasisinpregnancy.Retrieved20June,2015, from www.nhs.uk/conditions/pregnancy-and-baby/pages/itching-obstetric-cholestasis-pregnant.aspx.
NHS. (2016). Antenatal support: Meet the team. Retrieved 21 October 2016, from www.nhs.uk/conditions/pregnancy-and-baby/pages/antenatal-team-midwife-obstetrician-pregnant.aspx.
Oakley, A. (1980). *Women confined: Towards a sociology of childbirth*. Oxford: Martin Robertson.
Oakley, A. (1984). *The captured womb: A history of the medial care of pregnant women*. Oxford: Blackwell.
ONS. (2014a). *Births in England and Wales by parents country of birth, 2013*. From Office for National Statistics (ONS) www.ons.gov.uk/ons/rel/vsob1/parents--country-of-birth--england-and-wales/2013/stb-births-by-cob-2013.html.
ONS. (2014b). *Childbearing of UK and non-UK born women living in the UK—2011 census data*. From Office for National Statistics (ONS) www.ons.gov.uk/ons/dcp171766_350433.pdf.
ONS. (2016). *2011 Census aggregate data*. Retrieved 15 October 2016.
Pharoah, R. (2009). *Migration, integration, cohesion: New Chinese migrants in London*. London: The Chinese in Britain Forum.
Savage, M., Devine, F., Cunningham, N., Taylor, M., Li, Y. J., Hjellbrekke, J., … Miles, A. (2013). A new model of social class? Findings from the BBC's great British class survey experiment. *Sociology-The Journal of the British Sociological Association*, *47*(2), 219–250. doi:10.1177/0038038513481128.
Striley, K., & Field-Springer, K. (2014). The bad mother police: Theorizing risk orders in the discourses of infant feeding practices. *Health Communication*, *29*(6), 552–562.

Tahseen, M., & Cheah, C. S. L. (2012). A multidimensional examination of the acculturation and psychological functioning of a sample of immigrant Chinese mothers in the US. *International Journal of Behavioral Development*, *36*(6), 430–439. doi:10.1177/0165025412448605.

Theodorou, E., & Spyrou, S. (2013). Motherhood in utero: Consuming away anxiety. *Journal of Consumer Culture*, *13*(2), 79–96.

Zinn, J. O. (2008). Heading into the unknown: Everyday strategies for managing risk and uncertainty. *Health Risk & Society*, *10*(5), 439–450. doi:10.1080/13698570802380891.

7 Health Information Disparities and Medical Tourism Use among Korean Immigrants in the US

Jungmi Jun

Introduction

Korean-Americans (hereafter "KA") are the fifth-largest Asian-American subgroup, with more than 1.8 million living in the US as of 2013. They are also a rapidly increasing new immigrant group since the population has increased by 33 percent over the past ten years (US Census Bureau, 2013). More than 70 percent of KA adults are Korea-born, and about 25 percent of them arrived in the US in 2000 or later (Terrazas, 2009; US Census Bureau, 2010b). As a racial/ethnic minority and a new immigrant group in the US, KAs are reported to experience significant health disparities in multiple contexts. Given limited access to health care, some KAs travel to their home country, South Korea, to receive medical treatment. Based on a comprehensive review of relevant research, this chapter will (1) introduce the factors underlying KAs' health disparities and the socioeconomic barriers related to those disparities, (2) examine KAs' different health information seeking behaviors and cultural beliefs, and (3) discuss the South Korean medical tourism service, which is used by many uninsured and underinsured KAs as an alternative to health care in the US.

Health Disparities of Korean-Americans in the US

The mortality rates for KAs are the highest of any racial/ethnic group for several types of cancers (e.g. liver, uterine, cervix, and stomach; Jemal *et al.*, 2004; Miller, Chu, Hankey, & Ries, 2008). KAs are also at high risk of Type II diabetes, hypertension, and cardiovascular disease (Shin, Shin, & Blanchette, 2002), and their incidence rates for hepatitis B virus (HBV) infections are ten times higher than that of the general US population (Bastani, Glenn, Maxwell, & Jo, 2007). This population is also more susceptible to delayed care and death in the emergency room (NAKASEC, 2009). Additionally, the mental health literature describes elderly KAs as a particularly vulnerable group, with estimated depression rates four times greater than for non-Hispanic Whites (hereafter "Whites") or for African-Americans. KAs exhibit more depressive symptoms than any other Asian-American group does (Park, Jang, Lee, Haley, & Chiriboga, 2013).

Despite the high mortality rates and other health-related vulnerabilities, KAs' engagement in health behaviors is lower compared not only to Whites but also to other Asian sub-groups. Only 26 percent of KAs reported that they were regularly visiting a doctor (NAKASEC, 2009), and their frequency of visiting health professionals (2.78 visits per year) was much lower than for Whites (5.92), African Americans (3.75), or Hispanics (3.75; NIH, 2006). KA men reported a higher cigarette smoking prevalence (35.5 percent) than both Chinese (17.7 percent) and Indian American men (10.1 percent; Li, Kwon, Weerasingh, Rey, & Trinh-Shevrin, 2013). Also, the nutritional quality of elderly KAs' diets was reported to be poorer due to low intake of calories, calcium, vitamins A and C, riboflavin, and protein (Kim, Yu, Liu, Kim, & Kohrs, 1993). In addition, KA women's dietary intake did not meet general recommendations (Park, Murphy, Sharma, & Kolonel, 2005). KAs' cancer screening rates are consistently lower than the goal set by the US government in their Healthy People 2020 project (ODPHP, 2016). KA women's breast cancer screening rate was considerably lower than that of other racial/ethnic groups (Eun, Lee, Kim, & Fogg, 2009). KAs' colon cancer screening was also significantly lower despite the fact that colon cancer is the second most commonly diagnosed cancer within the KA population (Miller *et al.*, 2008). KA was the only Asian subgroup who demonstrated a decline in cancer screening rates in recent years (Maxwell *et al.*, 2010).

Socioeconomic Barriers

KAs' relatively lower income, lower employment rates, lack of English fluency, lower access to quality health educations/promotions, and lack of health insurance explain their perceived limited access to health care and poorer health outcomes (Maxwell *et al.*, 2010). KAs present the lowest rates for health insurance coverage and for having a regular source of health care among all racial/ethnic groups (Ryu, Crespi, & Maxwell, 2013a; Yoo & Kim, 2008). In 2010, 46 percent of KAs aged 18–64 had no health insurance compared to 22.3 percent of the US population (National Center for Health Statistics, 2011). One in five KAs is undocumented, and low-income undocumented immigrants are less likely to be insured (NAKASEC, 2009). This lack of health insurance could be the result of their recent immigration history combined with their engagement in retail businesses, which are unlikely to offer employee-sponsored health insurance, making health insurance premiums difficult to afford (Sohn & Harada, 2005). Only 48 percent of KAs are insured through employment, compared to 73 percent of Whites (APIAHF, 2006).

KAs' recent immigration history is another reason for their relatively high health risks. Maxwell *et al.* (2010) suggest that KAs' short residence in the US is a major factor associated with their lower cancer screening rates. For new Asian immigrants such as KAs, the incidence of chronic diseases increases within a few years of immigrating to the US. For instance, foreign-born Asian immigrants' breast cancer incidence rates were 30 percent–80 percent higher than that of their US-born counterparts. In addition, KAs' cancer incidence rates (e.g. colon, lung, breast, and prostate cancer) were considerably higher than those of native Koreans living in Korea (Lee, Demissie, Lu, & Rhoads, 2007). An adoption of westernized lifestyle (e.g. dietary change and low physical activity) may increase the risk of chronic diseases among Asian immigrants (Ryu, Crespi, & Maxwell, 2013b).

KAs' socioeconomic status and immigration history are also related to KAs' health information disparities. KAs' access to health professionals is limited due to their poor English proficiency, lack of health insurance, and expectations about interactions with health care professionals, which have motivated them to seek health information from alternative sources. The next section will discuss KAs' health information seeking behaviors and their relationship to language barriers and cultural beliefs. Then, it will introduce concerns regarding KAs' different information seeking behaviors and their negative consequences.

Korean-Americans' Health-Information Seeking

Communication Barriers

More than 70 percent of KAs speak the Korean language at home (APIAHF, 2006). Nearly 40 percent of KAs reported difficulties in communicating with their doctor (The Commonwealth Fund, 2002) and in understanding health information provided by doctors (New California Media, 2003). Even those KAs who speak English at an intermediate level and have high education levels reported that they do not feel comfortable communicating with English-speaking doctors (Oh, Jun, Zhou, & Kreps, 2014). As a result, 75 percent of KAs reported they prefer visiting Korean-speaking health care professionals (Shin & Robert, 2010); however, the availability of these providers is very limited, even in communities with a high KA population density (Shin *et al.*, 2002). Therefore, KAs may delay health care or must visit an English-speaking doctor. It is well documented that when language barriers exist in provider-patient communication, patients are significantly disadvantaged both during and after their interactions with providers. Patients with language barriers are less likely to understand health care providers' instructions, be satisfied with the quality of care, receive more diagnostic testing, follow doctors' recommendation, and make follow-up appointments (Hsieh, Pitaloka, & Johnson, 2013).

Cultural Barriers

In addition to the barriers related to language and communication, KAs' culturally-based health beliefs and expectations about interactions with health care providers may hinder them from using health care more frequently. KAs, as predominantly monolingual, first-generation immigrants, are likely to maintain cultural beliefs and attitudes after moving to the US (Barringer & Gardiner, 1993). These traditional cultural beliefs about health care and disease prevention are often at odds with the Western approach to medicine, which leads to negative impacts for KAs on seeking and engaging timely and quality health care in the US.

For instance, although health maintenance is very important among KAs, they tend to place less importance on preventive care. KAs are less familiar with the concept of routine screening or testing in the absence of symptoms to detect health problems before symptoms develop (Jo, Maxwell, Rick, Cha, & Bastani, 2009). Additionally, KAs reported that fear of finding cancer or other diseases through early screening as well as the expenditure of time and unavailability of transportation and their embarrassment and reluctance to request the procedure from their physicians were reasons to avoid preventive care (Lee, 2000; Maxwell, Bastani, & Warda, 1998).

An Asian cultural and prevalent religious value, fatalism, is also known to influence KAs' health behaviors. The fatalism rooted in Buddhism has influenced Koreans' perceptions and beliefs on diverse issues due to its long history in Korean society. For Koreans, the virtue of *Chenyum* (resignation) urges individuals to keep themselves away from all greed in life. An effort to live longer or possess more physical objects or materials is considered to be greedy (Jun & Oh, 2013). Fatal diseases are regarded as being destined by nature, so a human's effort to cure the disease in order to live longer is at odds with the concept of the giving-up spirit (Honda & Kreps, 2006). Fatalism was reported to influence Asian-Americans' attributions of disease and attitudes towards preventive care. Asian-Americans tend to believe that colon cancer is caused by unexplainable or uncontrollable reasons rather than by human behaviors or lifestyle. Therefore, they were less likely to believe in their ability to reduce their chances of developing colon cancer or that other methods to disrupt colon cancer would be successful (Jun & Oh, 2013).

Additionally, traditional gender role expectations embedded in the Confucianism culture of Korean society may underlie some health-related problems in KA women (Wong, Yoo, & Stewart, 2006). Men are dominant over women in Korean traditions, so emphasis is more likely to be placed on diseases occurring more frequently in men than in women (Shin *et al.*, 2002). Korean women are expected to be the caregiver for ill family members, including their husband's parents due to the cultural norm of filial piety, in which the first son and his wife are obliged to repay a debt by caring for parents (Lee & Farran, 2004). The emphasis on health for men and in-laws over women may explain some KA women's health problems. Many KA women reported that they do not have enough time to visit health professionals (Oh *et al.*, 2014) or to exercise because of family and work duties (Im & Choe, 2004). A majority of KA elderly women have experienced *Hwabyung*, a mental and physical illness that is believed to occur when they fail to open emotions and relieve stress during interpersonal or family conflicts (Pang, 1991).

KAs' preference of using *Hanbang* (traditional Korean medicines) may also have some negative impacts on their health. One in four KAs is reported to use acupuncture on a regular basis (The Commenwealth Fund, 2002). Elder and low-income KAs are much more likely to use *Hanbang* and its common treatment methods, such as acupuncture, herbs, moxibustion, and cupping, rather than to visit a doctor practicing the Western medicine (Han, Song, & Kim, 1996; NIH, 2006). Also, some KAs believe in spiritual causes of illness based on Christianity, animism, shamanism, or Confucianism (e.g. failure to pray, displeasure of ancestors with their burial place, or offenses displeasing folk spirits). They are more likely to trust their family or friends' views on their illness than that of health professionals (Shin *et al.*, 2002).

Collectively, KAs experience barriers in communicating with the Western health professionals, and some KAs hold inaccurate and/or fatalistic health beliefs derived from the traditional Korean culture. These barriers have led KAs to seek health information from alternative sources rather than from medically-trained health care professionals.

Korean-Americans' Health Information Sources

Health-information seeking is the purposive acquistion of information from selected sources that guide health-related decision-making (Kreps, 1988). Access to relevant, accurate health information is a critical factor in responding effectively to serious health challenges (Hesse *et al.*, 2005). Previous studies suggest that the Internet, KA community media, and Korean-speaking doctors are the primary sources of health information among KAs, though the accuracy and efficacy of information from these sources is questionable.

Internet

In accordance with the national trend of health information seeking by preferring and frequently using the Internet as a source for health information as well as a channel for communicating with health professionals (Hesse *et al.*, 2005), KAs also frequently use the Internet to seek health/medical information for themselves and to participate in online health/medical support groups. Compared to the national average, a higher percentage of KAs reported they had used email or the Internet to communicate with their doctors and to buy medicine or vitamins (Oh, Kreps, Jun, Chong, & Ramsey, 2012). KAs perceive the Internet to have immediate access and search ability as well as easy collection and tracking of important information, and to be a gateway to other forms of information (Oh, Jun, Zhao, Kreps, & Lee, 2015). The Internet is also where KAs most often receive cancer information (Oh, Kreps, Jun, & Ramsey, 2011).

Some scholars suggest that the Internet can be an especially valuable channel for racial/ethnic minorities to obtain inexpensive and culturally sensitive health information in their indigenous languages (Kim, Kim, & Kim, 2001; Kreps & Neuhauser, 2010). However, the reliability of online health information has been questioned, and the public's trust in online health information has decreased nationally (Hesse, Moser, & Rutten, 2010). KAs also raised concerns about the quality of online health information, and characterized it as biased, commercialized, and exaggerated (Oh *et al.*, 2015).

In general, trust in health care professionals is an important predictor of using the Internet as a health information source (Rains, 2007). When patients do not trust health care professionals as their health information source, they would rather use the Internet to seek that information. For KAs, however, trust in health care professionals may not always correlate with their actual source use. Although health care professionals remain as the most trusted information source among KAs (Oh *et al.*, 2012, 2015), only 10.9 percent visited their doctor first for health information, while 48.6 percent went to the Internet first (Oh *et al.*, 2012). This result was different from Whites, with 47 percent turning to their doctor first and 36.7 percent turning to the Internet first (Nguyen & Bellamy, 2006).

A recent study may explain the underlying causes of this discrepancy. According to Oh *et al.* (2015), KAs' evaluations of doctors versus the Internet as sources of health information, their accessibility, affordability, language proficiency, cultural sensitivity, ability to meet immediate needs, literacy, convenience, reliability, and collectability play the most important roles. KAs perceive information from health professionals as inaccessible and expensive because they feel that health professionals do not allow enough time to provide information during regular visits or that they overcharge for time spent on extra information. Many KAs reported relying on other information sources such as the Internet to fulfill their health information needs. Especially for KAs who are limited by lack of health insurance and poor English fluency, the Internet is often their only health information source. New immigrants, with limited interpersonal networks in the US, obtain health-related advice and information from online KA communities (Oh *et al.*, 2015). The most frequently asked questions in these online forums were about recommendations of Korean-speaking doctors and possible treatment methods without seeing a doctor (Kim & Yoon, 2012).

Korean Community Media

KA community media (hereafter "KA media") is another major source of health information among KAs. For instance, one-third of KAs reported that they have heard of cancer-related information from KA TV or KA newspaper/magazines in the past twelve months. KA TV was the second most trusted cancer information source following health care professionals (Oh *et al.*, 2012). KAs are known for their heavy use of KA media such as KA newspapers imported from Korea or printed locally in the US, satellite or cable TV aired from Korea or broadcasted from the local stations, and websites in the Korean language (Lee, 2004). KAs rely heavily on community media rather than US mainstream media (hereafter "US media") in order to receive or exchange information (Oh *et al.*, 2012).

Particularly, KA periodicals are considered to be a primary source of health information among KAs, especially for those with less education (Wismer *et al.*, 2001). KA newspapers and magazines are mostly free or can be purchased with a few coins. They are also readily available in Korean restaurants or grocery stores (Oh *et al.*, 2011). KAs highly trust health information from Korean media and perceive it to be more entertaining, understandable, convenient, diverse, comprehensive, reachable, and more reliable compared to US media (Lee, 2010; Oh *et al.*, 2015). Interestingly, some KAs perceive that the biggest benefit of Korean media is to provide health information in both the Western medicine and *Hanbang* (Korean traditional medicine) perspectives (Oh *et al.*, 2015).

KAs' use of US media as a health information source is extremely limited. Many KAs reported that they had never obtained cancer information from a US newspaper/magazine (45.7 percent) or US TV channels (40.2 percent). Health information from US media is perceived to be credible but not relevant to KAs. Some KAs believe that US mainstream media only targets middle-class Whites, who can afford the cost of health insurance, have time for regular check-ups and additional examinations, and enjoy an "American" lifestyle. They believe that preventive health strategies (e.g. diet and exercise) as recommended in the US media would not work for KAs (Oh *et al.*, 2015).

Korean-Speaking Doctors

More than 75 percent of KAs who are recent immigrants and less fluent in English reported visiting Korean-speaking doctors (Han *et al.*, 1996). Also, elder KAs who have extreme difficulty with English are more likely to use *Hanbang* and other over-the-counter Korean home remedies rather than seeking American health professionals (NIH, 2006).

When KAs visit English-speaking doctors, they may face cultural barriers (Kim, Cho, Cheon-Klessig, Gerace, & Camilleri, 2002). Most

US health care providers are unfamiliar with the unique health needs of KA immigrants, the specific barriers they face, and their views of health (Kim *et al.*, 2002). It is reported that KA patients feel that English-speaking doctors are not approachable and provide recommendations which often lack cultural sensitivity (Oh *et al.*, 2015). Nationally, only 24 percent of KAs strongly agree that their doctor understands their background and values, and only 28 percent were "very satisfied" with their health care (The Commonwealth Fund, 2002).

The patient-provider communication dissatisfaction was also observed among Chinese immigrants, also due to cultural incongruities (Chen, Kendall, & Shyu, 2010). Asian-American patients who place greater emphasis on their cultural values such as filial piety, collectivism, conformity, and humility may often feel that their doctors do not understand these values and thus are less satisfied with their medical care. Such patients may also be less likely to seek information from health care professionals (Ngo-Metzger, Legedza, & Phillips, 2004). KA patients experience more distrust and anxiety during communication with the Western doctors who show unconfident diagnoses in comparison with Korean doctors who tend to be authoritative and confident when communicating their diagnoses (Lee, Kearns, & Friesen, 2010).

Consequently, there are significant differences between KAs and the general US population in their level of trust in and use of various sources of health information. Internet, Korean media, and Korean-speaking doctors are primary sources of health information among KAs, while American health professionals were a primary source of health information for the general population (Hesse *et al.*, 2005). However, there are concerns as to whether KAs are currently obtaining high-quality health information from these sources and if the health information from these sources contributes to their appropriate use of preventive care while living in the US.

Concerns Regarding Korean-Americans' Health Information Sources

As previously discussed, the reliability of health information found online is questionable. Also, Korean newspapers and printed materials available free of charge from community centers often receive information subsidies from commercial partners, undermining the trustworthiness and reliability of health information from these sources. KA media provides limited information that is applicable to using health care services in the US. Oh *et al.* (2011) examined the relationship between KAs' media use and their awareness of valid national cancer information sources such as the National Cancer Institute (NCI) and the NCI's Cancer Information Service (CIS), which offer cancer screening and prevention guidelines. They found that the frequency of US media use was significantly related to awareness of the national cancer information resources because these sources are often promoted in the US media. However, the frequency of KA media use was not related to such awareness due to noticeable differences existing in the quantity and quality of cancer coverage in KA media compared to that found in US media. The KA media focused primarily on specific types of cancer, but US media provided diverse information surrounding cancers (e.g. people, politics, research; McDonnell, Lee, Kim, Kazinets, & Moskowitz, 2008).

Additionally, previous studies suggest that Korean-speaking doctors tend not to recommend preventive care as frequently as English-speaking doctors. According to Jo *et al.* (2009), KAs who received care from Korean-speaking doctors were less likely to have had a recent cancer screening than KAs who received care from a non-Korean-speaking doctor. The authors of this study suggested that this discrepancy may be explained by a variety factors: Korean-speaking doctors' lack of knowledge of US screening guidelines; KA patients' unfamiliarity with the concept of screening, as they generally equate a lack of symptoms with good health or having no disease; and the insufficient understanding of health care system referral networks and reimbursement for screening.

Another concern is that KAs are not obtaining health information from the source they trust the most. Although the Internet and KA media are used more frequently among KAs, they are not necessarily the most trusted sources. Health care providers remain the most trusted source, but immigration status and access to health care limit KAs' access to credible health information. In the context of health communication, trust is particularly important because a lack of trust in the information and its source could potentially push users further away from recommended health attitudes and behaviors (Hesse *et al.*, 2005).

As a result of limited access to quality health information sources and health literacy, KAs face significant deficits in health knowledge. For instance, KAs' awareness of cancer screening options and knowledge of cancer prevention strategies were reported to be significantly lower than in the national sample (Oh, Kreps, & Jun, 2013). Some KA women believe that women who reach menopause do not need Pap tests very often. Many elderly KA women think that a Pap test is only needed once in a lifetime (Juon, Choi, & Kim, 2000). Many KAs have never heard of the Pap smear test, even though cervical cancer is a significant health risk for KA women (Kim *et al.*, 1999).

These multiple barriers to accessing quality health care and health information in US as well as the inefficiencies of the US health care system have motivated many KAs to seek medical/health care in their home country, South Korea. The increasing availability of the South Korean medical tourism services targeting KAs encourages newer KA immigrants as well as those who are underinsured, uninsured, or uninsurable to opt for medical tourism. The next section describes (1) the rise of medical tourism in the US, (2) the status of the South

Korean medical tourism industry, (3) KAs' perceptions and use of the South Korean medical tourism, and (4) the KA media's selective presentation of medical tourism issues.

Medical Tourism Use among Korean-Americans

The Rise of Medical Tourism Use among Americans

Health expenses for Americans have increased in recent years and are projected to continue growing rapidly. US national health expenditures are expected to nearly double from US$8,680 per individual in 2011 to US$14,664 in 2022 (Centers for Medicare & Medicaid Services, 2012). The current US health expenditure of US$7,960 per individual is the highest among all nations included in a 2011 OECD study, followed by US$5,352 for Norway and a minimum of US$99 for Indonesia.

Despite the high cost, accessibility to quality health care in the US is relatively poor. For instance, US children show lower rates than the OECD average for all vaccinations, which were used as a quality health care indicator in the OECD study (OECD, 2011). Also, the proportion of the US population reporting difficulties gaining access to care is the highest among all countries included in that OECD study. Of the eight indicators measuring access to care, the US has the highest degree of unmet care due to out-of-pocket medical costs of US$1,000 or more, the third lowest percentage for health insurance coverage, inequity in the probability of scheduling a doctor visit, inequity in cervical cancer screening, and lower physician density in rural regions (OECD, 2011). Furthermore, one in every five US adults aged 18 to 65 is uninsured, and the likelihood of employment-based coverage declined from 64.4 percent in 1997 to 56.5 percent in 2010 (US Census Bureau, 2010a). Racial and ethnic minorities carry additional burdens in accessing quality health care.

Problems such as these have led Americans to become a part of the medical tourism industry. It is estimated that up to 750,000 US residents travel abroad for health/medical care annually (CDC, n.d.). A large number of medical tourists are immigrants to the US returning to their home country for health/medical care (Bergmark, Barr, & Garcia, 2010). Common destinations include Thailand, Mexico, Singapore, India, Malaysia, Cuba, Brazil, Argentina, and Costa Rica (CDC, 2013). South Korea has also established itself as a major host country for providing medical tourism services and has offered diverse services customized to KAs. As a result, KAs' use of South Korean medical tourism services is increasing rapidly.

The South Korean Medical Tourism Industry

South Korea has provided medical tourism services to foreign tourists since 2009, when the Foreign Patient Legislation Law was passed. The Korean government and the private sector have joined forces to promote the nation's medical services to foreign visitors. As a result, approximately 2,300 medical institutes across the country have registered to serve foreign patients (Shim, 2013). The number of foreign tourists visiting Korea for medical purposes surpassed 155,000 in 2012, and this number has risen more than fifteen times over the past five years (KHIDI, 2013b; Shim, 2013). The number of visitors is expected to reach more than 1.2 million by 2020 (KHIDI, 2013c). Concurrently, the revenue of international medical services in Korea has leaped from US$54.7 million in 2009 to US$103 million in 2010 (KHIDI, 2011, 2013a). The Korean Ministry of Health has set the goal for 2020 to host up to 1,000,000 international patients, and the Korea Health Industry Development Institute (KHIDI) estimates that this number will grow to more than 1,200,000 by 2020 (KHIDI, 2013c).

One-third of foreign patients receiving health care in Korea are from the US (32.4 percent), followed by China (19.4 percent) and Japan (16.8 percent; KHIDI, 2011). The number of US patients in Korea more than doubled from 2009 to 2011. Also, American patients are the second best source of revenue (25.7 percent) for the Korean medical tourism industry after China (26.8 percent). American patients spend more for medical services (US$1,556) during their stay in Korean medical institutes in comparison with other nationalities, such as Canadians (US$1,141) or Japanese (US$766; KHIDI, 2013a).

KAs are a prime target of the Korean medical tourism industry. Significantly lower costs of Korean medical services compared to those in the US are an important benefit. According to a study by Deloitte, major surgeries (e.g. heart bypass, heart valve replacement, hip replacement, knee replacement) are offered at prices two-to-eight times lower in Korea than in the US (Global Benefit Options, 2009). Additionally, fast, systematic, and customized medical services are offered to medical tourists in Korea (Jin, 2011). Easy scheduling, convenience, high quality health care services, and advanced medical technologies are additional benefits of Korean medical tourism as perceived by KAs (Oh *et al.*, 2014).

Major providers of the Korean medical industry are attempting to reach KAs with aggressive public relations and marketing strategies. For instance, in 2008, the Seoul National University Hospital opened an office in Los Angeles, where the majority of KAs reside, to recruit new consumers. They reported that approximately 1,000 KA consumers visited Korea through its programs in 2010 (Park, 2012). Other major Korean hospitals are also promoting medical tourism programs to KA communities (Kim, 2011).

KAs' Perceived Benefits of the South Korean Medical Tourism

As a result of the Korean medical tourism industry's aggressive marketing activities, KAs are heavily exposed to Korean medical tourism information through KA media, word-of-mouth, online, and printed materials. Oh *et al.* (2014) interviewed 40 KA women to examine their perceptions of medical tourism use. All respondents in the study were aware of Korean medical tourism products due to their advertisements and news materials available daily. Additionally, this study found that most KAs have a high opinion of the benefits of medical tourism and intend to use Korean medical services in the future.

Unfortunately, there are many risks and consequences of medical tourism. For example, a Canadian man receiving a controversial surgery in Costa Rica died from complications of the surgery (Morrow, 2010), and a Canadian woman lost the majority of her breast tissue because of a serious infection after breast augmentation abroad (Jacobs, 2010). When patients receive medical treatments or surgeries in a foreign country, they carry additional risks, including lengthy flights after a surgery, exposure to medical malpractice abroad, difficulties in obtaining follow-up care, and the danger of infectious disease transmission (Crooks, Kingsbury, Snyder, & Johnston, 2010; Penney, Snyder, Crooks, & Johnston, 2011). Additionally, medical tourists may lack health professionals' informational continuity about necessary treatment that is established through patient information being available over time and to multiple practitioners in different locations. Medical tourists may hold particular responsibilities in transporting hard copy records from the destination country to their home country and in ensuring that they find health care practitioners in their home country to continue supporting their health care. Medical records could become damaged during transit or the patient may choose not to share the details of the procedures with their local health care practitioners (Crooks *et al.*, 2010). Furthermore, given the lack of professional referrals, some people may have unnecessary treatment conducted abroad that can increase the risks of complications, costs, and anxiety (Oh *et al.*, 2014).

Despite these known risks, KAs highly perceive merits of medical/health services offered in Korea and have a high willingness to use such services in comparison to services in the US. These perceived benefits outweighed risks among KAs. They showed lower perceptions and fears of risks involved with travelling and getting medical services in Korea, such as delaying health care and possible negative health outcomes (Oh *et al.*, 2014).

KA Media Framing of Medical Tourism Risk and Benefit

KAs' overwhelmingly firm views on Korean medical tourism and their lack of risk perception may be a result of how the issue is framed in the group's primary information sources. Previous research found that KA newspapers, which are one of the primary sources of health information among KAs, frame Korean medical tourism as overwhelmingly positive and discuss the diverse benefits of Korean medical tourism. However, KA newspapers have little to no engagement in risk communication and lack sufficient information about the potential risks of medical tourism (Oh *et al.*, 2014). Most medical tourism information available to KAs via KA media reflects commercial sponsors and promotional offers, and many medical-tourism–related news articles may have been written based on information supplied by sponsors from the Korean medical tourism industry.

American medical tourists' satisfaction with services performed abroad were significantly lower than their expectations in many aspects, including up-to-date equipment, and service providers' knowledge, sympathy, communication skills, and billing processes. This gap may be due to unrealistic expectations regarding medical tourism, biased sources of information, and overpromising by the medical tourism industry (Guiry & Vequist, 2010). Obtaining health care through medical tourism rather than local health care providers can result not only in dissatisfaction with the services, but also serious negative health outcomes as medical tourists often fail to obtain appropriate and timely follow-up care (Oh *et al.*, 2014).

Conclusions

Racial/ethnic disparities in US health care are not novel issues as they have been represented as priority areas for research and public policies for over two decades. Rapid advances in medical technology and greater emphasis on preventive care have enhanced overall health and the life expectancy among many Americans. Despite these improvements, health disparities persist; racial/ethnic minorities continue to represent a disproportionate amount of preventable diseases (Kreps, 2006).Both as new immigrants and as racial/ethnic minorities, KAs face multiple barriers to accessing quality health information, which is reducing their access to timely, quality health care. More KAs are seeking alternatives to the US medical system from the Korean medical tourism industry. Noting this, the Korean medical tourism industry strategically communicates with KAs by exposing them to selective information that emphasizes the benefits but discounts the health risks of medical tourism. The US government and health care providers should make sufficient efforts to protect KAs and other medical tourists by fully informing KAs of the risks and benefits of obtaining health care through medical tourism, as well as strategies for accessing and utilizing the US medical/health care effectively. Such efforts would lead to more accurate evaluations of health services and more appropriate decision making that would result in healthier outcomes. At the same time, the benefits of medical tourism services deserve more attention, as they reflect KAs' and other immigrant populations' challenges of receiving quality medical care in the US.

The Affordable Care Act (ACA) was expected to bring significant changes to KAs' health insurance coverage rates and medical tourism use, as the insurance coverage was reported to increase among racial/

ethnic minorities during the first two open enrollment periods of the ACA (Sommers, Gunja, Finegold, & Musco, 2015). However, whether the health reform contributed to reducing the health disparities of KAs and other immigrants is still uncertain. The populations' language barriers and literacy problems with understanding the complex new health care system persist. Progress is contingent upon whether US health care providers effectively engage in communicating with KAs and other immigrants, gain their trust, and offer accessible and culturally sensitive information so that the groups may understand and effectively use the US health care system. For such efforts, understanding the patterns of racial/ethnic minorities' health information seeking and their barriers to positive health behaviors is critical. Although the importance of ethnic sources is undeniable in health information delivery to these populations, these sources contain limitations in providing reliable, credible, and applicable information for utilizing health/medical resources in the US. Therefore, future health communication programs should focus not only on enhancing credibility and applicability of health information delivered through ethnic sources, but also on developing culturally sensitive and accessible health information sources for racial/ethnic minorities and immigrants.

References

APIAHF (2006). Health belief: Koreans in the United States. Asian and Pacific Islander American health forum. Retrieved from www.apiahf.org/sites/default/files/APIAHF_Healthbrief08e_2006.pdf.

Barringer, H., & Gardiner, R. (1993). *Asians and Pacific Islanders in the United States*. New York: Russel Sage Foundation.

Bastani, R., Glenn, A., Maxwell, E., & Jo, M. (2007). Hepatitis B testing for liver cancer control among Korean Americans. *Ethnicity & Disease*, *17*(2), 365–373.

Bergmark, R., Barr, D., & Garcia, R. (2010). Mexican immigrants in the US living far from the border may return to mexico for health services. *Journal of Immigrant & Minority Health*, *12*(4), 610–614. doi:10.1007/s10903-008-9213-8.

CDC. (n.d.). Medical tourism: Getting medical care in another country, traveler's health. Centers for Disease Control and Prevention. Retrieved from http://wwwnc.cdc.gov/travel/page/medical-tourism.

CDC. (2013). Medical tourism: Travelers' health. Centers for Disease Control and Prevention. Retrieved from http://wwwnc.cdc.gov/travel/yellowbook/2014/chapter-2-the-pre-travel-consultation/medical-tourism.

Centers for Medicare & Medicaid Services. (2012). National health expenditure projections 2012-2022. Retrieved from www.cms.gov/Research-Statistics-Data-and-Systems/Statistics-Trends-and-Reports/NationalHealthExpendData/Downloads/Proj2012.pdf.

Chen, J., Kendall, J., & Shyu, L. (2010). Grabbing the rice straw: Health information seeking in Chinese immigrants in the United States. *Clinical Nursing Research*, *19*(4), 335–353. doi:10.1177/1054773810372542.

Crooks, V., Kingsbury, P., Snyder, J., & Johnston, R. (2010). What is known about the patient's experience of medical tourism? A scoping review. *BMC Health Services Research*, *10*, 266. doi:10.1186/1472-6963-10-266.

Eun, Y., Lee, E., Kim, J., & Fogg, L. (2009). Breast cancer screening beliefs among older Korean American women. *Journal of Geontological Nursing*, *35*(9), 40–50. doi:10.3928/00989134-20090731-09.

Global Benefit Options. (2009). Medical treatment abroad, affordable health-care options, travel health abroad. Retrieved August 29, 2013, from www.globalbenefitoptions.com/facts_about_medical_tourism.html.

Guiry, M., & Vequist, G. (2010). The role of professional values in determining U.S. medical tourists' expectations and perceptions of healthcare facility service quality: An exploratory investigation. *Journal of Tourism Challenges & Trends*, *3*(2), 115–140.

Han, E., Song, H., & Kim, S. (1996). Doctor visits among Korean Americans in Los Angeles County. *Asian American and Pacific Islander Journal of Health*, *4*, 1–3.

Hesse, B., Moser, R., & Rutten, L. (2010). Surveys of physicians and electronic health information. *New England Journal of Medicine*, *362*(9), 859–860. doi:10.1056/NEJMc0909595.

Hesse, B., Nelson, D., Kreps, G., Croyle, R., Arora, N., Rimer, B., & Viswanath, K. (2005). Trust and sources of health information: The impact of the Internet and its implications for health care providers: findings from the first Health Information National Trends Survey. *Archives of Internal Medicine*, *165*(22), 2618–2624. doi:10.1001/archinte.165.22.2618.

Honda, K., & Kreps, G. (2006). The relationship of media attention to colorectal cancer-related risk appraisals in older Japanese Americans: Using structural equation modeling to develop an explanatory model. *Californian Journal of Health Promotion*, *4*(3), 23–33.

Hsieh, E., Pitaloka, D., & Johnson, A. (2013). Bilingual health communication: Distinctive needs of providers from five specialties. *Health Communication*, *28*(6), 557–567. doi: 10.1080/10410236.2012.702644.

Im, E., & Choe, M. (2004). Korean women's attitudes toward physical activity. *Research in Nursing & Health*, *27*(1), 4–18. doi:10.1002/nur.20000.

Jacobs, M. (2010). Fixing foreign foul-ups. *Edmonton Sun*. Retrieved from www.edmontonsun.com/comment/columnists/mindelle_jacobs/2010/12/07/16465056.html.

Jemal, A., Tiwari, R., Murray, T., Ghafoor, A., Samuels, A., Ward, E., …, Thun, M. (2004). Cancer statistics, 2004. *CA: A Cancer Journal for Clinicians*, *54*(1), 8–29.

Jin, S. (2011). Explosive increase of Korean medical tourism among Americans. Retrieved from www.koreadaily.com/news/read.asp?art_id=1204058.

Jo, A., Maxwell, A., Rick, A., Cha, J., & Bastani, R. (2009). Why are Korean American physicians reluctant to recommend colorectal cancer screening to Korean American patients? Exploratory interview findings. *Journal of Immigrant & Minority Health*, *11*(4), 302–309. doi: 10.1007/s10903-008-9165-z.

Jun, J., & Oh, K. M. (2013). Asian and Hispanic Americans' cancer fatalism and colon cancer screening. *American Journal of Health Behavior*, *37*(2), 145–154. doi:10.5993/AJHB.37.2.1.

Juon, H., Choi, Y., & Kim, M. (2000). Cancer screening behaviors among Korean-American women. *Cancer Detection and Prevention, 24*(6), 589–601. doi:10.1002/(SICI)1099-1298(199907/08)9:4<247::AID-CASP500>3.0.CO;2-E.

KHIDI. (2011). Understanding of the foreign patients registration project. Retrieved from www.medicalkorea.or.kr/webzine/html/04.stats/02.html.

KHIDI. (2013a). Statistics on international patients in Korea, 2011. Retrieved from http://medicalkorea.khidi.or.kr/BOARD_FILE/B1/428_2011.

KHIDI. (2013b). The foreign patients status. Retrieved July 11, 2013, from http://khiss.go.kr/board/bbs_read.jsp?tname=MINBOARD358&bbsid=B205&bbs_seq=10&jkey=&jword=&pg=1&htxt_code=1253697688296185639109094980793O&wj_vcs=.

KHIDI. (2013c). The prospect of foreign patients. Retrieved July 11, 2013, from http://khiss.go.kr/board/bbs_read.jsp?tname=MINBOARD358&bbsid=B205&bbs_seq=11&jkey=&jword=&pg=1&htxt_code=1253697688296185639109094980793O&wj_vcs=.

Kim, H., Kim, E., & Kim, J. (2001). Development of a breast self-examination program for the Internet: health information for Korean women. *Cancer Nursing, 24*(2), 156–161.

Kim, K. (2011). Korean big hospitals' fierce competition in the US market. *Chosun*. Retrieved from http://news.chosun.com/site/data/html_dir/2011/04/09/2011040900102.html.

Kim, K., Yu, E., Liu, W., Kim, J., & Kohrs, M. (1993). Nutritional status of Chinese-, Korean-, and Japanese-American elderly. *Journal of the American Dietetic Association, 93*(12), 1416–1422.

Kim, K., Yu, E., Chen, E., Kim, J., Kaufman, M., & Purkiss, J. (1999). Cervical cancer screening knowledge and practices among Korean-American women. *Cancer Nursing, 22*(4), 297–302.

Kim, M., Cho, H., Cheon-Klessig, Y., Gerace, L., & Camilleri, D. (2002). Primary health care for Korean immigrants: Sustaining a culturally sensitive model. *Public Health Nursing, 19*(3), 191–200. doi:10.1046/j.0737-1209.2002.19307.x.

Kim, S., & Yoon, J. (2012). The use of an online forum for health information by married Korean women in the United States. *Information Research, 17*(2), 514.

Kreps, G. L. (1988). The pervasive role of information in health and health care: Implications for health communication policy. In J. Anderson (Ed.), Communication yearbook 11 (pp. 238–276). Newbury Park, CA: Sage.

Kreps, G. (2006). Communication and racial inequities in health care. *American Behavioral Scientist, 49*(6), 760–774. doi:10.1177/0002764205283800.

Kreps, G., & Neuhauser, L. (2010). Special issue editorial review board. *Journal of Computer-Mediated Communication, 15*(4), 682–682. doi:10.1111/j.1083-6101.2010.01527.x.

Lee, C. (2004). Korean immigrants' viewing patterns of Korean satellite television and its role in their lives. *Asian Journal of Communication, 4*(1), 68–80. doi:10.1080/0129298042000195161.

Lee, E., & Farran, C. (2004). Depression among Korean, Korean American, and Caucasian American family caregivers. *Journal of Transcultural Nursing: Official Journal of the Transcultural Nursing Society/Transcultural Nursing Society, 15*(1), 18–25. doi:10.1177/1043659603260010.

Lee, J. (2010). Channels of health communications used among Korean and Asian Indian older adults. *Social Work in Health Care*, *49*(2), 165–175. doi:10.1080/00981380903157997.

Lee, J., Demissie, K., Lu, S., & Rhoads, G. (2007). Cancer incidence among Korean-American immigrants in the United States and native Koreans in South Korea. *Cancer Control: Journal of the Moffitt Cancer Center*, *14*(1), 78–85.

Lee, Y., Kearns, R., & Friesen, W. (2010). Seeking affective health care: Korean immigrants' use of homeland medical services. *Health & Place*, *16*(1), 108–115. doi:10.1016/j.healthplace.2009.09.003.

Lee, M. (2000). Knowledge, barriers, and motivators related to cervical cancer screening among Korean-American women. A focus group approach. *Cancer Nursing*, *23*(3), 168–175. doi:10.1097/00002820-200006000-00003.

Li, S., Kwon, S., Weerasingh, I., Rey, M., & Trinh-Shevrin, C. (2013). Smoking among Asian Americans: Acculturation and gender in the context of tobacco control policies in New York City. *Health Promotion Practice*, *14*(5), 18S–28S. doi:10.1177/1524839913485757.

Maxwell, E., Bastani, R., & Warda, U. (1998). Mammography utilization and related attitudes among Korean-American women. *Women & Health*, *27*(3), 89–107.

Maxwell, E., Crespi, C., Antonio, C. & Lu, P. (2010). Explaining disparities in colorectal cancer screening among five Asian ethnic groups: A population-based study in California. *BMC Cancer*, *10*, 214–222. doi:10.1186/1471-2407-10-214.

McDonnell, D., Lee, H., Kim, Y., Kazinets, G., & Moskowitz, J. (2008). Cancer coverage in a mainstream and Korean American online newspaper: Lessons for community intervention. *Patient Education and Counseling*, *71*(3), 388–395. doi:10.1016/j.pec.2008.03.004.

Miller, B., Chu, K., Hankey, B., & Ries, L. (2008). Cancer incidence and mortality patterns among specific Asian and Pacific Islander populations in the U.S. *Cancer Causes & Control*, *19*(3), 227–256. doi:10.1007/s10552-007-9088-3.

Morrow, A. (2010). Man dies after controversial MS treatment, doctor says. *The Globe and Mail*. Retrieved from www.theglobeandmail.com/news/national/man-dies-after-controversial-ms-treatment-doctor-says/article1314585/.

NAKASEC. (2009). Why Korean Americans need responsible health reform. The National Korean American Service and Education Consortium (NAKASEC). Retrieved from http://nakasec.org/wp-content/uploads/sites/3/2009/05/health_reform_community_ed_material-final1.pdf.

National Center for Health Statistics. (2011). NHIS early release – health insurance – 2010. Retrieved May 10, 2012, from www.cdc.gov/nchs/nhis.htm.

New California Media. (2003). *Bridging language barriers in health care: Public opinion survey of California immigrants from Latin America, Asia and the Middle East*. New California Media. Retrieved from www.bendixenandassociates.com/studies/NCM percent20Health percent20Care percent20Report percent202003.pdf.

Ngo-Metzger, Q., Legedza, A., & Phillips, R. (2004). Asian Americans' reports of their health care experiences. Results of a national survey. *Journal of General Internal Medicine*, *19*(2), 111–119. doi:10.1111/j.1525-1497.2004.30143.x.

Nguyen, G., & Bellamy, S. (2006). Cancer information seeking preferences and experiences: Disparities between Asian Americans and Whites in the Health

Information National Trends Survey (HINTS). *Journal of Health Communication, 11*, 173–180. doi:10.1080/10810730600639620.

NIH. (2006). Women of color health data book. National Institutes of Health (NIH). Retrieved from http://orwh.od.nih.gov/pu bs/WomenofColor2006.pdf.

ODPHP. (2016). Health people 2020 topics and objectives. Office of Disease Prevention and Health Promotion. Retrieved from www.healthypeople.gov/2020/topics-objectives.

OECD, O. for E. C. and D. (2011). *Health at a glance 2011 OECD indicators.* Washington: Organization for Economic Cooperation & Development Brookings Institution Press. Retrieved from http://encompass.library.cornell.edu/cgi-bin/checkIP.cgi?access=gateway_standard percent26url.

Oh, K., Jun, J., Zhao, X., Kreps, G., & Lee, E. (2015). Cancer information seeking behaviors of Korean American women: A mixed-methods study using surveys and focus group interviews. *Journal of Health Communication*, 1–12. doi:10.1080/10810730.2015.1018578.

Oh, K., Jun, J., Zhou, Q., & Kreps, G. (2014). Korean American women's perceptions about physical examinations and cancer screening services offered in Korea: The influences of medical tourism on Korean Americans. *Journal of Community Health, 39*(2), 221–229. doi:10.1007/s10900-013-9800-z.

Oh, K., Kreps, G., Jun, J., Chong, E., & Ramsey, L. (2012). Examining the health information seeking behaviors of Korean Americans. *Journal of Health Communication, 17*(7), 779–790. doi:10.1080/10810730.2011.650830.

Oh, K., Kreps, G., Jun, J., & Ramsey, L. (2011). Cancer information seeking and awareness of cancer information sources among Korean Americans. *Journal of Cancer Education, 26*(2), 355–364. doi:10.1007/s13187-010-0191-x.

Oh, K., Kreps, G., & Jun, J. (2013). Colorectal cancer screening knowledge, beliefs, and practices of Korean Americans. *American Journal of Health Behaviors, 37*(3), 381–394. doi:10.5993/AJHB.37.3.11.

Pang, K. (1991). *Korean elderly women in America: Everyday life, health and illness*. New York: AMS Press.

Park, N., Jang, Y., Lee, B., Haley, W., & Chiriboga, D. (2013). The mediating role of loneliness in the relation between social engagement and depressive symptoms among older Korean Americans: Do men and women differ? *Psychological Sciences and Social Sciences, 68*(2), 193–201. doi:10.1093/geronb/gbs062.

Park, S. (2008, March 25). Medical tourism emerges as new growth engine. *Korean Times*. Retrieved from www.koreatimes.co.kr/www/news/special/2011/04/242_21375.html.

Park, S. (2012, May 21). Americans' use of Korean medical tourism services... 29 percent increase in the past year. *Koreadaily*. Retrieved from www.koreadaily.com/news/read.asp?art_id=1413177.

Park, S., Murphy, S., Sharma, S., & Kolonel, L. (2005). Dietary intakes and health-related behaviours of Korean American women born in the USA and Korea: The Multiethnic Cohort Study. *Public Health Nutrition, 8*(7), 904–911. doi:10.1079/PHN2005740.

Penney, K., Snyder, J., Crooks, V., & Johnston, R. (2011). Risk communication and informed consent in the medical tourism industry: A thematic content analysis of Canadian broker websites. *BMC Medical Ethics, 12*(1), 17. doi:10.1186/1472-6939-12-17.

Rains, S. (2007). Perceptions of traditional information sources and use of the world wide web to seek health information: Findings from the Health

Information National Trends Survey. *Journal of Health Communication*, *12*(7), 667–680. doi:10.1080/10810730701619992.

Ryu, S., Crespi, C., & Maxwell, A. (2013a). A bi-national comparative study of health behaviors of Koreans in South Korea and Korean Americans in California. *Journal of Immigrant and Minority Health*, *15*, 9706. doi:10.1007/s10903-012-9706-3.

Ryu, S. Y., Crespi, C. M., & Maxwell, A. E. (2013b). Colorectal cancer among Koreans living in South Korea versus California: incidence, mortality, and screening rates. *Ethnicity & Health*, *19*(4), 406–423. doi:10.1080/13557858.2013.801404.

Shim, J. (2013). Medical tourists increasing rapidly. *Korea Times*. Retrieved from http://koreatimes.co.kr/www/news/nation/2013/04/113_133635.html.

Shin, H., & Robert, A. (2010). Language use in the United States: 2007, American Community Survey Reports, ACS-12. U.S. Census Bureau, Washington, DC.

Shin, K., Shin, C., & Blanchette, P. (2002). Health and health care of Korean-American elders. Retrieved from http://web.stanford.edu/group/ethnoger/korean.html.

Sohn, L., & Harada, N. (2005). Knowledge and use of preventive health practices among Korean women in Los Angeles county. *Preventive Medicine*, *41*(1), 167–178. doi:10.1016/j.ypmed.2004.09.039.

Sommers, B. D., Gunja, M. Z., Finegold, K., & Musco, T. (2015). Changes in self-reported insurance coverage, access to care, and health under the Affordable Care Act. *Journal of the American Medical Association*, *314*(4), 366–374. doi:10.1001/jama.2015.8421.

Terrazas, A. (2009). Migration information source: Korean immigrants in the United States. Migration Policy Institute. Retrieved from www.migrationinformation.org/usfocus/display.cfm?ID=716.

The Commenwealth Fund. (2002). 2001 Health care quality survey. Retrieved from www.commonwealthfund.org/publications/surveys/2001/2001-health-care-quality-survey.

U.S. Census Bureau. (2010a). Highlights: 2010 – U.S Census Bureau. Retrieved November 6, 2011, Retrieved from www.census.gov/hhes/www/hlthins/data/incpovhlth/2010/highlights.html.

U.S. Census Bureau. (2010b). Race reporting for the Asian population by selected categories: 2010. Retrieved from http://factfinder2.census.gov/faces/tableservices/jsf/pages/productview.xhtml?pid=DEC_10_SF1_QT-P8&prodType=table.

U.S. Census Bureau. (2013). American fact finder: Results. Retrieved September 5, 2015, from http://factfinder.census.gov/faces/tableservices/jsf/pages/productview.xhtml?src=bkmk

Wismer, B., Moskowitz, J., Min, K., Chen, A., Ahn, Y., Cho, S., … Tager, I. (2001). Interim assessment of a community intervention to improve breast and cervical cancer screening among Korean American women. *Journal of Public Health Management and Practice*, 7(2), 61–70.

Wong, S. T., Yoo, G. J., & Stewart, A. L. (2006). The changing meaning of family support among older Chinese and Korean immigrants. *Psychological Sciences and Social Sciences*, *61*(1), S4–S9.

Yoo, G., & Kim, B. (2008). Korean immigrants and health care access: Implications for the uninsured and underinsured. *Research in the Sociology of Health Care*, *25*, 77–94. doi:10.1016/S0275-4959(07)00004-X.

Part III

ICTs and Migrants' Health Communication

8 Spheres of Influence and New Technological Trajectories

Olivia Guntarik, Marsha Berry, & Emsie Arnoldi

The Complex Topography of Health

The health care sector in Australia is a vast and complex terrain. Diverse networks of services, public and private practices, regulatory bodies, and government agencies jostle for position in a contested globalizing space. Beyond the panoply of providers that comprise this industry, there is also a virtual space—a moving panorama of viral-activity about health care, services, and professionals enabled by media technology. As more health information shifts from print to online forms, health care providers recognize the significance of stamping their digital footprint into a flourishing web-enabled economy.

In this chapter, we illustrate how navigating this topography can be both inviting and intimidating for new migrant communities. We demonstrate how negotiating this complex health care system can largely be determined by how people understand the local service provision network. While it is understood that accessibility is often restricted by cultural, linguistic, and financial constraints, we argue that a lack of access to health care and health-related information can be a significant aspect of a person's marginalization, exclusion, and isolation.

Our work in this area as social researchers explored this messy terrain of complex information-seeking experiences. We situate our analysis in the early years of a migrant's arrival to a new country, which is why our interest is in what the health care topography looks like to a new migrant negotiating this space for the first time. Our study examined the ways social media shapes migrants' views on health and their access to health care. Our findings support earlier studies that show how migrants place a significant emphasis on their social networks, as they seek to gain information about health-related issues (Albert, Becker, McCrone, & Thornicroft, 1998). The role online social support networks play in migrants' understandings of health during the early period of resettlement is crucial to the myriad ways in which they navigate the changing landscape of health care, but it remains little understood. Our findings indicate that migrants can be both socially enabled and impeded by their own social networks and communities. These outcomes point to the need to create culturally relevant ties between the communication strategies of health providers in a multicultural and increasingly competitive global context.

Communicating across Networks

In our research, we asked how new migrants sought information on significant health-related issues, focusing specifically on women's issues, such as maternity and pediatric health, and family planning. Within these health categories, we learnt that health communicators often struggle to understand the communities they want to reach and to promote their initiatives across diverse multicultural environments (Newman, Biedrzycki, & Baum, 2012). To gain insights into these health categories, we conducted an analysis of 10 websites of health care providers[1] targeting women's health in Dandenong, a region known for its cultural diversity in Australia. We found that much online promotional activity was designed to present generic information to the wider English-speaking populace. While this is unsurprising given Australia's predominant Anglo-Celtic heritage, it is evident that the country's changing multicultural mix and increasing fluctuations in ethnic makeup necessitates new ways of engaging the community.

Clearly, a number of these health services see the significance of making their mark and developing communication strategies that would be relevant to the growing multicultural community. At the local level, there are a range of initiatives across municipalities in Australia, which seek to foster social inclusion as a priority in service provision across different industry sectors. This includes incorporating a broad community engagement strategy for encouraging a whole community participation approach in supporting decision-making processes on health-related issues. Other health organizations are also producing resources, comprising of a mix of print and digital forms, which can be adapted across all communication and social media platforms. In some cases, providers are offering an interpreting service as part of their health care provision as they become attuned to the need for a more inclusive approach in health care. Several websites we looked at are also dedicated specifically to migrant and refugee needs. This included a number of providers offering referral or health services primarily targeting refugees and migrants or specific ethnic groups, such as Africans, Indo-Chinese, and Cambodian migrants.

Despite the strategic focus that health care providers are adopting at the local level to engage culturally and linguistically diverse communities, studies indicate that many migrants are challenged by the health care system and finding their own means to gain health information. For instance, some migrants are going online and joining social support networks, which act as important channels to share, exchange, and make recommendations on health issues and health care providers. This is most evident in the early years of migrants' settlement in a new country as they become familiar with the environment (Mackenzie & Guntarik, 2015; Renzaho & Oldroyd, 2014). This form of information-seeking behavior is further supported by existing research, which highlights how migrants can experience varying degrees of difficulty in understanding health care professionals and, as such, may hold different interpretations of their illness compared to the medical views of health (Bäärnhielm & Ekblad, 2000). In one instance, a study found that migrants who were unable to become pregnant were restricted by language barriers and cultural differences and regularly sought the advice of herbalist and spiritual healers from within their own cultural and social groups (Yebei, 2000).

Recent research on migrants reveals similar patterns where women's health was compromised due to language barriers, cultural differences and age (Goodall, Newman, & Ward, 2014; Hall, Chen, Wu, Zhou, & Latkin, 2014). One study found that even with easy and affordable access to health care providers, migrants did not view their health care professionals as a suitable resource for information and advice (Ahmad *et al.*, 2005). These women tended to find other means of addressing health problems, including general information seeking among their peers and using their social groups as a source of advice, rather than seeking help directly from professionals. Other results contradict this finding, revealing the increasing importance of caregivers in supporting migrants and their families, particularly among women transitioning into new roles for the first time, such as motherhood. However, the results highlight how the position of maternal caregivers can be compromised if the health care system has not adapted to the culturally diverse needs of migrants (Viken, Lyberg, & Severinsson, 2015).

While research has found a strong correlation between social networks and good health and wellbeing, much of the research in this area has tended to focus on community-based face-to-face social networks. This focus on 'physical' over 'digital' networks is expected given that work in this area only gained momentum in the pre-social media era of the 1980s (see Bryant, 1982; Kuo & Tsai, 1986; Valle & Bensussen, 1985). Studies in this earlier period suggest that the proximity of trusted peers, including friends and kin in a person's immediate social circle, reinforced positive experiences with the health care sector. The physical and close presence of peers had a significant impact on influencing an individual's decision-making processes around health choices and behavior. This finding indicates that people place considerable weight on the advice and support provided to them by those they trust in their extended circle of family and friends.

Over the past twenty-five years, research on the impact of social relationships on health has been broad and varied. For instance, the analytical focus of studies conducted during the 1990s to the New Millennium incorporated a wider range of age, gender and cultural groups. However, findings in this period reveal similar trends to studies undertaken in the previous decade of the 1980s and emphasized the importance of family and friendship networks, a strong relationship between good health and social connectedness and participation, and the vital need for culturally appropriate social support in the initial migration and acculturation period (Berkman & Glass, 2000; Dunkel-Schetter, Sagrestano, Feldman, & Killingsworth, 1996; Kim & McKenry, 1998). In all these studies, researchers have noted the role of social networks as a critical tool of communication, both in terms of *sharing* information about health-related issues and as an essential *influencing* factor to shaping how new migrants conceptualize their own and family's health, as well as understanding of the local health care system (also see Fox, 2011; Newman *et al.*, 2012).

More recent scholarship has centered on social networks as a form of social capital in the process of migrant acculturation (Perkins, Subramanian, & Christakis, 2014; Ryan, Sales, Tilki, & Siara, 2008), the importance of social networks in establishing social cohesion in the new homeland (Stansfeld, 2006), and the increasing value new migrants place on digital technology for ease of access, convenience and efficiency in accessing information (Chen & Choi, 2011). These studies reveal the kinds of anxieties produced as a consequence of contemporary migration, which illustrates that for newly arrived migrants the initial interval of transition into the host nation can be one of uncertainty, instability, stress and isolation. In Australia, the existence of a host of health services targeting specific migrant groups is a clear indication that many recent arrivals, particularly from refugee communities, suffer from physical and psychological trauma, and have experienced prolonged lengths of poverty, periods in detention, and poor access to appropriate health care prior to their arrival. While it might seem obvious that early intervention into these migrants' health problems can be addressed through relevant health care and support during the initial settlement phase, we found that migrants are often contending with other issues that prevent them from seeking immediate health care if required. This included the need to ensure appropriate housing and education for their families as among the most immediate priorities.

The need to understand how social networks can effectively support new migrants in the early stages of their settlement would be crucial to supporting their transition into community and social life. Researchers are only beginning to engage with the cultural and technological nuances that these social networks introduce, particularly the kinds of complexities that are to be taken into account in this era of media abundance and rapid digital content circulation. To this end, there is an apparent knowledge gap in our understandings about how the transmission of health information is mediated. This understanding is further complicated by digital technology as we experience shifts between physical face-to-face interactions and move into other social worlds, such as online and social media environments with their intricate and often invisible forms of sociality.

What has been noted in the literature is that social media should not simply be viewed as an emancipatory tool of communication, but understood simultaneously as a virtual environment that contains its own set of social rules—understood to be both socially inclusive and exclusive. Studies have highlighted the dangers of an online social environment where participants can remain anonymous or falsify their identities (O'Mara, 2013). For instance, anonymity may affect the quality of responses that people offer in public discussion forums, many of which may be un-moderated or not medically endorsed. This kind of environment can create a false sense of security around health information, which in turn can become an obstacle to effective health and wellbeing promotion. The dangers of this environment are further reinforced because the digital domain is also a highly individualized space, attracting opportunistic self-promoters of health and lifestyle services and products, which may run counter to a migrant's health needs, expectations, and priorities (Lupton, 2015). Digital technology, in other words, can enable or impede relevant access to health care. How an individual navigates the health care system can often be determined by whom they know and trust and the choices they make about what constitutes trustworthy and reliable content.

New Technological Trajectories

It is premature to assume that physical social networks function in the same way as the types of networks that evolve on the web. Emerging research tells us there are both similarities as well as vast differences precisely because of the viral nature of digital technology with its ability to incorporate greater reach, scale, and speed across multiple networks (see Lang, 2011). Yet what does remain obvious is that as an emergent field of study, the range of findings that exist on this topic will remain inconclusive for some time to come (Eysenbach, Powell, Englesakis, Rizo, & Stern, 2004; Miller & West, 2009). Contemporary studies point to the increasing significance of social networks as health-information seeking tools (see Newman, Lauterbach, Munson, Resnick, & Morris, 2011; Song, Yan, & Li, 2015). While it is clear that newly arrived migrants have differing views about their health that are highly heterogeneous, the process of migration and the effects of socialization in the receiving country can have a transformative impact on migrants' perceptions of health. The social networks that migrants carry with them from their previous homelands, and those they newly establish in their adopted one, provide vital links to their ongoing health care experience.

What remains unclear is the connection between offline and online sociality, as well as the particular features of online communities that help to empower or disempower a person's familiarity with the health care system. What is becoming clearer is that understanding how new migrants negotiate this system necessitates new approaches to scrutinizing this complex topography of online health communities as the evidence points to a surge in online health-seeking activity amongst this population.

Across the globe, the Internet is being used by a range of organizations and individuals to spread and access health and medical information across geographic, social, and cultural boundaries. In Ghana, traditional healers are using digital technology, drawing on a mix of local healing practices and Google searches, to increase their geographical reach (Hampshire & Owusu, 2013). In Australia, findings show that young women suffering from illness are more likely to seek online advice over other professional assistance, and that this increasing reliance on the Internet will have implications for democracy, equality, power, and ultimately women's health (Carroll & McCarthy, 2010). Such forms of digital information-seeking behavior have reshaped the health care delivery sector and continue to redefine how health information might be transmitted to the broader community into the future (Lober & Flowers, 2011). We are only just beginning to envisage the implications of this change to the health care sector. This points to the need for more critical investigations into the different assemblages of health promotion strategies and their relevance to online communities and digital communication networks across cultural differences.

The growing reliance on Dr Google as a form of health-information seeking should not be underestimated. This reliance on the Internet may reflect a lack of confidence among some members of new migrant populations to directly approach health care providers, and follow conventional routes to accessing health information by seeking the advice of doctors and other health care professionals. Not only does this reliance reinforce the notion that the Internet is a place of risk, it is also indicative of a digital and social environment that is more vulnerable to perpetuating myths and conspiracy theories about health and medical issues. This observation supports other studies, which highlight how migrants are increasingly seeking information about health issues online, either by conducting a Google search on their symptoms or posing (often anonymous) questions in online discussion forums (Ayers, Althouse, Allem, Rosenquist, & Ford, 2013; Bhandari & Jung, 2014). Further studies demonstrate that the phenomenon of 'Googling' symptoms or asking Dr Google, appears more acute among new migrant and ethnic communities often confronted with concomitant issues in the new homeland. These issues include a lack of confidence in negotiating the local health services environment, language barriers, and anxieties about health care, treatment, and access (Hechanova, Tuliao, Teh, Alianan, & Acosta, 2013).

The significance and nature of health and medical information when it is circulated in this context can be severely compromised and medical information, in turn, can be weakened or lose their value entirely. For new migrants, access to health care is not only restricted by cultural, linguistic and financial constraints, but the process of migration itself can transform how migrants come to conceptualize their own health and place in the community.

Final Analysis

This study offers a regional analysis of new migrant health issues in a contemporary context, by adopting a place-based focus on the multicultural site of Dandenong in Australia. We contextualized this site by reviewing scholarship located at the intersection of social networks, health and migration. This allowed us to critically explore the confluence of health information flows in relation to new migrant communities, both locally and in different parts of the world. We were then able to relate these findings to our localized conditions in Australia. We followed the challenges that migrants in general experience with the health care system as they move between the physical location of health services and into the digital world and back again. Our analysis of health and migrant adaptation issues has drawn attention to the initial timeframe of transition and instability experienced as a new arrival in a foreign culture. Migrants must learn to adjust before they can eventually become 'bicultural' citizens, so they can participate fully and in meaningful ways in the society to which they are expected to integrate (Furnham, 1988). While research on the role of social networks in migrant health has gained traction in communication studies, we learnt that much of this research gives primacy to face-to-face interactions and less attention has been paid to migrants' online social relations and communication practices (see Kristjánsdóttir & DeTurk, 2013). We discovered that there continues to be a great divide in investigative studies, which explore the contested relationship between online and offline socialities.

The boundaries between the online and offline dimensions of everyday life are becoming increasingly blurred. Postill and Pink (2012) argue that the distinction between the two realms is problematic. They suggest that in order to better understand the impacts of social media and the kinds of socialities these give rise to, one needs to look at how 'research participants navigate their wider social, material, and technological worlds' (Postill & Pink, 2012, p. 123). They point out the term 'community' is also problematic in sociological theory as an analytical unit or frame, and it is better understood through how participants in a particular research context define what community means to them. They argue that a focus on socialities 'permits us to attend to both "community" type feel-good-ness and the shifting and more transient encounters and co-routes between the Internet and offline experiences' (Postill & Pink, 2012, p. 127). We further suggest that the allusion to sociality here is important because sociality relates to people's tendencies to form groups and relate to one another along lines of co-operation, affinity and sense of identity and belonging—crucial considerations for promoting health in times of conflict and mass migration.

Our focus on migrant social support networks acknowledges the domain of the digital as an emergent field of study. Social networks adopt new forms and features in digital environments in contrast to their face-to-face counterparts. They have evolved in ways that complicate what it means to gain knowledge on significant health issues in competitive globalized economies. Information is now culturally, socio-politically and digitally mediated by a complex network of friends, family, strangers, and health professionals who share information and influence one another in multifaceted and subtle ways. This is a space of flux and flow, interconnections and disconnections, information and misinformation, which is technologically nuanced but which continues to redefine how people approach their own and family's health in unfamiliar settings. Furthermore, this health information-seeking activity is constrained by the process of migration and resettlement, which transforms migrants' conceptualizations of health and their status in the community. This experience is in turn conditioned by local contexts and complicated further by the simultaneity enabled by digital media.

Online social networks have emerged as a new galvanizing force in migrants' health information-seeking activities. These social relations are culturally and digitally-shaped; their online formations stand in contrast to their offline incarnations insofar as they are constituted as discrete collectives characterized by varying levels of trust, reciprocity, information-sharing, and influence. Yet as an emerging field, research on migrant digital social networks remains inconclusive, contradictory, and contestable. The relevance of earlier scholarship in the field of social networks and its impact on emerging social media investigations is still to be fully realized. In this light, our findings express the need to examine the new constellations of shared experiences and influences that drive people's interactions and social practices across transnational and local digital networks and their impact on the health-seeking efforts of migrants. Migrants engage with new technologies as a means of making sense of their experiences about their own and family's health. Through these engagements, they are able to redraw the connections they have with their former and existing home environments as they participate in multiple networks that are integrated into their everyday social realities. Perhaps what this means more generally is that, in the transition between home and new nation resettlement, the ties to authoritative health information can be lost, weakened or compromised as new engagements with health information are woven into migrants' own preferred interpretations, socialities, and spheres of influence.

Note

1 The list of 10 websites is provided below. These organizations are all broadly categorized as health care providers and offer either direct health care or health information with a focus specifically on migrant health or migrant women's health issues. All services are located within the municipality of Dandenong or make referrals to services in this area. Dandenong is a region of outer metropolitan Melbourne in Australia, covering an area of 130 square kilometers. With about 150,000 residents, this region has a highly multicultural population and more than half of its residents were born overseas.

www.monashhealth.org/page/Dandenong.
www.whise.org.au/.
headspace.org.au/headspace-centres/dandenong/.
humanservicesdirectory.vic.gov.au/SiteDetails.aspx?SiteID=27756.
www.smrc.org.au/.
www.refugeehealthnetwork.org.au/.
www.foundationhouse.org.au/.
www.health.vic.gov.au/diversity/refugee.htm.
www.asrc.org.au/.
www.ceh.org.au/health-literacy.

References

Ahmad, F., Shik, A., Vanza, R., Cheung, A. M., George, U., & Stewart, D. E. (2005). Voices of South Asian women: Immigration and mental health. *Women and Health*, *40*(4), 113–130. www.ncbi.nlm.nih.gov/pubmed/15911513.

Albert, M., Becker, T., McCrone, P., & Thornicroft, G. (1998). Social networks and mental health service utilization: A literature review. *International Journal of Social Psychiatry*, *44*(4), 248–266. doi:10.1177/002076409804400402.

Ayers, J.W., Althouse, B.M., Allem, J.P., Rosenquist, J.N. & Ford, D.E., (2013). Seasonality in seeking mental health information on Google. *American Journal of Preventive Medicine*, *44*(5), 520–525. doi:10.1016/j.amepre.2013.01.012.

Bäärnhielm, S., & Ekblad, S., (2000). Turkish migrant women encountering health care in Stockholm: A qualitative study of somatization and illness meaning. *Culture, Medicine and Psychiatry*, *24*(4), 431–452. www.link.springer.com/article/10.1023/A:1005671732703.

Berkman, L. F., & Glass, T. (2000). Social integration, social networks, social support, and health. *Social Epidemiology*, *1*, 137–173. www.ncbi.nlm.nih.gov/pmc/articles/PMC3455910/.

Bhandari, N.Y.S., & Jung, K. (2014). Seeking health information online: Does limited healthcare access matter? *Journal of the American Medical Informatics Association*, *21*(6), 1113–1117. doi:10.1136/amiajnl-2013-002350.

Bryant, C. A. (1982). The impact of kin, friend and neighbor networks on infant feeding practices: Cuban, Puerto Rican and Anglo families in Florida. *Social Science and Medicine*, *16*(20), 1757–1765. www.sciencedirect.com/science/article/pii/0277953682902696.

Carroll, J. A., & McCarthy, R. (2010, November). Geekdom for Grrrls health: Australian undergraduate experiences developing and promoting women's health in cyberspace. In *International Conference of Education, Research and Innovation Proceedings* (Vol. 3), Melia Castilla Madrid, Madrid.

Chen, W., & Choi, A. S. K. (2011). Internet and social support among Chinese migrants in Singapore. *New Media and Society*, *13*(7), 1067–1084. doi:10.1177/1461444810396311.

Dunkel-Schetter, C., Sagrestano, L. M., Feldman, P., & Killingsworth, C. (1996). Social support and pregnancy: A comprehensive review focusing on ethnicity and culture. In G. R. Pierceand & I.G. Sarason (Eds.), *Handbook of social support and the family* (pp. 375–412). New York: Springer.

Eysenbach, G., Powell, J., Englesakis, M., Rizo, C., & Stern, A. (2004). Health related virtual communities and electronic support groups: Systematic review of the effects of online peer to peer interactions', *British Medical Journal*, *328*(7449), 1166. doi:10.1136/bmj.328.7449.1166.

Fox, S. (2011). *The social life of health information 2011.* Pew Internet and American Life Project. Retrieved October 10, 2016 from www.pewinternet.org/files/old-media/Files/Reports/2011/PIP_Social_Life_of_Health_Info.pdf.

Furnham, A. (1988), The adjustment of sojourners. In Y. Y. Kim & W.B. Gudykunst (Eds.), *Cross-cultural adaptation: Current approaches* (pp. 42–61). Newbury Park, CA: Sage.

Goodall, K. T., Newman, L. A., & Ward, P. R. (2014). Improving access to health information for older migrants by using grounded theory and social network analysis to understand their information behaviour and digital technology use. *European Journal of Cancer Care*, *23*(6), 728–738. doi:10.1111/ecc.12241.

Hall, B. J., Chen, W., Wu, Y., Zhou, F., & Latkin, C. (2014). Prevalence of potentially traumatic events, depression, alcohol use, and social network supports among Chinese migrants: An epidemiological study in Guangzhou, China. *European Journal of Psychotraumatology,* [S.l.], 5, Dec. 2014. doi:10.3402/ejpt.v5.26529.

Hampshire, K.R., & Owusu, S.A. (2013). Grandfathers, Google, and dreams: Medical pluralism, globalization, and new healing encounters in Ghana. *Medical Anthropology*, *32*(3), 247–265. doi:10.1080/01459740.2012.692740.

Hechanova, M. R. M., Tuliao, A. P., Teh, L. A., Alianan Jr, A. S., & Acosta, A. (2013). Problem severity, technology adoption, and intent to seek online counseling among overseas Filipino workers. *Cyberpsychology, Behavior, and Social Networking*, *16*(8), 613–617. doi:10.1089/cyber.2012.0648.

Kim, H. K., & McKenry, P. C. (1998). Social networks and support: A comparison of African Americans, Asian Americans, Caucasians, and Hispanics. *Journal of Comparative Family Studies*, *29*(2), 313–334. www.jstor.org/stable/41603567?seq=1#page_scan_tab_contents.

Kristjánsdóttir, E. S., & DeTurk, S. (2013). Cultural insiders to cultural outsiders: Structure, identity, and communication in the adaptation of domestic, involuntary migrants. *Howard Journal of Communications*, *24*(2), 194–211. doi:10.1080/10646175.2013.776340.

Kuo, W. H., & Tsai, Y. M. (1986). Social networking, hardiness and immigrant's mental health. *Journal of Health and Social Behavior*, *27*(2), 133–149. www.jstor.org/stable/2136312.

Lang, T. (2011). Advancing global health research through digital technology and sharing data. *Science*, *331*(6018), 714–717. doi:10.1126/science.1199349.

Lober, W. B., & Flowers, J. L. (2011). Consumer empowerment in health care amid the internet and social media. *Seminars in Oncology Nursing*, *27*(3), 169–182. doi:10.1016/j.soncn.2011.04.002.

Lupton, D. (2015). Health promotion in the digital era: A critical commentary. *Health Promotion International*, *30*(1), 174–183. doi:10.1093/heapro/dau091.

MacKenzie, L., & Guntarik, O. (2015). Rites of passage: Experiences of transition for forced Hazara migrants and refugees in Australia. *Crossings: Journal of Culture and Migration*, *6*, 59–80. doi:10.1386/cjmc.6.1.59_1.

Miller, E. A., & West, D. M. (2009). Where's the revolution? Digital technology and health care in the internet age. *Journal of Health Politics, Policy and Law*, *34*(2), 261–284. doi:10.1215/03616878-2008-046.

Newman, L., Biedrzycki, K., & Baum, F. (2012). Digital technology use among disadvantaged Australians: Implications for equitable consumer participation in digitally-mediated communication and information exchange with health services. *Australian Health Review*, *36*(2), 125–129. doi:10.1071/AH11042.

Newman, M. W., Lauterbach, D., Munson, S. A., Resnick, P., & Morris, M. E. (2011, March). 'It's not that I don't have problems, I'm just not putting them on Facebook': Challenges and opportunities in using online social networks for health. *Proceedings of the ACM 2011 conference on Computer supported cooperative work*, 341–350. doi:10.1145/1958824.1958876.

O'Mara, B. (2013). Social media, digital video and health promotion in a culturally and linguistically diverse Australia. *Health Promotion International*, *28*(3), 466–476. doi:10.1093/heapro/das014.

Perkins, J. M., Subramanian, S. V., & Christakis, N. A. (2014). Social networks and health: A systematic review of sociocentric network studies in low-and middle-income countries. *Social Science and Medicine*, *125*, 60–78. doi:10.1016/j.socscimed.2014.08.019.

Postill, J. & Pink, S. (2012). Social media ethnography: The digital researcher in a messy web. *Media International Australia*, 145, 123–134. doi:10.1177/1329878X1214500114.

Renzaho, A. M., & Oldroyd, J. C. (2014). Closing the gap in maternal and child health: A qualitative study examining health needs of migrant mothers in Dandenong, Victoria, Australia. *Maternal and Child Health Journal*, *18*(6), 1391–1402. doi:10.1007/s10995-013-1378-7.

Ryan, L., Sales, R., Tilki, M., & Siara, B. (2008). Social networks, social support and social capital: The experiences of recent Polish migrants in London. *Sociology*, *42*(4), 672–690. doi:10.1177/0038038508091622.

Song, X., Yan, X., & Li, Y. (2015). Modelling liking networks in an online healthcare community: An exponential random graph model analysis approach. *Journal of Information Science*, *41*(1), 89–96. doi:10.1177/0165551514558179.

Stansfeld, S. A. (2006). Social support and social cohesion. In M. Marmot & R. Wilkinson (Eds.), *Social Determinants of Health* (pp. 148–171). Oxford: Oxford University Press.

Valle, R. O., & Bensussen, G. (1985). Hispanic social networks, social support, and mental health. In W. A. Vega & M. A. Miranda (Eds.), *Stress and hispanic mental health: Relating research to service delivery* (pp. 159–173). Washington, DC: US Government Printing Office.

Viken, B., Lyberg, A., & Severinsson, E. (2015). Maternal health coping strategies of migrant women in Norway. *Nursing Research and Practice*. (Article ID 878040, 11 pages), doi:10.1155/2015/878040.

Yebei, V.N. (2000). Unmet needs, beliefs and treatment-seeking for infertility among migrant Ghanaian women in the Netherlands. *Reproductive Health Matters*, *8*(16), 134–141. doi:10.1016/S0968-8080(00)90195-2.

9 Violence against Migrant Women Workers (MWWs) and the Role of Information Communication Technologies (ICTs)

Bolanle A. Olaniran

Theoretical Background and Overview

The past decades have seen a significant increase in the number of women migrants. However, the increase in the number is also accompanied by an increase in women autonomous migration as main economic providers for their families. Thus, the trend towards autonomous migration by women has justified the use of the feminization of migration theory. This theory called for increased attention to gender differences between male and female migration given that both genders have different migrant experiences (Boyd & Grieco, 2003; Internationalis, 2010; Peres & Baeninger, 2016). Furthermore, the transformations for both men and women migrant workers have different and profound effects on family structure, power, and identity (Peres & Baeninger, 2016). Similarly, men and women face different challenges and vulnerabilities especially regarding susceptibility to violence, human rights abuses, discriminations, and health risks. Notwithstanding, when it comes to migration policy in the political realms, framing and response appear to be along the line of male issue. The lack of specific policy on women migrants is believed to have led to the exploitation of women, where they become prey to smugglers and traffickers along with employment under poor working conditions. These issues are explored in depth within this chapter.

Most research and literature on the subject of violence and abuse have focused specifically upon the issue of domestic violence or specific abuses. In particular, one area that has garnered incredible interest is the violence against women from their husbands, domestic or intimate male partners (Olaniran & Rodriguez, 2013). This idea underscores the nature of emotion involved in abuses and violence when addressing migrant women workers (MWW). For instance, it has been discovered that women are more emotionally and economically dependent on the same individuals who abuse them to the extent that they often feel a sense of hopelessness due to the inability to escape their circumstances (Olaniran & Rodriguez, 2013).

The emotionality and economic dependency of women suffering from abuses and violence can be extended to the plight of women who are migrant workers. These plights are intensified by the abuses and violence these women suffer at the hand of their employers and their spouses. This is an area of research deserving increased focus, but to date an area that has not been adequately addressed. Furthermore, the notions of emotion and economic dependency among women, in particular migrant women (MW), can serve as a way to explore the complex dynamics of abuses and violence along with relevant coping mechanisms for migrant women workers. Therefore, this chapter explores why women become migrant workers along with the nature of violence against migrant women workers in general. Other issues addressed include: how international agencies deal with issues of violence against migrant women and the role information communication technologies (ICTs) play in addressing or alleviating the stress of violence on women migrant workers. Similarly, addressing violence against MWWs will extend the discourse about the issue beyond the mere categorization of it as a human rights issue to include issues that impact or undermine public health.

The use of ICTs to support and facilitate interactions on the Web has increased over the past ten years in the amount of actively involved users, communities, and organizations (Huysman, 2014). As far as migrant women workers are concerned, ICTs and especially mobile phones can empower migrants in meeting *existential needs*, more specifically, finding employment or housing. This is because the acquisition and low cost of mobile devices and, in particular, mobile phones facilitate their use in populations with many low income levels (Qui, 2014). At the same time, ICTs also allow MWW to stay in touch and fulfill parenting obligations with children or family left behind in the home country.

Similarly, support groups and services enabled through ICTs, web 2.0 applications, and mobile phones provide a unique type of community where individuals (i.e., migrant women workers) who have experienced violence can understand, access support, and interact with others—particularly victims/survivors—about the issues and resources for addressing violence against them (Olaniran & Rodriguez, 2013). The next section looks at the relationship between globalization and migration.

Globalization's impact on migration is very real and often explains its cause. For instance, as globalization continues to be the norm, individuals, like women, are in search of better economic opportunities that are not available or difficult to obtain in their countries of origin (Internationalis, 2010). There are other environmental structures such as war that necessitate a woman's need to flee her home country regardless of whether she wants to or not. This is quite often the case with those in ISIS and war-torn regions. Some women migrate independent of their spouses and/or family to seek work across the globe to support their families. This independent migration makes them vulnerable to violence.

Consequently, ICTs' role in providing support for MWWs as victims is important in navigating this potentially dangerous phenomenon. The next section examines the nature of violence against MWWs.

Nature of Violence against Migrant Women Workers

Regardless of ethnic categorization of MWWs, there appear to be common experiences among immigrant women in their host countries. Some of these include, but are not limited to, social class, limited host-language skills, isolation from family, lack of access to dignified jobs, uncertain legal status, and subsequent accruing rights (e.g. Berry, 2005). Together, all of these factors contribute to violence against women. Abraham (2000) reported in her study of South Asian women in the US that immigrant specific factors intensify the already vulnerable position due to gender, class, and race of immigrant women in domestic-violence situations. Furthermore, it needs to be said that there are two types of violence against MWWs: violence during employment and domestic violence. However, these two categories are not mutually exclusive.

Immigrants in general face some challenges when they resettle in a foreign country. A number of factors influence their experience, including the resources they bring to the host country and those they find when they arrive. These assets include their occupation, education, and, importantly, the social networks that await them (Menjívar, 2000). Hence, some studies found that immigrant women were able to establish informal networks accordingly (Menjívar, 2000). Others, however, observed that immigrant women arrive with disadvantages in social status and basic human capital resources relative to their male counterparts (Bui & Morash, 1999). Other times immigrant women find themselves unable to participate or navigate the same networks like their male cohorts (Abraham, 2000; Huysman, 2014; Rodriguez, 1993). In some instances, men serve as intermediaries between the women and community resources. Similarly, when women are able to navigate available resources on their own, their male partners may determine whether women can use those resources (Menjivar & Salcido, 2002). When MWWs enter a host country, they may not know the language and the culture that would further isolate them from interacting with members of the host environment. Such isolation has been suggested to exacerbate violence against MWW in the sense that it is easier for men to control these women, both emotionally and physically (Sabina, Cuevas, & Zadnik, 2015). Because of isolation, men are able to gain control over resources that could offer legal, financial, and/or emotional support to these women.

Therefore, conflicts often arise when women establish links in their communities. For instance, it was discovered that when Guatemalan and Salvadoran women in the United States received information on domestic violence and their rights at community organizations, their partners were not supportive of such knowledge (Menjívar, 2000). In other cases, isolation has proven to have fatal consequences. A case in point was when the Tamil women in Canada were faced with isolation—compounded by a sense of powerlessness, which led several Asian Indian women to jump to their deaths from their apartments (Morrison, Guruge, & Snarr, 1999). The authors of the study attributed these suicides to isolation culminating in a sense of helplessness, where the women felt that there were no other options, because other people in the community were not even aware of their existence until the suicide. Isolation also brings a sense of dependency on MWW where an abusive partner gains power and control, especially after immigration.

From a different standpoint is the role of culture (i.e., native culture and host culture) and its impact on MWW's predisposition to intimate partner violence (IPV). In particular, women seldom have the support of their family members who remain behind in their home countries (Mayock, Sheridan, & Parker, 2015). In some instance when MWWs live close to family and friends in the host countries, there is an expectation from family members that the MWW maintain cultural values and beliefs that are prevalent in the home countries. This is especially true when dealing with gender roles (Mayock *et al.*, 2015). Consequently, such cultural beliefs are deemed to be suspect to the acceptability of the domestic violence, and hence further isolate MWW even when surrounded by relatives and friends (Mayock *et al.*, 2015). Furthermore, when a migrant woman is involved in an abusive relationship, local shelters and/or organizations in charge of helping abusive women have the unrealistic expectations of wanting them to leave their homes in other to receive assistance or services. If a woman decides to leave her abusive partner, often she will need more support services than a shelter is able to provide (Mayock *et al.*, 2015; Tam *et al.*, 2015). There are other factors that may contribute to MWW domestic violence, including situations where the male or abusive partners are the sole income providers and hence decide to withhold economic support from the partner (Sabina, et al., 2015).

Non-drinking migrant women face increased pressure to drink and use drugs (Allan, Clifford, Ball, Alston, & Meister, 2012). However, increases in alcohol and drug use have been associated with stress and other trauma and violent behaviors (Lee, Sulaiman-Hill, & Thompson, 2014; Szaflarski, Cubbins, Ying, 2011). In this way, alcohol was being used as a stress-coping mechanism and as a way to socialize with members of the host nation (Lee *et al.*, 2014; see also, Amundsen, 2012). Also, MWWs are more likely to be abused, shouted at, embarrassed, and forced to have unwanted sex with individuals who had been drinking or under the influence of other drugs. There appear to be fewer reported physical and sexual abuse incidents among MWWs due to under reporting, because of the shame associated with such abuse.

Migrant Women Workers' Contexts and Types of Workplaces

MWWs and the nature of their job along with the contextual locations of such jobs put them at risk for abuse. For instance, MWWs who worked as domestic workers or in agricultural settings are often subject to abuses and domestic violence. Cheng (1996) found that MWWs who live and work in their employers' houses reported fear of making mistakes, being misunderstood, terminated, assaulted verbally and physically, and at times being raped. Unfortunately, there appear to be little recourse for MWW who work as domestic workers based on the complexity of issue surrounding their employment. For one, migrant women pay employment agencies to help them find work, thus, they are primarily indebted to these agencies for a long period (sometime a year) before they can start to see any income to send back home to their family. Hence, quitting is rarely an option. Employers also paid the same agencies to locate the workers, to the extent that employers can confiscate a MWW's passport, withhold salaries and other basic necessities to safeguard against their quitting. A Frontline documentary *Rape on the Midnight Shift* (PBS, 2015) provides a vivid illustration of this abuse in the janitorial service sector that are preponderantly serviced by MWWs. Employers often threaten employees with deportation to protect themselves from legal action or even to safeguard themselves against being reported.

According to Piper (2003), the dominance of domestic service as an occupation among female migrants creates a gender-specific problem. For example, in the Middle East, foreign domestic helpers (usually women) are categorized as "other" and are outside any legal protection (Piper, 2003). In other countries, too, domestic service is not covered by national labor laws because the domestic sphere is not defined as a workplace. An additional problem is that the idea of rights is novel, thus, no legal frameworks and enforcement is in place in certain "transition countries" such as Vietnam and Cambodia (Piper, 2003).

The one sided nature of the imbalance of power experienced by MWW is believed to explain why some MW reported fear and threats from the moment they entered their employer's residence. Hence, MW domestic workers are often put in their place as servants and/or slaves instead of welcome guests in employer's households. Cheng (1996) links the power imbalance to some aspects of culture. For instance, the Chinese culture operates on the basis of hierarchy or power distance, such that MW who are domestic workers are at the bottom of the hierarchy, cannot challenge their employers because it would be communicatively incompetent and socially unacceptable even if there was no fiduciary obligation to consider.

Trafficking and Migrant Women as Sex Workers

It is a well-established fact that trafficking of women is a burgeoning global business (PBS, 2015). It is a business that is not restricted or exclusive to women, but a majority of the victims are migrant women and children (Piper, 2003; Ucarer, 1999). MW are often trafficked for the sole purpose of engaging them in prostitution or serving as prostitutes who are otherwise referred to as sex workers (Piper, 2003; Ucarer, 1999). The aim in trafficking is to extort work or services from individuals through the use of deception, which may result in violence against MW.

As a case in point, studies on sex work in Southeast Asia show that women or young girls that were forced into sex work remain in it for several years (Rushing, Watts, & Rushing, 2005). In Arizona, it was reported that once MW arrive at their destination (i.e. the drop houses) it is not unusual for them to be kept against their will until family members agree to pay additional remunerations for their release (Simmons, Menjívar, & Téllez, 2015). Meshkovska, Siegel, Stutterheim, and Bos (2015) reported the plight of MWWs in both Argentina and the Dominican Republic where workers from lower social classes have little control in terms of the location of work, working conditions, and pay, and that they must comply with the terms of travel and work set by others even when they have reservations.

Young women who migrate for economic reasons are exceptionally vulnerable to sexual exploitation and violence (Meshkovska *et al.*, 2015; Rushing *et al.*, 2005). Consequently, many of the girls in this predicament suffer *physiological, emotional, and psychological* effects of sex work (Rushing *et al.*, 2005). For instance, Rushing *et al.* (2005) found sex workers in Vietnam reporting an inability to return home because they were considered as *city girls,* a connotation of tarnished reputations. Complicating the matter about trafficking is the law governing trafficking to the extent that there is no consensus on what counts as trafficking or labor exploitation. Meshkovska *et al.* (2015) alluded to this issue when they claimed that because of the fear of US government economic sanction, Argentina and the Dominican Republic label all forms of migrant labor exploitation as trafficking. At the same time, US trafficking law is believed to systematically disregard significant exploitation of migrants' labor. The same laws combine sex trafficking with trafficking in general (Meshkovska *et al.*, 2015).

Social Rights and Migrant Women

When MWWs take on the role as main income provider, they have a tendency to leave husbands and children behind in their country of origin. This can lead to a huge array of problems and strain on the women and families' lives. No Asian country, however, currently offers, or even contemplates providing, family reunification policies. However, Asian countries are not alone. Even in the US, reunification for migrants is predicated on citizenship for the most part, and the length of time to accomplish this may not make it worthwhile.

Also, when it comes to rights, the "rights of states" trumps the "rights of migrants" from an international law perspective. The states or countries usually reserve the right to set the conditions under which foreigners may enter and reside (Piper, 2003). Unfortunately, such laws often trample on certain social justice that MWW are entitled to. For example, migrants with a valid work permit tend to be in a better position than undocumented migrants in many parts of Asia and elsewhere around the globe. Furthermore, it has been shown that the nature of a country's economy and economic activities are important factors for MW when choosing a destination for residence. For instance, Piper (2003) noted that while Malaysia and Singapore receive proportionately more migrant laborers, Japan, because of its influential position within the regional political economy and its booming entertainment industries, absorb the majority of MWWs. Piper was quick to point out, however, that *entertainment* does not mean prostitution. In fact, Piper noted that all of the Filipino women he interviewed in 1997 had at least a college degree, but they made up the bulk of foreign entertainers in Japan.

Migrant Women Workers' Health & Well Being

As women migrate from rural areas to cities or cross borders for economic reasons, there is an increase in sex work as a global occurrence coupled with the level of HIV infections and other sexually transmitted diseases. For instance, the number of individuals infected with HIV is steadily increasing, and sex work has been attributed as the primary mode of transmission. This is especially true in Vietnam and Central Asia (Gilbert, Shaw, Terlikbayeva, McCrimmon, & Zhussupov, 2015). Similarly, Gilbert *et al.* (2015) found Central Asia as one of the few regions in the world where the HIV epidemic is on the rise, especially in heterosexual transmission (UNAIDS, 2012).

Perhaps one of the most notable finding in research is the association between intimate partner violence (IPV) and HIV/STI transmission in MWWs in Central Asia (Breiding, Chen, & Black, 2014; Gilbert *et al.*, 2015). For example, out of 225 participants, about 30 perhaps reported experiencing physical, sexual, or injurious IPV in their lifetime. Physical violence was most common, experienced by 28 percent of participants, while 18 percent reported sexual violence and 20 percent reported other forms of violence that caused injury (Gilbert *et al.*, 2015). The findings indicate that migrant women are at a significantly elevated risk of experiencing IPV compared to the general population of women in Central Asia.

Along the same line, young migrant women have been found to be exposed to high risk, aggressive behavior, physical violence, and forced sex (Raymond *et al.*, 2002). These women also feel they do not have control in how they choose to participate in sexual acts. This is especially true given that sex workers do not have the power to negotiate safe sexual practices and they often work under the threat of fear of violence (Breiding *et al.*, 2015; PBS, 2015).

Recommendations for MWWs

Obviously, the issues facing MWW are complex in nature. Thus, it will take a more comprehensive approach to deal with the problems. Two approaches may be of value in stemming the problems facing MWWs. One approach is to address individual needs, while the other is to focus on the group or societal concerns. However, it is important to understand that both of these approaches are not mutually exclusive propositions. The first looks at the role of information communication technologies (ICTs) in dealing with issues facing today's MWWs.

ICTs and MWWs

Earlier, this chapter held a discussion to explain that one of the primary reasons individuals migrate from their countries to another country is economic in nature. MWWs face challenges with qualification or issues of employability when they get to the host countries. Because some may not have the necessary or basic qualification to secure decent jobs, or jobs in their area of expertise, either due to lack of competence in the host language or lack of accreditation required for a specified job, MWWs must settle for low wage jobs or take whatever they can to sustain themselves. However, in the process of *abject coping or compliance* by migrants and especially MW, they open themselves to other forms of abuse such as isolation and, physical, emotional, along with sexual abuse in some instances.

ICTs like mobile phones with internet access capabilities offer MWs the opportunity to seek help on how to address their challenges. ICTs allow and can help MW break out of isolation, regardless of whether or not this isolation was self-imposed, to seek support from others who have similar experiences. These technologies can also allow MW the ability to call others' attention to their problem (Jin, Wen, Fan, & Wang, 2013; Olaniran & Rodriguez, 2013). For instance, women indicate that a mobile phone replaces the role of the family in reporting violence. Similarly, by encouraging the use of ICT for support and information services, MWWs can access, retrieve information, and develop their own understanding based on their own personal experiences and needs.

In 2006, an OECD report indicated that up to 30 percent of employability is somehow attributed to ICT skills and/or training (OECD, 2006). As increased globalization becomes the norm in both developed and developing countries, it is no surprise that there is increased penetration of ICTs even within industries that are not customarily known for their technological process (e.g. agriculture, construction, and service industries) (Garrido, Sullivan, & Gordon, 2010).

Beyond skill provision, ICTs also offer added value to the lives of MW in the areas of sociability, cultural adaptability, and other intangible benefits that may be difficult to measure. For instance, Madianou (2012) found in the ethnographic research of Filipina migrants in the UK that ICTs (i.e., internet, mobile phones, and social media networks) allow the MW to perform their motherly duties and obligations from a long distance. The study suggests that "ICTs can also be seen as solutions (albeit difficult ones) to the cultural contradictions of migration and motherhood and the 'accentuated ambivalence' they engender" (Madianou, 2012, p. 277). Similarly, a study of MW in Singapore found Filipina domestic workers reported mobile phone use alleviated their stress level by increasing the level of social and emotional support, which aided their psychological well-being (Chib, Wilkin, & Hua, 2013).

Along the area of socio-emotional support, ICTs in a way provide *microsolutions* to *macroproblems* through the different kinds of information they enable users to access (Qiu, 2014). Other instances of how ICTs can solve problems include how:

- ICTs allow Filipino migrant women to still perform their parenting duties remotely.
- ICTs facilitate polymedia—use of multiple media services.
- ICTs allow individuals to record events of poor working conditions.

Additionally, smartphones provide migrant women the opportunity to develop or produce *worker generated content* (WGC), which allows others to understand the plight of MWW (see Qiu, 2014).

Furthermore, ICTs can assist migrant women who are trying to break the cycle of violence and abuse by helping them to locate shelters such as Casa Rut (House of Ruth) that assist trafficked women in southern Italy (Caretta, 2015). In essence, ICTs empower migrant women to take better control of their lives and problems by increasing options, opportunities, and access to available resources in a way that is otherwise not available before.

At the same time, one needs to acknowledge the challenges to ICTs, especially as it relates to access and the digital divide. Olaniran (2007) alluded to general social challenges including, but not limited to the digital divide, illiteracy, and technology illiteracy. At times MW have access to ICTs in their own homes, but are afraid that their abusers may be monitoring their usage or may ultimately prevent them from using ICTs. After all, violence against MW revolves around control and power.

Similarly, given the socio-economic status of MWWs, access to technology may be difficult. Some may not be able to afford the cost of access to computers, mobile phones, or Internet service and thus, they may have to rely on public assistance through the library or local shelters (Garrido *et al.*, 2010; Olaniran & Rodriguez, 2013). For instance, when one talks about digital divide in ICT usage, traditionally one thinks of the haves and have-nots, which is often compounded by the fact that individuals from Economically Developed Countries (EDCs) usually enjoy more readily available access to ICTs than those from Less Economically Developed Countries (LEDCs) (Olaniran, 2007). However, there are times when individuals may have access and affordance to ICTs, yet they are unable to use them. This may be the case with victims of violence and, in particular, migrant women, whose abusers may deny them the opportunity to use ICTs either temporarily or in perpetuity (Olaniran & Rodriguez, 2013).

Group-Based Social Support for MWW

At the group level, social structures and the ways initiatives are offered affect how MW address their needs and the relevant challenges they face on a daily basis. Accordingly, given the lack of state sponsored programs or recognition of migrant workers, it is important that non-government organizations (NGOs) play an active role in helping MW. Garrido *et al.* (2010) found increased use of NGO services among MW. In essence, the researchers conclude that friends/families and NGOs are the most important networks through which MW are able to get jobs, improve their ICT skills, and have access to or use ICTs. Furthermore, NGOs can assist in promoting emotional, social, economic support, and cultural integration in advancing many of the required competences necessary in surviving the demands of today's labor markets (Caretta, 2015; Garrido et al., 2010). NGOs also serve as a channel for finding employment, either by employing women directly, or facilitating employment through a network of links (Garrido *et al.*, 2010). ICTs in particular can assist NGOs to create a database relating to employment opportunities, secure humanitarian visas, and locate/coordinate relevant services for MWWs. The Goodwill Company in USA promotes itself on how it helps migrant women and underprivileged people secure employment within its company. Similarly, NGOs can offer critical services including providing ICT training, as well as free or low-cost access to PCs and Internet. Furthermore, NGO ICT training could be even more valuable to MWs if the NGOs' services provide some form of official certification that might benefit the MWs.

NGO services are also critical in allowing MWW to access and navigate health care services and systems. It has been established that MWW often neglect or fail to seek health services. Hence, MW may not be getting the preventive health care services needed. Thus, by the time they seek such medical services their condition may already be too critical to be effectively addressed. For example, a lack of regular women exams may lead to terminal and infectious diseases like breast cancer, TB and HIV, among others. There are other consequences to such problems like the cost of treatment may be astronomical at the point of care and consequently overburden the host state's medical system. However, NGOs with ICTs can foster the deployment of e-health or mobile health and allow MWWs the necessary help they need before the problem impacts the society at large.

Similarly, NGOs can assist MW in the delivery of more efficient public services and, tailor to the needs of MW (Caretta, 2015; Rodriguez, 1993). For instance, NGO can assist health care professionals in screening for abuse among MW such that health care professionals are able to treat beyond the symptoms and address the primary issue. It is recommended that medical centers and those who care for MW should have information leaflets about abuse, along with contacts or referrals of where to seek help. In particular, Rodriguez (1993) recommends that once abuse is confirmed, documentation about the type, occurrence, location, and any other pertinent factors is essential in helping victims. There is also the need for health professionals and NGOs to figure out a way to develop trust with migrant women in order for them to provide accurate information (Caretta, 2015). In essence, proper screening is an important *intervention strategy* that can reduce *morbidity and mortality* from abusers (Rodriguez, 1993).

It is also imperative that health service providers balance culture with situations. For instance, Rodriguez (1993) suggests looking at power and control from the context of culture. She illustrates that

> while Hispanic farmworker women generally do not go out alone (without husbands and/or family members), male control over their use of health care resources is not an issue of cultural values—it is an issue of power and control.
>
> (p. 3)

Implications

The implications from this chapter are twofold. One is the technological and the other is political in nature.

ICTs

Being a migrant in a new land is challenging enough regardless of gender categories. However, being MW tend to be more complicated, given the added stress women must endure from the different roles they play as wife, mother, and income providers. These women face tremendous challenges in terms of violence and abuse from members of the host societies who are anti-immigrant. Abuses also stem from their own family members through the shunning of behaviors that do not reflect the role and culture a woman is believed to belong, including intimate partner violence.

Evidence have shown that ICTs can offer a way to acquire resources and help alleviate some of these problems (Olaniran & Rodriguez, 2013). Chib *et al.* (2013) found that mobile phones help reduce stress by increasing access to social support. However, this reduction occurs more so for women than for men migrant workers. Thus, the different findings for men and women regarding ICT as a resource suggests the need for both government agencies and other social groups to help migrant workers as individuals. Organizations providing assistants must remain careful not to treat all immigrant groups as homogenous, but rather as various groups with idiosyncratic needs. MWWs need additional type of services that do not apply to men.

The employability of MWWs has also come into question as a matter to help substantiate their socio-economic survival within their host country. A policy that considers and integrates international education of professionals such as nurses, teachers, and engineers may be of value (Salami & Nelson, 2014). There needs to be a measure that fosters recognition or provides accreditation for education obtained abroad. Although Canada is now putting in place policies for faster processing of work permits to address the situation, the level of deskilling across professions is not unique to Canada alone. Cuban (2010) and Tung (2000) found evidence of deskilling in the United Kingdom and the United States through the examination of other immigration programs in their respective countries. There is evidence to support the positive impact of ICT access and employment opportunities. NGOs can help MW figure a way to provide them with ICT training in an integrated manner where the focus is not just technical, but also in the development of needed social skills (Codagnone & Kluzer, 2011). Codaglone and Kluzer (2011) found that when ICTs skills are provided in a way where migrants are able to apply it to every aspect of their lives including language learning, social support and helping children with schoolwork.

Political

The social injustice and accruing damages in terms of racial and gender inequalities resulting from global capitalism is nonetheless vivid in the lives of migrant workers. Structurally, female migration flow reveals the underlining issue of the lack of economic opportunities in the home countries that drive women, especially professionals, to the conclusion that seeking a temporary job in a host country is more beneficial when compared to their current future prospects of continuation within their native country. Therefore, women from poor environments are willing to risk their lives to migrate to another country. Unfortunately, many of them are willing to downgrade their skills and take on jobs like cleaning hotel rooms and working as domestic caregivers in what has been termed as brain waste (Martin, 2004; Internationalis, 2010).

It is imperative as a part of the solution for governments in native countries to provide risk communication and public service announcements highlighting the dangers in the allure of overseas migrant workers (e.g. unstable nature, low wages, poor working conditions, and so on). Educating families about the challenges and dangers facing migrants should be a primary objective undertaken by any government. After all, it has been suggested that aside from women being able to gain increased freedom, when all things are considered, there remain no other accruing benefits to becoming migrant workers (Internationalis, 2010; Qiu, 2014). Governments must also take additional measures and steps to increase job opportunities such that individuals, especially women, would not want to leave their families to pursue dangerous migration.

Some host governments are putting in place laws to make it easier for migrant women to get help while grassroots local organizations are providing amenities where victims can seek services. However, certain barriers include, but are not limited to, language and culture and often make it difficult for migrant women to use those services (e.g. Tam *et al.*, 2015). There are some social services at the local level that take language and culture differences into consideration; Menjivar and Salcido (2002) argue that such services are seldom the exception. From another standpoint, government regulations such as Title VII that aim to protect MW from domestic violence are often counterproductive. Title VII is a provision that authorizes migrants to enter USA legally and work as seasonal workers. The regulation was designed to protect workers through the migrant and seasonal workers' protection (AWPA) provision if they ever want to file complain about harassment.

Title VII is considered inadequate in offering MW who are seasonal farmworkers protection. The lack of protection is due to the nature of their jobs (Conry, 2015). First, AWPA offers no protection for women against sexual violence or harassment. Second, a MW has to be in legal status to file complaints. However, about 80 percent of migrant women workers have either stayed past their required visa or have an illegal status (Conry, 2015). Hence, there is a need to amend the provisions of AWPA to specifically cover an illegal citizen's right as human beings and to specifically address sexual violence.

The same can be said for the International Labor Organization to pass a law such that there are no different interpretations among countries. MWWs need protection from sexual violence and other abuses. For instance, in 2008, Jordan amended its labor law to extend protections to migrant domestic workers (Human Rights Watch, 2009; Murray, 2012; Wilcke, 2011). Under the reform, domestic workers are required to have eight hours of continuous rest each day, limited to ten hours of work per day, and granted one day off per week (Human Rights Watch, 2011; Murray, 2012). Although this sets a precedent, the Jordanian law still lags behind other developed countries in terms of its employer stipulation. In Singapore, the law stipulates that employers would forfeit a $5,000 security bond for every migrant worker that they fail to pay in a timely manner (Human Rights Watch, 2011). Furthermore, the Singapore government, in contrast to Jordan, is considered to have a proven track record in enforcing the law by prosecuting the offending employers for non-payment or for offering sub-standard accommodations (Human Rights Watch, 2011).

The pervasiveness of partner violence against migrant women, necessitates the need for INS officers, immigration judges, and state court judges to undergo training and/or education programs in IPV (Raj & Silverman, 2002). Specifically, MWWs may be unable to seek protection under the existing Violence Against Women Act (VAWA) if they are not legal residents, but judges who are trained about IPV may be more sensitive to the need for MWWs to leave their abusers and access services/shelters in an attempt to protect themselves and their children (Raj & Silverman, 2002). Similarly, the collaboration among judges, INS, social workers, and other law enforcement officers, along with battered MWWs, may lead to designing an effective program to effectively help address IPV. It stands to reason, however, that any government or law can only go so far. It will be up to individuals and potential MW employers to operate in a moral and humane manner.

Perhaps ICTs may be of use in keeping employers accountable. Given the fact that the world is moving more towards the idea of a global village, the ability to digitize, access and store data via ICTs is essential. It may be necessary for governments or even grass roots organizations such as NGOs to keep a data base of employers who have violated or committed acts of violence against immigrants, in particular MWWs. Such a database can be accessed in a manner similar to the Better Business Bureau for migrants to see prior to a decision to commit to work for such employer. From this standpoint, ICTs can serve as means of empowering MWWs and perhaps protect them from potential harm.

Conclusion

Women experience migration in a different way than men. Thus, it is important that gender is factored in as one discusses issues facing migrant workers. Specifically, it is important that any social or political policy developed to address the plight of migrant workers take into consideration the fact that the specific needs of women, such as health and emotional well-being, that are different from men's. Furthermore, it is possible to consider women as having a higher risk than men when one considers the issues of trafficking and smuggling. Along this spectrum, some have reached the conclusion that the risk MW face in the process may not justify the risk they take on. However, when looking at possible solutions, ICTs may help empower women in alleviating some of the challenges in terms of networking with other women migrant workers, procuring or soliciting necessary help, speaking out against abuses they suffer to call public's attention to their concerns, and refusing to accept any form of abuses complacently or as powerless individuals would. After all, there is increasing need for MW to speak out and claim their rights (Internationalis, 2010).

There is also the need to approach the study of women migrant workers from interdisciplinary perspectives (Peres & Baeninger, 2016). The interdisciplinary gender study of migrant workers can elude the social processes in which the roles of women are modified and how these modifications interact or impacts other familial and relational roles. Finally, as populism and backlash against immigrants intensifies, it is imperative that studies on MW factor how this impacts policies and affects MWWs.

References

Abraham, M. (2000). *Speaking the unspeakable: Marital violence among South Asian immigrants in the United States*. New Brunswick, NJ: Rutgers University Press.

Allan, J., Clifford, A., Ball, P., Alston, M., & Meister, P. (2012). 'You're less complete if you haven't got a can in your hand: Alcohol consumption and related harmful effects in rural Australia: The role and influence of cultural capital. *Alcohol and Alcoholism*, *47*, 624–629.

Amundsen, E. J. (2012). Low level of alcohol drinking among two generations of non-Western immigrants in Oslo: A multiethnic comparison. *BMC Public Health*, *12*, Article 535. doi:10.1186/1471-2458-12-535.

Berry, J. W. (2005). Acculturation: Living successfully in two cultures. *International Journal of Intercultural Relations*, *29*(6), 697–712.

Boyd, M., & Grieco, E. (2003). Women and migration: incorporating gender into international migration theory. *Migration Information Source*, *1*, 1–7.

Breiding, M. J., Basile, K. C., Smith, S. G., Black, M. C., & Mahendra, R. R. (2015). Intimate partner violence surveillance: Uniform definitions and recommended data elements, version 2.0. *Atlanta, GA: National Center for Injury Prevention and Control, Centers for Disease Control and Prevention*, *18*.

Breiding, M. J., Chen, J., & Black, M. C. (2014). *Intimate Partner Violence in the United States—2010*. Atlanta, GA: National Center for Injury Prevention and Control, Centers for Disease Control and Prevention.

Bui, H. N., & Morash, M. (1999). Domestic violence in the Vietnamese immigrant community: An exploratory study. *Violence against Women*, *5*(7), 769–795.

Caretta, M. A. (2015). Casa rut a multilevel analysis of a "Good Practice" in the social assistance of sexually trafficked Nigerian women. *Affilia*, 30(4), 546–559.

Cheng, S. J. A. (1996). Migrant women domestic workers in Hong Kong, Singapore and Taiwan: A comparative analysis. *Asian and Pacific Migration Journal*, *5*(1), 139–152.

Chib, A., Wilkin, H. A., & Hua, S. R. M. (2013). International migrant workers' use of mobile phones to seek social support in Singapore. *Information Technologies & International Development*, *9*(4), 19.

Codagnone, C., & Kluzer, S. (2011). *ICT for the social and economic integration of migrants into Europe*. European Union Centre in Taiwan.

Conry, C. (2015). Forbidden fruit: Sexual victimization of migrant workers in America's farmlands. *Hastings Women's Law Journal*, *26*, 121–145.

Cuban, S. (2010). It is hard to stay in England: Itineraries, routes and dead ends: An (im)mobility study of nurses who became careers. *Compare: A Journal of Comparative and International Education*, *40*, 185–98.

Garrido, M., Sullivan, J., & Gordon, A. (2010, December). Understanding the links between ICT skills training and employability: An analytical framework. *Proceedings of the 4th ACM/IEEE International Conference on Information and Communication Technologies and Development* (p. 15). ACM.

Gilbert, L., Shaw, S., Terlikbayeva, A., McCrimmon, T., Zhussupov, B., *et al.* (2015). Intimate Partner Violence and HIV Risks among Migrant Women in Central Asia. *Journal of AIDS Clinical Research*, *6*, 428. doi:10.4172/2155-6113.1000428.

Human Rights Watch. (2009, July 10). *Saudi Arabia: Shura council passes domestic worker protections*. Press Release from www.hrw.org/news/2009/07/10/saudi-arabia-shura-council-passes-domestic-worker-protections.

Human Rights Watch. (2011). How Jordanian Law Officials, Employers, and Recruiters fail abused migrant domestic workers, 27.Huysman, M. (2014). Knowledge Sharing, Communities, and Social Capital. *Communities of Practice: A Special Issue of Trends in Communication*, 77–100.

Internationalis, C. (2010). *The female face of migration: Background paper*. Available online at www.caritas.org/includes/pdf/backgroundmigration.pdf.

Jin, L., Wen, M., Fan, J. X., & Wang, G. (2012). Trans-local ties, local ties and psychological wellbeing among rural-to-urban migrants in Shanghai. *Social Science & Medicine*, *75*(2), 288–296.

Lee, S. K., Sulaiman-Hill, C. M., & Thompson, S. C. (2014). Alcohol experiences and concerns of newly arrived migrant women. *Sage Open*, 4(2), 2158244014530727.

Madianou, M. (2012), Migration and the accentuated ambivalence of motherhood: the role of ICTs in Filipino transnational families. *Global Networks*, *12*, 277–295. doi:10.1111/j.1471-0374.2012.00352.x.

Martin, S. F. (2004, December). Women and migration. *Consultative Meeting on "Migration and Mobility and how this movement affects Women", Malmo*.

Mayock, P., Sheridan, S., & Parker, S. (2015). 'It's just like we're going around in circles and going back to the same thing…' The Dynamics of Women's Unresolved Homelessness. *Housing Studies*, (ahead-of-print), 1–24.

Menjívar, C. (2000). *Fragmented ties: Salvadoran immigrant networks in America*. CA: Univ of California Press.

Menjivar, C., & Salcido, O. (2002). Immigrant women and domestic violence: Common experiences in different countries. *Gender and Society*, 16(6), 898–920.

Meshkovska, B., Siegel, M., Stutterheim, S. E., & Bos, A. E. (2015). Female sex trafficking: Conceptual issues, current debates, and future directions. *Journal of Sex Research*, *52*(4), 380–395.

Morrison, L., Guruge, S., & Snarr, K. A. (1999). Sri Lankan Tamil immigrants in Toronto: Gender, marriage patterns, and sexuality. In *Gender and immigration* (pp. 144–162). Palgrave Macmillan UK.

Murray, H. E. (2012). Hope for reform springs eternal: How the sponsorship system, domestic laws and traditional customs fail to protect migrant domestic workers in GCC countries. *Cornell International Law Journal, 45,* 462–484.

Olaniran, B. A. (2007). Challenges to implementing E-learning and lesser developed countries. In A. Edmundson (Ed.), *Globalized e-Learning Cultural Challenges* (pp. 18–34). NY: Idea Group.

Olaniran, B. A., & Rodriguez, N. (2013). ICT and healthcare: A closer look at the role of ICTs in providing support for female victims/survivors of domestic violence (DV). In M. Cruz-Cunha, I. Miranda, & P. Gonçalves (Eds.) *Handbook of research on ICTs and management systems for improving efficiency in healthcare and social care* (pp. 720–733). Hershey, PA: Medical Information Science Reference.

OECD (2006). Innovation and Knowledge-Intensive Service Activities. OECD, Paris, France.

PBS (2015, June 23). Frontline—Rape on the Midnight Shift. From www.pbs.org/wgbh/pages/frontline/rape-on-the-night-shift/.

Peres, R. & Baeninger, R. (2016). *Female migration: A theoretical and methodological debate in gender studies*. Presented at the International Union for the Scientific Studies on Population (IUSSP). www.iussp.org/sites/default/files/event_call_for_papers/Abstract_Gender_IUSSP_2.pdf.

Piper, N. (2003). Feminization of labor migration as violence against women: International, regional, and local nongovernmental organization responses in Asia. *Violence against Women*, *9*(6), 623–629.

Qiu, J. L. (2014). Communication & global power shifts "power to the people!": Mobiles, migrants, and social movements in Asia. *International Journal of Communication*, *8*, 16.

Raj, A., & Silverman, J. (2002). Violence against immigrant women the roles of culture, context, and legal immigrant status on intimate partner violence. *Violence against Women*, *8*(3), 367–398.

Raymond, J., D'Cunha, J., Dzuhayatin, S., Hynes, P., Rodriguez, Z., & Santos, A. (2002). *A comparative study of women trafficked in the migration process: Patterns, profiles and health consequences in five countries*. From: www.action.web.ca/home/catw/readingroom.shtml?x//17062&AA_EX_Session//8a2a713d2cc7972ec06d0ea8ba61b60c.

Rodriguez, R. (1993). Violence in transience: Nursing care of battered migrant women. *AWHONN's Clifical Issues*, *4*, 437–440.

Rushing, R., Watts, C., & Rushing, S. (2005). Living the reality of forced sex work: perspectives from young migrant women sex workers in northern Vietnam. *Journal of Midwifery & Women's Health*, *50*(4), e41–e44.

Sabina, C., Cuevas, C. A., & Zadnik, E. (2015). Intimate partner violence among Latino women: Rates and cultural correlates. *Journal of Family Violence*, *30*(1), 35–47.

Salami, B., & Nelson, S. (2014). The downward occupational mobility of internationally educated nurses to domestic workers. *Nursing Inquiry*, *21*(2), 153–161.

Simmons, W. P., Menjívar, C., & Téllez, M. (2015). Violence and vulnerability of female migrants in drop houses in Arizona: The predictable outcome of a chain reaction of violence. *Violence against Women*, *21*(5), 551–570.

Szaflarski, M., Cubbins, L. A., & Ying, J. (2011). Epidemiology of alcohol abuse among US immigrant populations. *Journal of Immigrant and Minority Health*, *13*, 647–658.

Tam, K. P. (2015). Understanding intergenerational cultural transmission through the role of perceived norms. *Journal of Cross-Cultural Psychology*, *46*(10), 1260–1266.

Tung, C. (2000). The cost of caring: The social reproductive labor of Filipina live-in home health caregivers. *Frontiers: A Journal of Women Studies*, *21*: 61–82.

Ucarer, E. M. (1999). Trafficking in women: Alternative migration or modern slave trade? In M. Meyer & E. Pruegl (Eds.), *Gender politics in global governance*. Boulder, CO: Rowman and Littlefield.

UNAIDS. (2012). *Report on the Global AIDS Epidemic, 2012*. Geneva, Switzerland: UNAIDS.

Wilcke, C. (2011). *Domestic Plight: How Jordanian Laws, Officials, Employers, and Recruiters Fail Abused Migrant Domestic Workers*. Human Rights Watch.

Part IV

Culturally Grounded and Community-Based Health Intervention for Migrants

10 The PEN-3 Cultural Model

A Critical Review of Health Communication for Africans and African Immigrants

James O. Olufowote & Johnson S. Aranda

In the wake of the devastating impact of the Ebola crisis in West Africa, the international community is identifying areas of growth as it grapples with how to improve its response to health crises in African nations. These considerations extend beyond Ebola as African nations struggle with other health problems such as cardiovascular disease, HIV/AIDS, infant and maternal mortality, malaria, and polio (Airhihenbuwa, Ford, & Iwelunmor, 2014; Belue *et al.*, 2009; Birn, Pillay, & Holtz, 2009). One important focus and area of growth for the international community—in its response to recent health crises in Africa—is knowledge of African cultures and cultural practices (e.g. burial traditions, cultural taboos, kinship care roles and patterns) and their positive as well as negative impacts on community health. An existing cultural model, PEN-3, popular in global health research, is uniquely qualified to contribute to this area of growth. Although PEN-3 has had a broad impact on global health research (see Iwelunmor, Newsome, & Airhihenbuwa, 2014), it has had less of an impact on the development of health campaigns and interventions in African nations.

This chapter forwards PEN-3 as a useful tool—for both research and campaign interventions—in the contemporary response to health crises in African nations[1]. The PEN-3 cultural model was developed by Dr. Collins O. Airhihenbuwa to foreground the role of the sociocultural context in assessments of and interventions into community health problems (Airhihenbuwa, 1990; Olufowote & Airhihenbuwa, 2014). The model's emphasis on the sociocultural context (e.g. community health beliefs and values and cultural traditions involving family and friends that nurture health behaviors) highlights some absences and deficits in the international community's initial response to the Ebola crisis. The letters P, E, and N stand for the three dimensions within each of the model's three domains. One domain contains the dimensions of perceptions, enablers, and nurturers. Another domain contains the dimensions of positive, existential, and negative. A third domain consists of the dimensions of person, extended family, and neighborhood. Airhihenbuwa developed PEN-3 in reaction to limitations he perceived in traditional health communication theories such as the Health Belief Model. In his evaluation of the uses of such theories to stem the tide of the HIV/AIDS epidemic in Africa, Airhihenbuwa argued they contain assumptions (e.g. individualism, lack of attention to context) that limit their relevance to non-Western communities (Airhihenbuwa & Obregon, 2000). Rather than focus on individual and psychological determinants of health (common in traditional health communication theories), PEN-3 problematizes the sociocultural factors that shape community health (Airhihenbuwa *et al.*, 2014). Moreover, whereas previous researchers positioned culture as a barrier to health in non-Western communities, PEN-3 positions culture as both a barrier to and an enabler of health (Airhihenbuwa & Webster, 2004).

This chapter contends that the international community's response to the Ebola crisis in West Africa exposed absences and deficits in knowledge of the cultures and cultural practices of African communities. This type of knowledge is crucial for anticipating the sociocultural factors that shape community health and to formulating more effective responses to contemporary health crises in Africa. To forward PEN-3 as a viable tool for the conduct of research and for the development of contemporary health interventions in African nations, this chapter reviews the defining elements of the PEN-3 model, considers a corpus of knowledge developed from the model's uses in Africa, outlines interventions for the recent Ebola crisis based on this corpus of knowledge, and provides a critical evaluation of the PEN-3 model that yields future directions for health communication campaigns and research in African contexts.

The PEN-3 Cultural Model

The PEN-3 model is one of several culture-centered approaches to health communication (Airhihenbuwa *et al.*, 2014; Dutta, 2015; Singhal & Rogers, 2003). Communication researcher Dr. Arvind Singhal used a forest and tree metaphor to contrast a culture-centered approach to health communication with the traditional individual-level approach to health communication. Culture-centered approaches focus on how the form of the forest and the roles and relationships among trees, rather than a single tree, shape health beliefs and behaviors (Singhal, 2003).

PEN-3 is also one of several ecological models of health communication (e.g. Airhihenbuwa, Makinwa, & Obregon, 2000; Lammers, Barbour, & Duggan, 2003; Sharf, 1993; Street, 2003). In general, ecological models of health communication consider the influence of contextual factors such as the media environment and laws/policies on health practices and interactions such as those between caregivers and people living with HIV/AIDS (PLWHA).

The Three Domains

PEN-3 consists of three major domains that are visually represented as three separate, yet overlapping, concentric circles. One domain is labeled as "relationships and expectations." Another domain is labeled as "cultural empowerment," and the third domain is labeled as "cultural identity" (Airhihenbuwa, 1995).

The first domain of the PEN-3 model, "relationships and expectations," focuses analysts' attention on three dimensions of culture that relate to health (i.e. perceptions, enablers, and nurturers). The first dimension of this domain, *perceptions*, is concerned with culturally-indigenous attitudes, beliefs, and values about a health problem (e.g. HIV/AIDS as caused by witchcraft). Perceptions are widely shared yet unobservable aspects of the socio-cultural landscape. For example, Iwelunmor, Sofolahan-Oladeinde, and Airhihenbuwa (2015) conducted focus group interviews with twenty-seven male PLWHA in South Africa to explore sociocultural factors influencing HIV disclosures. They found participants' perceptions of male identity influenced the decision to hide one's HIV status. The second dimension, *enablers*, is concerned with the resources that communities and societies provide for health (e.g. health care systems/workers). An example comes from Airhihenbuwa *et al.* (2009) who interviewed four hundred fifty-three South Africans to explore the role of culture in HIV stigma. They found enablers such as community services and the health care system shaping participants' experiences of stigma. The third dimension, *nurturers*, focuses on traditions involving family and friends that shape health practices. For instance, Sofolahan-Oladeinde and Airhihenbuwa (2014) interviewed fifteen women living with HIV/AIDS in Nigeria to understand male partners' support in childbearing decisions. Their findings highlighted the nurturing practices of different forms of male partner support.

The second domain of PEN-3, the "cultural empowerment" domain, contains the three dimensions of positive, existential, and negative. The first dimension, "*positive*," requires that analysts acknowledge the ways that culture, in the communities of concern, contribute positively to health. Such knowledge not only challenges the ideology of culture as a barrier to health, but can also inform health campaigns in the communities of concern. For example, Airhihenbuwa *et al.* (2009) found participants reporting positive destigmatizing perceptions of HIV that were brought about by people being open about their HIV status and PWLHA receiving support from friends and loved ones. The second dimension, *existential*, asks analysts to recognize unique aspects of the community's culture that make neither positive nor negative contributions to health. Airhihenbuwa *et al.* (2009) also found existential perceptions of HIV grounded in the local terms and slang used to represent HIV. The third dimension, *negative*, requires analysts to provide knowledge of the negative cultural contributions to health. For example, Airhihenbuwa *et al.* (2009) found their study's participants largely blaming women for HIV/AIDS.

The third domain of PEN-3, the "cultural identity" domain, contains the three dimensions of person, extended family, and neighborhood. This domain directs researchers' attention to the sociocultural context and promotes multiple points of campaign or intervention entry. To move the focus for interventions beyond the individual, this domain points to the intervention entry points of *person, extended family*, and *neighborhood*. Points of entry decisions are to be made in consultation and in partnership with community members (Airhihenbuwa *et al.*, 2009).

The Two Areas of Application

PEN-3 has two major areas of application: (1) assessing cultural communities with a health problem and (2) implementing and evaluating health campaigns (Airhihenbuwa *et al.*, 2014; Iwelunmor *et al.*, 2014). The model has mainly been used in the first area of application. To assess cultural communities with a health problem, analysts are encouraged to foreground community members' points of view through crossing the "relationships and expectations" domain (perceptions, enablers, nurturers) with the "cultural empowerment" domain (positive, existential, negative), thus creating a three-by-three, nine-cell grid. Within this grid, analysts record community members' assessments of positive perceptions, enablers, and nurturers of a health problem; existential perceptions, enablers, and nurturers; and negative perceptions, enablers, and nurturers of a health problem (Airhihenbuwa *et al.*, 2014; Airhihenbuwa & Webster, 2004). Yet, analysts are not required to use all three domains and all of their dimensions (see Mieh, Iwelunmor, & Airhihenbuwa, 2013; Okoror, Belue, Zungu, Adam, & Airhihenbuwa, 2014).

Although PEN-3 can be used to implement and to evaluate health campaigns (Airhihenbuwa *et al.*, 2009), it has rarely been used in this way. One example comes from Kannan, Sparks, Webster, Krishnakumar, and Lumeng (2010), who used PEN-3 to develop, implement, and evaluate a thirteen-week nutrition education intervention to promote the diets, physical activities, and biomedical behaviors of one hundred two young African-American women. The intervention resulted in forty-five percent of participants adopting dietary and biomedical behaviors.

Applications of PEN-3 in African Nations

Iwelunmor *et al.* (2014) reviewed forty-five studies that were based on the PEN-3 model. The studies were of various cultural communities including African-Americans, Chinese-Americans, Ghanaians, Hawaiians, Latinas, Mexican-Americans, Nigerians, and South Africans.

The researchers found three themes across these studies: the role of culture and context, the role of families, and positive aspects of culture. To maintain a focus on knowledge generated from applications of the PEN-3 cultural model in African nations, this chapter elaborates on each of the three themes with examples from studies in African nations. Moreover, the chapter moves beyond these three themes to highlight other themes and knowledge pertinent to African nations.

Culture and Context

Studies using the PEN-3 model foreground, in various ways, the broader context and culture of health practices. For example, Green, Dlamini, D'Errico, Ruark, and Duby (2009) conducted individual and focus group interviews with one hundred seventeen traditional leaders and eighty youths from the countries of Botswanna, Lesotho, South Africa, and Swaziland to discover indigenous cultural resources for influencing sex-related norms. They found leaders discussing the revival of traditional customs such as initiation rites into adulthood and chiefs' councils as cultural vehicles for promoting HIV/AIDS prevention and gender sensitivity. Iwelunmor and Airhihenbuwa (2012) conducted focus group interviews with one hundred ten South African women affected and infected by HIV/AIDS to examine the cultural meanings of death and loss from HIV/AIDS. The women articulated various cultural meanings such as HIV is like any other disease and HIV as a death sentence. The theme of culture and context points attention to cultural and historical factors such as customs, meanings, and taboos.

Role of Families

Another theme that Iwelunmor *et al.* (2014) found across applications of PEN-3 is the important role of families in the experience of health/illness and in the shaping of health decisions. For example, Iwelunmor, Airhihenbuwa, Okoror, Brown, and Belue (2006) conducted focus group interviews with two hundred four participants in South Africa to examine the response by family systems to HIV/AIDS. They found family systems were sources of support (e.g. going with PLWHA to clinics and support groups), unique indigenous institutions (e.g. arranging family meetings to counsel members about HIV/AIDS), and sources of stress (e.g. rejecting members who disclosed their status). In another study, Williams and Amoateng (2012) conducted focus group interviews with twenty-nine men in Ghana on their beliefs and knowledge about cervical cancer and their willingness to encourage spousal cancer screening. They found most men were not aware of cervical cancer and held stigmatizing beliefs about its risk factors (e.g. caused by female promiscuity and poor hygiene). They concluded that men's lack of awareness and support may inhibit their spouses' cervical cancer prevention. In another study, Iwelunmor, Zungu, and Airhihenbuwa (2010) conducted interviews with 54 women living with HIV/AIDS in South Africa to explore the role of "motherhood" in women's HIV status disclosures to their mothers. Drawing on the notion of motherhood as a cultural construct, they found participants' motherhood roles predisposed disclosures and simultaneously created a dilemma that weakened their closeness with female family elders. The theme of role of families focuses on how communication in extended families and marriages shape members' health.

Positive Aspects of Culture

Iwelunmor *et al.* (2014) also found that applications of PEN-3 highlighted positive aspects of health practices that can be further harnessed in campaigns and interventions. For example, Mieh *et al.* (2013) conducted focus group interviews with forty-one female home-based caregivers for PLWHA in Limpopo, South Africa to examine their HIV/AIDS-related perceptions. They found caregivers possessing accurate knowledge about HIV/AIDS and reflecting on their evolution from initially stigmatizing patients to being supportive of them. Okoror *et al.* (2014) conducted seven focus group interviews with fifty-four female PLWHA in South Africa to examine their experiences with stigma in health care settings. Among various experiences, they found patients reporting positively about caregiver's supports and care and being able to see health care workers without an appointment. Sofolahan and Airhihenbuwa (2013) conducted four focus group interviews with thirty-five female PLWHA in South Africa to explore factors influencing their sexual and reproductive decisions about childbearing. They discovered positive perceptions (e.g. HIV status acceptance empowering healthy choices), positive enablers (e.g. health care workers' attentiveness and supportiveness) and positive nurturers (e.g. marital partners supporting use of condoms).

In addition to the three themes identified by Iwelunmor *et al.* (2014), applications of PEN-3 in African nations yield additional knowledge that further highlights the contextual and socio-cultural factors that shape health. The sections below elaborate on the role of elders, the impact of diverse social identities, and the theme of health care workers as family members.

The Role of Elders

Elders can be found in communities and extended families and are influential in shaping health decisions and practices. For example, Green *et al.* (2009) based their study of HIV prevention on traditional leaders (also referred to as "chiefs") in the countries of Botswanna, Lesotho,

South Africa, and Swaziland. They argued that these leaders hold strong influence, particularly in rural communities, and their influence persists despite modernization and Westernization. In another study, Iwelunmor *et al.* (2010) found that female elders in South African families usually manage the pregnancy and childbirth of younger family members and oftentimes oversee and guide new mothers' childrearing practices. Petros, Airhihenbuwa, Simbayi, Ramlagan, and Brown (2006), in their attempt at understanding HIV/AIDS "othering" practices (i.e. blaming and shaming) in broader South African society, turned to the local knowledge of key informants such as chiefs, traditional healers, and religious leaders. A theme from applications of PEN-3 is the important influence of elders who lead extended families and communities in shaping members' health decisions and practices.

Diverse Social Identities

Another theme that furthers our understanding of the sociocultural factors that inform health is the impact of diverse social identities (e.g. religion). PEN-3 studies highlight how social identities such as gender and race shape health in African nations. Gender concordance, particularly female-to-female, is found to create strong empathic bonds between health care workers such as nurses and female PLWHA (Sofolahan & Airhihenbuwa, 2013; Sofolahan, Airhihenbuwa, Makofane, & Mashaba, 2010). Gender inequality between females and males, on the other hand, has been found to stigmatize women and to constrain their health decisions in marriage. For example, Williams and Amoateng (2012) concluded that cervical cancer prevention was challenged by Ghanaian men's stigmatizing beliefs about females with cervical cancer and their lack of financial and spousal support for screening. In another example, Sofolahan and Airhihenbuwa (2013) found female PLWHA in South Africa reporting initial difficulties in gaining their partners' eventual support of condom use.

In addition to gender, studies have also considered the impact of racial identity on health in Africa. For example, Brown, Belue, and Airhihenbuwa (2010) surveyed four hundred people from two communities in South Africa to quantify the influence of racial identity on HIV/AIDS stigma in South African families. They found that Black Africans stigmatized family members living with HIV/AIDS due to cultural or spiritual values to a greater degree than Colored South Africans. Petros *et al.* (2006) found the practice of HIV/AIDS othering in South Africa to be based on racial identity. They wrote, "South Africans from different racial backgrounds blame each other as either being the source of HIV or being responsible for spreading the disease" (p. 70). They also found HIV/AIDS othering to be based on gender, homophobia, religion, and xenophobia. A theme that can be discerned from applications of

PEN-3 is the influence of diverse social identities (such as gender, race, and religion) on health behaviors and practices.

Health Care Workers as Family Members

Another theme found in applications of PEN-3 is the blurred role of the health care worker between that of a professional and a family member. For example, Mieh *et al.* (2013) asserted caregiving's centrality in African cultures when they found that home-based caregivers (volunteers who assisted family caregivers with PLWHA) possessed collective and communal identities that enabled them to assume the role of family for PLWHA who were rejected by their biological families. Sofolahan *et al.* (2010) conducted focus group interviews with seventeen female nurses in Limpopo, South Africa, to explore how nurses strike work-life balance in their care for PLWHA. They found nurses having difficulty drawing boundaries between their personal and professional lives. They wrote,

> Nurses can identify with patients at work when they test HIV positive. This induces empathy, because each time a patient tests positive, 'it reminds you of your own family members who died of AIDS or those who you care for because they are HIV positive'
>
> (p. 5)

Okoror *et al.* (2014) found participants having expectations of health care workers that exceeded policy mandates. Their study's participants described good health care workers as caring and supportive and uncaring health care workers as those who did not provide food for them. Knowledge from applications of PEN-3 suggests the role of health care workers is often blurred between that of a professional and an extended family member.

Applicability of the PEN-3 Model to the Ebola Crisis in West Africa

PEN-3 can inform the response to the recent Ebola crisis in West Africa. Use of the PEN-3 model requires the analyst to begin by assessing the cultural community with a health problem. The analyst is expected to begin by generating community members' viewpoints of positive perceptions, enablers, and nurturers regarding the Ebola virus (e.g. cultural traditions where elders immediately isolate and monitor those suspected of infectious diseases). The results may contain ideas and knowledge that can be further exploited and harnessed when devising a campaign or intervention. The analyst should also generate existential perceptions, enablers, and nurturers from community members. These are culturally-unique beliefs, assets, and practices that have neither positive nor negative impacts on health. Lastly, analysts are to generate negative perceptions, enablers, and nurturers of Ebola in the community. This provides the analyst with negative cultural factors surrounding the spread of the virus that need to be changed (e.g. burial traditions involving intimate contacts between the bereaved and the deceased).

After a thorough assessment, the analyst is encouraged to consult and partner with community members in developing solutions via campaigns and interventions (e.g. Ebola awareness, treatment, and prevention). These solutions should not only be based on community input and participation, but they should also seek to harness cultural strengths (positive perceptions, enablers, and nurturers) while confronting cultural barriers to health. One initial consideration is the intervention point of entry. Initiatives, for example, may consider the entry points of mothers/grandmothers. Although women are the primary caretakers and are the most engaged with health care systems, gender inequality and gender stigmatization may hamper their efforts. Initiatives may also consider the entry points of elders within families and within communities (e.g., religious and traditional leaders). Although these actors can play influential roles in family and community members' health decisions and practices, they may be distrustful of foreigners/outsiders and initially resistant to non-traditional health innovations and practices.

Initiatives can also consider the entry point of health care workers. PEN-3 research in African nations suggest health care workers play both strongly positive and negative roles in the health of community members. As such, they should be carefully screened before their participation in any intervention. The ideal health care worker would have a caring, supportive, and generous orientation. Such a worker believes he [*sic*] has an obligation to his community and regards patients and members of the community as extended family members.

Limitations and Future Applications of PEN-3

The following paragraphs elaborate on four areas for future applications of PEN-3: discovering uniquely African models of health and illness, examining how economic resource constraints shape health decisions and practices, implementing and evaluating health campaigns, and examining health problems in African immigrant groups residing in Western nations.

First, an important consideration in health communication is the models of health/illness that suggest prevalent assumptions and beliefs about the general causes of and solutions to health/illness (e.g. biomedical, biopsychosocial). Although PEN-3 contains the dimension of 'perceptions,' its applications in African nations have yet to generate prevalent culturally-unique models of health/illness among the indigenous communities studied. Future applications of PEN-3 can focus on eliciting these health/illness models' defining features as well examining how participants relate these models with more Western models of health/illness (e.g. biomedical).

Second, the PEN-3 dimension of enablers in the "relationships and expectations" domain is not only defined as health care systems and workers, but also as issues of access to and availability of economic resources (Airhihenbuwa & Webster, 2004). Studies of enablers in African nations tend to focus on health care systems and workers (e.g. Airhihenbuwa *et al.*, 2009; Okoror *et al.*, 2014; Sofolahan & Airhihenbuwa, 2013). Future applications may focus on how economic resource constraints shape community members' health decisions and practices.

Third, PEN-3 is designed not only for assessments of communities with a health problem, but also for developing and evaluating health campaigns. Yet, virtually all applications of PEN-3 in African nations focus on assessments to the detriment of implementing and evaluating health campaigns. Future applications of the model can harness the knowledge generated from community assessments to develop, implement, and evaluate health campaigns.

Fourth, although PEN-3 has been used to assess various immigrant groups in America such as Chinese and Latinas (e.g. Garces, Scarinci, & Harrison, 2006; Scarinci, Bandura, Hidalgo, & Cherrington, 2012; Yick & Oomen-Early, 2009), it is rarely used for African immigrants. A rare exception comes from De Jesus, Carrete, Maine, and Nalls (2015) who interviewed twenty-five East African immigrant women living in Washington DC to explore culture-specific perceptions of HIV testing. They found participants articulating both Western public health messages and East African sociocultural expectations. For example, along with reporting a Western theme of "One's friends/family/community would be supportive if one decided to get tested for HIV" (p. 606), they also reported a sociocultural theme of "Getting an HIV test brings shame to the person who got tested and to one's family; it implies one is engaging in immoral behavior" (p. 608).

Another rare exception of PEN-3 research on African immigrants comes from Whembolua, Conserve, and Tshiswaka (2015) who evaluated five episodes of an entertainment education health campaign for African immigrants in France for positive, negative, and existential uses of African identity; the episodes covered the health problems of emergency birth control, HIV stigma, home accidents, malaria, and nutrition. They found positive uses of African identity (e.g. traditional value of respect for elders, diversity of African identities, acceptance and support for PLWHA), existential uses (e.g. being treated like a foreigner in home and host countries, strong sense of community), and negative uses (e.g. fear of ridicule from home country preventing use of malaria prevention pills, HIV stigma and discrimination). In light of the rare applications of PEN-3 on African immigrants, future applications can focus on the health problems of African immigrants in Western nations.

Conclusion

This chapter forwarded the PEN-3 cultural model as both an assessment and intervention—development tool uniquely qualified to improve the international community's response to contemporary health risks and crises in Africa such as the Ebola crisis in West Africa. The chapter reviewed the PEN-3 cultural model by covering its three domains, its two areas of application, its applications in African nations, its applicability to the Ebola crisis, and limitations in its applications and directions for future applications.

PEN-3 is one of several culture-centered approaches to health. Although it is one of the earliest to have been offered in the literature (Airhihenbuwa, 1990), we have witnessed a chapter on cultural strategies in Singhal and Rogers (2003) and, more recently, Mohan Dutta's culture-centered approach to health communication (Dutta-Bergman, 2004), which has found expression in several key works (e.g. Dutta, 2007, 2008). Despite some similarities among these approaches, they also have important differences (e.g. central assumptions, considerations, and foci for interventionists and researchers). To assist future culture-centered applications, we can benefit from work that compares and contrasts all the available culture-centered approaches to health (e.g. fundamental tenets, extant applications to the health communication of cultural communities).

Note

1 The relative dearth of PEN-3 research on African immigrants in Western nations shapes our focus on applications of PEN-3 on the African continent. In the concluding sections, we call for more applications of PEN-3 on African immigrants in Western nations.

References

Airhihenbuwa, C. O. (1990). A conceptual model for culturally appropriate health education programs in developing countries. *International Quarterly of Community Health Education*, *11*, 53–62.

Airhihenbuwa, C. O. (1995). *Health and culture: Beyond the Western paradigm.* Thousand Oaks, CA: Sage.

Airhihenbuwa, C. O., Ford, C. L., & Iwelunmor, J. I. (2014). Why culture matters in health interventions: Lessons from HIV/AIDS stigma and NCDs. *Health Education & Behavior, 41*, 78–84. doi:10.1177/1090198113487199.

Airhihenbuwa, C. O., Makinwa, B., & Obregon, R. (2000). Toward a new communications framework for HIV/ AIDS. *Journal of Health Communication*, *5*, 101–111.

Airhihenbuwa, C. O., & Obregon, R. (2000). A critical assessment of theories/ models used in health communication for HIV/ AIDS. *Journal of Health Communication*, *5*, 5–15.

Airhihenbuwa, C. O., Okoror, T., Shefer, T., Brown, D., Iwelunmor, J., Smith, E., ... Shisana, O. (2009). Stigma, culture, and HIV and AIDS in the western cape, South Africa: An application of the PEN-3 cultural model for community-based research. *Journal of Black Psychology*, *35*, 407–432. doi:10.1177/0095798408329941.

Airhihenbuwa, C. O., & Webster, J. D. (2004). Culture and African contexts of HIV/AIDS prevention, care, and support. *Journal of Social Aspects of HIV/AIDS Research Alliance*, *1*, 4–13.

Belue, R., Okoror, T. A., Iwelunmor, J., Taylor, K. D., Degboe, A. N., Agyemang, C., & Ogedegbe, G. (2009). An overview of cardiovascular risk factor burden in sub-Saharan African countries: A socio-cultural perspective. *Globalization and Health*, *5*, 10–22. doi:10.1186/1744-8603-5-10.

Birn, A., Pillay, Y., & Holtz, T. H. (2009). *Textbook of international health: Global health in a dynamic world* (3rd ed.). Oxford: Oxford University Press.

Brown, D. C., Belue, R., & Airhihenbuwa, C. O. (2010). HIV and AIDS-related stigma in the context of family support and race in South Africa. *Ethnicity & Health*, *15*, 441–458. doi:10.1080/13557858.2010.486029.

De Jesus, M., Carrete, C., Maine, C., & Nalls, P. (2015). "Getting tested is almost like going to the Salem witch trials": Discordant discourses between Western public health messages and sociocultural expectations surrounding HIV testing among East African immigrant women. *AIDS Care*, *27*, 604–611. doi:10.1080/09540121.2014.1002827.

Dutta, M. J. (2007). Communicating about culture and health: Theorizing culture-centered and cultural sensitivity approaches. *Communication Theory*, *17*, 304–328. doi:10.1111/j.1468-2885.2007.00297.x.

Dutta, M. J. (2008). *Communicating heath: A culture-centered aproach.* Malden, MA: Polity Press.

Dutta, M. J. (2015). Decolonizing communication for social change: A culture-centered approach. *Communication Theory*, *25*, 123–143. doi:10.1111/comt.12067.

Dutta-Bergman, M. J. (2004). The unheard voices of Santalis: Communicating about health from the margins of India. *Communication Theory*, *14*, 237–263.

Garces, I. C., Scarinci, I. C., & Harrison, L. (2006). An examination of sociocultural factors associated with health and health care seeking among Latina immigrants. *Journal of Immigrant Health*, *8*, 377–385. doi:10.1007/s10903-006-9008-8.

Green, E. C., Dlamini, C., D'Errico, N. C. D., Ruark, A., & Duby, Z. (2009). Mobilising indigenous resources for anthropologically designed HIV-prevention and behaviour-change interventions in southern Africa. *African Journal of AIDS Research*, *8*, 389–400.

Iwelunmor, J., & Airhihenbuwa, C. O. (2012). Cultural implications of death and loss from AIDS among women in South Africa. *Death Studies*, *36*, 134–151. doi:10.1080/07481187.2011.553332.

Iwelunmor, J., Airhihenbuwa, C. O., Okoror, T., Brown, D., & Belue, R. (2006). Family systems and HIV/AIDS in South Africa. *International Quarterly of Community Health Education*, *27*, 321–335. doi:10.2190/IQ.27.4.d.

Iwelunmor, J., Newsome, V., & Airhihenbuwa, C. O. (2014). Framing the impact of culture on health: A systematic review of the PEN-3 cultural model and its application in public health research and interventions. *Ethnicity & Health, 19*, 20–46. doi:10.1080/13557858.2013.857768.

Iwelunmor, J., Sofolahan-Oladeinde, Y., & Airhihenbuwa, C. O. (2015). Sociocultural factors influencing HIV disclosure among men in South Africa. *American Journal of Men's Health, 9*, 193–200. doi:10.1177/1557988314535235.

Iwelunmor, J., Zungu, N., & Airhihenbuwa, C. O. (2010). Rethinking HIV/AIDS disclosure among women within the context of motherhood in South Africa. *American Journal of Public Health, 100*, 1393–1399. doi:10.2105/AJPH.2009.168989.

Kannan, S., Sparks, A. V., Webster, J. D., Krishnakumar, A., & Lumeng, J. (2010). Health eating and Harambee: Curriculum development for a culturally-centered bio-medically oriented nutrition education program to reach African American women of childbearing age. *Maternal and Child Health Journal, 14*, 535–547. doi:10.1007/s10995-009-0507-9.

Lammers, J. C., Barbour, J. B., & Duggan, A. P. (2003). Organizational forms of the provision of health care: An institutional perspective. In T. L. Thompson, A. M. Dorsey, K. I. Miller, & R. Parrott (Eds.), *Handbook of health communication* (pp. 319–345). Mahwah, NJ: Erlbaum.

Mieh, T. M., Iwelunmor, J., & Airhihenbuwa, C. O. (2013). Home-based caregiving for people living with HIV/AIDS in South Africa. *Journal of Health Care for the Poor and Underserved, 24*, 697–705.

Okoror, T., Belue, R., Zungu, N., Adam, M. A., & Airhihenbuwa, C. O. (2014). HIV positive women's perceptions of stigma in health care settings in Western Cape, South Africa. *Health Care for Women International, 35*, 27–49. doi:10.1080/07399332.2012.736566.

Olufowote, J. O., & Airhihenbuwa, C. O. (2014). Nigeria. In T. L. Thompson (Ed.), *The Encyclopedia of Health Communication* (Vol. 2, pp. 944–945). Thousand Oaks, CA: Sage.

Petros, G., Airhihenbuwa, C. O., Simbayi, L., Ramlagan, S., & Brown, B. (2006). HIV/AIDS and 'othering' in South Africa: The blame goes on. *Culture, Health & Sexuality, 8*, 67–77. doi:10.1080/13691050500391489.

Scarinci, I. C., Bandura, L., Hidalgo, B., & Cherrington, A. (2012). Development of a theory-based (PEN-3 and health belief model), culturally relevant intervention on cervical cancer prevention among Latina immigrants using intrvention mapping. *Health Promotion Practice, 13*, 29–40. doi:10.1177/1524839910366416.

Sharf, B. F. (1993). Reading the vital signs: research in health communication. *Communication Monographs, 60*, 35–41.

Singhal, A. (2003). Focusing on the forest, not just the tree. *MICA Communications Review, 1*, 21–28.

Singhal, A., & Rogers, E. M. (2003). *Combating AIDS: Communication strategies in action.* Thousand Oaks, CA: Sage.

Sofolahan, Y., & Airhihenbuwa, C. O. (2012). Childbearing decision making: A qualitative study of women living with HIV/AIDS in Southwest Nigeria. *AIDS Research and Treatment, 2012*, 1–8. doi:10.1155/2012/478065.

Sofolahan, Y., & Airhihenbuwa, C. O. (2013). Cultural expectations and reproductive desires: Experiences of South African women living with HIV/AIDS (WLHA). *Health Care for Women International, 34*, 263–280. doi:10.1080/07399332.2012.721415.

Sofolahan, Y., Airhihenbuwa, C. O., Makofane, D., & Mashaba, E. (2010). "I have lost sexual interest..."—Challenges of balancing personal and professional lives among nurses caring for people living with HIV and AIDS in Limpopo, South Africa. *International Quarterly of Community Health Education*, *31*, 155–169. doi:10.2190/IQ.31.2.d.

Sofolahan-Oladeinde, Y., & Airhihenbuwa, C. O. (2014). "He doesn't love me less. He loves me more": Perceptions of women living with HIV/AIDS of partner support in childbearing decision-making. *Health Care for Women International*, *35*, 937–953. doi:10.1080/07399332.2014.920022.

Street, R. L. (2003). Communication in medical encounters: An ecological perspective. In T. L. Thompson, A. Dorsey, R. Parrott, & K. I. Miller (Eds.), *Handbook of health communication*. Mahwah, NJ: Lawrence Erlbaum Associates.

Whembolua, G. S., Conserve, D. F., & Tshiswaka, D. I. (2015). Cultural identity and health promotion: Assessing a health education program targeting African immigrants in France. *The Journal of Pan African Studies*, *8*, 23–39.

Williams, M. S., & Amoateng, P. (2012). Knowledge and beliefs about cervical cancer screening among men in Kumasi, Ghana. *Ghana Medical Journal*, *46*, 147–152.

Yick, A. G., & Oomen-Early, J. (2009). Using the PEN-3 model to plan culturally competent domestic violence intervention and prevention services in Chinese American and immigrant communities. *Health Education*, *109*, 125–139. doi:10.1108/09654280910936585.

11 Women, Polarization, and Communication for Social Change

Breast Cancer Policy in Venezuela

Isaac Nahon-Serfaty and Mahmoud Eid

Introduction

From 2009 to 2013, we developed an action-oriented research project[1] in Venezuela in partnership with the non-governmental organization SenoAyuda that aimed at empowering community activists and patients in their fight against breast cancer (BC) through the development of their communication and social advocacy skills.[2] Inspired by the principles of a dialogic educational process (Freire, 1970, 2000), this project was structured around an ecological vision of health communication that integrates the personal, organizational, and social levels (Street, 2003). Based on the premise that communication has an emancipatory potential (Beltrán Salmón, 2010) as a process to promote social change (Figueroa, Kincaid, Rani, Lewis, & Gray-Felder, 2002), we put together a series of activities (workshops, planning sessions, dialogue tables, among others) that contributed to develop the communication and leadership skills of community activists, patients, physicians, researchers, journalists, and other actors involved in BC policy and care.

First, we present the context in which the action-oriented research has taken place in Venezuela amidst what is so-called "Bolivarian revolution," marked with high levels of political and social polarization and changes in the public health care system. Second, we discuss the theoretical framework that guides the action-oriented research from the perspective of social mobilization and cooperation among all stakeholders. Next, we explain the methodological approach based on the concept of collective learning by doing. Finally, we discuss the results of this project and consider the limitations of the method and the context where the action-oriented research has been implemented.

Research Context: Marginalization and Polarization

The right to health care in Latin America faces several challenges that manifest in the existing disparities to access basic services (Yamin, 2000). The case of Venezuela confirms that trend, where an important portion of the population is excluded from quality and efficient health care services. Even though the government claims that poverty has been reduced, some indicators still show that 40 percent of Venezuelans are poor and 12 percent among them live at the level of extreme poverty (Ponce, 2009). Being poor and a woman at the same time represents a double challenge of exclusion and marginalization. The unemployment is higher among women (Boza, 2004), and their income is lower than men's (Orlando & Zúñiga, 2000). The exclusion is also a consequence of the geography, since some regions of the country have higher birth and mortality rates with important differences between the center, the east, and the south-west of Venezuela (Freitez, 2003). Non-communicable diseases account for 80 percent of all deaths, and the mortality among women in the ages between 45 and 64 is mainly due to cervical cancer and BC (OPS, 2011).

Even though BC incidences are lower among Latin American women than non-Hispanic women (Cancer mortality, 2005), the growing rate is more important among the Latinas than in other groups (Buki, Borrayo, Feigal, & Carrillo, 2004). The increase in BC incidences is due to changes in lifestyle, beliefs and prejudices influenced by their culture, and a lack of awareness about the disease (e.g. Andersen *et al.*, 2004; Harvard Medical School's Center of Excellence in Women's Health, 2007; Schutt *et al.*, 2008). In Venezuela, BC has a significant incidence (42.5 cases per 100K), a relatively high mortality rate (13.7 deaths per 100K), and an important impact on lost productive years (International Agency for Research on Cancer, 2008; MPPS, 2008). Between 2005 and 2011, mortality rates show an increase of BC deaths by 19.08 percent for all ages and 21.92 percent in those below 40 (MPPS, 2011). Twenty years ago, cervical cancer was the first cause of death among all the cancers affecting women. Since 1985, cervical cancer mortality has been decreasing, thanks to a national program of early detection (MPPS, 2008, 2011). On the contrary, the incidences of BC have been increasing since 1990, becoming the first cause of cancer-related mortality among women. The latest mortality report of the Venezuelan Ministry of Health (MPPS, 2011) states 1.697 deaths attributed to BC and 1.238 deaths due to cervical cancer.

When compared with other Latin American countries, Venezuela presents some institutional weaknesses. The country does not have a national program against BC, even though it has made some progress in the inclusion of civil society organizations in the early detection initiatives (Nigenda, González-Robledo, González-Robledo, & Bejarano, 2011). The expert opinion is that the government has neglected the prevention of BC (Sociedad Venezolana de Mastología, 2010). In fact, the lack of governmental resources can create obstacles that hinder or completely impede citizens' access to proper care (Eid & Nahon-Serfaty, 2015a).

Culturally, the *macho* prejudices are still very much present in the public sphere as shown by the controversy that emerged among the supporters of a soccer team who protested when the players wore pink shirts during the BC awareness month on October 12, 2012. According to media reports, the match between *Deportivo Táchira* and *Atlético Venezuela* was cancelled because a group of supporters did not want to leave the soccer field protesting against the use of "pink shirts" (Bailey, 2012).

The Venezuelan constitution has three articles that secure the right to health care. These articles consider health care as a fundamental social right that should be guaranteed by the state in the context of the right of life (Feo & Siqueira, 2004). The constitution establishes two mechanisms to enforce the right to health care: the creation of national public health care service guided by principles of universal access and inclusion, and the public financing of this system. Theoretically, the public health care system should be decentralized, intersectoral, and participatory (Feo & Curcia, 2004). The participatory principle prescribes an active role of society and civil organizations in the design, implementation, and management of health care policies and programs. This is in line with the empowerment notion that has guided our project.

The constitutional change resulted in some policies that improved the access of the population, especially the poor sectors, to primary care services. The government under Hugo Chávez put the accent on some programs through the so-called *Misión Barrio Adentro* (MBA) with the help of the Cuban government (Briggs & Mantini-Briggs, 2009). According to some evaluations, the MBA—with the participation of 33,000 Cuban health care workers—was able to overcome some inequalities in health care, combining theoretical perspectives of social medicine, critical epidemiology, and "popular knowledge" ("*saberes populares*" in Spanish) in the communities (Briggs & Mantini-Briggs, 2008).

Nevertheless, the impact of the MBA is not entirely positive. This program contributed to the already historical fragmentation of the public health care service and had a negative impact on the global financing and organization of the system proposed in the constitution (Díaz Polanco, 2006; Nahon-Serfaty, 2005). According to some assessments, health care policies in Venezuela have been mismanaged and lacked sustainability, a reality that is reflected in an increase of infant and maternal mortality rates (González, 2005). More recently, public officials have denounced equipment and infrastructure deficiencies in the Ministry of Health's primary care clinics, and the need to reinstitute 40,000 beds in public hospitals (Villasmil, 2015). A coalition of NGOs declared in a public statement: "health care in the country is in intensive care, and that's a reality that anybody can deny" (Alvarado, 2014, our translation).

Since 1999, when Hugo Chávez was first elected president, Venezuela has been under an intense process of social and political polarization. The division between what is so-called "*chavistas*" and the opposition has manifested in political violence, repression, and attacks against freedom of speech and hate discourse. Even though the conflict has contributed to the activation of the political participation and reinforcement of social and political identities within some groups, it has also resulted in many barriers for dialogue and consensus building (Lozada, 2008).

Human Rights Watch (2008) has denounced the inability of the Venezuelan government to properly address human rights issues and its tendency to confront and attack human rights advocates and civil society organizations. Reyna (2013) has noticed the political will of the Bolivarian regime to manipulate the notion of "popular power" ("*poder popular*" in Spanish) by framing it in different legal instruments and executive decrees:

> *Poder popular* is not a direct means for popular participation nor strengths the power of the citizens in public decision making. On the contrary, is another power in a new form of State that concentrates and exerts vertically the power, the so-called "Communal State" ["*Estado Comunal*"] that does not consider democracy or autonomy. There are no citizens or civil society, only organizations and structures of the Popular Power that are forced to comply with the goals of the State.
>
> (Reyna, 2013, p. 181, our translation)

In the Venezuelan socio-political context, the leader (particularly Hugo Chávez) symbolizes "*el pueblo*" and becomes the vehicle of the people's aspirations and hopes (Smilde, 2011), having both empowering and disempowering effects on society. The leader empowers—at least rhetorically—the poor or marginalized by referring constantly to their rights in his speeches; meanwhile, disempowers them by promoting a paternalistic view on the role of the government as a "benefactor of the people". The media have played an important role in the dynamics of polarization. The government put in place a strategy to achieve "hegemonic communication" ("*hegemonía comunicacional*") through direct and indirect control of the media and the Internet (Bisbal, 2009; Pino Iturrieta, 2013).

Several organizations have emerged in the country to fill the gap left by the public sector in health care provision and services. The Venezuela Cancer League (*Sociedad Anticancerosa de Venezuela*) was founded in 1948 to promote the education about, and prevention of, cancer and to reinforce the access to proper diagnostic and treatment, especially for the poor. Recently, many NGOs have been established to work in the field of BC: SenoSalud, Funcamama, Fuccam, Famac, Fundamama, Fundaseno, Senosestima, Unicam, and SenosAyuda, among many others.

In 2007, SenosAyuda launched the Organizational Capacity Building Program (OCBP) aimed at collaborating with other NGOs working in the area of BC in Venezuela. The OCBP had two main goals: (1) to help develop these organizations, with particular focus on those operating in the provinces and areas where access to health care is more difficult; (2) to provide community leaders and spokespersons in these organizations with the knowledge and management tools to achieve their objectives.

In the context of social divisions and political tensions, we proposed a plan to overcome some of the barriers between social actors and institutions, particularly between civil society organizations working in health care and patients' rights and the central government that defines itself as "revolutionary". The action-oriented research project discussed here was also part of the OCBP, contributing to the multi-organizational co-operation and multidisciplinary integration between patients, activists, physicians, researchers, journalists, and health public officials.

Theoretical Framework: Communication, Activism, and Social Change

Two theoretical premises guided this action-oriented research. The first states that an ecological approach of communication (Street, 2003) should integrate the interpersonal, organizational, and social levels in health care activism. The second premise acknowledges the emancipatory potential of communication (Beltrán, 1994), following a Latin American tradition of citizenship mobilization and community action. Communication in this project is viewed as a political action in the broadest meaning of the concept, since communication is a way to empower groups who are traditionally marginalized and unable to get their voices heard. In this regard, the speech (Freire, 1970, 2000) and communication, in its different forms, are practices that contribute to achieve positive results for the individual and society.

The Role of NGOs

The Latin American activism in BC has expanded in recent years. Many NGOs have been established, social research has been used as an intervention tool, and networks of cooperation and exchanges have facilitated the emergence of consensus for the implementation of public policies (Nigenda *et al.*, 2011). In almost all Latin American countries, the constitutional provisions consecrate health care as a fundamental human right. However, this normative formality does not always translate into real improvements for the population. NGOs and community action programs fill the gap left by the public and the traditional private sectors. Some positive results have been observed in the area of health care program sustainability and the overall well-being of communities where NGOs operate (Zoller, 2005). These organizations help to reduce disparities in the access to health care services and respond to the needs of the most vulnerable populations. One of the most positive aspects is the NGOs' ability to create communication spaces for health education and deliberation of health care issues (De Souza, 2009). Early detection of BC has been improved in groups and communities usually marginalized through the action of these groups (Durstine & Leitman, 2009). However, the influence and impact of NGOs confront some limitations. The participation of civil society and community-oriented research that encompasses a wide variety of actors and variables, could lead to confrontations and tensions with political connotations (Israël *et al.*, 1998), as we have observed in the Venezuelan context. Moreover, some organizations in Latin America have difficulties in demonstrating clear results of their actions (Durstine & Leitman, 2009).

Collective Learning and Collective Action

Learning and diffusion of knowledge are key elements of social activism in health care. The Communication for Social Change (CFSC) model (Figueroa *et al.*, 2002) approaches this process as a dialogue through which the citizens define their identities, identify their needs, and set their objectives to improve their quality of life. CFSC is a decision-making and collective action dynamic intended to find solutions to problems that affect society. This process is based on certain principles: the objectives of communication are multiple and are not only focused on persuading the "other"; all participants in the process have the right to give and receive information coming from different sources; the dialogue is defined as the right to be heard; participation means the right to set the change agenda and the goals of the intervention; finally, communication should aim at achieving individual changes and transforming social norms, policies, and culture (Beltrán, 1980).

Puntos de Encuentro is an emblematic CFSC experience that was born in Nicaragua in 1991 that combined research and communication designed to achieve "the transformation of oppressive cultures that are present in the daily life. The objective of the NGO is not to change behaviours but transform cultural norms" (Rodríguez, 2004, p. 116, our translation). Throughout fourteen years of different actions that included public campaigns, narrative interventions in *telenovelas* and other TV and radio shows, community workshops, training programs, and public forums, *Puntos de Encuentro* has integrated the two dimensions of CFSC: communication and mobilization.

> Historically, the communication for social change has been in the hands of organizations of communication for social change, government institutions and scholars in communication. The mobilization has been the fief of the organized civil society, popular organizations, and political science scholars. In this NGO

> (*Puntos de Encuentro*) the two spheres are seemingly integrated assuming the dialectic between communication and mobilization.
> (Rodríguez, 2004, p. 132, our translation)

The model of CFSC, which refers to an iterative process where community dialogue and collective action synergize to produce social change in a community, improving health and quality of life for all its members, is also useful (Byrne *et al.*, 2005). Similarly, the Integrated Model of Communication for Social Change refers to a "dynamic, iterative process that starts with a 'catalyst/stimulus' that can be external or internal to the community" (Byrne *et al.*, 2005, p. 6). Perhaps the most important aspect of this model lies in the goal of knowledge equity; substantial emphasis is placed on the extent to which the knowledge is shared within a community rather than being hoarded or monopolized by just a few.

The CFSC emphasizes the collective action, but also values the individual learning understood as a cognitive, emotional, and social process (Figueroa *et al.*, 2002). In that regard, communication should contribute to the development of certain individual skills and capabilities intended to achieve a more egalitarian and inclusive participation, while facilitating the acquisition of knowledge aligned with the social change objectives. Additionally, this process should help the emergence of individual "emotional responses" such as solidarity, empathy, and trust to strengthen the social linkage.

Participation in health and developmental communication programs not only strengthens the voice of citizens, but also ensures their involvement in decisions that affect them, their families, and their communities (Brasington, Tapia, & van Lith, 2007). This approach favors mutual learning rather than top-down practices to change implementation, thereby respecting local traditions and refusing to undermine cultures and values of affected communities. Nowadays, the social networks contribute to empower the voice of citizens, promoting alternative sources of information in a context of lack of legitimacy or mistrust of traditional information sources (Cancelo Sanmartín & Gadea Aldave, 2013). In the case of health care, "polyphonic discourses" have challenged the managerial perspectives that are focused mainly on efficacy and efficiency (Iedema, Degeling, Braithwaite, & White,, 2003; Iriart, Merhy, & Waitzkin, 2001), opening a space for the voices of patients, users, and social activists (Kim & Willis, 2007; Vasconcellos-Silva, Uribe Rivera, & Siebeneichler, 2007). In some cases, the "marginal voices" have captured the attention of the media and the public, bringing a human angle to health care policies (Hivon, Lehoux, & Rock, 2010).

Achieving inclusion and participation, though, requires careful consideration and planning to carry out network relations effectively; network integration must be intensive, involving multiple and overlapping links both within and across the organizations that compose the core of a network (Provan & Sebastian, 1998). Moreover, it is especially important to ensure that health care communication strategies take into account contextual and cultural factors, such as moral and religious values. Such principles form the foundation of social groups, villages, cities, and nations alike, and may affect patient, physician, and authority perceptions and evaluations of health care. In a Latin American context, many cultural values need to be considered when developing public health campaigns. For instance, the values of collectivism, family, religion, trust, respect, and interpersonal relationships are deemed significant (Borrayo, 2004).

In the Venezuelan case, the CFSC presented practical and ethical challenges to overcome the barriers of social exclusion and political polarization, and to integrate diverse stakeholders in a network of different organizations while being culturally sensible. The action-oriented research method helped us to address all these issues, as we explain in the next section.

Method: Understanding and Doing

Action-oriented research is a collective, self-reflective, and participatory enquiry undertaken by participants (stakeholders) in social interactions to improve some condition in which they are all involved. It is "a methodological approach for doing collaborative research with practitioners and community partners that can inform practice, programs, community development, and policy while contributing to the scientific knowledge base" (Small & Uttal, 2005, p. 936). It promotes a critical consciousness that exhibits itself in political and practical action to make some type of change. Its agenda mainly includes "producing research that can address practical concerns" (Small, 1995, p. 942), aiming to "have some type of change" (Small & Uttal, 2005, p. 938). It helps to: (1) increase the closeness between the day-to-day problems encountered by practitioners in specific settings and the theories used to explain and resolve problems; and (2) assist practitioners in lifting their veil of clouded understandings to better understand fundamental problems by raising their collective consciousness (Berg, 2009).

Action-oriented researchers "believe that the process of conducting research should be empowering for research participants" (Esterberg, 2002, p. 141). They "value collaboration with non-researcher participants" in that while they bring "to the research process theoretical knowledge, experience, and the skills of conducting social science research, the participant collaborators bring practical knowledge and experience about the situations that are being studied" (Small, 1995, p. 942). Together, researchers and community partners "combine their different kinds of knowledge and skills to produce insightful and usable findings" (Small & Uttal, 2005, p. 938). Ultimately, action-oriented research aims to "generate knowledge that can be used to address practical concerns of local communities, organizations, and groups and incorporate local understandings of specific practices and issues" (Ibid).

Within the context of SenosAyuda's OCBP initiative, our project was based on six guiding principles: inclusion and equity, gender sensitivity, dialogue and interaction, social change, networking, and ethical standards. Inclusion and equity are fundamental because all the stakeholders should have a voice in defining their priorities and needs, and all have the potential of becoming advocates and spokespersons of their own cause (Eid & Nahon-Serfaty, 2015b). Gender sensitivity takes into account that on top of all the traditional barriers to accessing proper health care services, women in Venezuela face additional obstacles due to cultural and social obstacles, as they are frequently the subjects of a double marginalization process (being poor and women). Dialogue and interaction are ways to promote an open conversation about the goals, strategies, and tactics of the project, inspired by the conviction that communication is a two-way and horizontal process. Social change is understood here as a gradual process that entails the development of capabilities and abilities of the individuals and organizations to improve their access to information, health care services, and participation in policymaking. Networking is a way to promote solidarity among different actors, including those who are marginalized (i.e. regional activists) and to create synergies among them. Ethical standards are essential to respect human dignity, promote transparency, encourage responsibility, and demand accountability of all stakeholders (Eid, 2008; Eid & Nahon-Serfaty, 2008).

Our action-oriented research has aimed to achieve four objectives: (1) to contribute to the development of communication and social mobilization knowledge and skills among community activists; (2) to fill in the existing gap between activists, patients, physicians, and public officials by collaboration for BC awareness and education; (3) to promote a dialogue between social and institutional actors to define a consensual framework for a BC's national policy; and (4) to strengthen the relationships between activists, patients, and journalists to improve the diffusion of information about BC's early detection, treatment, and social support.

To achieve these objectives, we co-organized in partnership with SenosAyuda five workshops in Caracas (Venezuela) between 2009 and 2013. The workshops were consecrated to the following subjects: communication and social mobilization capabilities (June 5–6, 2009); patient-doctor communication in BC (June 11–12, 2010); building a consensus about a national response in BC (May 20–21, 2011); improve the diffusion of information about BC through media (February 24–25, 2012); and setting the priorities of a BC national response (July 27, 2013). In total, 142 persons participated in the activities, including activists representing various organizations (i.e. patients and cancer survivors), physicians, journalists, researchers, public officials, a member of parliament, representatives of the private sector, and instructors (in the areas of interpersonal communication, media relations, health journalism, communication ethics, and advocacy). We should note that many activists, physicians, and researchers participated in all the activities, contributing to consolidate the networks of cooperation and advocacy. Table 11.1 contains the details of all types of participants in each activity and the organizations that were represented in the workshops.

The first two activities and the workshop about media diffusion were quantitatively and qualitatively evaluated in terms of what the participants have learned, the organization of the workshop, and the interaction between them and the facilitators. The first two workshops (communication and social mobilization, as well as the doctor-patient communication) were also assessed post facto through a reflexive report that some participants answered between two and three months after the activities. The reflexive reports detailed the type of communication and advocacy the participants were involved in, the skills and capabilities that they put in practice, and their perception about their performance. Furthermore, the researchers worked with SenosAyuda to write the organization's code of ethics, a collaborative process that included the participation of university students.[3]

The participants decided that the subjects of all workshops following the dialogic and iterative principles of CFSC. During the first workshop, where the action-oriented research program was presented and discussed, the participants identified the doctor–patient communication and the relationship with media and journalists as priority subjects.

The interactions during the first activity also helped participants to identify the social and political polarization as the main barrier in the relationship between activists and the central government. This prompted the decision of summoning a workshop to build a consensus about BC policy with the participation of all the stakeholders. This activity was preceded by a consultation with three physicians and three social activists who identified the main obstacles, the priorities, and the actions for a future national policy on BC. During that workshop, all participants contributed to fill a situational matrix (current situation, barriers, drivers for change, and desired situation) that allowed them to set the core ideas for a consensus. These ideas were compiled and edited in a consensus document by an *ad hoc* committee (two physicians, two public officials, and two activists). The action-oriented research project was completed with a dialogue roundtable among social and political stakeholders, including for the first time public officials from the Ministry of Health and the Venezuelan Institutes of Social Security. The roundtable focused on three priorities: education about BC for physicians and health care personnel; improving the quality of

Table 11.1 Activities of the Action-Oriented Research

Activity	*Date*	*Number of Participants*	*Organizations Represented*
Communication and social mobilization workshop	June 5–6, 2009	37	SenosAyuda (Activists/Patients); Unicam (Activists/Patients); Fundamasol (Activists/Patients); Funcamama (Activists/Patients); Asomasol (Activists/Patients); FAVE (Activists/Patients); Fundaseno (Activists/Patients); Acción Solidaria (Activists/Patients); Servicio de Oncologia Hospital Padre Machado (Hospital); Centro de Salud Santa Inés (Community Clinic); Asoc. Civil Don Bosco (Community Clinic); Sociedad Venezolana de Mastologia (Medical Association); Sociedad Anticancerosa (Activists/Patients); Universidad Católica Andrés Bello (University); Chucky Reina Comunicaciones (PR Firm).
Doctor-patient communication workshop	June 11–12, 2010	34	Physicians (oncologists, mastologist, surgeons, gynecologists); Sociedad Venezolana de Mastologia (Medical Association); SenosAyuda (Activists/Patients); Funcamama (Activists/Patients); Asomasol (Activists/Patients); Universidad Católica Andrés Bello (University); Avon Venezuela (Private Corporation/Sponsor)
Consensus building workshop	May 20–21, 2011	21	SenosAyuda (Activists/Patients); Fuccam (Activists/Patients); Funcamama (Activists/Patients); Funcamamas (Activists/Patients); Famac (Activists/Patients); Asomasol (Activists/Patients); Sociedad Venezolana de Mastologia (Medical Association); Asociación Venezolana de Servicios de Salud de Orientación Cristiana (NGO); Cendes-Universidad Central de Venezuela (University); Universidad Católica Andrés Bello (University); Centro de Salud Santa Inés (Community Clinic); Salud Miranda (Regional Gov.); Corposalud Aragua (Regional Gov.); Salud Sucre (Municipal Gov.); Salud Chacao (Municipal Gov.); Salud Baruta (Municipal Gov.)

(*Continued*)

Activity	*Date*	*Number of Participants*	*Organizations Represented*
Media relations workshop	February 24–25, 2012	34	SenosAyuda (Activists/Patients); Funcamama (Activists/Patients); Asomasol (Activists/Patients); Sociedad Venezolana de Mastologia (Medical Association); Colegio Nacional de Periodistas (NGO); Globovisión (TV Station); El Nacional (Newspaper); Ciudad CCS (Newspaper); 2001 (Newspaper); Entre Vecinos (Newspaper); Estética y Salud (Magazine); Revista Claro (Magazine); Vecino Saludable (Magazine); Vivir Mejor (Magazine); Vecino Saludable (Magazine); La Región (Newspaper); El Siglo (Newspaper); El Sol de Margarita (Newspaper); El Norte (Newspaper); El Informador (Newspaper); Radio Capital 710 (Radio Station); Kiss FM (Radio Station); Mágica FM (Radio Station); Roche (Pharma Company/ Sponsor)
Roundtable about the BC national response initiative	June 27, 2013	16	SenosAyuda (Activists/Patients); Funcamama (Activists/Patients); Famac (Activists/Patients); Sociedad Venezolana de Mastologia (Medical Association); Sociedad Venezolana de Oncologia (Medical Association); Sociedad Venezolana de Radiologia (Medical Association); Colegio Nacional de Periodistas (NGO); Sociedad Anticancerosa (NGO); Instituto Venezolano de los Seguros Sociales (Central Gov.); Ministerio del Poder Popular de la Salud (Central Gov.); Universidad Católica Andrés (University); Facultad de Medicina, Universidad Central de Venezuela (University); Novartis (Pharma/Sponsor); Roche (Pharma/Sponsor); Instituto Venezolano de Investigaciones Cientificas (Research Institute); Comisión de Familia, Asamblea Nacional (Parliament)

mammograms; and the diffusion of reliable and useful information about BC diagnostic, treatment, and social support.

In the context of this project, an "activist" is someone who plays a role of leadership and advocacy in a NGO representing the interests of people suffering from BC. Many of the activists who participated in this action-oriented research were also cancer patients (most of them BC patients, but some of them suffered from other type of cancers). SenosAyuda acted in this project as a federative platform of different NGOs and associations, facilitating the networking and connection between them. Members of SenosAyuda also actively participated in the workshops. The researchers facilitated the activities in collaboration with other colleagues, designed the evaluation tools, contributed to edit the documents, and participated in activities of scholarly and media diffusion of information.

Outcomes: Empowerment and Cooperation

The findings of this action-oriented research project could be summarized as follows: (1) we observed an empowerment of groups traditionally marginalized in Venezuela (women, and particularly sick women from certain regions); (2) we created the conditions to expand the networking among social activists, patients, physicians, public officials (from the central, regional, and municipal governments) that improved the relationship between the stakeholders and their understanding of BC issues; (3) we facilitated the participation of activists and patients in the design of a consensual view about a national response on BC; and (4) we contributed to a better understanding from social advocates, physicians, and journalists about the media's role in shaping opinions and public perceptions about BC in Venezuela.

The direct observation during the various activities allowed us to see how participants improved their communication performances. From a highly emotional communication, frequently marked by their own personal experience with the disease, many women developed their skills to convey their ideas and messages more clearly and persuasively. From a more systematic point of view, the evaluations of the first two workshops ($n = 37$ and $n = 25$, respectively) and the activity with journalists ($n = 34$) showed that the participants retained some basic notions of effective communication and social advocacy. In the first workshop, most participants said that the activity was useful, stressing that they learned important communication and advocacy skills, and declared to have a better understanding of the issues and challenges that they are facing as BC advocates.

In the workshop consecrated to doctor-patient communication, most participants reported that the subjects covered were useful, they gained a better understanding of the challenges that they have to overcome as physicians or patients when communicating with each other, and that they learned skills to improve their interpersonal interactions. Finally, in the workshop about media relations, most participants said that they learned useful concepts and techniques to improve their work as communicators or spokespersons. They also declared to have a better understanding of the issues and obstacles to improve media coverage of cancer in general and BC in particular.

During the first workshop, "strategic planning," "key messages techniques," and "risk communication" were identified as the participant's main cognitive gains. The doctor–patient workshop revealed main gains in the affective and relational levels: fundamental notions about a good "interpersonal communication", the "value of empathy", the "right way" to announce a diagnostic of cancer, and the "ethical considerations" in the doctor–patient interaction were retained as the most important subjects that were learned The journalists mentioned the "ethics of information" and the need to use a "more accessible language" to different audiences as the most important subjects.

The self-reflexive follow-up after the workshops (n = 8 after the first workshop and n = 8 after the second one) provided us with a deeper understanding about how the participants used the skills learned during the activities in their roles as social activists, advocates, or physicians. The activists, including some patients, mentioned that they were able to better define their objectives and messages in their diffusion and awareness activities in society. The doctors declared that they have changed some routines in their practice to overcome some of the physical and perceptual barriers when interacting with patients (e.g. remove the desk to avoid that barrier to communicate). They also mentioned to be more aware of the psychological factors influencing their encounter with patients (e.g. apply the active listening technique to better respond to patients' needs).

The action-oriented research project expanded SenosAyuda's collaboration network with different stakeholders, including other NGOs from the regions, physicians, public officials from the central, regional, and municipal governments, journalists, and scholars. The declaration entitled "Towards a Common Vision for the Design and Implementation of a National Policy against BC in Venezuela" was a direct outcome of this collaboration.[4] Those who participated in the third workshop (n = 20) initially subscribed in the declaration. After one year (May, 2012), one hundred one organizations signed the declaration, including eight community-based BC organizations, six medical associations, four human rights NGOs, and stakeholders such as the Venezuelan Red Cross and National College of Journalists.

The declaration presents a reference framework about the principles that should guide a future national policy on BC. These principles are:

- Educate and train the health care personnel in the diagnostic, treatment, and support of those suffering from BC.
- Develop a national system to compile, analyze, and facilitate the access to reliable data about the real impact of BC.

- Establish the mammogram as the key element for an early detection and diagnostic of the disease that will contribute to a better integration of all the actors involved in patient care.
- Convey messages and information associated with the solutions available to the public in connection with the diagnostic, treatment and palliative care, taking into account the needs and sociocultural realities of different patients.
- Secure the financial protection of those affected with BC through social security funding and private insurance.
- Promote the integration of public and private health care services to improve the access to BC diagnostic and treatment all over the country.
- Provide proper palliative care as a humane, ethical and moral duty of the State and society towards the persons with BC.

The declaration triggered a social mobilization that resulted in five thousand signatures supporting the document (last quarter of 2014), the diffusion of the principles and action calls of the consensual vision, and institutional cooperation agreements between SenosAyuda and different organizations such as the Universidad Central de Venezuela (UCV)[5]—the most important in the country—to improve BC education and training of the health care personnel (medicine students, residents, and nurses). The process of social mobilization included a media campaign,[6] meetings, and forums in different regions,[7] and the diffusion of the declaration through the NGO website[8] and social networks.[9]

The dialogue roundtable in July 2013 followed-up on the recommendations of the declaration.[10] Social activists, patients, doctors, scholars, and public officials from the Ministry of Health and the Venezuelan Institutes of Social Security agreed in that meeting: (1) to improve the quality of the mammogram as a way to improve the diagnostic and overall care of the disease; (2) to educate physicians (GPs, family doctors, gynecologists, etc.) to improve their BC knowledge and their ability to better guide patients seeking specialized care; and (3) to convey key information about diagnostic and treatment services and the patient support organizations throughout the country.

Conclusions

Individuals who face the burden of BC are bombarded by a variety of factors that interact with one's disease path. Patients are forced to wade through their own emotions and those of others, information regarding treatment, and a multitude of health care practitioner personalities. While this process can be extremely daunting for many women, the enactment of certain behaviors and social mechanisms can act as useful coping techniques. These tactics are intrinsically linked to empowerment and are centralized around one's ability to enact self-advocacy, which are facilitated through patient-centered care, self-efficacy, and strategic health promotion and coping strategies. Such empowerment can boost feelings of self-efficacy, which may promote healthy preventative behaviors (Errico & Rowden, 2006). Particularly in Latin America, NGOs are involved in the instigation of these endeavors; however, they commonly face obstacles that obstruct their success. Thus, research surrounding health behaviors is identified as a useful tool in guiding health interventions. The techniques and ideologies extracted from such research are subsequently complimented by networking, which fosters interactions and community involvement necessary for breast cancer awareness among women.

Activism initiatives function with the help of both health care providers and social influences. Health care providers play a unique role in activism and raising awareness, as they have the ability to interact with patients on a personal and intimate level. However, this opportunity for enacting satisfaction and healthy behaviors among patients relies on health care providers' communicative abilities. A detailed analysis of physician–patient communication reveals the highly complex nature of such interactions and the need for ongoing training and development. The role of society, specifically familial and cultural influences, has a strong impact on women's BC awareness, ultimately affecting how patients choose to navigate their healing journey. In fact, Latin American women respond more positively to physicians and the outreach that is sensitive and attuned to their specific cultural context (e.g. Larkey, 2006; Warren, Londoño & Wessell, 2006).

This action-oriented research illustrates the double impact of a dialogic approach in the empowerment of social activists in health care. By helping to enhance a systematic and continuous communication among different stakeholders, those who participated in this project developed their own skills as advocates of the cause (empowered for the activism), while at the same time applied these skills in the field working with the community (empowered by activism). In this regard, we share White's (2004) view on empowerment not only as a process of personal growing and influence, but as a social action to improve human rights, including the right to health care. The empowerment that we observed during the five-year collaboration with NGOs in Venezuela has been translated also into outcomes to defend the right of access to proper health care services and has set the foundations of a BC national policy.

This process of participation and inclusion helped overcome the barrier of social and political polarization, even though it did that in a limited way. The tensions and conflicts are still present in Venezuela,[11] but this project opened a dialogue between civil society and the central government breaking the dynamics of social division. The project made evident the political dimension—as action in the public sphere—of the empowerment process that implies the questioning of traditional social roles (e.g. doctor vs. patient; public official vs. citizen). We observed in several occasions during the workshops, at least in the framework of this research, a more horizontal and egalitarian relationship among all stakeholders.

Communication also had a disruptive effect on some participants who traditionally play the role of expert. For example, during the doctor-patient communication workshop it was evident that physicians did not like to be challenged by patients in simulation exercises. What we observed in the field confirmed that the traditional asymmetry in doctor–patient communication is often criticized by patients during their face-to-face and virtual interactions with health care professionals (Espinàs Olvera, 2003).

The encounter among activists, patients, doctors, and journalists opened a discussion about the challenges and opportunities regarding the diffusion of information on BC in Venezuela. The workshop participants identified two priorities about the role of media: the promotion of the breast self-exam, especially among young women, and the need to link reproductive health strategies and BC's early detection.

Something that is more difficult to assess corresponds to the empathy and solidarity that eventually emerged among the participants. Clearly after five years of collaboration and networking, the action-oriented research set the foundations of a "minimal solidarity" that allowed to build-up a consensual view about BC policy. However, this solidarity is more visible in the exchanges and communication that are still underway through the network of formal and informal collaborations. These networks have today a global and regional reach, as illustrated by the *Unión Latinoamericana Contra el Cáncer de la Mujer* (ULACCAM),[12] where SenosAyuda is a member, which brings to reality the motto "act locally, connect globally" of women organizations (Women in Sync, 2000).

This project has also some limitations, particularly in relationship to the inclusion of some organizations and activists living in remote areas. We encountered some difficulties in the self-reflexive follow-up as well. Some of the actions decided in the dialogue roundtable have not been implemented yet. Nevertheless, the general balance of the project is positive.

This action-oriented research is a modest contribution to better integrate civil society networks in their fight for the right to health care in Venezuela and eventually could inspire similar projects in other countries. The ecological model of communication and social activism in health care can be applied to disease prevention strategies, health promotion programs, and patient education initiatives. This model can certainly contribute to achieve the participation of citizens and communities in the design of health care policies through empowerment and a more horizontal and egalitarian communication.

Notes

1 The action-oriented research was possible thanks to grants from the Canadian Institutes of Health Research and the support of Avon Venezuela, Roche, and Novartis.
2 This action-oriented research was done in partnership with the NGO SenosAyuda and the support of professors Andrés Cañizales, Alfredo Poggi, José Rafael Briceño, Acianela Montes de Oca, and Néstor Garrido from the School of Social Communication, Universidad Católica Andrés Bello (Caracas, Venezuela), professor Jorge Díaz Polanco from CENDES (Universidad Central de Venezuela), and Feliciano Reyna and Joli D'Elía from the NGO *Acción Solidaria*. Various community and professionals also contributed to this project: the *Sociedad Venezolana de Mastología*, the *Sociedad Anticancerosa de Venezuela*, the *Colegio Nacional de Periodistas*, the community clinic *Centro de Salud Santa Inés*, and the breast cancer NGOs Fundamama, Funcamama, Famac, and Asomal.
3 SenosAyuda's Code of Conduct can be read here: www.senosayuda.org.ve/Nosotros.aspx.
4 The consensus declaration can be read here: www.senosayuda.org.ve/senosayuda/media/bibliotecaglobal/pdf/documentconsenso.pdf.
5 The cooperation agreement between SenosAyuda and the UCV can be read here: www.ucv.ve/fileadmin/user_upload/dicori/Documentos_Nacionales_pdf/10-13.pdf.
6 An example of the media campaign where SenosAyuda's spokesperson promoted the declaration: www.noticias24.com/venezuela/noticia/201206/en-vivo-tania-sarabia-conversa-con-noticias24-sobre-el-dia-internacional-del-cancer-de-mama/.
7 A meeting with community activists and patients in Margarita Island: www.facebook.com/media/set/?set=a.10151555871973182.1073741863.66899768181&type=1.
8 People can subscribe the on-line declaration here: www.senosayuda.org.ve/Redes/Documento-Consenso.aspx.
9 The declaration was promoted via Twitter: https://twitter.com/senosayuda/status/177417375119978496.
10 The dialogue roundtable was announced via Twitter: https://twitter.com/SenosAyuda/status/350259518145445889/photo/1.
11 The *Alianza social por la salud* was created in March 2014 to denounce the crisis of the health care system in Venezuela. Various members of this coalition were part of the action-oriented research project: www.derechos.org.ve/2014/03/27/marino-alvarado-alianza-social-por-la-salud/.
12 The ULACCAM website explains the mission and actions of this regional network: http://ulaccam.org/.

References

Alvarado, M. (2014). *Alianza Social por la Salud. Provea, 27 de marzo.* Retrieved April 23, 2015, from www.derechos.org.ve/2014/03/27/marino-alvarado-alianza-social-por-la-salud/.

Andersen, M. R., Ankerst, D. P., Bowen, D. J., McGregor, B. A., McTiernan, A. & Yasui, Y. (2004). Optimism, perceived risk of breast cancer, and cancer worry among a community-based sample of women. *Health Psychology, 23*(4), 339–344. doi:10.1037/0278-6133.23.4.339.

Bailey, R. (2012, October 29). *Deportivo Tachira match abandoned after fans riot over pink Breast Cancer Awareness kit.* Yahoo News. Retrieved November 11, 2012, from http://sports.yahoo.com/blogs/soccer-dirty-tackle/deportivo-tachira-match-abandoned-fans-riot-over-pink-181919490--sow.html.

Beltrán Salmón, L. R. (2010). Comunicación para la salud del pueblo. Una revisión de conceptos básicos, *Estudios sobre las Culturas Contemporáneas. Época II*, *XVI*(31), 17–65.

Beltrán, L. (1980). A farewell to Aristotle: Horizontal communication. *Communication*, *5*, 5–41.

Beltrán, L. R. (1994). La salud y la comunicación en Latinoamérica: Políticas, estrategias y planes. In UNESCO – OPS, *Por una política de comunicación para la promoción de la salud en América Latina* (pp. 29–90). Quito, Ecuador: OPS.

Berg, B. L. (2009). *Qualitative research methods for the social sciences.* Boston, MA: Allyn & Bacon.

Bisbal, M. (Ed). (2009). *Hegemonía y control comunicacional.* Caracas, Venezuela: Editorial Alfa-UCAB.

Borrayo, E. A. (2004). Where's Maria? A video to increase awareness about breast cancer and mammography screening among low-literacy Latinas. *Preventive Medicine*, *39*(1), 99–110. doi:10.1016/j.ypmed.2004.03.024.

Boza, M. E. (2004). *Desempleo en primera persona.* Caracas, Venezuela: IESA.

Brasington, A., Tapia, M., & van Lith, L. (2007). *Involving those directly affected in health and development communication programs.* Baltimore: Health Communication Partnership based at the John Hopkins Bloomberg School of Public Health/Center for Communication Programs.

Briggs, C. L., & Mantini-Briggs, C. (2009). Confronting health disparities: Latin American social medicine in Venezuela. *American Journal of Public Health*, *99*(3), 549–555. doi:10.2105/AJPH.2007.129130.

Briggs, C. L., & Mantini-Briggs, C. (2008). "Misión Barrio Adentro": Medicina Social, Movimientos Sociales de los Pobres y Nuevas Coaliciones en Venezuela. *Salud colectiva*, *3*(2), 159–176.

Buki, L. P., Borrayo, E. A., Feigal, B. M., & Carrillo, I. Y. (2004). Are all Latinas the same? Perceived breast cancer screening barriers and facilitative conditions. *Psychology of Women Quarterly*, *28*(4), 400–411. doi:10.1111/j.1471-6402.2004.00157.x.

Byrne, A., Gray-Felder, D., Hunt, J., & Parks, W. (2005). *Who measures change? An introduction to participatory monitoring and evaluation of communication for social change.* UK: Department for International Development, the Rockefeller Foundation, and Communication for Social Change Consortium.

Cancelo Sanmartín, M., & Gadea Aldave, G. (2013). Empoderamiento de las redes sociales en las crisis institucionales. *Revista de Comunicación Vivat Academia*, *124*, 21–33.

Cancer mortality: Researchers compare Latin American cancer mortality to other countries. (2005, October 6). *Women's Health Weekly*, p. 65.

De Souza, R. (2009). Creating "communicative spaces": A case of NGO community organizing for HIV/AIDS prevention. *Health Communication*, *24*(8), 692–702. doi:10.1080/10410230903264006.

Díaz Polanco, J. (2006). Salud y Hegemonía Regional: Las relaciones Venezuela-Cuba, 1999–2006. *Foreign Affairs en español*, *6*(4), 10–12.

Durstine, A., & Leitman, E. (2009). Building a Latin American cancer patient advocacy movement: Latin American cancer NGO regional overview. *Salud Publica Mexico*, *51*(2), 316–322. doi:10.1590/S0036-36342009000800023.

Eid, M., & Nahon-Serfaty, I. (2008). Transparency in direct-to-consumer pharmaceutical marketing: Crucial ethical standards. *IMC Review: Journal of Integrated Marketing Communications*, *7*(1), 6–14.

Eid, M., & Nahon-Serfaty, I. (2015a). Ethics, risk, and media intervention: Women's breast cancer in Venezuela. *International Journal of Risk and Contingency Management*, *4*(3), 49–69. doi:10.4018/IJRCM.2015070104.

Eid, M., & Nahon-Serfaty, I. (2015b). Risk, activism, and empowerment: Women's breast cancer in Venezuela. *International Journal of Civic Engagement and Social Change*, *2*(1), 43–64. doi:10.4018/IJCESC.2015010104.

Eid, M. (2008). *Interweavement: International media ethics and rational decision-making*. Boston, MA: Pearson.

Errico, K. M., & Rowden, D. (2006). Experiences of Breast Cancer survivor-advocates and advocates in countries with limited resources: A shared journey in breast cancer advocacy. *The Breast Journal*, *12*(1), S111–S116. doi:10.1111/j.1075-122X.2006.00208.x.

Espinàs Olvera, L. (2003). *Análisis psicosocial de la interacción "profesional de la salud"/"paciente"/"familiar". Un ejemplo: el caso de los foros virtuales de autoayuda en cáncer*. Athenea Digital, 4. Retrieved April 23, 2015, from http://atheneadigital.net/article/view/112/112.

Esterberg, K. G. (2002). *Qualitative methods in social research*. Boston, MA: McGraw-Hill.

Feo, O., & Curcio, P. (2004). La salud en el proceso constituyente venezolano. *Revista Cubana de Salud Pública*, *30*(2). Retrieved April 23, 2015, from http://scielo.sld.cu/scielo.php?pid=S0864-34662004000200008&script=sci_arttext&tlng=pt.

Feo, O., & Siqueira, C. E. (2004). An alternative to the Neoliberal model of health: The case of Venezuela. *International Journal of Health Services*, *34*(2), 365–375. doi:10.2190/NHFK-GHQW-AQLA-YC5D.

Figueroa, M. E., Kincaid, L. D., Rani, M., Lewis, G., & Gray-Felder, D. (2002). *Communication for social change: An integrated model for measuring the process and its outcomes*. Baltimore: Health Communication Partnership based at the John Hopkins Bloomberg School of Public Health/Center for Communication Programs and Rockefeller Foundation as part of their Communication for Social Change Grant making Strategy.

Freire, P. (1970, 2000). *Pedagogy of the Oppressed*. New York: The Continuum International Publishing Group.

Freitez, A. (2003). La situación demográfica de Venezuela a inicios del tercer milenio. *Temas de Coyuntura, IIES-UCAB*, *47*, 45–92.

González, M. J. (2005). Políticas de salud en Venezuela: Ni lo urgente, ni lo importante, *Anales Venezolanos de Nutrición*, *18*(1), 39 http://scielo.sld.cu/scielo.php?script=sci_isoref&pid=S0864-34662004000200008&lng=es&tlng=es–44.

Harvard Medical School's Center of Excellence in Women's Health. (2007). *Black women's attitudes about the links between breast cancer and obesity.* Boston, MA: Harvard Medical School.

Hivon, M, Lehoux, P., Denis, J.-L., & Rock, D. M. (2010). Marginal voices in the media coverage of controversial health interventions: How do they contribute to the public understanding of science? *Public Understanding of Science, 19*, 34–51. doi:10.1177/0963662508088668.

Human Rights Watch. (2008). *A Decade under Chávez. Political Intolerance and Lost Opportunities for Advancing Human Rights in Venezuela.* Washington, D.C.: Human Rights Watch.

Iedema, R., Degeling, P., Braithwaite, J., & White, L. (2003) "It's an interesting conversation I'm hearing": The doctor as manager. *Organization Studies, 25*, 15–33. doi:10.1177/0170840604038174.

International Agency for Research on Cancer. (2008). *Globocan 2008: Fast stats.* Retrieved November 11, 2012, from http://globocan.iarc.fr/factsheet.asp#WOMEN.

Iriart, C., Merhy, E. E., & Waitzkin, H. (2001). Managed care in Latin America: the new common sense in health policy reform. *Social Science & Medicine, 52*, 1243–1253. doi:10.1016/S0277-9536(00)00243-4.

Israël, B.A., Schulz, A.J., Parker, E.A., & Becker, A.B. (1998). Review of community- based research: Assessing partnership approaches to improve public health. *Annual Review of Public Health, 19*(1), 173–202.

Kim, S. H., & Willis, L. A. (2007). Talking about obesity: News framing of who is responsible for causing and fixing the problem. *Journal of Health Communication, 12*, 359–376. doi:10.1080/10810730701326051.

Larkey, L. (2006). Las mujeres saludables: Reaching Latinas for breast, cervical and colorectal cancer prevention and screening. *Journal of Community Health, 31*(1), 69–77. doi:10.1007/s10900-005-8190-2.

Lozada, M. (2008). ¿Nosotros o ellos? Representaciones sociales, polarización y espacio público en Venezuela. *Cuadernos del CENDES, 25*(69), 89–105.

MPPS. (2008). *Anuario de Mortalidad*, Ministerio del Poder Popular de la Salud, Caracas, Venezuela.

MPPS. (2011). *Anuario de Mortalidad*, Ministerio del Poder Popular de la Salud, Caracas, Venezuela.

Nahon-Serfaty, I. (2005). *Le discours sur la réforme de la santé au Vénézuela: la transition Chávez (1999–2001).* (Thèse de doctorat en Communication). Université de Montréal, Montréal, Canada.

Nigenda, G., González-Robledo, M. C., González-Robledo, L. M., & Bejarano, R. M. (2011). *Políticas y programas gubernamentales de atención al cáncer de mama en América-Latina: México, Colombia, Venezuela, Brasil y Argentina. Informe Final.* Cuernavaca, México: Instituto Nacional de Salud Pública y American Cancer Society.

OPS. (2011). *Género, salud y desarrollo: Venezuela.* Retrieved November 11, 2012, from www.paho.org/cdmedia/ge_cp/Venezuela.pdf.

Orlando, M. B., & Zúñiga, G. (2000). Situación de la mujer en el mercado laboral en Venezuela: Participación femenina y brecha de ingresos por género. *Temas de Coyuntura, IIES-UCAB, 41*, 59–97.

Pino Iturrieta, E. (2013). La revolución bolivariana: principio ó fin de una época? In M. Bisbal (Coordinador), *Saldo en rojo. Comunicaciones y cultura en la era bolivariana* (pp. 13–18). Caracas, Venezuela: Ediciones UCAB – Konrad Adenauer Stiftung.

Ponce, M. G. (2009). La pobreza en Venezuela: Mediciones y diversidades. *Presentación realizada en el taller sobre salud, mujer y telefonía celular.* Caracas, Venezuela: UCAB.

Provan, K. G., & Sebastian, J. G. (1998). Networks within networks: Service link overlap, organizational cliques, and network effectiveness. *Academy of Management Journal, 41*(4), 453–463. doi:10.2307/257084.

Reyna, F. (2013). La sociedad civil en el contexto post electoral. In M. Bisbal, (Coordinador-Ed.), *La Política y sus tramas. Miradas desde la Venezuela del presente* (pp. 180–189). Caracas, Venezuela: Ediciones de la UCAB.

Rodríguez, C. (2004). De la revolución sandinista a las telenovelas: el caso de «Puntos de Encuentro» (Nicaragua). *Investigación y desarrollo, 12*(1), 108–137.

Schutt, R. K., Cruz, E. R., & Woodford, M. L. (2008). Client satisfaction in a breast and cervical cancer early detection program: The influence of ethnicity and language, health, resources, and barriers. *Women & Health, 48*(3), 283–302. doi:10.1080/03630240802463475.

Small, S. A., & Uttal, L. (2005). Action-oriented research: Strategies for engaged scholarship. *Journal of Marriage and Family, 67*(4), 936–948. doi:10.1111/j.1741-3737.2005.00185.x.

Small, S. A. (1995). Action-oriented research: Models and methods. *Journal of Marriage and Family, 57*(4), 941–955. doi:10.2307/353414.

Smilde, D. (2011). Participation, politics, and culture. Emerging fragments of Venezuela's bolivarian democracy. In D. Smilde & D. Hellinger (Eds.) *Venezuela's bolivarian democracy: Participation, politics, and culture under Chávez* (pp. 1–27). Durham, NC: Duke University Press.

Sociedad Venezolana de Mastología. (2010). La Sociedad Venezolana de Mastología en tiempo de dificultades. *Carta Mastológica: Organo Divulgatorio de la Sociedad Venezolana de Mastología, 1*(28), 1–8. Retrieved January 12, 2013, from http://svmastologia.org/portal/images/stories/Cartas_Mastologicas/CM201007.pdf.

Street, R. L. (2003). Communicating in medical encounters: An ecological perspective. In T. L. Thomson, A. M. Dorsey, K. I. Miller, & R. Parrott (Eds.), *Handbook of health communication* (pp. 63–89). London: Lawrence Erlbaum Associates.

Vasconcellos-Silva, P. R., Uribe Rivera, F. J., & Siebeneichler, F. B. (2007). Health care organizations, linguistic communities, and the emblematic model of palliative care. *Cad. Saúde Pública, 23*, 1529–1538. doi:10.1590/S0102-311X2007000700003.

Villasmil, G. (2015). 5 consejos (no solicitados) de Gustavo Villasmil para Henry Ventura, el nuevo Ministro de Salud. *Prodavinci, 19 de marzo.* Retrieved April 25, 2015, from http://prodavinci.com/2015/03/19/actualidad/5-consejos-no-solicitados-de-gustavo-villasmil-para-henry-ventura-el-nuevo-ministro-de-salud/.

Warren, A., Londoño, G. E., & Wessel, L. A. (2006). Breaking down barriers to breast and cervical cancer screening: A university-based prevention program for Latinas. *Journal of Health care for the Poor and Underserved*, *17*(3), 512–521. doi:10.1353/hpu.2006.0114.

White, R. A. (2004). Is "empowerment" the answer? Current theory and research on development communication. *International Communication Gazette*, *66*(1), 7–24. doi:10.1177/0016549204039939.

Women in Sync. (Ed.). (2000). *Acting locally, connecting globally stories from the regions*. Manila, The Philippines: APC Women's Networking Support Programme.

Yamin, A. E. (2000). Protecting and promoting the right to health in Latin America: Selected experiences from the field. *Health and Human Rights*, *5*(1), 116–148. doi:10.2307/4065225.

Zoller, H. M. (2005). Health activism: Communication theory and action for social change. *Communication Theory*, *15*(4), 341–364. doi:10.1111/j.1468-2885.2005.tb00339.x.

12 Social Support, Social Control, and Dietary Acculturation among Asian Immigrants Living in the United States

Zheng An

Asians (populations originating from East Asia, Southeast Asia, or the Indian subcontinent, including, for example, China, Korea, Japan, Vietnam, Thailand, and India) have been the fastest-growing population during the past decade in the United States. Between 2000 and 2010, the number of Asians living in the US grew 46 percent from 11.9 to 17.3 million (Census, 2012). Long-term Asian immigrants and US-born Asian-Americans are more likely to be overweight than newly arrived Asian immigrants (Corlin, Woodin, Thanikachalam, Lowe, & Brugge, 2014; Singh, Siahpush, Hiatt, & Timsina, 2011). Asian immigrants have a higher risk of developing weight-related diseases (e.g. Type 2 diabetes, cardiovascular disease, and high blood pressure) if their body mass index increases slightly (Chiu, Austin, Manuel, Shah, & Tu, 2011). The increased risk for being overweight among long-term Asian immigrants and US-born Asian-Americans is partly caused by their adoption of the unhealthy diets of the host country (Rosenmöller, Gasevic, Seidell, & Lear, 2011; Satia *et al.*, 2001). Existing research on dietary acculturation has focused on a number of environmental and individual determinants, but has paid limited attention to sociocultural factors that play a central role in the lives of Asian immigrants.

Research shows that social relationships protect individuals' health by promoting health-enhancing behaviors (Berkman, Glass, Brissette, & Seeman, 2000; Tsai & Papachristos, 2014; Umberson, 1987). Social support (i.e. help from others) and social control (i.e. regulation from others), which are important and distinctive elements of social relationships, serve to encourage healthy eating, and limit the consumption of unhealthy foods. Functions of social relationships are especially important for Asian immigrants who are from predominantly collectivistic cultures. According to Hofstede (1980), collectivistic cultures, as opposed to individualistic cultures, place a great emphasis on social relationships. Among the various types of social relationships, family and close friends are at the center of the social structure. Immigrants from a predominantly collectivistic culture may be more likely to encounter social influence attempts and may thus be more susceptible to social influence than those from an individualistic culture (Liou & Contento, 2001).

The purpose of this chapter is to review the role of social support and social control from strong ties (i.e. family and friends) in promoting healthy eating behavior among Asian immigrants living in the United States. This chapter starts with an overview of overweight prevalence and dietary acculturation among Asian immigrants. Following that, this chapter reviews two important functions of social relationships, namely social support and social control, and their impact on dietary behavior. Next, this chapter discusses the implications of social relationships for family intervention programs. Finally, this chapter addresses the limitations of applying individualistic assumptions about social support and social control to the study of Asian immigrants and suggests opportunities for future research.

Overweight and Dietary Acculturation

Research consistently shows a healthy immigrant effect: immigrants in North America are generally healthier than the native-born Americans (Corlin *et al.*, 2014; McDonald & Kennedy, 2005). Immigrants tend to lose their health advantages within a decade of living in the United States. The healthy immigrant effect is evidenced by the fact that immigrants' overweight and obesity rates are significantly lower than that of the native-born (Singh *et al.*, 2011). Overweight and obesity rates of immigrants converge to those of the native-born within a decade of US residency (McDonald & Kennedy, 2005). For example, the National Health Interview Survey shows that the observed overweight prevalence in 2003–2008 was 19.8 for recent Chinese immigrants and 40.1 for US-born Chinese (Singh *et al.*, 2011). Cho and Juon (2006) surveyed 492 Korean Americans in California and found that about 46 percent were overweight and obese. The overweight prevalence was as high as 40 percent among US-born Chinese boys aged 6–12 years (Au, Kwong, Chou, Tso, & Wong, 2009). Overweight and obesity increase the health risks of Type 2 diabetes, hypertension, cardiovascular disease, fatty liver disease, and some types of cancer (Kumanyika *et al.*, 2008). According to the World Health Organization (2004), Asian immigrants and Asian-Americans may underestimate the health risks associated with being overweight, because a large proportion of them misclassify their body fatness status. The body mass index (BMI) estimates body fat based on weight and height. Asians have a higher percentage of body fat than whites with the same BMI (WHO, 2004). Asians whose BMI is less than but close to the cut-off point for being overweight may also have health risks associated with being overweight (Chiu *et al.*, 2011). For example, Shih, Du, Lightstone, Simon, and Wang (2014) analyzed the Los Angeles County Health Survey between 1997 and 2011 and found that the diabetes prevalence among Asians increased more rapidly than that of whites, even though Asians had lower BMIs. Oza-Frank and Narayan (2010) analyzed the 1997–2005 National Health Interview Survey and found that immigrants from the Indian subcontinent had a higher diabetes prevalence at lower BMIs than did European immigrants.

Changes in dietary patterns and lifestyles are believed to increase the risks of being overweight among immigrants (Sussner, Lindsay, Greaney, & Perterson, 2008). Satia *et al.* (2001) used the term *dietary acculturation* to describe the process by which immigrants adopt the eating patterns of the host country. Immigrants experience both favorable and unfavorable dietary changes after arriving in North America. Lesser *et al.* (2014) found that immigrants of South Asian origin increased their intakes of fruits and vegetables and reduced their use of deep-frying after immigration. Rosenmöller *et al.* (2011) reported similar findings among Chinese immigrants who increased fruit and vegetable consumption and awareness about healthy foods after they immigrated to North America. Despite such positive changes, dietary acculturation mostly involves the adoption of unhealthy food choices and eating patterns (Satia, 2010). Batis, Hernandez-Barrera, Barquera, Rivera, and Popkin (2011) found that many newly arrived immigrants maintained the favorable health behaviors (e.g. having low-fat and low-calorie diets) they had acquired prior to immigration. However, dietary choices based on traditional eating habits and food practices were lost within one generation of immigrants living in the United States. The US-born from various ethnic groups are acculturated to the typical American diet, which is characterized by high intakes of sugar, salt, saturated fat, red meat, and processed meat (Daniel, Cross, Koebnick, & Sinha, 2011; Wells & Buzby, 2008). The American diet has a high concentration of calories per serving. High consumption of highly processed and energy-dense foods has been linked to an increased risk of being overweight (Sussner *et al.*, 2008). Studies have shown that Asian immigrants increase their consumption of high-fat diets and convenience foods, increase portion sizes, and increase their frequency of dining out after immigration to North America (Lesser *et al.*, 2014; Rosenmöller *et al.*, 2011; Satia *et al.*, 2001). For example, Pan, Dixon, Himburg, and Huffman (1999) surveyed sixty-three Asian students on their dietary patterns before and after immigration to the United States. They found that the majority of Asian students increased their consumption of salty and sweet snacks and fast foods after immigration. In a longitudinal study of three hundred twelve Chinese immigrant women, Tseng, Wright, and Fang (2015) assessed participants' dietary intakes once a year between 2005 and 2008. They found that a longer US residency was associated with increases in sugar intake, consumption of energy-dense foods, and the percentage of energy acquired from fat. Jasti (2011) surveyed one hundred ninety-five

Korean immigrants living in the US and found that acculturated immigrants increased their consumption of fast foods and salted and sweet snacks. Mulasi-Pokhriyal, Smith, and Franzen-Castle (2012) used the twenty-four–hour dietary recall method to collect detailed information about food and beverage consumption among Southeast Asian children aged 9–18 years in Minnesota. They found that acculturated immigrant children increased their consumption of saturated fat and trans fatty acids. Unger *et al.* (2004) surveyed six hundred nineteen Asian adolescents in Southern California and found a significant association between acculturation and fast-food consumption.

A number of factors may contribute to dietary acculturation, such as nutrition knowledge, taste preferences, affordability, time constraints, financial insecurity, new interpersonal relationships, and the availability of traditional ingredients (Sanou *et al.*, 2014; Satia, 2010). For example, a review article on acculturation and nutritional health reveals that unavailability of traditional ingredients, low socioeconomic status, lack of nutrition knowledge, and lack of transportation were associated with the adoption of unfavorable dietary changes (Sanou *et al.*, 2014). Existing research on dietary acculturation recognizes the importance of multiple levels of influence, such as environmental and individual determinants, but has paid limited attention to sociocultural factors that play a central role in determining dietary and other health behaviors among Asian immigrants. If sociocultural factors are not considered important determinants of behavioral change, nutrition-related health promotion may be ineffective for Asian immigrant populations.

Many Asian immigrants share common cultural values that place great emphasis on interdependence and collectivism despite the heterogeneity that exists within each subgroup (Hofstede, 1980; Triandis, 1995). Asian cultures of origin have a tendency to define the self in terms of social relationships. Strong ties form an individual's social core. Interdependence normalizes behaviors involving others in exercising agency and making decisions (Morling, Kitayama, & Miyamoto, 2003). Relational boundaries are blurred. In-group members have a moral obligation to take care of each other (Kim, Sherman, Ko, & Taylor, 2006). Unwanted or excessive help may be perceived as showing love and protection rather than as undermining a person's agency (Gao & Ting-Toomey, 1998). Therefore, Asian immigrants are more likely to encounter social influence attempts from strong ties and are more susceptible to these attempts than members of individualistic cultures (Liou & Contento, 2001).

Social relationships protect health by promoting health-enhancing behavior (Berkman *et al.*, 2000; Durkheim, 1967). The protective function of social relationships is often practiced in the form of communicative activities (Umberson, Crosnoe, & Reczek, 2010). The following section discusses two functional contents of social relationships, social support and social control, and their impact on dietary behavior among Asian immigrants.

Social Support and Dietary Behavior

Social support is the "verbal and nonverbal communication between recipients and providers that reduces uncertainty about the situation, the self, the other or the relationship, and functions to enhance a perception of personal control in one's life experience" (Albrecht & Adelman, 1987, p. 19). Individuals may receive various types of support, such as information, empathy, tangible aid, and constructive feedback, from social relationships that promote better health and well-being. Sallis *et al.* (1987) developed a measure of social support specific to dietary behaviors. Supportive acts from the support provider may include, but are not limited to, discussing dietary patterns with the recipient, reminding the recipient not to eat high-fat foods, offering the recipient healthy snacks, and encouraging the recipient to eat low-salt, low-fat foods.

Received support is often distinguished from perceived support (Uchino, 2009). Perceived support is an individual's belief that he or she will be helped by others, whereas received support emphasizes the behavioral component. In a review article on social support and chronic illness self-management, Gallant (2003) found that regimen-specific support (e.g. improving diets among people with diabetes) was more effective when it was actual, whereas general support was more effective when being perceived. Uchino (2009) also found that received support has direct relevance for health behavior and physical health outcomes, and perceived support has been shown to be more effective in buffering the effects of stressful events and improving individuals' psychological health.

Social support can come from many sources, including family members, friends, coworkers, acquaintances, neighbors, online support groups, and health care professionals. The amount and type of support may vary widely depending on its source of support. Strong ties are more likely to provide long-term support and emotional support than weak ties such as neighbors and coworkers (Heaney & Israel, 2008). In cultures that are oriented towards interdependence and collectivism, family members and close friends are primary sources of diet-specific social support (Choi, 2009; Thrasher, Campbell, & Oates, 2004). Female family members play a significant role in providing support such as cooking for others and disseminating nutrition knowledge (Choi, 2009; Thornton *et al.*, 2006).

Diet-specific social support has been linked to healthy dietary behavior, which, in turn, leads to many health benefits (Anderson, Winett, & Wojcik, 2007). For example, Choi (2009) surveyed 143 Korean immigrants with Type 2 diabetes and found that higher levels of diet-specific family support, such as praise for following one's diet and eating together, were significantly associated with better glucose control. Larson, Eisenberg, Berge, Arcan, and Neumark-Sztainer (2015) surveyed 2374 ethnically diverse adolescents and their parents in a metropolitan area in the United States and found that parental encouragement of healthy eating lowered Asian youths' intake of sugar-sweetened beverages. Scholz, Ochsner, Hornung, and Knoll (2013) surveyed 252 overweight and obese individuals at baseline and 12 months later. They found that receiving instrumental support from one's partner was associated with eating a low-fat diet one year later. Anderson *et al.* (2007) surveyed 712 churchgoers in Virginia and found that family support increased participants' consumption of fiber, fruits, and vegetables. Stanton, Green, and Fries (2007) surveyed 1942 rural adolescents' diet-specific social support from family and friends and found that family and friend support was positively associated with fiber intake. Harley and Eskenazi (2006) found that social support could counter the negative effect of acculturation of diets; that is, acculturated immigrants who received high levels of social support had better diet quality.

Numerous pathways exist by which social support exerts influence on health behavior. One possible mechanism explaining the link between social support and dietary behavior is self-efficacy. Perceived self-efficacy refers to one's belief that he or she is able to perform a certain behavior (Bandura, 2004). Individuals with high levels of perceived self-efficacy are motivated to control impulses and avoid unhealthy eating habits (Stroebe, Papies, & Aarts, 2010). Social support may increase individuals' efficacy beliefs by informing, modeling, and motivating the adoption of eating a healthy diet (Bandura, 2004). For example, Stanford *et al.* (2015) surveyed 182 adolescents and found that social support from friends increased nutritional self-efficacy beliefs, which, in turn, increased their consumption of healthy foods. Even earlier, Anderson *et al.* (2007) had also found that family social support increased self-efficacy, which then increased the intake of fruits and vegetables and decreased fat consumption. Rosland *et al.* (2008) surveyed 164 diabetic patients and found that self-efficacy mediated the relationship between support from family and friends and adherence to diabetic-diet meal plans. Increasing self-efficacy is particularly important for maintaining healthy eating behavior in the long term, otherwise individuals may not stick to a healthy behavior once social influence factors are removed from their social environment (Rook, Thuras, & Lewis, 1990).

Social Control and Dietary Behavior

Individuals are attracted to energy-dense foods for survival (Drewnowski & Almiron-Roig, 2010). These foods are usually highly palatable and stimulate a desire to eat. Before coming to the United States, some immigrants may live in a resource-constrained environment, where limited access to food is a restraint in itself. After they come to the United States, immigrants are exposed to an environment with abundant energy-dense foods and may more or less lose their control over food intake. The desire for tasty but unhealthy foods may be constrained by social relationships.

Social control refers to communication that helps regulate individuals' thoughts, feelings, and behaviors in an attempt to gain conformity (Umberson, 1987). The concept of social control at the interpersonal level has been developed from the tradition of research on social relationships and health (Berkman *et al.*, 2000; House, Umberson, & Landis, 1988; Lewis & Rook, 1999; Umberson, 1987). Social control is a function of social relationships that provide external regulation of health behaviors (Umberson, 1987). Social control has direct and indirect forms. Direct control takes place when members of social relationships make explicit attempts to monitor, remind, or physically intervene in an effort to change a person's health-related behavior. For example, a father may limit sweets and cookies available to his children, or a wife may remind her husband to eat green vegetables. Indirect social control occurs when an individual internalizes norms of behavior for the relationship and consequently avoids risky behaviors in order to fulfill his or her responsibilities to others. For example, parents may eat at regular times throughout the day to set a good example for their children. Vilaro, Barnett, Mathews, Pomeranz, and Curbow (2016) interviewed 20 rural adult women and found that they experienced both direct and indirect control from their social network members. Spouses, boyfriends, and close relatives persuaded these women to eat a healthy diet by reminding, sanctioning, and modeling.

Although social control as a constraint on risky behavior can theoretically be distinguished from social support that focuses on the positive, affirming, and encouraging aspects of social relationships, the two concepts are both functional contents of social relationships and have considerable overlap in the ways they are measured (House *et al.*, 1988; Lewis, Butterfield, Darbes, & Johnston-Brooks, 2004). Social control has been assessed as members of social relationships providing information, giving advice, reminding or pressuring an individual to do something for his or her health, and rewarding or praising an individual for performing a health-enhancing behavior (Lewis & Rook, 1999; Rook *et al.*, 1990). Lewis *et al.* (2004) explored a wide range of social control tactics in close relationships (e.g. marriage) and concluded that social control might be best conceptualized and measured as a continuum of tactics ranging from direct coercion to subtle forms of influence (e.g. discussion, modeling, and making suggestions). Social control actions can be both unwelcome (e.g. nagging and policing) and positive (e.g. expressing support and praising). Positive social control overlaps with some forms of social support such as informational support (i.e. the provision of information and advice) and emotional support (i.e. the provision of empathy, praise, and love).

The tradition of research on the regulatory functions of social relationships is rooted in Durkheim's (1967) seminal work on social integration. Durkheim viewed human desire as unlimited and believed that satisfaction stimulates rather than fulfills desires. In his view, desires can only be regulated by external controls. Society exerts the controlling influence and puts limits on individuals' behavior. When social control is weakened, individuals are more prone to deviant behavior or suicide. Durkheim stressed the importance of family relationships (e.g. parent-child and husband-wife) as sources of social integration and found that family ties reduced suicide. Durkheim's contribution influenced major theoretical developments in linking social relationships with health behavior through social control.

Umberson (1987) viewed social control as a dimension of social integration. She proposed that the relationships of marriage and parenting provide external regulation and facilitate the self-enforcement of norms of health behaviors. When individuals are attached to family ties, they are likely to engage in health behaviors that promote health and reduce mortality. House *et al.* (1988) explicitly defined the social regulation or control function of social relationships, noting that it overlaps with that of social support but emphasizes the constraining influence on individuals' behavior. They argued that social regulation and social support are important functional contents of social relationships that promote individual or collective health-enhancing behaviors. Berkman *et al.* (2000) proposed a conceptual model for thinking about social networks and health. Constraining influences are one of the pathways through which social networks affect health behaviors (e.g. diet and exercise). In another review paper, Thoits (2011) viewed social control as a direct and active form of social influence and a key mechanism through which social ties affect physical health outcomes.

Although little research has focused on the influence of social control on dietary behavior among Asian immigrant adults, relevant research examining parental control provides some empirical evidence linking social control to healthy eating behavior for the immigrant population. Lv and Brown (2010) interviewed 20 Chinese households with at least one child aged five years old or older in Pennsylvania. They found that most parents urged their children to eat vegetables and limited their children's consumption of unhealthy foods (e.g. potato chips, popcorn, and soda). High levels of parental control and frequent family meals have been linked to healthy food choices for collectivistic youth (Chang & Halgunseth, 2014). Larson *et al.* (2015) also found that parental modeling of healthy food choices increased adolescents' fruit and vegetable intake. Another line of research, on spouse control and health behavior, yields mixed findings. Some studies report positive associations between spouse control and partners' health-enhancing behavior, whereas other studies find that spouse control increases partners' psychological stress or has no impact on partners' health behavior (Helgeson, Novak, Lepore, & Eton, 2004; Sullivan, Pasch, Bejanyan, & Hanson, 2010). The following section discusses a potential explanation for inconsistencies in the relationship between social control and health behavior that are specifically relevant to the immigrant population.

Costs of Social Support and Social Control

It is important to note that social support and social control from strong ties do not always produce desirable effects. Several studies have reported some levels of distress experienced by the person who receives social support or social control from social networks (Thornton *et al.*, 2006; Vilaro *et al.*, 2016). Sources of distress include harsh criticism about fat gain and comments about one's eating habits. Although social support and social control are intended by the sender to be beneficial, the act itself may have a negative impact on the recipient if it is not carried out tactfully. Individuals have needs for both connectedness and autonomy. They constantly try to balance the two contradictory needs in interpersonal relationships (Baxter, 1988). If social support or social control is implemented without tact, it may be perceived as controlling and may threaten one's autonomy (Lewis *et al.*, 2004). The psychological reactance theory suggests that a threat to one's freedom could trigger reactance (Brehm & Brehm, 1981). Individuals may be motivated to resist or act counter to social influence attempts in order to restore freedom. For example, Gough and Conner (2006) interviewed twenty-four men about barriers to healthy eating. Participants perceived the persuasive messages about healthy eating as intrusive and wanted to restore freedom by claiming eating as a personal choice.

According to the normative approach, the extent to which well-intentioned social support and social control acts trigger psychological stress may depend on how well these acts achieve multiple goals, such as instrumental, relationship, and identity goals (Goldsmith & Fitch, 1997). For example, advice about healthy eating can be informative; alternatively, it could be perceived as intrusive and might undermine the recipient's self-worth. Social support and social control acts should be instrumentally helpful as well as emotionally sensitive if they are to achieve multiple goals (An, 2016).

The extent to which a social support or social control attempt provokes psychological distress may depend on immigrants' levels of acculturation. For example, in a longitudinal study with Hispanic adolescents who are influenced by collectivistic values, Chang and Halgunseth (2014) found that parental control protected against unhealthy weight change only for less acculturated Hispanic youth. They speculated that parental control was culturally contextualized. In less acculturated Hispanic families, parental control sets a structured home environment, which is perceived as a positive influence on regulating adolescents' eating behavior. In more acculturated Hispanic families, parental control may be perceived as criticism of weight and eating habits or suppression of alternative views on what is considered healthy eating, both of which can be associated with stress and rejection.

Computer-Mediated Social Support and Social Control

The Internet has facilitated immigrants' communication with family and friends who may reside in different time and geographic zones. A recent study reports that the majority of immigrants have at least one transnational tie in their social support networks (Herz, 2015). The Internet allows family and friends to provide social support and social control in many different ways, such as reminding a person not to eat high-fat, high-salt foods using online chat applications, showing concerns about one's diet in text messages, or giving suggestions on where to buy healthy produce through emails. Furthermore, strong ties are drivers of news. In 2013, about 21 percent of US adults received news from family and friends through social media or emails (Enda & Mitchell, 2013). Family and friends may spread news and information about dietary guidelines, healthy recipes, or food safety by sharing it on social networking sites.

The relationship between face-to-face (FTF) and computer-mediated support/control may be placed within a larger context that concerns the relationship between FTF and computer-mediated communication (CMC). Early research proposed the displacement hypothesis—that FTF is negatively associated with CMC (Putnam, 1995). An individual's total channel use is relatively constant. Time spent using one channel will reduce time spent using another. The channel complementarity theory, however, posits a competing hypothesis, that is, FTF is positively associated with CMC (Dutta-Bergman, 2006). According to this theory, the functions of interactions affect how individuals use specific communication channels to fulfill their goals. An individual may use both FTF and CMC to serve a specific functional need, such as providing or receiving support from family and friends. Therefore, the functions of social relationships may be delivered in both FTF and in computer-mediated contexts. For example, An (2015) surveyed five hundred five Chinese immigrants living in the United States and found that immigrants who received high levels of face-to-face support from family and friends also received high levels of computer-mediated support in the context of healthy eating.

Implications for Practice

Social support interventions for Asian immigrants should prioritize enhancing support from family and friends, who are among the most influential social network members. Immigrants and their family members may benefit from workshops on improving communication skills that are used to deliver instrumentally helpful and emotionally sensitive support in multicultural contexts. These skills may include, but are not limited to, praising a family member for making healthy choices, redirecting a family member to a healthier choice, and turning negativity or criticisms about unhealthy behavior into shows of support. With such skills, family members may be helpful to each other in setting limits on food without being overly intrusive. Such workshops may also help immigrants and their family members raise awareness of the relationship between social support and healthy eating behavior, as well as increase support for each other if they are currently not providing enough support.

Computer-mediated networks offer great potential for individuals to gain access to social support from strong ties (Wright, 2009). For example, food is a widely used topic with which to start conversations for ethnic Chinese. Supportive messages can be conveyed in small talks on a regular basis. Health practitioners could design interventions that help Asian immigrants increase their contact with family and close friends through emails, instant messaging, video chatting applications, and social networking sites. Frequent interactions may increase the likelihood of providing and receiving social support, such as sharing healthy recipes, discussing places to buy healthy produce, and showing concerns about one's diet. In addition, health professionals could work with application software developers to design diet-related applications that help increase the participation of family members and close friends in grocery shopping and meal planning.

Future Research

Existing literature utilizes Western conceptualizations of social support to study immigrant populations. The process of seeking and receiving support is based on individualistic assumptions in which individuals are responsible for seeking resources and coping with health issues (Kim *et al.*, 2006). When applying individualistic assumptions to the study of immigrants with collectivistic orientations, it may appear that these immigrants are reluctant to seek support. Some studies have reported that Asians are less likely than Caucasians to seek support from their social networks, because Asians do not want to burden others (e.g. Kim, Sherman, & Taylor, 2008). It is also possible that immigrants with collectivistic orientations may receive high levels of support without explicitly asking for it. Members of their social networks, especially family and friends, are expected to interpret things left unsaid and take actions to help. For Asian immigrants, support recipients and providers may exchange a few words that convey complex meanings, such as asking for help without explicitly saying so. This process may not be accurately captured by existing assessments of social support. More research is needed using collectivistic perspectives in which supportive interactions are implicit and relational.

Another area of potential research involves the relationship between acculturation and diet-specific social support/social control. It has been reported that social support or social control from strong ties may not be easily available to newly arrived immigrants, because their family and friends live in geographically dispersed locations (Salinero-Fort *et al.*, 2011). This may be true under some circumstances, such as instrumental support that requires physical presence or acculturation-related support that requires knowledge of the host country. However, some forms of diet-specific social support and social control, such as reminding a family member to eat fruits and vegetables, can be practiced without location constraints. A recent study found that foreign-born Chinese in the United States received higher levels of diet-specific support from family and friends than did US-born Chinese in both face-to-face and computer-mediated contexts (An, 2015). The findings suggest that social support, social control, and many other indicators of social influence may be embedded in collectivistic ways of living. Immigrants may slowly lose their exposure and conformity to social influence as they assimilate into the US culture, which places high values on self-reliance and independence. Future research could potentially examine how acculturation alters frequencies, practices, and consequences of social influence attempts for Asian immigrants.

Conclusions

Social relationships are an important driving factor to target nutrition-related health promotion and intervention among Asian immigrants living in the United States. Social support and social control, as important functions of social relationships, play an essential role in affecting Asian immigrants' dietary behavior, which, in turn, prevents overweight and weight-related diseases. Social support and social control from strong ties provide external regulation and facilitate internal regulation of healthy eating behavior. Asian immigrants may be more susceptible than other ethnic groups to social influence attempts because of their collectivistic orientations. The amount of support and control that Asian immigrants receive and their willingness to conform may decrease as they assimilate into the US culture. The decreased level of social support and/or social control experienced after immigration may, in part, contribute to the loss of healthy eating habits, particularly when immigrants have not developed self-oriented values such as self-reliance and self-regulation. This chapter also raises questions about the individualistic approach in social support and social control research. Future research should examine the ways in which social support attempts are made without expressive communication and how social control tactics are embedded in collectivistic ways of living.

References

Albrecht, T. L., & Adelman, M. B. (1987). Communicating social support: A theoretical Perspective. In T. L. Albrecht & M. B. Adelman (Eds.), *Communicating social support* (pp. 18–39). Newbury Park, CA: Sage.

An, Z. (2015). *The role of social control in promoting healthy eating behavior among Chinese immigrants: An ecological approach* (Doctoral dissertation).

University of Southern California Digital Library. Retrieved from http://digitallibrary.usc.edu/cdm/ref/collection/p15799coll3/id/543319.

An, Z. (2016). Emotional and relationship well-being for post-1980s Chinese mothers receiving family support for childcare: Comparing tangible support and supportive communication. *Chinese Journal of Communication*, *9*, 422–439. doi:10.1080/17544750.2016.1202852.

Anderson, E. S., Winett, R. A., & Wojcik, J. R. (2007). Self-regulation, self-efficacy, outcome expectations, and social support: Social cognitive theory and nutrition behavior. *Annals of Behavioral Medicine*, *34*, 304–312. doi:10.1007/BF02874555.

Au, L., Kwong, K., Chou, J. C., Tso, A., & Wong, M. (2009). Prevalence of overweight and obesity in Chinese American children in New York City. *Journal of Immigrant and Minority*, *11*, 337–341. doi:10.1007/s10903-009-9226-y.

Bandura, A. (2004). Health promotion by social cognitive means. *Health Education & Behavior*, *31*, 143–164. doi:10.1177/1090198104263660.

Batis, C., Hernandez-Barrera, L., Barquera, S., Rivera, J. A., & Popkin, B. M. (2011). Food acculturation drives dietary differences among Mexicans, Mexican Americans, and Non-Hispanic Whites. *Journal of Nutrition*, *141*, 1898–1906. doi:10.3945/jn.111.141473.

Baxter, L. A. (1988). A dialectical perspective on communication strategies in relationship development. In S. Duck (Ed.), *Handbook of personal relationships* (pp. 257–273). London: Wiley.

Berkman, L. F., Glass, T., Brissette, I., & Seeman, T. E. (2000). From social integration to health: Durkheim in the new millennium. *Social Science & Medicine*, *51*, 843–857. doi:10.1016/S0277-9536(00)00065-4.

Brehm, S. S., & Brehm, J. W. (1981). *Psychological reactance: A theory of freedom and control*. New York, NY: Academic Press.

Census. (2012). *2010 Census shows Asians are fastest-growing race group*. Retrieved from www.census.gov/newsroom/releases/archives/2010_census/cb12-cn22.html.

Chang, Y., & Halgunseth, L. C. (2014). The association between family meals and early-adolescents' weight status change in the context of parental discipline practices: The moderating roles of ethnicity and acculturation. *Journal of Immigrant and Minority Health*, *17*, 450–458. doi:10.1007/s10903-014-0084-x.

Chiu, M., Austin, P. C., Manuel, D. G., Shah, B. R., & Tu, J. V. (2011). Deriving ethnic-specific BMI cutoff points for assessing diabetes risk. *Diabetes Care*, *34*, 1741–1748. doi:10.2337/dc10-2300.

Cho, J., & Juon, H.-S. (2006). Assessing overweight and obesity risk among Korean Americans in California using World Health Organization body mass index criteria for Asians. *Preventing Chronic Disease: Public Health Research, Practice, and Policy*, *3*, 1–11. Retrieved from www.cdc.gov/pcd/issues/2006/jul/pdf/05_0198.pdf.

Choi, S. E. (2009). Diet-specific family support and glucose control among Korean immigrants with type 2 diabetes. *The Diabetes Educator*, *35*, 978–985. doi:10.1177/0145721709349220.

Corlin, L., Woodin, M., Thanikachalam, M., Lowe, L., & Brugge, D. (2014). Evidence for the healthy immigrant effect in older Chinese immigrants: A cross-sectional study. *BMC Public Health*, *14*, 603. doi:10.1186/1471-2458-14-603.

Daniel, C. R., Cross, A. J., Koebnick, C., & Sinha, R. (2011). Trends in meat consumption in the USA. *Public Health Nutrition, 14*, 575–583. doi:10.1017/S1368980010002077.

Drewnowski, A., & Almiron-Roig, E. (2010). Human perceptions and preferences for fat-rich foods. In J.-P. Montmayeur & J. le Coutre (Eds.), *Fat detection: Taste, texture, and post ingestive effects*. CRC Press. Retrieved from www.ncbi.nlm.nih.gov/books/NBK53528/.

Durkheim, E. (1967). *Le suicide: etude de sociologie* (2nd ed.) Presses Universitaires de France (1st ed., 1897), Paris.

Dutta-Bergman, M. J. (2006). Community participation and Internet use after September 11: Complementarity in channel consumption. *Journal of Computer-Mediated Communication, 11*, 469–484. doi:10.1111/j.1083-6101.2006.00022.x.

Enda, J., & Mitchell, A. (2013). *Friends and family – important drivers of news*. Retrieved from www.stateofthemedia.org/2013/special-reports-landing-page/friends-and-family-important-drivers-of-news/.

Gallant, M. P. (2003). The influence of social support on chronic illness self-management: A review and directions for research. *Health Education & Behavior, 30*, 170–195. doi:10.1177/1090198102251030.

Gao, G., & Ting-Toomey, S. (1998). *Communicating effectively with the Chinese*. Thousand Oaks, CA: Sage.

Goldsmith, D. J., & Fitch, K. (1997). The normative context of advice as social support. *Human Communication Research, 23*, 454–476. doi:10.1111/j.1468-2958.1997.tb00406.x.

Gough, B., & Conner, M. T. (2006). Barriers to healthy eating amongst men: A qualitative analysis. *Social Science & Medicine, 62*, 387-395. doi:10.1016/j.socscimed.2005.05.032.

Harley, K., & Eskenazi, B. (2006). Time in the United States, social support and health behaviors during pregnancy among women of Mexican descent. *Social Science & Medicine, 62*, 3048–3061. doi:10.1016/j.socscimed.2005.11.036.

Heaney, C. A., & Israel, B. A. (2008). Social networks and social support. In K. Glanz & B. K. Rimer (Eds.), *Health behavior and health education: Theory, research, and practice* (4th ed., pp. 189–210). San Francisco, CA: Jossey-Bass.

Helgeson, V. S., Novak, S. A., Lepore, S. J., & Eton, D. T. (2004). Spouse social control efforts: Relations to health behavior and well-being among men with prostate cancer. *Journal of Social and Personal Relationships, 21*, 53–68. doi:10.1177/0265407504039840.

Herz, A. (2015). Relational constitution of social support in migrants' transnational personal communities. *Social Networks, 40*, 64–74. doi:10.1016/j.socnet.2014.08.001.

Hofstede, G. (1980). *Culture's consequences: International differences in work-related values*. Beverly Hills, CA: Sage Publications.

House, J. S., Umberson, D., & Landis, K. R. (1988). Structures and processes of social support. *Annual Review of Sociology, 14*, 293–318. doi:10.1146/annurev.so.14.080188.001453.

Jasti, S. (2011). Gender, acculturation, food patterns, and overweight in Korean immigrants. *American Journal of Health Behavior, 35*, 734–745. doi:10.5993/AJHB.35.6.9.

Kim, H. S., Sherman, D. K., Ko, D., & Taylor, S. E. (2006). Pursuit of comfort and pursuit of harmony: culture, relationships, and social support seeking. *Personality and Social Psychology Bulletin*, *32*, 1595–1607. doi:10.1177/0146167206291991.

Kim, H. S., Sherman, D. K., & Taylor, S. E. (2008). Culture and social support. *The American Psychologist*, *63*, 518–526. doi:10.1037/0003-066X.

Kumanyika, S. K., Obarzanek, E., Stettler, N., Bell, R., Field, A. E., Fortmann, S. P., ... Hong, Y. (2008). Population-based prevention of obesity: the need for comprehensive promotion of healthful eating, physical activity, and energy balance: A scientific statement from American Heart Association Council on epidemiology and prevention, interdisciplinary committee for prevention. *Circulation*, *118*, 428–64. doi:10.1161/CIRCULATIONAHA.108.189702.

Larson, N., Eisenberg, M. E., Berge, J. M., Arcan, C., & Neumark-Sztainer, D. (2015). Ethnic/racial disparities in adolescents' home food environments and linkages to dietary intake and weight status. *Eating Behaviors*, *16*, 43–6. doi:10.1016/j.eatbeh.2014.10.010.

Lesser, I. A., Gasevic, D., Lear, S. A., Lauderdale, D., Rathouz, P., Lee, M., ... Wong, P. (2014). The association between acculturation and dietary patterns of South Asian immigrants. *PLoS ONE*, *9*, e88495. doi:10.1371/journal.pone.0088495.

Lewis, M. A., Butterfield, R. M., Darbes, L. A., & Johnston-Brooks, C. (2004). The conceptualization and assessment of health-related social control. *Journal of Social and Personal Relationships*, *21*, 669–687. doi:10.1177/0265407504045893.

Lewis, M. A., & Rook, K. S. (1999). Social control in personal relationships: Impact on health behaviors and psychological distress. *Health Psychology*, *18*, 63–71. doi:10.1037/0278-6133.18.1.63.

Liou, D., & Contento, I. R. (2001). Usefulness of psychosocial theory variables in explaining fat-related dietary behavior in Chinese Americans: Association with degree of acculturation. *Journal of Nutrition Education*, *33*, 322–331. doi:10.1016/S1499-4046(06)60354-0.

Lv, N., & Brown, J. L. (2010). Chinese American family food systems: Impact of Western influences. *Journal of Nutrition Education and Behavior*, *42*, 106–114. doi:10.1016/j.jneb.2009.04.005.

McDonald, J. T., & Kennedy, S. (2005). Is migration to Canada associated with unhealthy weight gain? Overweight and obesity among Canada's immigrants. *Social Science & Medicine*, *61*, 2469–2481. doi:10.1016/j.socscimed.2005.05.004.

Morling, B., Kitayama, S., & Miyamoto, Y. (2003). American and Japanese women use different coping strategies during normal pregnancy. *Personality and Social Psychology Bulletin*, *29*, 1533–1546. doi:10.1177/0146167203256878.

Mulasi-Pokhriyal, U., Smith, C., & Franzen-Castle, L. (2012). Investigating dietary acculturation and intake among US-born and Thailand/Laos-born Hmong-American children aged 9–18 years. *Public Health Nutrition*, *15*, 176–85. doi:10.1017/S1368980011001649.

Oza-Frank, R., & Narayan, K. M. (2010). Overweight and diabetes prevalence among US immigrants. *American Journal of Public Health*, *100*, 661–668. doi:10.2105/AJPH.2008.149492.

Pan, Y. L., Dixon, Z., Himburg, S., & Huffman, F. (1999). Asian students change their eating patterns after living in the United States. *Journal of the American Dietetic Association*, *99*, 54–57. doi:10.1016/S0002-8223(99)00016-4.

Putnam, R. D. (1995). Bowling alone: America's declining social capital. *Journal of Democracy*, *6*, 65–78. doi:10.1353/jod.1995.0002.

Rook, K. S., Thuras, P. D., & Lewis, M. A. (1990). Social control, health risk taking, and psychological distress among the elderly. *Psychology and Aging*, *5*, 327–334. doi:10.1037/0882-7974.5.3.327.

Rosenmöller, D. L., Gasevic, D., Seidell, J., & Lear, S. A. (2011). Determinants of changes in dietary patterns among Chinese immigrants: a cross-sectional analysis. *The International Journal of Behavioral Nutrition and Physical Activity*, *8*, 42. doi:10.1186/1479-5868-8-42.

Rosland, A. M., Kieffer, E., Israel, B., Cofield, M., Palmisano, G., Sinco, B., … Heisler, M. (2008). When is social support important? The association of family support and professional support with specific diabetes self-management behaviors. *Journal of General Internal Medicine*, *23*, 1992–1999. doi:10.1007/s11606-008-0814-7.

Salinero-Fort, M. Á., del Otero-Sanz, L., Martín-Madrazo, C., de Burgos-Lunar, C., Chico-Moraleja, R. M., Rodés-Soldevila, B., … Gómez-Campelo, P. (2011). The relationship between social support and self-reported health status in immigrants: An adjusted analysis in the Madrid cross sectional study. *BMC Family Practice*, *12*, 46. doi:10.1186/1471-2296-12-46.

Sallis, J. F., Grossman, R. M., Pinski, R. B., Patterson, T. L., & Nader, P. R. (1987). The development of scales to measure social support for diet and exercise behaviors. *Preventive Medicine*, *16*, 825–836. doi:10.1016/0091-7435(87)90022-3.

Sanou, D., O'Reilly, E., Ngnie-Teta, I., Batal, M., Mondain, N., Andrew, C., … Bourgeault, I. L. (2014). Acculturation and nutritional health of immigrants in Canada: A scoping review. *Journal of Immigrant and Minority Health*, *16*, 24–34. doi:10.1007/s10903-013-9823-7.

Satia, J. A. (2010). Dietary acculturation and the nutrition transition: An overview. *Applied Physiology, Nutrition, and Metabolism*, *35*, 219–223. doi:10.1139/H10-007.

Satia, J. A., Patterson, R. E., Kristal, A. R., Hislop, T. G., Yasui, Y., & Taylor, V. M. (2001). Development of scales to measure dietary acculturation among Chinese-Americans and Chinese-Canadians. *Journal of the American Dietetic Association*, *101*, 548–53. doi:10.1016/S0002-8223(01)00137-7.

Scholz, U., Ochsner, S., Hornung, R., & Knoll, N. (2013). Does social support really help to eat a low-fat diet? Main effects and gender differences of received social support within the health action process approach. *Applied Psychology: Health and Well-Being*, *5*, 270–290. doi:10.1111/aphw.12010.

Shih, M., Du, Y., Lightstone, A. S., Simon, P. A., & Wang, M. C. (2014). Stemming the tide: Rising diabetes prevalence and ethnic subgroup variation among Asians in Los Angeles County. *Preventive Medicine*, *63*, 90–95. doi:10.1016/j.ypmed.2014.03.016.

Singh, G. K., Siahpush, M., Hiatt, R. A., & Timsina, L. R. (2011). Dramatic increases in obesity and overweight prevalence and body mass index among ethnic-immigrant and social class groups in the United States, 1976–2008. *Journal of Community Health*, *36*, 94–110. doi:10.1007/s10900-010-9287-9.

Stanford, J., Jacksonville, F., Lee, J., Fort Worth, T., Doldren, M., & Rathore, M. (2015). Teacher and friend social support: Association with body weight in African-American adolescent females. *Journal of Racial and Ethnic Health Disparities*, 2, 358–364. doi:10.1007/s40615-014-0081-8.

Stanton, C. A., Green, S. L., & Fries, E. A. (2007). Diet-specific social support among rural adolescents. *Journal of Nutrition Education and Behavior, 39*, 214–218. doi:10.1016/j.jneb.2006.10.001.

Stroebe, W., Papies, E. K., & Aarts, H. (2010). The psychology of dieting and overweight. In R. Schwarzer & A. Frensch, Peter (Eds.), *Personality, human development, and culture: International perspectives on psychological science* (Vol. 2, pp. 17–27). New York, NY: Psychology Press.

Sullivan, K., Pasch, L., Bejanyan, K., & Hanson, K. (2010). Social Support, Social Control, and Health Behavior Change in Spouses. In K.T. Sullivan & J. Davila (Eds) *Support processes in intimate relationships* (pp. 219–239). New York, NY: Oxford University Press.

Sussner, K. M., Lindsay, A. C., Greaney, M. L., & Peterson, K. E. (2008). The influence of immigrant status and acculturation on the development of overweight in Latino families: A qualitative study. *Journal of Immigrant and Minority, 10*, 497–505. doi:10.1007/s10903-008-9137-3.

Thoits, P. A. (2011). Mechanisms linking social ties and support to physical and mental health. *Journal of Health and Social Behavior, 52*, 145–161. doi:10.1177/0022146510395592.

Thornton, P. L., Kieffer, E. C., Salabarría-Peña, Y., Odoms-Young, A., Willis, S. K., Kim, H., & Salinas, M. A. (2006). Weight, diet, and physical activity-related beliefs and practices among pregnant and postpartum Latino women: The role of social support. *Maternal and Child Health Journal, 10*, 95–104. doi:10.1007/s10995-005-0025-3.

Thrasher, J. F., Campbell, M. K., & Oates, V. (2004). Behavior-specific social support for healthy behaviors among African American church members: Applying optimal matching theory. *Health Education & Behavior, 31*, 193–205. doi:10.1177/1090198103259184.

Triandis, H. C. (1995). *Individualism and Collectivism.* Boulder, CO: Westview Press.

Tsai, A. C., & Papachristos, A. V. (2014). From social networks to health: Durkheim after the turn of the millennium. *Social Science & Medicine, 125*, 1–7. doi:10.1016/j.socscimed.2014.10.045.

Tseng, M., Wright, D. J., & Fang, C. Y. (2015). Acculturation and dietary change among Chinese immigrant women in the United State. *Journal of Immigrant and Minority Health, 17*, 400–407. doi:10.1007/s10903-014-0118-4.

Uchino, B. N. (2009). Understanding the links between social support and physical health: A life-span perspective with emphasis on the separability of perceived and received support. *Perspectives on Psychological Science, 4*, 236–255. doi:10.1111/j.1745-6924.2009.01122.x.

Umberson, D. (1987). Family status and health behaviors: Social control as a dimension of social integration. *Journal of Health and Social Behavior, 28*, 306–319.

Umberson, D., Crosnoe, R., & Reczek, C. (2010). Social relationships and health behavior across the life course. *Annual Review of Sociology, 36*, 139–157. doi:10.1146/annurev-soc-070308-120011.

Unger, J. B., Reynolds, K., Shakib, S., Spruijt-Metz, D., Sun, P., & Johnson, C. A. (2004). Acculturation, physical activity, and fast-food consumption among Asian-American and Hispanic adolescents. *Journal of Community Health*, *29*, 467–481. doi:10.1007/s10900-004-3395-3.

Vilaro, M. J., Barnett, T. E., Mathews, A., Pomeranz, J., & Curbow, B. (2016). Income differences in social control of eating behaviors and food choice priorities among southern rural women in the US: A qualitative study. *Appetite*, *107*, 604–612. doi:10.1016/j.appet.2016.09.003.

Wells, H. F., & Buzby, J. C. (2008). Dietary assessment of major trends in U.S. food consumption, 1970–2005. Retrieved from www.libertyparkusafd.org/NatureFirst USA/Special Reports percent5CUSDA percent5CDietary Assessment of Major Trends in US Food Consumption-1970–2005.pdf.

World Health Organization. (2004). Appropriate body-mass index for Asian populations and its implications for policy and intervention strategies. Retrieved from www.who.int/nutrition/publications/bmi_asia_strategies.pdf.

Wright, K. B. (2009). Increasing computer-mediated social support. In J. C. Parker & E. Thorson (Eds.), *Health communication in the new media landscape* (pp. 243–265). New York: Springer Publishing Co.

Part V

Methodological Reflections

13 Mobilities in/and Nomadic Health Research

Health Communication Scholarship and Flows across Migratory Landscapes

Benjamin R. Bates

Much of the research on global migration as it impacts understandings of health focuses on the way that migrant populations adopt, refuse or adapt to the cultural health beliefs and behaviors of the host nation-state in which they arrive. Many of the chapters in this book attest to these phenomena. However, as Appadurai (1996) reminds us, however, mobility and migration are not just the flow of people from one set of regions to another, from one nation-state to a different one, and back, but a complex set of flows across and among ethnoscapes, technoscapes, financescapes, mediascapes, and ideoscapes (see also Lofland, 1998). When individuals migrate, they also activate complex networks of the flow of people and culture, of innovations and technologies, of capital and goods, of representations and images, and of thoughts and ideologies. And, as they traverse physical spaces, they traverse the ethnoscape, the technoscape, the mediascape, and the ideoscape as they activate each of these respective flows.

Each chapter in this volume, in some ways, has reflected and enacted these flows, but each has also tended to focus on global migrants as Others engaged in enacting these flows, particularly as their flowing has impacted migrants' understanding or performance of health and healing. We, as researchers and academics, however, are also part of these migratory flows. And, although we may engage in reflexive research practices, we may also wish to reflect on how our own movement from region to region, or state to state, also illustrates how our movement as a particular kind of global migrant impacts the ways we engage issues of health and healing.

As an academic, I view myself as a particularly advantaged kind of global migrant. I am a privileged global nomad out of choice; my research and teaching is in the area of health communication, and my travels have allowed me to teach, research, and perform service in multiple national contexts, as well as within several regions of my home nation and state.

Because academics may observe global migrants without recognizing their own participation in particular forms of migration, turning our lens on ourselves to understand how our own movement in the migratory spaces shapes us as researchers and informs our research practices may be a significant site for reflection as investigation. Drawing on Michel de Certeau's (1984, 1998) claim that our "practice of everyday life" articulates the way that we navigate landscapes—both physical and conceptual—this chapter seeks to access these multiple flows across - scapes through a self-reflexive engagement. These intersecting flows create confluences and turbulences that re-articulate the way mobilities both reveal structures that guide our movements across these landscapes and how we participate (sometimes resistively) in the maintenance of conceptual structures built on these landscapes (see also Cresswell, 2006; Urry, 2007). Indeed, as Shortell and Aderer (2014) note, through this quotidian mobility, "we enact structured social relations by interacting with others in the course of moving around and through the vernacular landscape. Through these interactions, we form interpretations of ourselves and others" (p. 112).

To access a set of these interpretations, this chapter articulates a series of vignettes where mobile methodologies are used. In a mobile methodology, one focuses on not on the fixed artifacts and structures that make up a physical landscapes, but instead on the ways that individuals can navigate through physical and conceptual landscapes (see e.g. Hall, 2009; Phillips, 2005; Mendoza & Moren-Alegert, 2013). Although places in each vignette are material, the mobilities by which I navigate them are not through the landscape only, but, to varying degrees, through ethnoscapes, technoscapes, financescapes, mediascapes, and ideoscapes. I relate four vignettes that take place within a few months of one another. First, I consider the flows and blockage of mobilities encountered by a visiting faculty member in urban Bangkok during the evening of and days following the 2014 regime change. Second, I listen in on a conversation between an Indonesian maid and an Indian professor, both working in Singapore, as the latter attempts to help the former recover a passport so that she can go home. I turn then to a stroll through Manama, Bahrain, on the night before a collegiate recruiting fair, and then meet a former student. The final vignette presents a run through farming fields near the town of Mikumi, Tanzania, and ends with the roar of a lion. Drawing together these vignettes, I reflect on how each reveals implications for how we might understand global migration as it relates to health.

Mobile Methodologies

To explore these spaces, I employ ideas drawn from mobile research methodologies. Specifically, I reflect on a series of encounters with people and places to offer some reactions to how I, as a particular global migrant, encounter physical and conceptual landscapes in four distinct spaces. These specific places were chosen for two reasons. First, they are temporally close to one another. If the researcher is the instrument in a mobile methodology (Bendiner-Viani, 2005; Leyshon, 2011), then a consistency in that instrument among experiences should allow greater reflection on how those experiences, individually and collectively, allow interpretations of peoples and spaces to emerge. Second, it is important to engage multiple spaces within that selection of time, As Edensor (2010) reminds us, encountering a new place, or at least a partially new place, allows for a different engagement:

> Place is experienced as the predictable passing of familiar fixtures under the same and different conditions. But this may also emerge through a mindful passage across unfamiliar terrain through which the body adapts to land underfoot, and the peculiarities of place are apprehended at a slower rhythm
>
> (2010, p. 70)

I engage each space slowly and, thus, intentionally.

It is also important to disclaim generalizability and reproducibility. Rather than seeking to abstract meaning from each encounter in a statistical or ethnographically representative sense, I employ these methods precisely because they are not reproducible or generalizable. Mobile methods reflect a commitment "to understanding *through* the local and particular. Here the very arbitrariness of place, its particularity, is what matters: an explicitly partial window on totalizing description which tests and challenges the coherence of models" (Hall, 2009, p. 574). Instead of attempting to produce a coherent model, this compilation of experience is meant to be generative of other possibilities. Each engagement allows a larger story of how mobility across these spaces allows different possible narratives to emerge. Hetherington (2013) puts it well when he claims that mobile methods are "about movement through space in a more fluid and dynamic way allowing little stories, neighbourhood stories to emerge and creating a series of tactics of resistance" (p. 28) that are disallowed in more traditional methods.

Turning to specific experiences of spaces and places as they inform broader understandings and reflections is common. There have been many investigations, mostly in North America and Europe (Cresswell, 2010), investigating how people move across and understand the countryside (Lorimer & Lund, 2008; MacPherson, 2009; Yarwood, 2010), through major cities (Hall, 2009; Moles, 2008; Sidaway, 2009), or how they might compare the two (Ingold & Vergunst, 2008). While some claim that reports on an experience risk translating the singular experience into the way that all persons would experience that space, the better lesson to be drawn from is that a single person's experience of a place might inspire or generate alternative understandings of how spaces and places might influence beliefs and actions (Wylie, 2005).

Although I find this work on mobility in the global north informative and inspiring, I also find that it tends to focus on well-planned journeys. Some work emphasizes hikes, tours, and pilgrimages, the kinds of things that one puts planning into to make sure that specific places are encountered in specific ways at specifics times. But, as Edensor (2010) argues, "While much walking literature and art focuses upon certain exceptional walking experiences, most walking is mundane and habitual. Familiar places are the unquestioned settings for daily tasks, pleasures and rhythmically apprehended routines" (p. 70). A strong body of work on the daily commute and the everyday walk also exists.

To the side of the exceptional journey and the daily commute exist another way of moving through landscape: the improvisational. An individual may visit a space, intentionally, yet leave herself open to new and unanticipated encounters with people, things, and places within that space. By opening herself to this encounter and recording actions, feelings, impressions, and observations, she can create data from her experiences in that space. She becomes, as it were, the recorder of experience and the interpreter of experience so as to make meaning from it. As Hester and Francis (2003) argue,

> Competent participation in any social setting demands that those involved pay attention to, and make sense of, the visual availability of what is happening around them. Consequently, observation is not so much a sociological method as an inevitable and necessary part of everyday social life
>
> (p. 37)

Having gathered together these observations, the mobile researcher can then turn to a "first person analysis" of these observations. This analysis, as Hester and Francis (2003) claim, "involves the researcher engaging in self-reflection, in which the researcher's own experiences and activities are turned into data for analysis. … [she] can legitimately employ his or her own observations of public activities as a form of usable data" (p. 37). With this guidance in mind, I offer some encounters and reflections as I engage in some transnational movements as an academic nomad.

Movements

Thursday, May 22, 2014, Bangkok, Thailand

Sitting in a small conference room on the ninth floor of a building at Bangkok University, I was about to begin my class on empirical research methods in communication. My PowerPoint presentation was ready; the students were on time. The only thing missing was a small goblet of water, a goblet usually brought by the housekeeping staff to every visiting professor immediately before the start of their class. It was 5:30 P.M.; usually the water was there. Although it was nice to have a glass of water, given the blasting air conditioning and extremely dry air in the room, it was not entirely necessary.

I appreciated the glass of water because it was also refreshing to have after my afternoon stroll. Although it was unusual for visiting professors to do so, I walked most afternoons from my flat to the campus. The journey from the top of Soi Phumichit and then down Rama IV Road to campus only took fifteen minutes on foot, but, in the 95-degree heat, 95 percent humidity of Bangkok, my students thought it odd that I would not take a taxi for the 1.37 kilometer trip.

I soon learned the reason for the missing goblet. One of the grey-clad housekeepers came into the room, and whispered something in a student's ear. The student began packing her bag, turned to the class and announced that Bangkok University was closing at six. General Prayuth Chan-o-cha had announced martial law was to be imposed. The student announced that everyone was to be home by eight; anyone out after that risked detention and prosecution.

The other students flew into action. The packed their materials as quickly as they could. Seeing that one of their classmates was wearing red—the color representing the populist government that was soon to be ousted from power—they gave her a white jumper and covered her with scarves of many colors so that she would not be hassled on the bus. Two students, sisters, then told me that they needed to drive me home.

The practice in this class had been that visiting professors could arrive at campus any way they chose, but they were always to be driven home. Our class usually let out near ten in the evening, and, although the walk home would only take fifteen minutes, it was not well-lit in many places, had uneven sidewalks, and there were concerns held by the campus administration about petty crime in the neighborhood. The landscape was navigable for Thai people, but I was considered unable to navigate it. I could not walk this ethnoscape; my person did not fit for reasons of ethnicity. I was further burdened by an ideoscape in which teachers at all levels are to be served and protected, even against the student's own interest.

Although the students themselves had to be home by 8, they insisted that I must be driven home. We left the building and got into their recent model Mercedes and pulled left onto Kluai Nam Thai Road. There, a sea of red taillights confronted us. Faculty, staff and students from the University, employees of the shipping companies from the nearby port, and clients and vendors from the now-cancelled Aajarong night market were all pulling onto the same street to get home by 8. With the closure of all business, the financescape was no longer navigable for any worker, be it the knowledge worker, the laborer, or the vendor. And, with financial mobility no longer a concern, they poured into the street to go home.

We crawled toward Rama IV road, moving a few car lengths every time the light changed ahead. I told my students that I could walk home, but they replied it was not safe. There were army and police about; the professor might not know how to get home. We crept, and crept, and eight minutes later we had traversed the three hundred meters to the light at Rama IV Road.

On a good night, with no martial law about to be imposed and no impending coup, the remainder of the journey would take twenty minutes. Traffic on Rama IV, although not nearly as dense as that on Sukhumwit or other major thoroughfares, was never good. But tonight it was especially not good. It was bad. Motorcycles weaved around us; drivers, desperate to get home, darted into any opening to make space; pedestrians crossed wherever they could. Horns sounded; lights flashed; harsh words were exchanged. Collectively, we challenged the law of physics that no two objects could occupy the same space. Miraculously not a single accident occurred on Rama IV that night.

We passed condominiums and apartments filling their lots early, and guards smoking cigarettes as they checked tags so that only people who belonged could come in. Shutters were pulled at businesses large and small. The 7-Eleven at the petrol station turned its "Closed" sign on for the first time in a decade. As night fell, the taillights grew brighter, the traffic denser, and the time later.

The clock turned to seven as we arrived at the U-turn just before Soi Phumichit. A tank with soldiers sat at the intersection with Sukhumwit; thankfully we did not need to go any further forward. My students had only an hour to get home. They needed to go four or five kilometers; it had taken us an hour to go one. They insisted that we drive up the Soi, that they be able to drop me at my flat. The traffic in the Soi was prohibitive. It would take them another hour to drive it.

I insisted that I would get out and walk. I knew everyone on the Soi. It was lit well enough, and I knew the shopkeepers and doormen along the way. I had navigated this space before and, as *farang*, or foreigner, I stood out well enough to be remembered by my neighbors. Over my students' protestations, I enacted my physical mobility and alit. I ordered them, using my social mobility, to drive home and email me or call me when they arrived. I headed up my Soi.

Five minutes later, I was at the 7-Eleven in the Soi, one owned and operated by a family who lived just next door. The 7-Eleven didn't need to close until the curfew was in place. They sold me a few microwavable meals, a bottle of beer, and some crisps. They then updated me on what was happening. Schools and universities would be closed Friday, perhaps through the weekend. No groups larger than three could get together. There would be a curfew from sundown to sunrise. Television and radio would probably be shut down.

All these things came to pass in the next six days. Educational, social, and media mobilities were limited, just as physical mobilities became limited. My class moved online for the next week; my news came across the Internet. The next few days were comprised of making breakfast, lounging at the condo pool, walking to 7-Eleven to buy lunch supplies, reading and posting to my online class, walking to Tesco-Lotus Express to buy dinner supplies, and not leaving the Soi. Although I had been in Thailand as a highly mobile individual, the constrictions of the landscape by the curfew, accompanied by a constricted mediascape and technoscape, limited this mobility. Only my home university's extension of my purchasing card limit, just in case I needed to leave in the midst of the coup, afforded more mobility. The possibility, a possibility engendered by the ethnoscape of Western, *farang* privilege and the financescape of a multinational credit card company, provided offsetting mobilities.

The flows and blockages of mobility that I experienced were not as challenging as those faced by the Thai people. Their physical, technological, and media mobilities were as constricted as mine, but compounded by limits on financial mobility though currency control and ethnic mobility whereby they could not leave Thailand on as short a notice. Although my students made it home that night, and although the greatest concern was expressed over my ability to navigate this new political space, I remained the one who was mobile through the advantages afforded to me.

Monday, September 22, 2014, Singapore

As part of my sabbatical from Ohio University, I served as an academic visitor at the Center for Culture-Centered Approach to Research and Evaluation (CARE) at the National University of Singapore. One of the many benefits of my employment and profession is that, we are encouraged to grow and develop as scholars by taking extended time to focus on teaching projects, research projects, and projects that improve our ability to serve our community.

In late 2013, asked the Director of CARE if I would be able to visit with his program to observe how the "culture-centered approach" to research and evaluation in health and development communication projects differs from the "culturally sensitive approach" to these projects. Fortunately, the Director agreed. Not only was office space and help with finding accommodations provided by the National University of Singapore, but I was invited to observe CARE projects to see the culture-centered approach in action at multiple stages of implementation. It is easy, for an academic worker, to gain impressions of new theories and new approaches to doing research by reading, but moving to the field—becoming academically mobile—may be the best way to understand the practical differences between the new approaches and the old approaches. The Director had developed this new approach; as an Indian-born, US citizen who had now migrated to Singapore, he was particularly well-suited to recognize gaps in our old acultural or supposedly-culturally sensitive approaches to communication.

During the four weeks I was resident at NUS, I was able to observe, and in some ways participate in, different stages of culture-centered research projects being conducted by CARE. I had been invited to participate in discussions at the formative stages of a campaign that would focus on the health needs of transgendered sex workers. By being in the room with these workers, as they interacted with CARE academics, to set an agenda for social change communication, some of these differences in how formative research differs among acultural, culturally sensitive and culture-centered approaches to communication interventions. Their articulation of needs outside of HIV care (privileged by the government) for transgendered sex workers allowed different, community-centered issues to emerge, issues primarily surrounding sex worker-police interaction and gaps in a national health system that assumed gender was assignable at birth.

I was also allowed to participate in mid-research discussions, after the agenda had been set but before materials had been developed or tested, among CARE researchers and migrant Bangladeshi construction workers. As we ate mishit pulao and chicken curry together, the construction workers shared stories of food shortages, residential overcrowding, and safety shortcuts that endangered both their immediate health and their long term safety. As they ate, the first complete meal for many of them in days, they articulated additional layers of meaning that the CARE team would engage in trying to build messages that would change corporate behaviors to better meet the needs of workers.

But, the most impactful experience occurred for me after the Director invited me to a reveal meeting in a small office building off of Orchard Road on September 22. The reveal meeting was one where Indonesian maids, migrant workers resident in Singapore, would be able to see, for the first time, the messages advocating to employers the concept of domestic workers rights that they had helped to develop. Monday was the day that most of the workers had off; having cooked for their employers large Sunday meals, their employers would be able to eat leftovers and the house had not yet had a chance to get dirty.

The domestic workers watched the video that had been produced with their help, commented on placards and social media items, and offered input on a press release announcing the campaign. The mood was largely celebratory. These migrant women, whose lives had been limited by employers that chose to violate the rights of migrant workers, were enacting their voice to restore some of their social and physical mobility.

As the meeting wound down, one of the workers asked to speak to the Director, and the rest of us listened to her story and their conversation.

The maid's employer had been a particularly cruel mistress, a pattern of behavior familiar to many of the women in the room. There was denial of food, imprisonment in the maid's room at night, beatings and brandings, and other denials of basic rights. But, after having worked with CARE, this domestic worker had become more aware of her rights. She insisted to her employer that she be paid on time, that her food and housing be adequate, and that she be allowed to visit family. In response, the employer reported to police that the maid had stolen some jewelry.

The police confiscated the maid's passport during their investigation. The police interviewed the employer. They interviewed the maid. The police issued a finding that they could not establish that any jewelry was missing, let alone that the maid had stolen anything. Yet, the police would not return the passport, as the accusation had not been formally resolved in court. The police also said that, if they pressed charges for a false report against the employer, they could not return the impounded passport. The maid's passport was due to expire in three weeks, and there would probably not be a court hearing before the new year. The maid was in a particularly pernicious limbo: she could pay a human smuggler to return her to Indonesia without a passport, an illegal act; overstay her employment visa, also an illegal act; or she could confess to stealing, receive her passport, and be expelled from the country.

As he listened, the Director became more concerned. He asked for the police officer's badge number and the location of the police station where the passport had been impounded. He requested the name of the employment agency that had obtained the original immigration approval for the maid. He inquired whether the maid had obtained legal representation. Throughout his sensitive, yet incisive questioning, the other domestic workers remained silent. Whereas before they had loudly agreed with one another, talked over one another, and been lively, here they listened to the story and its explication with little comment. After the Director's queries had been answered, he then asked if the maid would like him to contact the police station; through previous CARE projects, the Director had built an extensive network across the lower levels of police leadership. He asked if the maid would like him to put pressure on the employment agency; the Director knew many of these agencies and people who had hired from these agencies, and would be able to use his social capital. The Director offered legal representation; as a professor at the National University, he had connections with the campus legal clinic. Some of these offers the maid accepted; others, she declined.

Because I left Singapore six days later, I do not know whether the maid received her passport back. I do not know whether the employer was ever prosecuted. But, what I do know is that, although both the maid and the Director are migrant workers, their mobilities are very different. To be Indian is different from being Indonesian; these different identity markers enabled the Director to move more smoothly across the ethnoscape, as Indians constitute a large portion of the Singaporean population, but Indonesians are nearly always assumed to be migrant domestic workers. The Director's political-legal knowledge and his secure financial position, both results of having completed a doctorate and subsequent employment at the National University, enable him to challenge police and companies in ways that are denied to the domestic worker; he is on higher ground in this technoscape and financescape. Although both the Director and the domestic worker are migrant, their migration is different. Each landscape—whether it is physical or conceptual—is more porous to and navigable by the Director, and this enables him to have a greater mobility.

Wednesday, October 22 and Thursday, October 23, 2014, Manama, Bahrain

Night has set in on this desert island, and our college recruiting fair is scheduled for tomorrow for this particular nation. I am in the middle of a recruiting tour where I am accompanying my spouse as she finds students for our University, and where students can meet with representatives from twenty institutions of higher learning in the US. Each nation we stop in on—Morocco, Qatar, Kuwait, Jordan, so far—is facing opportunities and challenges of calls for economic diversification, democratization, and liberalization of their media sector. Allegedly, the Arab Spring ended in late 2012, but someone forgot to tell high school students in Bahrain. Occasionally, they take to the street. But, tonight, they are not out. Soon, our recruiting tour group will divide up. Some people are going home to the US, some people are continuing on to Saudi Arabia for the last leg, and my spouse and I are continuing to Oman to meet with some admitted students. One member of our group does not own an *abaya*, and, if she is going to be admitted to Saudi, she will need one.

Although this might seem like an important challenge to global mobility—how is a woman of Korean descent to acquire Middle Eastern dress when she resides in the Midwestern United States?—this challenge is easily answered. It is a twenty-minute walk from the Sheraton Bahrain, where our fair will be held, to the *souk* behind Bab al-Bahrain. There will be dozens of stalls at this market, and we will surely find an appropriate *abaya* for our colleague to wear. To get there, all we have to do is walk down Government Avenue. It is a cool night, only 65 degrees. It isn't very humid; the exercise will do us good.

Government Avenue is appropriately named. As we turn right onto the street, banks, business establishments, and government offices flank both sides. We pass ordinary office buildings housing the Ministries of Information and Telecommunications, courtyards for the Ministries of Foreign Affairs and of Consultative Council Affairs, the Banks of Bahrain and Kuwait, and post offices. As we cross Isa al Kabeer Avenue, we see a lone man, dressed in a tan uniform, sitting in a folding chair, a chair placed in the middle of a roundabout access. Across his lap sits a multishot shotgun, its metal gleaming. Unmarked on our maps, we have stumbled across the Ministry of National Security, newly empowered in the wake of the Arab Spring to preserve law, order, and the Kingdom. But the guard barely notices us. He is there to impede flow into the Ministry of National Security, to block those who merely pass by. Perhaps because it is night, but perhaps also because we are distinctly non-Arab, we need not be challenged. We may be on our way. This man, the results of the Arab Spring (insofar as we Americans can understand them), and the need to purchase an *abaya* become our conversational materials for the night.

The next day, at our recruitment fair, we encounter another Bahraini man who becomes quite memorable. We are in the ballroom of the Sheraton, at about 6:00 PM. We have a group photograph with the American ambassador as he opens the fair, and then hurry to our tables to prepare for an onslaught of teenagers and their parents. We ensure that our table is well-stocked with brochures, business cards, and recruitment materials designed for a 17-year-old looking at colleges in the United States, and charts showing tuition, fees, and national rankings for their parents. Then, we see man, wearing a t-shirt emblazoned with the name of our school, holding in one hand his iPhone with a case with our school name and holding in the other his wallet flipped open to his student ID card from 1992. He comes to our table, sharing stories of his time at our school. When mothers are concerned about how safe and secure their daughters will feel in the US, he tells them about his and his wife's experiences living there and the general acceptance of Muslims in our small town. When fathers ask about the reputation of the school, our alum relates how his experiences at our school helped prepare him for his current role as a dean in one of the largest colleges at the University of Bahrain. This alum invites my spouse and I to dinner, where we are whisked into the small neighborhoods of Manama, a restaurant is kept open just for us, and we learn more about our alum, his family and studying at Ohio University. Our bellies full of food, and our ears full of stories, he drives us back to the Sheraton where, the next morning, we will pack and head off to Qatar.

These two Bahrainis—the soldier and the dean—reveal two different ways, out of many possible ways, that they can engage a migratory landscape. Bahrain is one of the first post-petroleum countries in the Persian Gulf, having developed strong banking and tourism centers. Yet, it is also economically tied to traditional economic resources like pearl diving and oil shipping. Bahrain has an elected parliament under a constitutional monarchy, but an upper house appointed by the King that must approve all legislation. Bahrainis are encouraged to go abroad to study, but also encouraged to come back home. They are taught to be tolerant of all races and religions, but there are enacted preferences for particular kinds of Gulf Arabs and for particular sects within Islam. The two Bahrainis exist at opposite ends of a mobility spectrum, perhaps embodying much of the country. The soldier is stable, stationary, armed with a symbol of military authority. He is dressed in a uniform, designed to suppress individuality. The soldier may embody larger blockages of mobilities toward democratization and free flows across the ideoscape of Bahrain. The dean is moving, a migrant from Bahrain to the US and back again (and again, and again, as he helps his own children choose colleges). The dean wears university t-shirts, eschewing both the uniform and the suit that would characterize many educated Bahrainis. The dean may embody larger flows of mobility toward educational and other systems of regulation that integrate Bahrain into the world educational order.

Monday, January 11, 2015, Mikumi, Tanzania

A cool breeze blows across the Uluguru mountain valley, clearing dust away from our lodge next to the A7 highway. After a day of riding in the back of a safari truck, our eyes strained from the bright sun, the dry air, and the need to pick out well-camouflaged animals, some of us are eager to stretch our legs and exercise before dinner. The truck drops us inside the lodge compound; the vehicle gate closes behind it and a door in the chain link fence is opened to us. We pass inside, drink some water, and prepare for the evening. One of my travelling companions and I change from our safari gear into running clothes and walk out the back gate, opening the rear door in the chain link fence. We clasp the lock closed on an empty part of the fence, ensuring that the hasp will not keep us out when we return.

Although our team knows that we are due back for dinner, we are about to head across small holding farm fields, and our team will not know precisely where we are. Until the lock is replaced on the hasp, they know that we have yet to return. My companion and I walk past the small tire fire that has been lit to ward off insects and animals, passing an abandoned farmstead. Our map has told us that there is a narrow trail that crosses a dozen small holdings between the lodge and a small stream that marks the western edge of Mikumi National Park. We jog out under the late afternoon sun, plodding across the well-worn path. Many people have walked from small village as Kidatu to their fields, most of them using these same paths.

The people of Kidatu come not for exercise, but to tend their crops. The land here is dry, nearly arid. The farmers pull buckets of water from the stream, hang them on staves across their back, and lug the water to plants that need it most. Manioc, sweet potato, and beans sprout and struggle through the land. The farmers have been staggering their crops; some of the beans are ready for harvest and others are just beginning their growth. We pass a farmer. He shouts out a greeting to us as we pass his field. He strikes his hoe into the ground, breaking space for the next seed. My companion points out a fork in the road and she directs us to turn right, heading toward the stream. As we approach the stream, the crops change from drought-resistant crops to maize and bananas. The closer to water they are, the thirstier the plants the land can support.

A more well-to-do farmer comes up the path toward us, leading a scrawny cow. His buttoned shirt implies that he buys clothes from the shop rather than weaving them at home. He has been furrowing longer rows for maize; his plow has been turned so he can take it back to Kidatu. Brushing some of the ever-present dust from his shirt, he warns us that the sun will set in an hour or so; he tells us we don't want to stay out once night begins to fall. We continue on deciding that another twenty minutes of jogging will allow us plenty of time to heed his warning.

A few minutes later we come to the stream. Although the stream is only a meter wide, my running partner and I decide not to cross it. The stream is in a deep downcut; over the years, the stream has moved from being level with the land to being in a rut six or seven feet below the surface of this alluvial plain. We could go down, cross the stream, and clamber up the mud on the other side. We choose not to do so, in part to avoid the mud, but also because, deep in the downcut, we see a paw print. The print in the mud, made when an animal has leaned over the stream to drink, is comprised of a heart-shaped pad with four gumdrops in front. This is the paw print of a lion. The farmer's warning comes into focus. We are at the border of the National Park, but this border is meant to keep man out, not animals in.

We turn back. It is still daylight, and, regardless of what the Tokens sang, lions do not sleep at night. When the sun sets, this lion, and the rest of her pride, will seek prey. Passing through the same fields, all of the farmers that we have passed are no longer present; they have gone back to Kidatu, Mikumi, or another village for the evening. Insects begin to emerge, toads croak, birds gather. The closer the sun comes to the horizon, the more animals appear. They avoid us, Rachel and I are the largest predators right now. We are the top of the food chain, but not for long. We come arrive at the chain link fence, unlock the lock, step through the portal, and put the lock on the hasp. The lodge caretaker will arrive soon to close the gate for the night, and we have signaled our return. Were the lock not restored to the hasp, he would have to organize a search party. He knows that we have safely returned. As we walk from the rear gate to the lodge proper, a rumbling roar crosses the fields. The lion has awoken, and she has announced the beginning of her hunt to the pack.

Running, jogging, and exercise are why my running partner and I entered the fields. Our use of the fields stands in contrast to that of the farmers. Our use of the space was recreational; for the farmers the space is for production. Although both Rachel and I are here for work, as part of a faculty development seminar, at this moment, we are tourists, using the space in unintended ways. The farmers may also become more physically fit from their labors, but their interest is in feeding their families and producing crops for sale. They know not only the use of the land, which crops grow best in which soils and which need additional care, but also the other users of this land. They know that the land can be used by humans during the day, but when night falls the land is ruled by the lion. They must make way for the lion, and they have shared this knowledge with us. Our use of the land as recreational and exercise space is compatible with their use of the land; farming and running go together well. However, neither of our uses is compatible with what the land is for at night. The night does not belong to us. As Rachel and I have dinner with the rest of the team at the lodge, we note that night is a time for human to be indoors. Trucks do not use the road next to the lodge at night, the villages nearby do not broadcast light or noise, all of the travelers turn in early. There's no reason to be awake at night.

Reflections and Lessons

Each of these vignettes relates an experience as I moved through different national spaces as an academic nomad. And, each one can be characterized by the way that it fits into my research, teaching, and service on health communication as a global practice. Indeed, in proposing a sabbatical project that encompassed three of the four vignettes, each experience had to be described within a justification of how it fit into that scholarly agenda. The story told at an administrative level is that the contributions to my scholarly agenda through this academic nomadism would be transparent and knowable at the time of application. Teaching health communication to Thai students in Thailand would enhance my teaching of health communication by incorporating a new context; learning the culture-centered approach to health communication in Singapore would enhance my health communication research capabilities; accompanying an international recruiting tour in the Middle East would allow our school to better recruit student-scholars of health communication; and, participating in an international faculty development seminar on the topic of HIV/AIDS in Tanzania would allow me to connect with other scholars of health communication. All of these anticipated outcomes were supported.

The results of enacting health communications scholarship as a global nomad, however, are not comprised only of transparent and predictable outcomes. Drawing on Hall's argument that, because we live in "a world gone mobile" wherein "the mobility turn is also a part of a broader theoretical project aimed at undermining an established and sedentary social science" (p. 573), and Sheller and Urry's (2006) argument that mobility no longer "treats as normal stability, meaning and place, and treats as abnormal distance, change and placelessness" (p. 208), what becomes more significant are the obscure and unanticipated outcomes of performing health communication scholarship as a global nomad. The counters described here could not have been predicted or proposed as part of a sabbatical to develop health communication scholarship; we cannot plan coups, predict human rights violations, or control wild beasts. Yet, each encounter informs how we might understand the nomadic academic as she engages issues of health and healing in her own mobility and migration.

Each of the vignettes offered could offer a specific lesson for thinking through issues of health and healing as a named academic. Cresswell (2010) correctly reminds us

> Facts in the world—increased levels of mobility, new forms of mobility where bodies combine with information and different patterns of mobility, for instance—combine with ways of thinking and theorizing that foreground mobility (of people, of ideas, of things) as a geographical fact that lies at the centre of constellations of power, the creation of identities and the microgeographies of everyday life.
> (p. 551)

Each encounter is made up of these facts in the world, but they also help constitute power, identity, and everyday life.

In Thailand, as with many Southeast Asian countries, social health is predicated on respect for roles and hierarchy and, specifically, the needs of the *ajaan* are placed before the needs of the student because doing so maintains this social health. The students, even in the midst of a coup that disrupted social health and order, put the health and safety needs of the teacher before their own. At the same time, because I too was constrained by these roles and hierarchies, I placed the educational needs of the students ahead of my own possible return to the United States. Although my home university saw the military takeover as a threat to my own health and safety, to maintain the relations of social health my migratory position required me to participate in particular ways within that challenging social (dis)order. The ideoscape and ethnoscape interact such that the mobility of knowledge become primary, the mobility of the teacher secondary, and of the student, tertiary. To spread knowledge is judged more significant than bodily safety in their conceptual landscape. The short lesson to be drawn here: the globally nomadic scholar of health communication is both enabled and constrained by her participation in the production of knowledge and the sharing of knowledge about health and healing.

In Singapore we saw that there is differentiation within migrant workers. The Indonesian maid faced obvious health threats; she risked being beaten by her mistress, she was less able to eat, her freedom of movement was restricted. Her physical health was endangered by her employment, and her mental health endangered by how she was retreated by employment agencies and government offices. Although it is tempting to argue that migrant workers always face health challenges, it is significant that two other migrants were also in the room. The Indian professor saw that he would be able to mobilize resources on behalf of the maid. Despite being a global migrant, he needed not worry about his physical and emotional health. Yet, he was constrained in some ways by his need to participate in various Singaporean systems. To be able to maintain his research position with domestic worker communities, he sought to challenge various systems of power that injured workers' health, but to maintain that position in terms of external support and funding, his challenges had to be strategic and partial. The third migrant in the room (me) was able to move in and out of the situation; although perhaps I had the least risk to health and position as a worker, I was also the one who would not be able to navigate well the channels of power in that migratory system. Here, the financescape becomes differently navigable than the ideoscape, and it is the ability to navigate both effectively that becomes central to accessing system of power than enable individual and collective health. The lesson to be drawn here: the globally nomadic scholar of health communication must attend to which global migrants are advantaged by, and which are disadvantaged by, the conceptual landscapes of a nation-state; she must not assume that all migrants in that landscape are equally advantaged or disadvantaged.

In Bahrain we encountered two individuals, the soldier and the dean. Health and development communication scholarship often argues that economic and political liberalization and strong determinants of individual and collective health (for a review, see DeLaet & DeLaet, 2012). And, although there are some trends to support this argument, it must be remembered that different parts of the conceptual landscape respond to these social influences in different ways. The dean, with his high social, educational, and financial mobility is better able to participate in the larger neoliberal system, and he can thrive more easily in it than can the soldier. That is, the dean is advantaged and can employ resources drawn from the ideoscape, financescape, and mediascape privileged within the neoliberal model of economic and political liberalization. The soldier, although less mobile in the parts of the landscape that the dean navigates well, is enabled by the ethnoscape underlying Bahraini political systems and the technoscape that empowers military armaments. That is, the soldier has better access to these resources that may limit the extent to which economic and political liberalization can be enacted. While it might seem easy for us to prefer the dean's navigation of conceptual landscapes (after all, he, like us, is an academic), the soldier's alternative navigation may be important to preserving other possibilities for economic and political change should the neoliberal project fail or become harmful. The lesson: the globally nomadic scholar of health communication should not assume that all parts of the conceptual landscape are navigated together when understanding health practices; she must attend to what layers of the conceptual landscape enable or constrain particular enactments in the overall landscape.

Finally, in Tanzania, we encountered two sets of users of the land. Once set were the Tanzanian farmers; the other two US-based health communication academics. Taken from a position in the global north, the academics were making healthy use of the land and the farmers' unhealthy use: the academics were using the land as exercise space, getting their recommended minutes of aerobic activity for the week; the farmers were using the land to grow calorie-dense, nutritionally-incomplete, high-starch foods. Yet, this view, when taken from a more local perspective is clearly absurd. There is no need to schedule exercise to create a special time and space for it when one's quotidian activity is physical activity; these farmers need not seek health through exercise, their labor is exercise. Moreover, the judgment that these crops—manioc, sweet potato, beans, maize, and banana—are nutritionally incomplete becomes falsified in at least two ways. First, although the colonial perspective might regard each separate crop as incomplete, when eaten together, these crops form a complete nutritional profile, a combination developed from experience living in and working, rather than merely visiting, this land. Second, although the colonial perspective might seek to adjust the land to allow a broader variety of crops to grow, the choice of these particular crops for an arid landscape represents a way for peoples to fit their practices into the land. Thus, rather than a navigation controlled by technological and financial intervention, a privileging of the technoscape and the financescape as the best ways to navigate terrain, local knowledge privileged in the ideoscape and ethnoscape of Tanzania becomes an alternative, and perhaps more sustainable, means of navigation. The final lesson to be learnt: the globally nomadic scholar of health communication must not impose a definition of health or healthy behaviors from her own context; she must, rather, come to understand how health and healthy behaviors become defined by peoples as they operate in their contexts.

Although these are the lessons that I would offer from this mobile engagement with these four places, there are likely others. And, as with any examination of health phenomena and contexts, particularly ones that we encounter from outsider positions, the strength of the lesson learned is also variable. When using a mobile methodology, "the methodological question relates to the efficacy of relying on one individual's personal account" (Morris, 2011, p. 335). Although studies, such as this one, that draw on a single personal account make textured meaning drawn from details, these non-representational accounts must be understood as approximations of immediate experience. Other individuals, even if they were in the same time and place, might attend to different details and articulate different lessons. My experience does not stand in for all experience, yet I need not defend my experience as failing to present a full ethnographic truth of these events or a places. Rather than a focus on whether the representation is sufficient, mobile engagements by nomadic scholars create opportunities for changing our approach to research and ourselves. By recognizing that we are migrant nomadic, mobile researchers, we may become more open to the newness and possibility of experience, of encountering other migrant populations in new ways that fully acknowledge our transitory positioning just as much as we acknowledge theirs.

References

Appadurai, A. (1996). *Modernity at large: Cultural dimensions of globalization.* Minneapolis, MN: University of Minnesota Press.

Bendiner-Viani, G. (2005). Walking, emotion, and dwelling. *Space and Culture, 8*(4), 459–471. doi:10.1177/1206331205280144.

Cresswell, T. (2010). Mobilities I: Catching up. *Progress in Human Geography, 34*(4), 550–558. doi:10.1177/0309132510383348.

Cresswell, T. (2006). *On the move: Mobility in the modern western world.* New York: Routledge.

De Certeau, M. (1984). *The practice of everyday life.* Berkeley, CA: University of California Press.

De Certeau, M. (1998). *The practice of everyday life. Vol. 2, Living and cooking.* Minneapolis, MN: University of Minnesota Press.

DeLaet, D. L., & DeLaet, D. E. (2012). *Global health in the 21st century: The globalization of disease and wellness.* New York: Routledge.

Edensor, T. (2010). Walking in rhythms: Place, regulation, style and the flow of experience. *Visual Studies, 25*(1), 69–79. doi:10.1080/14725861003606902.

Hall, T. (2009). Footwork: Moving and knowing in local space(s). *Qualitative Research, 9*(5), 571–585. doi:10.1177/1468794109343626.

Hester, S., & Francis, D. (2003). Analysing visually available mundane order: A walk to the supermarket. *Visual Studies, 18*(1), 36–46. doi:10.1080/14725860320001000056.

Hetherington, K. (2013). Rhythm and noise: The city, memory and the archive. *The Sociological Review, 61*, 17–33. doi:10.1111/1467-954x.12051.

Ingold, T., & Vergunst, J. (2008). Introduction. In T. Ingold & J. Vergunst (Eds.), *Ways of walking: Ethnography and practice on foot* (pp. 1–19). Aldershot: Ashgate.

Leyshon, M. (2011). The struggle to belong: Young people on the move in the countryside. *Population, Space and Place, 17*(4), 304–325. doi:10.1002/psp.580.

Lofland, L. H. (1998). *The public realm: Exploring the city's quintessential social territory.* Piscataway, NJ: Transaction.

Lorimer, H., & Lund, K. (2008). A collectable topography: Walking, remembering and recording mountains. In T. Ingold & J. Vergunst (Eds.), *Ways of walking: Ethnography and practice on foot* (pp. 185–200). London: Ashgate.

Macpherson, H. (2009). The intercorporeal emergence of landscape: Negotiating sight, blindness and ideas of landscape in the British countryside. *Environment and Planning A, 41*(5), 1042–1054. doi:10.1068/a40365.

Mendoza, C., & Morén-Alegret, R. (2013). Exploring methods and techniques for the analysis of senses of place and migration. *Progress in Human Geography*, *37*(6), 762–785. doi:10.1177/0309132512473867.

Moles, K. (2008). A walk in thirdspace: Place, methods, walking. *Sociological Research*. [Online]. Retrieved 2 May 2016 from: www.socresonline.org.uk/13/4/2.html.

Morris, N. (2011). Night walking: Darkness and sensory perception in a night-time landscape installation. *Cultural Geographies*, *18*(3), 315-342. doi:10.1177/1474474011410277.

Phillips, A. (2005). Cultural geographies in practice: Walking and looking. *Cultural Geographies*, *12*(4), 507–513. doi:10.1191/1474474005eu342xx.

Sheller, M., & Urry, J. (2006). The new mobilities paradigm. *Environment and Planning A*, *38*, 207–226. doi:10.1068/a37268.

Shortell, T., & Aderer, K. (2014). Drifting in Chinatowns: Toward a situationist analysis of polyglot urban spaces in New York, Paris, and London. In T. Shortell & E. Brown (Eds.), *Walking in the city: Quotidian mobility and urban ethnography* (pp. 109–128). New York: Routledge.

Sidaway, J. (2009). Shadows on the path: Negotiating geopolitics on an urban section of Britain's South West Coast Path. *Environment and Planning D: Society and Space*, *27*(6), 1091–1116. doi:10.1068/d5508.

Urry, J. (2007). *Mobilities*. New York: Polity.

Wylie, J. (2005). A single day's walking: Narrating self and landscape on the South West Coast Path. *Transactions of the Institute of British Geographers*, *30*(2), 234–247. doi:10.1111/j.1475-5661.2005.00163.x.

Yarwood, R. (2010). Risk, rescue and emergency services: the changing spatialities of Mountain Rescue Teams in England and Wales. *Geoforum*, *41*(2), 257–270. doi:10.1016/j.geoforum.2009.10.004.

14 International Collaboration on Health Research

Strengths, Challenges, and Future Opportunities

Solina Richter and Kimberly Jarvis

Introduction

International collaboration is a fundamental part of scholarly development. This has become particularly true with the advent of globalization, which has accelerated the scope, rate, and importance of international, collaborative, cross-national, and cross-cultural research. International collaboration and health research offer unique and innovative opportunities for scholars who are willing to stretch their comfort zone beyond that of national studies (Buttigieg, Rathert, D'Aunno, & Savage, 2015).

As we move toward the Sustainable Development Goals (SDG) post 2015 era, the focus has shifted to sustainable development, and partnerships to address health inequities. Globalization and internationalization have affected the physical, psychosocial, and environmental factors associated with health, increasing the need to conduct collaborative research across countries, cultures, and diversities in order to share and enhance knowledge and best practices in all aspects of health policy and service delivery (Buttigieg *et al.*, 2015). Accordingly, we need evidence "to compare countries as to the strengths and weaknesses of health outcomes, health services, and other factors related to health," as well as "to validated knowledge on best practices programs and other factors that could be used to guide policy recommendation or decisions" (Richter & Botha, 2012, p. 117). The advancement of professional health care practices is needed to build a global knowledge society that is key to address the "increased complexity, diversity, and insecurity brought by the amplified flow of people and information in a globalizing world" (Andreotti & de Souza, 2008, p. 7; Lombe, Newransky, Crea, & Stout, 2013; Opollo, Opollo, Gray, & Spies, 2014).

It is essential that researchers combine resources and expertise on an international scale to adequately address complex and interconnected global issues (Freshwater, Sherwood, & Drury, 2006). International research on complex global issues that cross transnational borders and allowing cross-cultural comparisons is necessary to improvement of health, reduce disparities, and protect against global threats that often disregard national borders (Macfarlane, Jacobs, & Kaaya, 2008).

However, quality, useful, and relevant global research efforts are difficult to coordinate between and among countries. This is especially true in relation to engaging interdisciplinary or cross-sectoral research teams (Freshwater *et al.*, 2006) and to confronting issues of equitable access to health and social services. Establishing international research partnerships requires sustained, long-term investment in people, research institutions, and research infrastructure if development is to be made feasible.

Understanding the Local Context and Building the Team

Rolfe *et al.* (2004) outline a number of stages in building sustainable collaborative research partnerships. These stages encompass the sharing of information, resources, and skills, and multidisciplinary involvement. An essential first step is to develop an in-depth understanding and awareness of the context in which the research is to be conducted. As such, Zheng, Hinshaw, Yu, Guo, and Oakley (2001) argue that "cross national collaboration requires flexibility and sophistication" and elaborated that "international work requires an understanding of cultural differences, including language, lifestyle, and assumptions about health, economic resources and political systems" (p. 117). This often requires additional resources of time, money, and an awareness of appropriate interactions and local customs best provided and confirmed by adding local researchers and stakeholders to the team from the planning phase onwards. Local researchers and stakeholders ensure that the research processes are relevant and responsive to their needs. They can challenge stereotypes and bring new perspectives as the team interact with different cultures (Lombe *et al.*, 2013). It is essential to seek variety in membership in terms of gender, culture, and discipline to enhance the diversity of perspectives (Buttigieg *et al.*, 2015).

Reciprocal Advantages and Equal Partnerships

The development of partnerships is emphasized in the SDG post-2015. The term 'partnership' can be used interchangeably to describe a variety of different collaborative activities such 'collaboration' or 'shared' projects (Africa Unit, 2010). Partnerships are essential to ensure and sustain effective health interventions in low-resource settings. However, the process of developing and promoting partnerships can be complex and multifaceted.

Historical patterns are just one consideration that may give rise to tensions within and between local communities and to the involvement of foreign researchers (Stenson, Kapungu, Geller, & Miller, 2010). Colonization had a profound impact on the history of many countries and research practices should be attentive to ensure that recolonization is not occurring, for example, by ignoring traditional patterns of knowledge development such as personal, ethical, aesthetic, and emancipatory knowing (Mogale, 2012).

Challenges arise when there are differing expectations between the foreign researchers, funders, and the global partners. Full engagement of local partners and stakeholders, and clear communication between partners, are crucial elements in overcoming these tensions and challenges. A community-based participatory approach is essential to engage local communities and stakeholders in the research and development process. This involves the creation of a community advisory board which "comprises of [*sic*] key community stakeholders, health providers, local researchers, and foreign investigators, can serve to generate research ideas, ground the research in real world experiences, [and] aid in interpretation of findings" (Stenson *et al.*, 2010, p. 2102). This base of community involvement provides effective knowledge-dissemination activities. A team approach that includes joint planning and decision-making, sharing of ideas, and clear communication, asserting project goals and objectives, ensures the development of partnerships that are equal and reciprocal. Sustainable partnerships require long-term commitment and investment on the part of both local and international stakeholders.

Practicalities

It is important to attend to certain practicalities before conducting international research. Careful planning during the predeparture, gaining entry, and reentry phases will prevent possible negative outcomes. Mindful cross-cultural communication is an important aspect of a successful international project.

Pre-Departure Preparation

To decrease frustration and ensure a smooth beginning to your research project, pre-plan your accommodations, organize your visa and travel health insurance, and become familiar with the vaccination requirements of the host country. In addition, ensure that you are acquainted with the risk management (safety and security) procedures of your employer. Prior to departure, decide how you will transfer money for your basic needs while travelling; credit cards and traveler's checks are not accepted everywhere. Become knowledgeable about the historical, cultural, political, social, and economic background of the host country before departure to inform your understanding of the context in which the research will be conducted.

Academic preparation prior to the beginning of the project includes making contact with the local research institution through a formal written notice of the intent of your research. Making such contact beforehand can support and establish access to libraries, and to administrative assistance and other assistance that the research might need (Barrett & Cason, 1997). The researcher should ensure what research equipment and technologies are available in the host country and which ones should be budgeted for and purchased prior to departure. Plan how data will be stored and shared with co-researchers ahead of time.

Gaining Access

Gaining access into a country and a community is the first step in conducting international research. It is advisable to plan how to gain entry during the project development phase. An essential step to gaining entry is early identification of gatekeepers or gate openers (the local people who have influence and control of access to research participants), combined with open, honest communication with them about the purpose of the project. Before a research project can begin, gatekeepers must be convinced of the benefits of conducting the research.

Further, the emic and etic (inside and outsider perspective) position of the researchers should be considered when entering the field. The term 'emic' "typically represents the internal language and meaning of a defined culture" and 'etic' "encompasses an external view on a culture, language, meaning associations and real-world events" (Olive, 2014, The Emic Perspective, para. 1). This is important to ensure that all members of the research team understand each other's subjectivity and the perspectives that each one brings to the research from his or her past experiences.

Gaining access to potential participants is one of the most challenging tasks associated with starting an international research project. It requires identifying research partners and stakeholders who can help provide access to study participants. Gatekeeper(s) vouch for researchers and this may potentially compromise their (gatekeeper's) status in the community. Therefore, researchers should respect the cultural knowledge and wisdom of gatekeepers and work with them.

Gaining access involves hard work and strategic planning. Buchanan, Boddy, and McCalman (1988) provide a four-stage model of getting in, getting on, getting out, and getting back, to gain access to organizations. This model focuses on interpersonal communication and mutual respect for persons.

The getting-in phase is about setting clear objectives and building a trusting relationship that is nonthreatening to the gatekeeper(s). The getting-on phase is renegotiating entry into the lives of participants once initial entry has been obtained. This can be time-consuming and requires exceptional communication skills. The getting-out phase, which includes setting deadlines for the closure of data gathering, should be discussed early in the research project, especially if the research involves vulnerable or marginalized populations. Finally, as part of the getting-back phase, researchers always want to leave the research setting on a positive note in order to facilitate revisiting a study site or participants at a later date. It is important the research honor the project objectives and not make promises that might compromise the researcher's position in the community.

Cross-Cultural Communication

Effective communication with people of different cultures can be challenging, a basic knowledge of cross-cultural communication practices of the host country is indispensable. People from different cultures have various ways of seeing, hearing, and interpreting the world. The possibility of communication barriers and misunderstandings is further increased by diversity of languages and the use of interpreters and translators. Ting-Toomey (1999) describes three types of cultural constraints which interfere with effective cross-cultural understanding and communication: cognitive, behavioral, and emotional. Cognitive constraints refer to the frames through which we view the world and which provide the background to how we interpret all new information. Behavioral constraints are the cultural rules controlling verbal and nonverbal communication. Practices related to making eye contact or observance of personal space vary from culture to culture. Emotional constraints refer to the various ways that cultures encourage or discourage emotional expression. Some cultures can get very emotional, while others try to keep emotions hidden. All these differences can lead to communication difficulties (Cultural Barriers to Effective Communication, n.d).

Mindful intercultural communication includes an understanding of both differences and similarities between members of different groups, and an awareness that individual members have her/his/their own unique communication style and habits. To become a mindful communicator you have to become aware of the value systems that influence your own and others' self-conceptualization. A mindful communicator understands a behavior or problem from others' cultural and personal standpoint. Furthermore, as Ting-Toomey (1999) stresses, "mindful communication needs to be on the alert that multiple perspectives typically exists in interpreting a basic phenomenon" (p. 46).

For international research teams, competent communication requires attention to appropriate and effective interactions. Culturally sensitive communication develops through an openness to learning about the new culture by using a range of methods such as conscious learning, personal experiences, observations, and reflexivity.

Reentry or Coming Home

Leaving the field can be emotional for researchers, and it is not uncommon for them to experience reentry shock. Reentry shock refers to the difficulties a researcher might experience when reentering their own culture. Reentry shock is often more difficult than culture shock as it is often unexpected. Knell (2007) suggests the word "reentry" makes the assumption of returning to "something" a person left and wanting to return. When that "something" is different from what the person previously recalls, reverse culture shock occurs. International researchers can and do experience reverse culture shock, especially when they have been in the field for prolonged periods immersed in another culture. When researchers are engrossed in another culture, it is difficult not to be changed or influenced by what was observed and experienced, since people are the sum of their experiences. Many researchers transition and manage reverse culture shock successfully. It is not uncommon, however, to experience feelings of disorientation, withdrawal, boredom, a need for excessive sleep, as well as feelings of separation from and resistance to family and friends. Coping strategies can include getting together with others who have a shared experience, maintaining a healthy diet, looking for ways to make meaning of the new skills and knowledge learned, and keeping in touch with the friends and contacts you have made during your experience (Knell, 2007).

Challenges

There are many financial and operational challenges to be faced when conducting international research, such as financial constraints, funding body mandates, and time management.

Financial Costs and Fluctuation in Currencies

In addition to the usual research expenses of research assistant(s), equipment, and material and participant compensation, conducting international research incurs additional cost related to travelling and accommodation. As well, unexpected expenses may arise, such as customary gifts and payment for the review of the ethics protocol by local ethics review board(s). Currency fluctuations and differences during the lifetime of research projects need careful attention and transparency, for example, it can have budget implication for certain research activities if less money is available than planned.

The finances of an international research project are often controlled by the country from which the project is funded and this can contribute to power imbalances and inequities. These problems can be overcome by supporting the partnering researchers to apply for local funding.

To further complicate the financial responsibilities of conducting international research, transactional practices often differ globally, making it difficult to comply with foreign accounting requirements. As an example, it may not be customary to issue official receipts for services delivered, such as transportation and sundries, but the donor institution requires an official receipt for reimbursement of expenses.

Funding Body Mandates

International research is more likely to be ethical and successful if the mandate of the funding agency addresses the research needs of the partnering country. Open communication between the researchers and funding bodies are necessary to ensure that the research answers to the local needs of the country in which the research is conducted, and that it contributes to better outcomes for their communities. Complex systems for transferring funds and underdeveloped banking systems in low-income countries are hurdles that should be anticipated. Strategies should be considered beforehand to overcome these difficulties.

Time Management

Rigid timelines do not fit well with international research. It is important to be flexible and build in extra time for unexpected procedures such as adjustment of the ethics application, availability of translator, and training of local transcribers and research assistants.

Ethics and Ethical Approval

Research ethics have been defined as "the study of what a researcher ought or ought not to do or the set of ethical principles that should be taken into account when doing research" (Hammersley & Traianou, 2012, p. 17). Throughout history there have been a number of documented examples of unethical research practices involving human subjects. Whiteford and Trotter (2008) draws attention to the Tuskegee Syphilis Study (1932 to 1972), the "Nazi experiments" which emerged after the German Nuremberg War trials (1946 to 1948), and Skloot (2011) highlights the story of Henrietta Lack whose tissue sample in 1951, known as the HeLa cells, raised important ethical concerns about cell/tissue harvesting. Ethical tragedies such as these have called for national and international guidelines to safeguard against unethical breaches and mishaps. The Nuremberg Code developed in 1947 became known as the basis for many international codes such as the Declaration of Helsinki in 1964, the Belmont Report in 1979, United Nations Council for International Organization of Medical Science (CIOMS) Research Ethics (1981, revised in 2002), and the International Ethical Guidelines for Biomedical Research Involving Human Subjects (1993, revised in 2002) (Whiteford & Trotter, 2008). All of these reports, codes, and guidelines uphold the core principles of respect, beneficence, and justice that represent the cornerstone of research ethics (Snežana, 2001). These ethical tragedies gave rise, as well, to the implementation of the institutional review board (IRB), known as independent ethics committee (IEC), ethical review board (ERB), or research ethics board (REB). These boards act as formal committees designated to approve, monitor, and review biomedical and behavioral research involving humans. IRBs are associated with academic institutions, but can be linked within the community (Moon & Khin-Maung-Gyi, 2009).

When conducting international research, it is important to seek out local IRBs and to be aware of the criteria and timelines required to obtain ethics approval. It is important to understand that ethics approval needs to be received in the donor country as well as the partnering country where the research will take place. Ethics approval can either be obtained sequentially or concurrently. Partnering with research team members in the host country is important to ease the process of seeking and obtaining ethical approval. Assumptions about how IRBs function in other countries should be curtailed, since ethical matters and protocols may be handled differently for cultural and/or political reasons.

Whether research is quantitative or qualitative, the ethical requirements are the same. Biomedical or applied research may be less complicated in terms of describing and understanding ethical issues (Morse, 2007), but social science research can present unique ethical matters since researchers seek to understand more abstract concepts about human behavior, the human condition, and the concepts of culture, social life, and/or relationships between individuals and groups. The complexity and level of risk to participants are often unknown and are intensified with international research. This is especially true when research is conducted in low resource countries where global disparities in wealth, health, and lifestyle are most evident (Benatar, 2002). Ethical guidelines for international research are historically rooted in Western ideology, which has created many ethical dilemmas and challenges for those who do research in non-Western countries (Whiteford & Trotter, 2008).

Practical Wisdom

When discussing ethical approaches in research, there is no one approach that fits all situations. Being ethical requires a researcher to take into account factors such as culture, gender, ethnic origin, and geography. Research and methodology courses emphasize the ethical rules and guidelines for how to conduct research, but knowing the ethically correct "thing" to do in a particular situation demands experience, or what Aristotle calls *phronesis* or practical wisdom. The term *practical wisdom* is an oxymoron since we often think of wisdom as being the opposite of practical. However, if we reflect on the core ethical principles of respect, beneficence, and justice in different environments and within different cultures, we realize there must be an element of both. Culture shapes our beliefs and behaviors as well as contextualizes our way of thinking. Cultural relativism is an important concept to consider when undertaking an international project, since research conducted with human participants should take into account a person's beliefs and practices. Nagengast and Velez-Ibanez (2004) points out the concerns about embracing cultural relativism in research and the steps taken in the 1940s addressing a person's basic rights as set out in the Universal Declaration of Human Rights (UDHR). It is essential to understand that western ethical principles cannot be extended to all human behaviors and/or practices. International researchers may encounter unpredictable ethical issues calling for phronesis. Cross-cultural matters arise concerning issues of respect for participants especially pertaining to privacy, confidentiality and informed consent, minimizing harm, maximizing justice, and data access, control, and dissemination.

Respect for Participants

In order to conduct ethical research researchers must have respect for people as well as for cross-cultural difference in conceptualization of autonomy and self-determination. The concept of respect in Western philosophy stresses the rights and obligations of the individual rather than society as a whole. Respect acknowledges a person's individuality and the right to make decisions which affect them. In some cultures, however, age and gender restrict a person's ability to be autonomous. For example, in patriarchal societies, men make important decisions affecting the health and welfare of women, and in communal societies decisions are frequently made by the community. In such societies, how do researchers determine a participant's level of autonomy to make decisions about participating in a research study? Decisions must be made of a person's free will, for this is embedded in the United Nations (1948) UDHR.

There is no firm way to know if a participant's decision to participate is entirely autonomous; researchers can use instinctive sense to identify when there is resistance. When this is the case, the researcher should explore the reason for the resistance and/or terminate the researcher–participant relationship out of respect for the participant. Researchers must explain to potential participants the terms and conditions of the researcher–participant relationship, the expectations of the participant including any risks and benefits, the meaning of privacy and confidentiality in the context of the research project, what will happen to the data collected, and that participation is voluntary. These ideas are usually outlined in a written document which participants are asked to sign, acknowledging their understanding, providing informed consent.

Informed Consent

Consent is considered informed when a competent participant has sufficient information about the study to make an informed, voluntary, and rational decision to participate. Informed consent protects potential research participants from a researcher's overzealous attempts to promote science and their careers at the expense of participants' safety and well-being. Informed consent builds trust, since participants witness transparency in the research process. This is particularly important for cultural groups where past research experiences have resulted in negative consequences.

The processes for obtaining informed consent vary cross-culturally. Participants may be asked to sign a consent form in writing or use their thumb print. Participants who are illiterate may be asked to sign an "X" and have it witnessed by a third party. In some oral cultures, written consent may not be appropriate. In this case, the participant's consent may be audio recorded or oral consent may be witnessed by a third party. Inevitably, there will be instances in the field where oral consent will be given, but not witnessed. If this should happen, it is suggested that the researcher document the encounter (date, time, place of interview) in their field notes.

Participants should always be provided with information about the research study in their local language and in a medium that is understandable and appropriate to the culture. This may not be written text, but in the form of an audio recording, pictures, and so forth.

While participants must be of legal age to consent, the legal consenting age can differ between countries. Researchers conducting international projects are ethically obligated to follow the requirements of the country with the greatest consenting age. Persons under the consenting age require parental or guardian permission to be involved in the research project. An underage participant who verbally or nonverbally indicates unwillingness to participant always overrides a consenting guardian. In some remote areas, births and deaths are not recorded, leaving participants with no knowledge of their chronological age. This can lead researchers to question a participant's capacity to consent. A researcher can attempt to approximate the age of potential participants by linking their age to important events within the country (for example, who was the president when you were born?). Nevertheless, there are many times when researchers must use practical judgment to assess a participant's ability to consent by considering each of the participants' individual life experiences and maturity.

Privacy and Confidentiality

Privacy and confidentiality is another vital component of respect for persons when conducting ethical research. Privacy is a participant's ability to have control over their own personal information. Confidentiality is a participant's right to have private information divulged in the course of a professional relationship with a researcher kept private. When conducting international research, it is important to recognize that terms such as privacy and confidentiality can have different meanings in communal societies. Additionally, in societies where power imbalances are particularly evident, participants may feel obliged to disclose information to researchers because of their "status" and not because they freely choose to do so. Issues pertaining to privacy and confidentiality may need additional explanation and creative accommodation in order for the researcher to meet the ethical obligations of the donor and host countries.

Minimizing Harm and Maximizing Justice

Researchers who conduct international projects, especially those who have projects in low to middle income countries, must identify the benefits and risks to participants. The Declaration of Helsinki declares that all health research must benefit the population and/or community (World Medical Association, 2015). Bhutta (2002) suggests this "would avoid unnecessary and curiosity-driven research as well as undue exploitation of vulnerable population in undeveloped countries" (p. 116). It is important for researchers to reflect on how their research impacts, positively and negatively, participants and the communities in which the research takes place. Partnering with local researchers and community stakeholders can help to keep your project genuine and well grounded. The benefits of the research projects, as well as how participants, community stakeholders, and local institutions are selected, must be equitable to both the donor and host country. Though this is usually based on the type of data required, difficult choices may sometimes be required. For example, a decision about which community will participate in the research needs to be made when several communities meet the inclusion criteria and would potentially benefit socially, economically, and politically.

Data Access, Control, and Dissemination

An international researcher should not be observed as "swooping in and out", exporting valuable knowledge. There needs to be open and transparent communication at the start of the project with participants, community stakeholders and research team members about who can access the data and who controls it. Guidelines about data management must be discussed early, since data storage methods can differ between countries. When disseminating findings, you have to think about your target audience. All too often researchers strive to publish their findings in high impact journals which boost their prestige and opportunities for future funding and promotion. It is equally important to disseminate where it will make the greatest impact in benefiting participants and the research community. The cultural context in which the research takes place should be considered during the dissemination plan. In some countries, alternative ways of dissemination, such as storytelling and arts-based approaches, are required.

Methodological Considerations

Researchers design their methodological approach based on their inquiry. When conducting international research, there is a need to consider whether the methodological design can be supported in the host country to predict and prevent potential methodological pitfalls. Areas which require forward thought include selection of suitable cross-cultural frameworks, recruitment of participants, selection and testing of data collection tools, maintaining rigor, data analysis, and how to overcome cultural differences.

Conceptual Frameworks and Philosophical Underpinnings

There are numerous frameworks, theories, and models upon which to build your research. Many of them, however, are grounded in Western ideology and are not applicable in other countries. Religion, spirituality, myths, and superstitions can occupy a significant place in the lives of many cultures, particularly in East and West Africa, Latin America, and the Middle East. Language, and the use of metaphors and parables, shape our reality and are embedded in our life practices. They influence the ways in which we understand the world and reveal the realities of global inequalities. Such differences compel researchers who conduct international research to look beyond Western ideologies and to explore frameworks, theories, and models proposed by non-Western philosophers (Santos-Salas, 2005).

Sampling and Recruitment

When developing recruitment strategies, it is important to collaborate with local stakeholders and community partners. These people are experts with valuable knowledge about where to focus recruitment efforts and what types of strategies will have the best results. As with any research project, knowing the type of sample you need, setting the inclusion and exclusion criteria, and then devising a recruitment plan is essential to obtain rich data.

When conducting international research, obtaining and accessing the sample can be challenging. Challenges are related to geographic and cultural accessibility, lack of resources, or being an outsider to the research community. Accessing extremely vulnerable populations such as the homeless can be difficult and time consuming and is often cited by researchers as the reason for small sample sizes. In countries with low economic status, communities can view their ability to participate as an opportunity for income generation. In these countries, a small "gift," a token of appreciation for participation, may be given and participants may participate to benefit financially or to receive the "gift." This has the potential to cause an ethical conflict and should be carefully handled to correspond with the cultural context. Care needs to be taken to ensure that your sample suits your inquiry.

Methods

When designing data collection tools, it is key to understand that tools may need to be adapted to fit the cultural context. Depending on the degree of cultural diversity among countries, this may require working alongside a cultural broker or a linguist. Researchers frequently opt to test or pilot their data collection tools with smaller samples before implementation. It is not unusual for data collection tools to evolve as the study advances, especially when there are significant language, behavioral, and value differences.

Validation of Data

Researchers ensure a study's rigor by confirming that the data is collected and interpreted correctly while addressing the goals and objectives of the inquiry. A good practice is to collect and analyze data simultaneously. Despite the importance of fully understanding the cultural context, project timelines often impact a researcher's ability to sufficiently immerse themselves in the culture and to be physically present in the host country for extended periods of time. International researchers must take every opportunity to maximize their time spent in the field, asking critical questions about emerging data and surrounding themselves with a knowledgeable research team that communicates effectively. Attaining a qualified translator or interpreter is imperative. The gender of the translator or interpreter can be crucial, depending on the culture and sensitivity of the questions being asked. It is a good practice to use local translator(s). Investing in the training of translator(s), interpreter(s), transcriptionist(s), and research assistance(s) prior to the commencement of the research is important. This can be time consuming and costly, but will lead to fewer difficulties and more successful results. Data collected in a different language must be forward and backward translated to ensure accuracy of the translation and rigor of the study (Dhamani & Richter, 2011). Language translation may involve the first level of data interpretation, as words and phrases can have different meanings. Careful attention must be given to language translation as it can impact the quality of the data.

Analysis and Findings

It is preferable that data collection and analysis occur concurrently, and it is recommended that data analysis start within the environmental context in which it was collected. "Naïve 'touristic' approaches that stereotype the result" (Steen, 1999, p. 110) can be avoided by seeking instant clarification from interpreters and your local research team members.

Data storage and how the research team, who potentially reside in different geographical sites, access data must be considered when conducting international research. Secure and confidential systems or environments, known as Virtual Research Environments, Science Gateways, Collaboratories, Digital Libraries and Inhabited Information Spaces, allow researchers, community members, and/or stakeholders to collaborate remotely (Candela, Castelli, & Pagano, 2013). Access to an optimal internet connection can be challenging and may not be available in countries with poor infrastructures. Using these virtual resources often have associated fees; researchers should budget for these expenses during the planning phase.

Research findings should always be brought back to the community and participants to ensure accuracy of the interpretation of the findings. This is especially true when vast cultural differences exist. The community's and participants' suggestions related to the best medium for dissemination of the research findings should be considered during the knowledge translation phase. This may be outside the normal or traditional modes of disseminating, but it is important to disseminate the findings where they will make the greatest impact.

Key Learnings

- Intimate knowledge of the cultural, historical, language, political, and economic structure of the country where you are conducting the research is critical.
- Cultural sensitivity is essential to develop effective and mindful communication.
- Researchers should allow for flexibility in their timelines when conducting international research.
- International researchers may encounter unpredictable ethical issues, calling for phronesis (practical wisdom).
- Collaboration with gatekeeper(s) and community stakeholder(s) is key to the success of the research.
- In any research project, the expert is the participant. Listen carefully and clarify what is heard.

References

Africa Unit. (2010). *Good practices in educational partnerships guide: UK-Africa higher and further education partnerships*. London, UK: The Africa Unit.

Andreotti, V., & de Souza, L. M. T. M. (2008). Global learning in the 'knowledge society'. Four tools for discussion. *ZEP: Zeitschrift für internationale Bildungsforschung und Entwicklungspädagogik*, *31*(1), 9–14.

Barrett, C. B. & Cason, J. W. (1997). *Overseas research. A practical guide.* Baltimore, MA: John Hopkins University Press.

Belmont Report (1979). *The Belmont report: Ethical principles and guidelines for the protection of human subjects of research.* Retrieved from www.hhs.gov/ohrp/humansubjects/guidance/belmont.html.

Benatar, S. R. (2002). Reflections and recommendations on research ethic in developing countries. *Social Science and Medicine, 54*, 1131–1141.

Bhutta, Z. A. (2002). Ethics in international health research: A perspective from the developing world. *Bulletin of the World Health Organization, 80*(2), 114–120.

Buchanan, D. A., Boddy, D., & McCalman, J. (1988). Getting in, getting on, getting out and getting back. In A. Bryman (Ed.), *Doing research in organizations* (pp. 53–67). London, UK: Routledge.

Buttigieg, S. C., Rathert, C., D'Aunno, T. A., & Savage, G. T. (2015). International research in health care management: Its needs in the 21st century, methodological challenges, ethical issues, pitfall, and practicalities. *Advances in Health Care Management, 17*, 3–22. doi:10.1108/S1474-823120140000017001.

Candela, L., Castelli, D. & Pagano, P., (2013). Virtual Research Environments: An Overview and a Research Agenda. *Data Science Journal, 12*, GRDI75–GRDI81. doi:10.2481/dsj.GRDI-013.

Council for International Organizations of Medical Sciences (CIOMS) & World Health Organization (WHO). (2002). *International ethical guidelines for biomedical research involving human subjects.* Retrieved from www.cioms.ch/publications/layout_guide2002.pdf.

Cultural Barriers to Effective Communication. (n.d). Retrieved from www.colorado.edu/conflict/peace/problem/cultrbar.htm.

Dhamani, A. K., & Richter, M. S. (2011). Translation of research instruments: Process, pitfalls and challenges in health services. *African Journal of Nursing and Midwifery, 13*(1), 3–13.

Freshwater, D., Sherwood, G., & Drury, V. (2006). International research collaboration: Issues, benefits and challenges of global network. *Journal of Research in Nursing, 11*, 295–303.

Hammersley, M., & Traianou, A. (2012). *Ethics in qualitative research.* Newbury Park, CA: SAGE Publications Inc.

Knell, M. (2007). *Burn-up or splash down: Surviving the culture shock of re-entry.* Atlanta, USA: Authentic Publishing.

Lombe, M., Newransky, C., Crea, T., & Stout, A. (2013). From rhetoric to reality: Planning and conducting collaborations for international research in the global south. *Social Work, 58*(1), 31–40. doi:10.1093/sw/sws056.

Macfarlane, S. B., Jacobs, M., & Kaaya, E. E. (2008). In the name of global health: Trends in academic institutions. *Journal of Public Health Policy, 29*(4), 383–401.

Mogale, R. S. (2012). The epiphany of Ubuntu in knowledge development: An African way. *The Journal of Pan-African Studies, 4*(10), 240–246.

Moon, M. R., & Khin-Maung-Gyi, R. (2009). The history and role of institutional review boards. *American Medical Association Journal of Ethics, 11*(4), 311–321.

Morse, J. (2007). Ethics in action: Ethical principles for doing qualitative health research. *Qualitative Health Research, 17*, 1003–1005.

Nagengast, C. & Velez-Ibanez, C. G. (2004). *Human rights: The scholar as activist*. Oklahoma City, USA: Society for Applied Anthropology.

Olive, J. L. (2014). Reflecting on the tensions between emic and etic perspectives in life history research: Lessons learned [35 paragraphs]. *Forum Qualitative Sozialforschung/Forum: Qualitative Social Research*, *15*(2), Art. 6. Retrieved from www.qualitative-research.net/index.php/fqs/article/view/2072/3656.

Opollo, J., Opollo, D., Gray, J., & Spies, L. (2014). Conducting international nursing research challenges and opportunities. *Nurse Researcher*, *22*(2), 29–33.

Santos-Salas, A. (2005). Towards a North-South dialogue: Revisiting nursing theory (from the South). *Advances in Nursing Science*, *28*, 17–24.

Skloot, R. (2011). *The immortal life of Henrietta Lacks*. Portland, USA: Broadway Books.

Snežana, B. (2001). The Declaration of Helsinki: The cornerstone of research ethics. *Archive of Oncology*, *9*(3), 179–184.

Steen, M. (1999). Qualitative research methods in cross-national settings. *International Journal of Social Research Methodology*, *2*(2), 109–124.

Stenson, A. L., Kapungu, C., Geller, S. E., & Miller, S. (2010). Navigating the challenges of global reproductive health research. *Journal of Women's Health*, *19*(11), 2101–2107.

Richter, M. S., & Botha, A. D. H. (2012). New research initiatives: Addressing global homelessness. *Canadian Journal of Nursing Research*, *44*(S4), 117–121.

Rolfe, M. K., Bryar, R. M., Hjelm, K., Apelquist, J., Fletcher, M., & Anderson, B. L. (2004). International collaboration to address common problems in health care: Process, practicalities and power. *International Nursing Review*, *51*, 140–148.

Ting-Toomey, S. (1999). *Communication across cultures*. New York, NY: The Guilford Press.

United Nations. (1948). *The Universal Declaration of Human Rights*. Retrieved from www.un.org/en/documents/udhr/index.shtml.

Whiteford, L. M., & Trotter, R. T., (2008). *Ethics for anthropological research and practice*. Long Grove: IL, Waveland Press Inc.

World Medical Association. (2015). *Declaration of Helsinki, ethical principles for medical research involving human subjects*. Amended by the World Medical Association 64th WMA General Assembly, Fortaleza, Brazil, and October 2013. Retrieved from www.wma.net/en/30publications/10policies/b3/.

Zheng, X. X., Hinshaw, A. S., Yu, M. Y., Guo, G. F., Oakley, D. J. (2001). Building international partnerships. *International Nursing Review*, *48*, 117–121.

List of Contributors

Rukhsana Ahmed (PhD, Ohio University) is Associate Professor, Department of Communication, University of Ottawa, Canada, with specialization in health communication, focusing on culture and media. She is co-author and co-editor of *Health literacy in Canada: A primer for students* (2014); *New media considerations and communication across religions and cultures* (2014); *Health communication and mass media: An integrated approach to policy and practice* (2013); and *Medical communication in clinical contexts* (2012; Distinguished Edited Book Award by the Applied Communication Division, National Communication Association [NCA]). She has been recognized with the Top 3 Paper (Applied Communication, Eastern Communication Association [ECA], 2017), Top Paper (Game Studies, NCA, 2016), and Top 5 Paper (Health Communication, ECA, 2006) Awards from national and regional conventions for her co-authored papers at the intersection of health communication, culture, and media. She is associate editor of *Health Communication,* specialty section of *Frontiers in Communication*, and past chair of the Health Communication Interest Group of ECA.

Zheng An, PhD, is an Assistant Professor in the Department of Communication at the University of Hawaii at Hilo. Zheng completed her PhD from the Annenberg School for Communication and Journalism at the University of Southern California. She received her MA in communication from the University of New Mexico and BA in journalism from Tsinghua University. Zheng specializes in interpersonal and health communication. Her research centers on the ways social support and social networks affect immigrant health and health behaviors. Her current research examines social support and dietary acculturation among Chinese immigrants. Zheng's research has been published in *Communication Research Reports*, *Chinese Journal of Communication*, *Health Communication*, *International Journal of Communication, and Telecommunications Policy.*

Johnson S. Aranda is a PhD candidate in communication at the University of Oklahoma. He studies global health within contextual domains such as race, culture, politics, and socioeconomics. He uses a critical approach to examine the discourses surrounding global health. His interest is in exploring how structural power—as rooted in moral authority, epistemic/scientific universalism, and economic asymmetry—determines the formulation of global health knowledge, which in turn leads to prioritization of specific health issues and pursuance of certain policies and interventions.

Emsie Arnoldi teaches research in the School of Media and Communication at RMIT University. Her research interests include mobile media technologies and the relationship between communication and multiculturalism, health and well-being, and sustainable practice and migrant communities. She plays an active role in leading research, teaching, professional activities, and policy development and has helped to establish RMIT's unique position as a Fair Trade organization, highlighting her commitment to social responsibility and collaborative practice.

Benjamin R. Bates teaches and researches in the areas of public understanding of health and healing. Although first trained as a rhetorical scholar, Dr. Bates appreciates and uses critical, qualitative, and quantitative methods to address questions at the intersection of health, medicine, and public need. Specifically, he investigates communication campaigns in the context of public health and public understanding of health and healing. In addition to extensive teaching in Athens, Ohio, Dr. Bates has also taught and researched in southeast Asia, sub-Saharan Africa, and South America. Dr. Bates's research, teaching, and service were recognized by the Eastern Communication Association when they awarded him the Past Presidents' Award, named him an ECA Distinguished Research Fellow, and, most recently, elected him to head the organization.

Marsha Berry teaches creative writing and digital media in the School of Media and Communication, RMIT University. She is co-editor of the book *Mobile media making in an age of smartphones (2014).* Since 2004, she has been researching connections between mobile media, place, memory and migration, and creative practices and has published her work extensively in international journals and edited books. She is also an ethnographer, writer, and artist whose practice includes filmmaking, participatory and locative media art projects, and poetry.

Jefferey G. Cox is a PhD candidate in the Department of Communication at Michigan State University. His research focuses on health and risk communication, including projects on the perception of risk from prescription medications, environmental contamination, and health-based social networks. He received his M.A. in journalism from

Indiana University. He has published in *Cyberpsychology, Behavior, and Social Networking*, *American Behavioral Scientist*, and *Journal of Communication*.

James W. Dearing (Ph.D., University of Southern California) is Professor and Chairperson of the Department of Communication at Michigan State University in the U.S. Dearing studies the diffusion of innovations, including the adoption and implementation of new evidence-based practices, programs, and technologies. His research and teaching spans dissemination science, implementation science, and program sustainability. Dearing was senior scientist with Kaiser Permanente, the largest nongovernmental health care provider in the U.S., where he was the principal investigator for a National Cancer Institute Center of Excellence in Cancer Communication Research. Currently he collaborates in a National Institute for Environmental Health Sciences Superfund Research Center.

Mohan J. Dutta is Provost's Chair Professor and Head of the Department of Communications and New Media at the National University of Singapore (NUS), Adjunct Professor at the Interactive Digital Media Institute (IDMI) at NUS, and Courtesy Professor of Communication at Purdue University. At NUS, he is the Founding Director of the Center for Culture-Centered Approach to Research and Evaluation (CARE), directing research on culturally-centered, community-based projects of social change. He teaches and conducts research in immigrant health, international health communication, critical cultural theory, poverty in health care, health activism in globalization politics, indigenous cosmologies of health, subaltern studies and dialogue, and public policy and participatory social change. Currently, he serves as editor of the "Critical Cultural Studies in Global Health Communication Book Series" with Routledge and sits on the editorial board of seven journals. Before arriving to NUS, he served as Associate Dean of research in the College of Liberal Arts at Purdue University, a Service Learning Fellow, and a fellow of the Entrepreneurial Leadership Academy. Also at Purdue, he served as the Founding Director of the Center for Poverty and Health Inequities (COPHI), where he holds an affiliate appointment.

Mahmoud Eid is an Associate Professor of communication, University of Ottawa, Canada. Dr. Eid is editor-in-chief of the *Global Media Journal—Canadian Edition* and serves on the editorial boards of several academic journals and on the organizing committees of various international conferences. He has contributed over twenty books and journal issues, fifty book chapters, journal articles, and reviews, and fifty international conference presentations. His research interests focus on global communication and media ethics, terrorism and media representations, crisis management and conflict resolution, and political decision-making and international relations.

Qian (Sarah) Gong is a Lecturer at the School of Media, Communication and Sociology at the University of Leicester, UK. Her previous research in the field of health communication investigated media, parenting culture and children's health issues within the context of 'risk society' in urban China. She is the author of *Children's healthcare and parental media engagement in urban china: A culture of anxiety?* Her current research is concerned with communication, migration, and health, and she is the chief investigator of the project "Health communication for pregnant Chinese women in Northern England".

Olivia Guntarik teaches on popular culture in the School of Media and Communication at RMIT University. She has researched on social mobility and social change in migrant and Indigenous communities in Australia and southeast Asia. Her current research examines the intersections of immersive digital technologies and environments with a focus on co-creative practices. This includes the use of geo-locative mobile media incorporating virtual and augmented reality, digital stories, and interactive history apps.

Kimberly Jarvis RN; PhD is a postdoctoral fellow at the University of Alberta, Alberta, Canada. She has a keen interest in global health and has lived and worked and been involved in research projects in Qatar, Ethiopia, Ghana, and Canada. Her research is not placed in one specific country but rather focuses on the interdependencies and entanglements of women's health globally. She has a vested interest in health and how it is produced through social, political, and cultural practices. Her research interests focus on women's maternal and reproductive health, social determinants of health (particularly gender and culture), health equity, and global health.

Jungmi Jun (PhD, George Mason University) conducts research in health and strategic communication. She is interested in examining health/cancer information and communication disparities and their impacts on underserved populations' cancer prevention and other health behaviors. You may find her research publications in influential medical, health, communication, and PR journals including *American Journal of Health Behaviors, International Journal on Advances in Life Sciences, Journal of Health Communication, Health Communication, Journal of International and Intercultural Communication, Asian Pacific Journal of Cancer Prevention, Journal of Cancer Education*, and *Public Relations Review*.

Lenore Manderson, PhD, FASSA, FWAAS, MASSAf, is Distinguished Professor of public health and medical anthropology in the School of Public Health, the University of the Witwatersrand, Johannesburg, South Africa, and Visiting Distinguished Professor, Institute at Brown for Environment and Society and Visiting Professor of anthropology, Brown University, Providence, RI, USA. In addition, she is an honorary professor at Khon Kaen University, Thailand, and adjunct professor in the School of Social Sciences at Monash University. She is current editor of the international journal *Medical Anthropology*. Her research focuses on infectious diseases of poverty, chronic conditions, and disability, and on questions of inequality, technologies, and access to care. She is the author, editor, and co-author of nearly six hundred books, articles, book chapters, and reports. Email: lenore.manderson@wits.ac.za.

Sarah Mantwill, PhD, is a coordinator in the Swiss Learning Health System (SLHS) and a postdoctoral researcher at the Department of Health Sciences & Health Policy at the University of Lucerne (Switzerland). Prior to joining the University of Lucerne, she was a postdoctoral research fellow at the Harvard T.H. Chan School of Public Health and the Dana-Farber Cancer Institute, Boston (MA). Her research explores the concept of health literacy and its applicability to different cultural contexts. More specifically, in how far health literacy contributes to disparities in health and the mediating role of health literacy in creating health communication inequalities. Besides, her current research also explores the role of social networks in health information exposure and access among minority and low-income populations.

Yuping Mao (Ph.D., Ohio University) is Assistant Professor in the Department of Communication Studies at California State University, Long Beach. Her research focuses on intercultural and health communication. Her research interests in health communication focus on the following areas: cross-cultural communication between patients and health professionals, health information diffusion among different cultural groups, and media effects on health behaviors. She is particularly interested in health communication issues among migrants. She is the co-editor of *Handbook of research on citizen engagement and public participation in the era of new media*. She has published a few book chapters, and her work has also been published in peer reviewed journals such as *Communication Research, Canadian Journal of Communication, Journal of Intercultural Communication Research, Journal of Substance Use*, and *Advances in Public Health*. She *has made more than 50 research presentations in regional, national, and international academic conferences.*

Milica Markovic, BSoc (Hon), MSoc, PhD, is a sociologist, trained both in Serbia and Australia. Her research and policy interests have included immigrant health, women's health, chronic illness, provision of health care in the multicultural context, and hospital-based care. Email: milicaaustralia@gmail.com.

Isaac Nahon-Serfaty is Chair and Associate Professor at the Department of Communication, University of Ottawa (Ontario, Canada). His current research studies the role of the visually grotesque in public communication campaigns, including public health, political communication, and environmental activism. He has also extensively researched on the relations between health care policies and communication in Latin America. Dr. Nahon-Serfaty has developed action-research projects to enhance the advocacy capabilities of non-governmental organizations in the region, with particular focus on Venezuela and Mexico.

Bolanle A. Olaniran is a Professor in the Department of Communication Studies. He is an internationally acclaimed scholar. His research includes the use of information communication technologies in the workplace and organization communication, cross-cultural communication, crisis communication, and collaborative decision-making and technologies. He has authored several peer-reviewed articles in discipline focus and interdisciplinary journals (i.e., regional, national, and international) and authored several edited book chapters in each of these areas. He also serves as consultant to organizations and universities at the local, national, international, and government levels. His works have gained recognition such as the American Communication Association's "Outstanding Scholarship in Communication field," among others.

James O. Olufowote (PhD, Purdue University) is an Assistant Professor of communication at the University of Oklahoma. His research interests lie at the intersections of health communication and organizational communication. For example, he has focused on how non-profit organizations communicate and collaborate in confronting health epidemics such as HIV/AIDS and polio.

Solina Richter, RN, DCur, is a Professor and the Academic Director of the Global Nursing Office in the Faculty of Nursing, University of Alberta. Dr. Richter believes that global collaboration has always been a fundamental part of scholarly development. Globalization is accelerating the scope, rate, and importance of international research. It is essential that researchers combine resources and expertise on an international scale to adequately address complex and interconnected global issues. Her research program focuses on the social determinants of health, and particularly on building capacity for partnerships and collaboration to address global health. Current projects focus on homelessness in rural communities in Canada, and a study in Ghana, Africa, related to maternal health, how people within or across cultures share the same understanding of health, what it means to be healthy, and practices for maintaining health.

Peter J. Schulz, PhD, is the Director of the Institute of Communication and Health at the University of Lugano, Switzerland, and Professor of communication theories and health communication. In his work he brings together thinking from the humanities, social sciences, and information technology to investigate important issues in health communication. His recent research has focused on health literacy and empowerment, doctor-patient communication, and media effects in the health domain. He has published more than one hundred forty articles in peer-reviewed publications and important volumes. He currently holds several research grants from the Swiss National Science Foundation (SNF) and other funding bodies. Further, he was granted a doctoral school on adaptivity in communication & health by the SNF. Together with Paul Cobley, London, he is the editor of the series Handbooks of Communication Science (DeGruyter & Mouton). He is also the deputy editor of *Patient Education and Counseling* and associate editor of *BMC Medical Informatics and Decision Making*.

Victoria Team, MD, MPH, DrPH, is a medical anthropologist and a public health researcher with broad interests in women's health. She currently works in the School of Social Sciences and the School of Nursing and Midwifery at Monash University, Melbourne, Australia and manages the editorial office of international journal *Medical Anthropology: Cross-Cultural Studies in Health and Illness*. Her doctoral research projects were conducted at the University of Melbourne and focused on health of immigrant Australians. Her publications focus on body image, solarium tanning, caregiving, disability, reproductive screening, motherhood and breastfeeding. She can be contacted at victoria.team@monash.edu.

Index